ALLOCATION OF LIABILITY FOR DANGEROUS GOODS UNDER INTERNATIONAL TRADE LAW

This book explores the allocation of risk and liability of dangerous goods between the seller and the buyer under CIF (Cost, Insurance and Freight) and FOB (Free on Board) contracts, providing an in-depth study of the issue of carriage of dangerous goods in the context of international trade law. In addition to offering specific solutions to issues arising in the context of the contract of sale, the book provides a non-contractual angle, putting forward suggestions under non-contractual mechanisms. Importantly, the book incorporates case law examples from the Commonwealth and the US.

Dangerous goods that are carried by sea can cause potential risks of losses and damages to the vessel, other cargoes and lives on board. The allocation of liability arising out of the carriage of dangerous goods has recently attracted unwelcome attention because of mis-declared cargoes leading to fires on board ships. Thus the book fills a gap in the literature by addressing the issue in detail with examples from multiple jurisdictions, and proposing solutions. In particular, the book analyses whether and to what extent the law of international sale of goods can provide any assistance in the re-allocation of liability between the buyer and the seller.

This book will be of great interest to all those involved in the research as well as legal practice of international trade law and the law of carriage of goods by sea.

Allocation of Liability for Dangerous Goods under International Trade Law

CIF and FOB Contracts

Ahmet Gelgeç

•HART•
OXFORD • LONDON • NEW YORK • NEW DELHI • SYDNEY

HART PUBLISHING

Bloomsbury Publishing Plc

Kemp House, Chawley Park, Cumnor Hill, Oxford, OX2 9PH, UK

1385 Broadway, New York, NY 10018, USA

29 Earlsfort Terrace, Dublin 2, Ireland

HART PUBLISHING, the Hart/Stag logo, BLOOMSBURY and the Diana logo are trademarks of Bloomsbury Publishing Plc

First published in Great Britain 2022

A catalogue record for this book is available from the British Library.

A catalogue record for this book is available from the Library of Congress.

Library of Congress Control Number: 2022944267

ISBN: HB: 978-1-50995-019-5
ePDF: 978-1-50995-021-8
ePub: 978-1-50995-020-1

Typeset by Compuscript Ltd, Shannon

To find out more about our authors and books visit www.hartpublishing.co.uk. Here you will find extracts, author information, details of forthcoming events and the option to sign up for our newsletters.

ACKNOWLEDGEMENTS

This work is the product of a few years of research. Writing is by no means an easy task but preparing and writing this book has turned into a joy with the support of several people to whom I would like to express my gratitude with more than conventional sincerity for their invaluable professional, motivational and substantial help and assistance throughout the whole process. My gratitude goes first to Filippo Lorenzon for his immense help, support and comments on much of the material in the earlier version of the manuscript. I am extremely grateful to the Institute of Maritime Law at the University of Southampton for providing access to resources throughout the earlier stages of preparing the manuscript. I am also very grateful to Paul Myburgh and Simone Lamont-Black, Academic Advisors for Shipping Law at Hart Publishing, for their invaluable constructive comments and suggestions on the manuscript, from which I have benefited greatly. I also owe a debt of gratitude to Roberta Bassi, Senior Commissioning Editor at Hart Publishing, for her precious help and assistance in the entire process of preparing the manuscript for publication. I would like to avail myself of the opportunity to thank my family, my parents-in-law and above all my wife, Berrak Genç-Gelgeç for supporting, encouraging and putting up with me so tirelessly during the whole process. Without them this work would not have been possible. I must also express my gratitude and love to the pet members of our family, Sütlaç and Panda, for their timely intrusions during the writing process.

Also grateful acknowledgement is made to the following publisher for their permission to reproduce or revise some of the texts from the article that I have previously published:

- A Gelgeç, 'Identifying the Shipper under Bills of Lading' (2020) 26 *Journal of International Maritime Law* 229.

Ahmet Gelgeç
July 2022

CONTENTS

ABBREVIATIONS

All ER	All England Law Reports
CISG	United Nations Convention on Contracts for the International Sale of Goods
CJQ	Civil Justice Quarterly
CLC	International Convention on Civil Liability for Oil Pollution Damage
CLJ	Cambridge Law Journal
CMI	Comité Maritime International
COGSA	Carriagc of Goods by Sea Act
EWHC	High Court of England and Wales
EWCA (Civ)	Court of Appeal of England and Wales
ER	English Reports
ETL	European Transport Law
FOSFA	Federation of Oils, Seeds & Fats Associations
GAFTA	The Grain and Feed Trade Association
HNS	International Convention on Liability and Compensation for Damage in Connection with the Carriage of Hazardous and Noxious Substances by Sea
HR	International Convention for the Unification of Certain Rules of Law relating to Bills of Lading, 1924 (The Hague Rules)
HVR	Brussels Protocol amending The Hague Rules relating to Bills of Lading, 1968 (The Hague-Visby Rules)
IBL	International Business Lawyer
ICCLR	International Company and Commercial Law Review
ICLQ	International Comparative Law Quarterly
IJMCL	International Journal of Marine and Coastal Law
IJOSL	International Journal of Shipping Law
IMDG Code	International Maritime Dangerous Goods Code

IMO	International Maritime Organization
Int'l ML	International Maritime Law
JBL	Journal of Business Law
JIBL	Journal of International Business Law
JIBFL	Journal of International Banking and Financial Law
JIML	Journal of International Maritime Law
JITLP	Journal of International Trade Law and Policy
JMLC	Journal of Maritime Law and Commerce
Ll L Rep	Lloyd's List Law Reports
Lloyd's Rep	Lloyd's Law Reports
LMCLQ	Lloyd's Maritime and Commercial Law Quarterly
LQR	Law Quarterly Review
MARPOL	The International Convention for the Prevention of Pollution from Ships
MLR	Maritime Law Review
MSA	Merchant Shipping Act
MSR	Merchant Shipping Regulations
NYPE	New York Product Exchange Time Charter
OJLS	Oxford Journal of Legal Studies
RLR	Restitution Law Review
RR	United Nations Convention on the Contracts for the International Carriage of Goods Wholly or Partly by Sea (The Rotterdam Rules 2009)
SOGA	Sale of Goods Act
SOLAS	Convention for the Safety of Life at Sea
STL	Shipping and Trade Law
S&TLI	Shipping and Transport Lawyer International
Tul Mar LJ	Tulane Maritime Law Journal
TLR	Times Law Reports
UKHL	United Kingdom House of Lords
UNCITRAL	United Nations Commission on International Trade Law

TABLE OF CASES

Australia

Canada

Denmark

Hong Kong

Malaysia

New Zealand

Norway

Singapore

South Africa

United States of America

England & Wales

1

Introduction

I. General

Dangerous goods that are carried by sea carry along with them potential risks of loss and/or damage to the vessel, other cargoes and lives on board. When the carrier has not been enabled to take necessary precautions against the dangerous nature and character of the goods prior to shipment, the risks of damage and loss will vastly increase. Under English law, there is no exhaustive definition of 'dangerous goods' given in legislation.[1] Obviously substances such as explosives and radioactive materials can be classified as dangerous. An example of a classification for these can be found in 1(2) of the Merchant Shipping (Dangerous Goods and Marine Pollutants) Regulations 1997 in which dangerous goods are defined by reference to 'goods classified in the Blue Book, the IMDG Code[2] or any IMO publication specified below as dangerous carriage by sea …'[3]

This is not, however, entirely sufficient to grasp the scope of dangerous goods. The approach adopted under English law is that goods can be dangerous not only in consequence of their inherent nature but also as a result of surrounding circumstances.[4] For instance, grain, which is normally regarded as innocuous, can create danger if it overheats. Similarly, although some liquids may not normally pose any danger, their risk may lie in inappropriate packing, which may cause leakage and damage to the vessel or other cargoes on board.[5] The risks associated with dangerous goods are varied based on their inherent nature, characteristics and surrounding circumstances, and those risks may vary from minor incidents such

[1] But see the Merchant Shipping (Dangerous Goods and Marine Pollutants) Regulations 1997, SI 1997/2357.

[2] The International Maritime Dangerous Goods (IMDG) Code. A comprehensive list of dangerous substances and guidelines for the safe carriage or shipment of them can be found in the IMDG Code. Chapter VII of the International Convention for the Safety of Life at Sea (SOLAS) 1974 makes the IMDG Code mandatorily applicable for the contracting states. See generally, Chapter 2.

[3] The Merchant Shipping Regulations 1997 give effect to the International Convention for the Safety of Life at Sea (SOLAS) 1974 and its protocol as amended.

[4] *Brass v Maitland* (1856) 6 E & B 470; 119 ER 940; *Ministry of Food v Lamport & Holt* [1952] 2 Lloyd's Rep 371; *The Athanasia Comninos* [1990] 1 Lloyd's Rep 277; *Effort Shipping Co Ltd v Linden Management SA (The Giannis NK)* [1998] AC 605. In *Chandris v Isbrandsten-Moller Co Inc (The Eugenia Chandris)* [1951] 1 KB 240, Devlin J refused to read 'other dangerous cargo' restrictively by reference to the *eiusdem generis* rule.

[5] *Brass v Maitland* (1856) 6 E & B 470; 119 ER 940; *Ministry of Food v Lamport & Holt* [1952] 2 Lloyd's Rep 371.

as damage to other goods, damage to the container or clean-up expenses because of leakage, to serious incidents resulting in fire or even explosions on account of chemical substances. Indeed, the burden of this work is to provide a legal analysis on the allocation of liability for dangerous goods between to the parties to the sale contract. But prior to this, it is vital to provide a practical overview of some of the dangers and risks presented by these goods during their sea carriage in order to have a better understanding of the legal framework surrounding dangerous goods which is to be covered in the following chapters.

A. Practical Overview of Commonly Shipped Dangerous Goods

(i) Goods in Packaged Form

It would be only right to start with dangerous goods in packaged form, sea transportation of which is governed by the International Maritime Dangerous Goods (IMDG) Code. The IMDG Code is the primary international instrument that has, since 2004, set out the mandatory general provisions for the safe carriage of dangerous goods in packaged form, which will be covered in the following chapter. Although the Code provides extensive guidance on dangerous goods in packaged form, ironically in the last couple of decades, the majority of incidents involving dangerous goods have been caused by misdeclared/undeclared goods and improper, inadequate or poor packing. Even just one item of poorly packed or misdeclared cargo stowed in a container may suffice to cause a total loss of a vessel, loss of lives and of other cargoes on board, as well as damage to the environment. In the 1990s, *Recife, Aconcagua, CMA Djakarta, Kapitan Sakharov* and in the 2000s *Maersk Seoul, Cape Moreton, APL Austria, DG Harmony* and, most recently, *Maersk Honam* are some of the incidents attributed to misdeclared or improperly packed goods. According to the Container Inspection Safety Initiative (CISI) launched by the US National Cargo Bureau (NCB), an inspection was conducted recently on 500 containers loaded from South America, Europe and Asia. The data collected showed that 55 per cent of the containers failed to comply with dangerous goods regulations of which 43 per cent failed owing to improper securing of goods within the container. The results also proved that approximately 6.5% of the containers packed with dangerous goods had been misdeclared.[6] Evidently, one of the most common causes of incidents arising from dangerous goods is associated with goods poorly or improperly packed into containers. Packaging used could be poor or even unsuitable for the intended cargo. For instance, some cargoes are prone to self-heating. If they are poorly packed or inadequate packaging is

[6] US National Cargo Bureau, 'A white paper by National Cargo Bureau', 5, www.natcargo.org/Holistic-Approach-For-Undeclared-Misdeclared-And-Other-Non-compliant-Dangerous-Goods_White-Paper-by-NCB.pdf.

used, due to the lack of air circulation such cargoes may ignite causing fire or even explosion. Dangers presented by some goods can be sometimes attributable to the use of damaged packaging, due to negligence or faults of packers during the packing process. Where this is the case, regardless of whether goods are dangerous or not, leaks or spills from the cargo can react with the base of the container, timber pallets or other goods in the container in such a way to give rise to serious risks such as fire, explosion, spoiling or harming other goods and the vessel. For instance, inadequate stowing of liquids above solids may cause serious risks due to potential leaks or spills. If a poorly packed liquid drum is over-stowed a solid cargo, when the liquid drum leaks or spillage occurs, leaks or spills may dangerously react with the solid cargo stowed below, leading to a fire or even explosion. However, stowing solids over properly packed liquid drums will reduce the chance of such a potentially dangerous reaction for two reasons: first, even if the solid cargo above is defectively packed, it would be unlikely to leak or spill; and second, in case a leak occurred from the liquid drum, it would be unlikely to make contact with the solid cargo stowed above. This method may not entirely eliminate the risk of potentially dangerous reaction between the cargoes though. For instance, containers might be exposed to high temperatures either as a result of absorbing direct sunlight if carried over deck, or if carried below deck where they could be exposed to sources of heat like the fuel bunker. Where this is the case, the walls of plastic drums will soften and lose resistance, eventually leading to spillage inside the container, posing serious risks if over-stowed heavily.[7]

Non-declaration or misdeclaration of cargoes is also one of the major underlying reasons in sea transport resulting in catastrophic incidents such as loss of lives, the total loss of or damage to the vessel, other cargoes on board or the environment. As containerships' capacities are higher than ever today – some of the largest ones have the capacity to carry around 20,000 20ft containers – the likelihood of incidents involving undeclared or misdeclared cargoes occurring is greater than ever. A dangerous substance could be accidentally or even sometimes fraudulently declared as non-dangerous. Similarly, a cargo could be accidentally or fraudulently misdeclared as well. An accidental misdeclaration may occur if the wrong shipping name or UN number of a certain substance is erroneously declared. Calcium hypochlorite is a good example of this, as it is classified under three different classes and has eight different UN numbers with eight different descriptions under the IMDG Code. As for fraudulent misdeclarations, this is when the information or documentation provided to carriers inaccurately identifies the shipping name of a cargo on purpose. The reasons for misdeclaration are not exhaustive but there are some common motives of shippers for this. Where carriers refuse to carry certain dangerous goods or where tighter port restrictions are applied, this may lead to a rise in the numbers of misdeclarations. Alternatively, a cargo may be misdeclared to bypass the rigours of the dangerous goods regulations, quotas or

[7] See generally, 'Packing dangerous goods: a burning issue', *Maritime Risk International* (March, 2020).

stiff surcharges imposed by carriers. Calcium hypochlorite is once again one of the most popular examples of fraudulently misdeclared cargoes, which is often declared as bleaching powder, chloride of lime or disinfectant to avoid carriers' bans or ports' restrictions.[8] After a misdeclared cargo has been packed into a container, it is unlikely that it will be properly marked, labelled or secured in accordance with the relevant schedule. Dangerous goods are often segregated from each other, as a certain dangerous cargo may react with another certain substance, if they are adjacent to each other. As a result of misdeclaration, strict segregation and stowage procedures set out in the IMDG Code are unlikely to be followed. Accordingly, a misdeclared or an undeclared cargo that is not stowed safely and correctly in compliance with the IMDG Code will represent serious risks to the vessel, lives and the environment.

The tragic incident on *The Kapitan Sakharov* is a good example of this practice. An undeclared dangerous cargo, which was in fact calcium hypochlorite, was carried on deck *Kapitan Sakharov* packed in a container. There were also eight containers stowed below deck loaded with isopentane. During transit in the Arabian Gulf in July 1993, the undeclared calcium hypochlorite exploded causing fire, which spread down to where the eight containers of isopentane were stowed in an unventilated hold. Isopentane is a highly flammable liquid substance with a flashpoint well below 0°C and a boiling point around 28°C. As a highly flammable liquid giving off dangerous vapours, isopentane must be stowed in a mechanically ventilated space or on deck. Considering the ambient temperature in the Gulf in July and the fact that the initial fire spread below, the isopentane packed into the eight containers with a boiling point around 28°C was under pressure, and subsequently it escaped through the containers' pressure valves in vapour form. As there was no mechanical ventilation in the hold, the isopentane in the form of vapour acted as a source of ignition, caught fire and exacerbated the existing fire, causing an explosion leading to the sinking of the vessel and the loss of two lives.[9]

As aforesaid, calcium hypochlorite is an infamous chemical in shipping trade that is, for various reasons, widely misdeclared or undeclared, and which may cause a fire or explosion on board the vessel. Fires or explosions on *Recife, Aconcagua, CMA Djakarta, DG Harmony* and, most recently, on *APL Austria* were all caused by misdeclared or undeclared cargoes of calcium hypochlorite packed into containers. Calcium hypochlorite is a white or yellow water treatment chemical in granular, powder or tablet form that is widely used as a disinfectant and a bleaching agent. At commonly encountered temperatures, it constantly but gradually decomposes and releases heat and oxygen. As a result of being an unstable and self-reactive substance, at elevated temperatures – particularly at anything above 30°C – decomposition accelerates, which will also increase the heat in a confined space like a container. This increase of the temperature in the container will in

[8] See US National Cargo Bureau, n 6 above, 6.

[9] *Northern Shipping Co v Deutsche Seereederei GmbH and Others (The Kapitan Sakharov)* [2000] 2 Lloyd's Rep 255, 258.

turn also increase the decomposition. Eventually, it will undergo an exothermic chain reaction causing serious fires, explosions and emissions of toxic gases like chlorine. Decomposition of calcium hypochlorite can also be initiated or accelerated by impurities like iron or cobalt, by reacting with organic materials like oil, or even by moisture. When reacting with organic substances, calcium hypochlorite can catch fire even without the presence of an external ignition source. Because of these factors, calcium hypochlorite must be carried in reefer or dry containers on deck, away from sources of heat like bunker tanks or under direct sunlight, in adequately ventilated areas. Where this substance is misdeclared or undeclared, it will be likely that it will be mishandled and necessary precautions – particularly the stowage and segregation requirements set out in the IMDG Code – will not be followed by carriers. As a result, it could be stowed either in a hold, where it will be exposed to elevated temperatures, or on deck under direct sunlight, where it will cause fire or explosion leading to catastrophic incidents like total loss of the vessel, other cargoes on board, loss of life and pollution to the environment.[10] This is in fact what happened in *The Aconcagua*, where a cargo of calcium hypochlorite packed into a container had an abnormally high thermal instability, which made it prone to be explosive at ordinary sea transit temperatures around as low as 30°C. It was stowed in a position in the hold where it was surrounded on three sides by a fuel bunker tank that had been heated during transit, and due to being liable to self-ignite around 30°C, the cargo exploded causing catastrophic damage to the vessel and the other cargoes on board.[11]

Seedcake is another cargo which can be potentially misdeclared or undeclared in practice when presented to carriers. It is mainly used as animal feed or fertiliser after the oil has been extracted from seeds, cereals or similar commodities. Seedcake can be in flake, pulp, cake, pellets or meal form and consignments that are presented for shipment might be commonly named as 'animal feed', 'groundnut meal', 'peanut cake', 'soya bean meal', 'sunflower seed' or 'copra extraction pellets'.[12] Oil from seeds could be extracted either by a solvent process or by mechanically crushing the seeds. Neither process extracts the oil entirely. Depending on the remaining oil and moisture content and the process of oil extraction used, the necessary requirements for safe carriage may differ from one cargo to another. And in case of misdeclaration or non-declaration involving a seedcake cargo, whereby the cargo is likely to be mishandled, the presence of oil and moisture in the cargo can create microbiological activity leading to self-heating of the seedcake and spontaneous combustion. Where the oil is removed by the use of solvent, seedcake cargoes are generally said to contain no more than 1.5 per cent oil and no

[10] See generally, www.cinsnet.com/wp-content/uploads/2018/01/Calcium-Hypochlorite-Guidelines-CINS-IGPI-Version-3-January-2018.pdf, 3–7; 'Misdeclared beware', *Maritime Risk International* (May 2014); 'Putting out the fires', *Maritime Risk International* (December 2019).

[11] *Compania Sud Americana de Vapores SA v Sinochem Tianjin Import and Export Corporation (The Aconcagua)* [2011] 1 Lloyd's Rep 683.

[12] www.cinsnet.com/wp-content/uploads/2021/04/CINS-IG-Seed-Cake-Guidelines-Version-3-April-2021.pdf, 3.

more than 11 per cent moisture. On the other hand, mechanically extracted seedcake cargoes have a far higher oil and moisture content, which together increase the likelihood of self-heating and spontaneous combustion. The excessive moisture content can elevate the temperature of the cargo to a point where oxidation of the remaining oil occurs. Unlike microbiological self-heating, particularly with the presence of an excessive amount of oil, oxidative self-heating may quickly elevate the temperature of the cargo to the point where it may combust spontaneously. Solvent extracted seed cake cargoes may also present additional risk. Where the oil is expelled by the use of solvent, there might be some residual flammable solvent communicating with the cargo. If the cargo is not substantially free from such flammable solvent, it may ignite spontaneously. To prevent the risk of fire, seedcake containers should be stowed away from sources of heat and kept dry, in accordance with the requirements set out in the IMDG Code. Misdeclaration or non-declaration of the seedcake cargo presented for shipment may lead to mishandling of the cargo, including inadequate stowage near sources of heat, causing fire, eventually leading to damage to the vessel, other cargoes on board and loss of lives.[13]

Charcoal is another substance that may prove to be troublesome when misdeclared or undeclared. Charcoal is a black residue composed of carbon, commonly used to fuel barbecues or for similar purposes. As a self-heating cargo, it is prone to spontaneous combustion when reacting with oxygen. If carbon in the charcoal communicates with oxygen, it produces carbon dioxide and carbon monoxide as a result of oxidation. This in turn causes production of heat, elevating the temperature and the level of oxidation, which leads the cargo to self-ignite.[14] The quality of charcoal, packaging, handling, and even the quantity of the cargo could be one of the underlying factors to pose serious risks during transit. For instance, if there are partial wood pieces left in the cargo, this may render the charcoal chemically unstable, accelerating the carbonising process even at lower temperatures. Alternatively, some types of charcoal may contain some flammable solids, giving rise to combustion of the cargo at lower temperatures. Charcoal cargoes require heat treatment and a subsequent cooling process prior to packing. This will cause the charcoal to oxidise under controlled conditions. This process in turn helps minimise the reactivity of the cargo in the container. If the cargo is wet as a result of inadequate heat treatment or it is exposed to the rain prior to loading, or it is not adequately packaged with a water-resistant material, this will mobilise an exothermic reaction, accelerating the self-ignition of charcoal. The quantity of charcoal packed into the container may also have an important role to play in the safe carriage of charcoal. A high volume of dead space in the container will increase the chance of air circulation. As a result of not packing the container with the maximum amount allowed, the interior atmosphere will be filled with a high volume of oxygen in the dead space, causing air circulation which will increase the

[13] ibid, 3–5.
[14] www.gard.no/Content/24227347/CINS_IGPI_GuidelinesCarriageCharcoalCarbon.pdf, 3.

possibility of the oxidation of charcoal, leading to self-ignition of the cargo.[15] For all these reasons, charcoal cargoes should be stowed on deck, away from sources of heat, and kept as cool as possible during transport. If a cargo of charcoal is misdeclared or non-declared, the cargo is unlikely to be handled or stowed according to the requirements set out in the IMDG Code. Once it is mishandled or stowed in a hold where the temperature of charcoal quickly elevates, it is likely that the cargo will spontaneously combust, resulting in a fire that may lead to damage to the vessel, loss of lives and of other cargoes on board.[16]

There are also other cargoes that may appear to be entirely innocuous but still present certain hazards during transit. Fishmeal is probably one of the best examples of such cargoes. Fishmeal is manufactured from fish, the bones and offal from processed fish. It is a solid product with most of the water and oil removed. It is primarily used as animal feed or fertiliser. There are two types of fishmeal: antioxidant treated fishmeal and non-antioxidant treated fishmeal. Whereas the former is spontaneously combustible,[17] the latter falls within miscellaneous dangerous goods.[18] The acceptable amount of moisture content in both types is between 5 and 12 per cent. In terms of the oil content for antioxidant treated fishmeal, the maximum amount permitted should not exceed 15 per cent, while that of non-antioxidant treated fishmeal should not exceed 12 per cent. If the moisture and oil content exceed the permitted levels, fishmeal may start heating, resulting in fire. To prevent fishmeal with excessive oil and moisture from becoming heated, it should be dried out for a certain period of time prior to shipment. In any case, non-antioxidant treated fishmeal cargoes should be weathered for at least 28 days prior to shipment so as to enable the cargo to oxidise unsaturated oils left within. On the other hand, unlike non-antioxidant treated fishmeal, antioxidant treated fishmeal cargoes do not require weathering.[19] Also, as non-antioxidant treated meal is more prone to heating, certain methods of stowage and ventilation set out in the IMDG Code must be followed, whereas the same methods may not be applicable to antioxidant treated meal. This does not necessarily mean that antioxidant treated meal cargoes are free from hazards though. Quality or quantity of the cargo, improper application of antioxidant treatment, inefficient packing or improper stowage due to misdeclaration or non-declaration are common underlying reasons causing heating and combustion of the cargo. For example, if the container is not packed with the maximum amount permitted, the free space within the container will be filled with oxygen causing air circulation, which will increase the likelihood of spontaneous combustion, resulting in fire.[20] Whether it is antioxidant treated or not, fishmeal cargoes are naturally bound to heat during transit. The remaining unoxidised particles of oil in the cargo are likely to

[15] ibid, 3–5.
[16] ibid, 5–6.
[17] See Class 4.2 under the IMDG Code.
[18] See Class 9 under the IMDG Code.
[19] On fishmeal cargoes see generally, www.cargohandbook.com/Fishmeal.
[20] ibid.

oxidise because of the vessel's motion and weather conditions during transport. Unless the antioxidant applied to the cargo is sufficient, the cargo will consume the treatment before it is stabilised. As a result, oxidation will not be subdued, and subsequently the cargo will become heated and the temperature will elevate to the point of combustion.[21] In *The Amphion*,[22] a cargo of 'anti-oxidant treated fishmeal', packed into a container, was shipped on board the vessel. The cargo in question had not been properly treated, despite the fact that it was declared as 'antioxidant treated fishmeal'. As it was misdeclared, the cargo was improperly stowed in the lower part of the hold where it was exposed to heat, and not ventilated during transport. As a result, during discharge, the cargo caused a fire in the hold, which required the carrier to undertake the costly process of smothering the fire and ventilating the smoke in the hold.[23] Similarly to fishmeal, divinylbenzene (DVB) is another substance that may present a risk of fire when mishandled. DVB is a liquid chemical, which is at risk of polymerisation (a form of self-reaction) when heated. When the container is exposed to heat, DVB may produce a flammable gas as a result of polymerisation, and once that gas communicates with a certain amount of oxygen, the DVB may catch fire, which may lead to an explosion. This is in fact what happened on board *MSC Flaminia* where the shipment of DVB was only loaded onto the ship after sitting on the dock for 10 days in hot weather conditions. The poorly handled cargo, owing to its exposure of heat, generated flammable gas that led to an explosion, causing damage to the vessel, the cargo on board and the loss of lives.[24]

(ii) Petroleum Products and Liquefied Gases

The carriage of petroleum products, such as fuel oil, is generally assumed one of the safest in practice. Many common types known in the trade have a particular flashpoint associated with the relevant product, and the safe carriage of the intended cargo is provided by carrying it at temperatures generally within 10°C of its particular flashpoint. However, some types could be partly composed of some residual fuel oils from previous cargo, which might cause explosion unless the tanks of the vessel are pumped with carbon dioxide. Such fuel oils might have a propensity to give off inflammable light hydrocarbon vapours, which may lead the lower explosive limit (LEL) to exceed the acceptable level in the headspace of the vessel, regardless of the flashpoint temperature. If the necessary precautions are not taken, the inherent flammability of such fuel oils can cause devastating explosions.[25] Sometimes, it might be that all the relevant characteristics associated with the intended cargo are known but the danger might lie within the tank's floor. It

[21] ibid; www.bulkcarrierguide.com/fishmeal-loading.html.

[22] *General Feeds Inc v Burnham Shipping Corporation (The Amphion)* [1991] 2 Lloyd's Rep 101.

[23] ibid.

[24] *In re M/V MSC Flaminia* 339 F Supp 3d 185 (SDNY 2018).

[25] See *Mediterranean Freight Services Ltd v BP Oil International Ltd (The Fiona)* [1993] 1 Lloyd's Rep 257, affirmed in [1994] 2 Lloyd's Rep 506.

is not uncommon in oil trade that the residues of the previously carried cargo are left in the tank. The practical solution is to clean the tanks to remove residues by carrying out a proper line and duct wash before loading the next cargo. A failure to do so will likely lead to contamination of the residues from the previous cargo with the loaded fuel oil, and accordingly this will increase the likelihood of explosion, as the vapour mixture could change the flashpoint and the LEL of the fuel oil in question.

So far as liquefied petroleum gases (LPGs) and liquefied natural gases (LNGs) are concerned, they may cause direct physical dangers as well as indirect ones. LPGs and LNGs are carried in special tanks under pressure at very low temperatures in liquid form. Although LPGs such as butane and propane and LNGs are types of hydrocarbons, which render them highly combustible, in liquid form they do not burn or explode. However, LPGs boil at ambient temperature, which would generate flammable vapour, and accordingly in confined spaces like tanks they may increase the likelihood of fire or explosion.[26] Once they mix with other flammable vapour residues from previous cargoes in tanks, or with oxygen, they may also ignite, causing fire or explosion. Similarly, LNG does not burn in liquid form. It may create vapour only if it is mixed with a residue from previous loads of LNG of a different density or if it is contaminated by water. Air in the tanks is forced out by applying inert gas into the tanks. Otherwise in cargo tanks, as LNGs are highly combustible in vapour form, they are likely to cause fire or explosion when mixed with oxygen.[27] Also such liquid gases may cause indirect damage. For instance, if butane contains high sulphur content, it might be regarded as of inferior quality, or off specification. Due to an unacceptable amount of sulphur content, butane may cause contamination in the tanks of the vessel. So as not to contaminate the next cargo with sulphur residues from the previous cargo, a detailed decontamination should be carried out to clean tanks of the vessel.[28] Similarly, hydrogen sulphide compounds might be present in propane. Hydrogen sulphide is a corrosive and flammable substance, which could be explosive if mixed with air. An extensive decontamination must be carried out in the tanks of the vessel so that explosions are avoided and subsequent consignments are not contaminated.[29] In the carriage of gasoil, a similar problem may arise. Gasoil might produce colony-forming units (CFUs) of bacteria, yeasts or moulds if it is stored in a contaminated tank. Gasoil becomes more prone to hydrocarbon-eating bacterial infection if water is present in the cargo or if it is exposed to different temperatures. Hydrocarbon-eating bacteria generate hydrogen sulphide. Where this is the case, an extensive decontamination might be required to clean the tanks of the vessel.[30]

[26] 'Making bunkering safe', *Maritime Risk International* (December 2019).

[27] ibid.

[28] See *Sig Bergesen DY & Co and Others v Mobil Shipping and Transportation Co (The Berge Sund)* [1993] 2 Lloyd's Rep 453. See also *American Overseas Marine Corp v Golar Commodities Ltd (The LNG Gemini)* [2014] EWHC 1347.

[29] *Marimpex Mineralöl Handelsgesellschaft mbH v Louis Dreyfus et Cie Mineralöl GmbH* [1995] 1 Lloyd's Rep 167.

[30] *Borealis AB v Stargas Ltd (The Berge Sisar)* [2001] UKHL 17; [2002] AC 205.

(iii) Non-inherently Dangerous Goods

Just because a cargo is not inherently dangerous does not necessarily mean that it may not present danger. Biofuels such as vegetable oils and biodiesels are not classified as dangerous goods, as vegetable oil and most biodiesels have a flashpoint above 100°C. However, for instance, if a cargo of biodiesel with a flashpoint above 100°C happened to be contaminated with water or residues from previous cargoes with a lower flashpoint such as chemicals, oxidising substances, methanol, diesel or gasoline, such mixing would cause fire or explosion, as it would drop the flashpoint of the biodiesel in question.[31] To avoid such incidents, a proper cleaning must be carried out to remove the remains of water and residues of previous cargoes in the tanks for safe carriage. Cocoa butter is another good example of goods that do not have to be inherently dangerous to be troublesome during transport. Cocoa butter is produced from cocoa beans which contains around 57–54 per cent saturated fats and 36–43 per cent unsaturated fats. It is a product that softens around 30–32°C and its melting point is 37°C. Once melted, it preserves the latent heat and its molten form even around as low as 17°C.[32] It is predominantly shipped from equatorial and tropical countries and carried through hot climate zones where it is exposed to high ambient temperatures during transit. The interior temperature of the container is said to reach 50°C or even higher when the ambient temperature outside the container is around 30°C.[33] Cocoa butter cargoes are often shipped in dry containers. However, considering the countries where cocoa butter is exported from, packing it into 'reefer' (refridgerated) containers increases the possibility of safe carriage, as they will protect the cargo from radiant heat by reducing the transfer of heat from outside into the container. However, packaging is as important as choosing the right container type for cocoa butter cargoes, particularly when shipped in dry containers. They should be packaged in plastic bags and sealed properly and subsequently put into carton boxes. If cocoa butter is not packaged properly or exposed to high temperatures due to the wrong container choice, it is liable to expand and burst the packaging, causing spillage inside the container and leakage outside the container on board the vessel, which may result in damage to the container as well as damage to the vessel by clogging the vessel's bilges.[34]

As with biofuels and cocoa butter, grains such as barley, oats, rice, corn, seeds and their processed forms are not considered inherently dangerous either. Accordingly, their carriage is regulated under the International Code for the Safe Carriage of Grain in Bulk (International Grain Code).[35] However, this does

[31] www.gov.uk/government/publications/carriage-of-dangerous-goods-guidance-note-16/thameslink-southern-and-great-northern-tsgn-2014-franchise-agreement.

[32] www.cinsnet.com/wp-content/uploads/2017/11/CINS-Cocoa-Butter-Guidelines-January-2018-Final.pdf, 3.

[33] ibid.

[34] ibid, 3–4.

[35] See generally, Chapter 2, section III.B.

not mean that grain cannot pose danger to the vessel, the lives of crew, or other cargoes on board. Most grains are carried in large quantities in bulk. They can only be carried at certain temperatures, and under certain moisture and ventilation conditions, as the majority of them are shipped in a damp state, which may cause spontaneous combustion. Often the nature and characteristics of usual types of grains are known to the carrier. Therefore, safe carriage is provided with the usual precautions known in the trade. However, if the cargo in question is different from the usual type, it may require different temperatures and different ventilation conditions during carriage. The centre of grain shipped in bulk has a tendency to natural heating, as ventilation will not reach the centre of the cargo. Accordingly, the centre, as a result of self-heating, will spontaneously combust and smoulder. When air reaches the smouldering parts, the cargo will simply burst into flames leading to fire. Wheat is one of the grains most commonly transported by sea and the carriage temperature of its usual type is around 20°C. If the usual type is carried at over 25°C, it will produce excessive carbon dioxide in the hold, causing self-heating.[36] Some types of wheat may have higher level of moisture. Wheat with a moisture content above 15 per cent is considered moist or wet and as a result, it may require a cooler atmosphere. Ventilation replaces moist air with drier air, which helps control and reduce the moisture within the hold. Such a cargo of wheat will release more water vapour than usual. Therefore, if extensive ventilation is not applied, depending on the nature and characteristics of the cargo, wheat will easily cause damp in the hold even at around 20°C, stimulating activity of the respiratory enzymes. Subsequently, respiration will lead the cargo to self-heat, which may cause spontaneous combustion in the end. As well as self-heating, such high levels of moisture may cause swelling in wheat, which may also give rise to swelling in the hold causing structural damage to the vessel.[37] Apart from these risks, grains may pose a different type of danger to the vessel or other cargoes on board. Insect infestation is not uncommon in many types of grain. The presence of insects, as a result of their metabolic activity, will contribute to respiration in the hold, which will cause a rise in temperature, subsequently leading to self-heating of the cargo. Such cargoes will require fumigation either prior to or after loading to fully eliminate insects within the hold. Otherwise the presence of insects or pests in the cargo will not only give rise to damage to the cargo itself, but also to the vessel, other cargoes on board and any subsequent cargo to be shipped.[38]

(iv) Solid Bulk Cargoes

There are also solid bulk cargoes carried by sea, such as coal, iron ore, wood products, fertilisers and cement, etc, that may pose serious risks to the vessel,

[36] www.skuld.com/topics/cargo/solid-bulk/agricultural-cargoes/transportation-of-wheat.
[37] ibid; www.tis-gdv.de/tis_e/ware/getreide/weizen/weizen-htm/#schaedlingsbefall.
[38] See *The Giannis NK* [1998] AC 605.

other cargoes and lives on board. The main risks associated with these goods are instability, capsizing, structural damage to the vessel and fire or explosion. The main authority setting out the standards for safe carriage of solid bulk cargoes is the International Maritime Solid Bulk Cargoes (IMSBC) Code.[39] The IMSBC Code divides solid bulk cargoes into three main groups: Group A, Group B and Group C.

(a) Group A Cargoes

Group A includes cargoes that are liable to liquefy if they are shipped with a moisture content exceeding their Transportable Moisture Limit (TML).[40] When liquefaction occurs, it may cause the cargo to shift resulting in the vessel capsizing or total loss of the vessel and her crew. Although cargoes that are liable to liquefy are in dry and granular form, they contain a certain amount of moisture and particles. Most common examples of such cargoes are iron ore concentrates, iron ore fines (small particles of ore), nickel ore and bauxite fines, which caused tragic incidents on board *Bulk Jupiter, Vinalines Queen, Jian Fu Star*, and *Asian Forest* due to liquefaction.[41] Iron ore concentrates can be produced by two different processes: wet and dry processing. In dry processing, the ore is crushed to subtract the waste material within. Following this, iron ore concentrate is produced in powder form with a low amount of moisture. Iron concentrate contains oxygen and it may react with sulphur within the cargo, creating heat. As a result, it may be liable to spontaneously combust. In wet processing, iron ore is washed by water to remove sulphides. The concentrate produced from the wet processing contains a high amount of moisture. When the vessel is at sea, the constant motion of the vessel and vibrations of the engine cause mobility in the cargo of iron ore. Due to such movement, the volume of space between the particles within the cargo reduces. This, in return gives rise to an increase in the pore water pressure (the pressure of water in gaps between particles) meaning that the cargo may reach its flow moisture point (FMP). When this happens, liquefaction occurs, and subsequently the cargo may react like fluid shifting to one side of the bulkheads, which in the end is likely to capsize the vessel.[42]

(b) Group B Cargoes

So far as Group B cargoes are concerned, they may give rise to dangerous situations on the vessel owing to chemical hazards. The most common dangers posed by Group B cargoes are fire, explosion and corrosion. Wood products like wood pellets or wood chips are one of the most popular Group B cargoes carried by sea. Despite the fact that incidents are rare in wood product shipments and these cargoes appear to be innocuous, there are still some serious dangers

[39] See generally, Chapter 2, section III.A.
[40] The TML is the maximum moisture content allowed for safe carriage of the particular cargo.
[41] See also *Micada Compania Naviera SA v Texim (The Agios Nicolas)* [1968] 2 Lloyd's Rep 57.
[42] 'Cargo liquefaction – still a problem; still taking lives', *Maritime Risk International* (May 2012).

associated with the carriage of wood products. Wood pellets are composed of timber shavings in a pelletised form. There are two main types of wood pellets: the pellets with additive/binder which may emit flammable gas and the pellets without binder.[43] Both types are liable to self-heat and 'off-gas' in bulk form. Self-heating or self-ignition of wood pellets may occur as a result of chemical oxidation or microbiological decay. Wood pellets are composed of fibrous material, which is produced from wood shavings. The fibres generate heat by oxidation. When they are exposed to the air, they are liable to oxidise, leading to the depletion of the oxygen in the hold, which will eventually cause wood pellets to release heat. Depending on the moisture content, the temperature and age of the biomass, wood pellets may quickly self-heat causing fire.[44] Depending on their moisture content, wood pellets are also prone to self-ignition owing to microbiological decay. A high moisture content gives rise to the development of microorganisms, which in turn causes the generation of heat as a result of chemical oxidation. Such self-heating of wood pellets may escalate to the point of fire.[45] Similarly to wood *pellets*, although wood *chips* seem to be harmless, they may also pose danger as a result of being prone to self-ignition. Depending on the age of biomass and the moisture content of the cargo in question, oxygen depletion and the growth of carbon dioxide may occur in the space, leading wood chips to spontaneously combust by friction.[46]

Direct reduced iron (DRI) as a Group B cargo, is also prone to spontaneous combustion and emitting toxic gases. DRI, which has a very low moisture content, is produced from iron ore without having any contact with air. When carried in bulk, these cargoes are kept separated by magnets to preserve the low moisture content within the cargo. If DRI reacts with air, as a result of oxidation, it starts to produce hydrogen and heat, leading the cargo to spontaneously combust and emit toxic gases, causing explosions.[47] Like DRI, metal sulphide concentrates like zinc, lead or nickel sulphide concentrates may also cause a chemical hazard, as they are also liable to self-heat and emit toxic fumes as a result of oxygen depletion. Depending on the moisture level in the cargo, metal sulphide concentrates may generate sulphuric acid, which may give rise to corrosion problems in the vessel.[48] Coal is another material that is widely known as a Group B cargo, as it is flammable and prone to self-heating, due to the combustible chemicals like carbons and hydrocarbons present in it. However, as some types of coals are liable to liquefy, where 75 per cent of the cargo comprises particles less than 5mm in size, it could be classed as Group A as well as Group B under the IMSBC Code.[49] Coal slurry is one of the liquefiable coal types. It has a high moisture content and is in very fine

[43] See generally, www.skuld.com/topics/cargo/solid-bulk/general-advice/wood-pellets-and-risk-of-fire; www.irclass.org/technical-circulars/fire-safety-hazards-associated-with-wood-pellets.

[44] ibid.

[45] ibid.

[46] ibid.

[47] www.bulkcarrierguide.com/iron-ore.html.

[48] www.nautinst.org/uploads/assets/uploaded/d865b674-d59d-4255-8d7b462811d48043.pdf, 11.

[49] A cargo of coal will not be deemed as a Group A cargo, if it contains more than 10% fine particles less than 1mm in size and more than 50% fine particles less than 10mm in size. In case of exceeding either of these limits, the cargo will be classified as both Group A and B under the IMSBC Code.

form, often less than 1mm in size. Thus, it is liable to liquefy and may pose dangers associated with Group A cargoes. Another type is coal duff, which is composed of particles around 7mm in size. Although this type is less likely to liquefy due to the presence of large particles, it may still present a risk of liquefaction, as its moisture content can be sometimes higher than usual.[50] It is therefore important to inform the carrier adequately of the nature and the type of the cargo to be loaded, as some types of coal may liquefy, resulting in catastrophic incidents, if mishandled. On the other hand, even if not liable to liquefy, coal may present other types of dangers. Some types may emit methane which is an explosive gas, creating a flammable atmosphere. Since even an isolated spark could spontaneously ignite methane, bunker or fuel tanks adjacent to the hold carrying the cargo of coal may not be allowed to be used during transport. Methane, as it is lighter than air, moves upward and may even travel to adjacent holds, expanding the explosive atmosphere on board the vessel.[51] Therefore, the temperature of coal and the methane level must be monitored prior to and after loading to see whether these figures are within the acceptable limits. Unless the hold is ventilated adequately, the excessive amounts of methane in the hold may lead to an explosion resulting in the total loss of the vessel, loss of lives and damage to other cargoes on board.[52] The dangers created by coal are not limited to liquefaction or methane-related explosions. Some types may also be liable to self-heating, causing the cargo to spontaneously combust, given the presence of moisture. A cargo of coal shipped in bulk with a high moisture content may give rise to exothermic oxidation in the centre of the cargo. Due to the presence of a high level of moisture, the oxygen in the cargo will be confined in the centre causing exothermic oxidation, which in turn generates heat and smouldering at ambient temperature, building up to a point that the cargo bursts into flames causing major fires and explosions.[53] Coal may also cause severe corrosion to the surfaces of the hold carrying the cargo. If it comes into contact with water or has high level of moisture or contains sulphur, it will produce acid leachate, leading to severe corrosion in the vessel's structure.[54]

(c) Group C Cargoes

Unlike Groups A and B, Group C cargoes are classified as neither liable to liquefy nor possessing chemical hazards. Although their carriage may appear to be safe at first sight, they may nevertheless pose great risks to the vessel, lives and other cargoes on board. Bauxite and cement are popular examples of Group C cargoes. Bauxite is considered to carry no risk of liquefaction, as it is considered not liable

[50] www.bulkcarrierguide.com/coal-hazards.html.

[51] ibid.

[52] 'An insight into the causes and prevention of cargo fires', *Maritime Risk International*, (December 2017). See also, *the Athanasia Comninos and Georges Chr Lemos* [1990] 1 Lloyd's Rep 277.

[53] www.bulkcarrierguide.com/coal-hazards-&-safety-considerations.html; www.bulkcarrierguide.com/coal-hazards.html.

[54] www.bulkcarrierguide.com/cargo.html; www.bulkcarrierguide.com/corrosion.html.

to liquefy as a Group C cargo. However, in 2015 *Bulk Jupiter* carried 46,400 tonnes of bauxite fines of which the moisture content was around 21 per cent. Although according to the IMSBC Code, the acceptable moisture limit is below 10 per cent for the cargo in question, the Bauxite Schedule of the Code showed no 'special hazard' associated with the carriage of bauxite if the amount of moisture in the cargo is in excess of the allowed moisture level in the Code.[55] In the event, however, owing to its high moisture content, *Bulk Jupiter's* cargo of 46,400 tonnes of bauxite fines liquefied, leading to the total loss of *Bulk Jupiter* along with the tragic loss of 18 lives on board.[56] Cement is another example of a cargo that seems innocuous but may present certain risks to the vessel. Cement is not a combustible cargo. Thus, it does not carry the risk of fire. However, the temperature of cement may pose some serious risks to the vessel. It is important to check the temperature of cement prior to loading. If a cargo of cement with a temperature over 100°C is loaded, it may cause serious damage to the hold coatings. A cargo of cement with such a high temperature, or even a cargo of cement with a higher temperature than that of the hold, may produce water vapour within the hold when loaded. This may result in water vapour condensing, leading the cement in the hold to dampen. When the wet cement dries, it is liable to solidify in the hold, giving rise to significant delays to the vessel owing to the necessary extensive cleaning process, which could be costly.[57]

B. The Law Surrounding the Shipment of Dangerous Goods

Following from the previous section, it would not be wrong to say that whether it is inherently dangerous or not, any cargo can create hazards, and dangerous goods come in any shape, size, form and kind. They present serious risks to the vessel, safety of life, other cargoes on board and the environment. Of great significance in avoiding and preventing the risks that may potentially arise from these goods, are knowledge of the nature of the cargo to be shipped, and taking all the necessary precautions required by the intended cargo. It would not be practical to expect carriers to be an 'expert chemist'[58] and to be aware of all the necessary information and precautions in relation to each cargo that they accept to carry on board. Consequently, shippers, who are often the sellers of the goods to be shipped[59] – having a superior means of knowledge of the nature of their goods that they present for shipment to carriers, and having a closer nexus with their own goods

[55] See Appendix 1 of the IMSBC Code.

[56] Bauxite fines are classified within Group A cargoes, following IMO Resolution MSC.462 (101). See Chapter 2 below.

[57] www.bulkcarrierguide.com/cement-handling.html.

[58] *Brass v Maitland* (1856) 6 E & B 470; 119 ER 940.

[59] On this see generally, Chapter 4.

to know the dangers associated with them – are justifiably subject to strict liability under English law, which will be discussed in Chapter three below.[60]

In order to make the carrier aware of the nature or the circumstances that may create danger, at common law the shipper is under an implied duty to warn the carrier of the dangerous nature and character of the goods prior to loading.[61] Therefore if goods are loaded without such notice given of their dangerous nature and character, the shipper of the goods will be subject to strict liability for damage or loss caused to the vessel, any other cargo or lives on board.[62] The concept of the common law duty also extends to cases where there is no physical danger whatsoever. The shipper of the goods can have liability imposed on him for economic losses resulting from 'legally' dangerous goods which lead to legal obstacles and delay to the vessel.[63] For instance, a cargo of rice, which itself was physically innocuous, was held to be legally dangerous, because the shipper failed to obtain the permission for discharge (unloading of cargo) from the British government, thus causing delay to the vessel and to the discharge of other cargoes on board.[64] When the Hague Rules or the Hague-Visby Rules[65] (the Rules) are applicable to the carriage contract evidenced or contained in the bill of lading, the common law duty is supplanted.[66] However, pursuant to article IV rule 6 of the Rules, when the carrier 'has not consented, with knowledge of their nature and character' to 'goods of an inflammable, explosive or dangerous nature', the carrier is entitled to an indemnity from the shipper of the goods in respect of 'all damages and expenses directly or indirectly arising out of or resulting from such shipment'.[67] Similarly to the common law obligation, the word 'dangerous' in article IV rule 6 is given a broad interpretation in the sense of physical danger and is not restrictively qualified by the preceding words 'inflammable, explosive'.[68]

[60] *Brass v Maitland* (1856) 6 E & B 470; 119 ER 940; *The Giannis NK* [1998] AC 605.

[61] However the shipper is not under such a duty where the shipowner knows or ought reasonably to be aware of the nature and character of the goods: *Brass v Maitland* (1856) 6 E & B 470; 119 ER 940; *Bamfield v Goole and Sheffield Transport Co Ltd* [1910] 2 KB 94; *Great Northern Railway Co v LEP Transport & Depository Ltd* [1922] 2 KB 742; (1922) 11 Ll L Rep 133. A similar duty may arise under a charterparty, even though in most situations there will be an express clause in relation to this duty therein.

[62] *Great Nothern Railway Co v LEP Transport & Depository Ltd* [1922] 2 KB 742; *Micada v Texim* [1968] 2 Lloyd's Rep 57; *Mediterranean Freight Services Ltd v BP Oil International Ltd (The Fiona)* [1993] 1 Lloyd's Rep 257 (High Ct), affirmed in [1994] 2 Lloyd's Rep 506 (CA); *The Giannis NK* [1998] AC 605.

[63] *Mitchell Cotts & Co Ltd v Steel Brothers & Co Ltd* [1916] 2 KB 610.

[64] ibid.

[65] The Hague-Visby Rules have the force of law in England by virtue of the Carriage of Goods by Sea Act 1971.

[66] *The Fiona* [1993] 1 Lloyd's Rep 257, affirmed in [1994] 2 Lloyd's Rep 506. The common law duty is superseded in respect of physically dangerous goods. The common law duty arising from legally dangerous goods is not supplanted by the Rules. See *Bunge SA v ADM do Brasil Ltda and Others (The Darya Radhe)* [2009] EWHC 845 (Comm); [2009] 2 Lloyd's Rep 175; *Mitchell Cotts & Co Ltd v Steel Brothers & Co Ltd* [1916] 2 KB 610.

[67] See art IV r 6 of the Rules. It should be noted that there is no material difference between the Hague Rules and the Hague-Visby Rules in terms of the wording of this provision.

[68] *The Giannis NK* [1998] AC 605; [1998] 1 Lloyd's Rep 337, 341. In the case, it was held that the provision is also applicable where the goods cause indirect physical loss. Nevertheless, art IV r 6 is

The carrier is therefore entitled to indemnity even if the goods cause indirect physical damage to the vessel, other cargo or crew on board.[69]

However, this formulation only provides a partial picture of the allocation of liability for dangerous goods, which is only from the perspective of the law of carriage of goods by sea, and only attaches this liability vis-à-vis the carrier to whoever falls within the term 'shipper'. The shipper is a party that enters into a carriage contract with the carrier under the bill of lading.[70] The term 'shipper', however, does not signify any real party or identity under the law of carriage of goods by sea. Nor is it concerned with anything beyond that. Therefore, there is the question of who is the real party contracting for the carriage of goods by sea. Perhaps the answer to this question lies within the law of international trade, as there is a complex but a reciprocal relationship between the law of carriage of goods by sea and the law of international trade. Thousands of commercial ships sail daily across the seas for one main reason: in order to carry goods that are purchased and sold internationally under sale contracts. The vast majority of reported cases on international sale of goods appear to prove that those contracts are contextually in a direct nexus with marine transportation. Although no rigorous definition has been given, contracts for the international sale of goods can be divided into sub-headings according to the mode and place of delivery of the goods: *ex works* contracts,[71] *ex ships* contracts,[72] and contracts of sale on *shipment terms*. However, the focus of this book is on sale contracts on shipment terms only, on the grounds that first, the former two do not raise similar legal issues and in practice almost have nothing in common with contracts on shipment terms; and second, an overwhelming majority of contracts for international sale of goods are concluded on shipment terms, namely CIF (cost, insurance and freight) and FOB (free on board) or variations thereof.[73] These contracts are called sale contracts on shipment terms, as the seller's physical obligations in relation to the goods end at the loading port rather than at the arrival port. However, it does not necessarily follow that the seller's physical obligations end when he loads the goods as agreed in the sale contract at the port of shipment. Under these sales, someone must also make transport arrangements and conclude a contract of carriage for the goods. Depending on the stipulation in the contract, this could be either the seller or the buyer. Even though there is no invariable rule in that respect, under CIF sales and often FOB sales, due to the development of international trade, responsibility for making shipping arrangements is often shifted onto the seller rather than the buyer.[74]

confined to physically dangerous goods and not applicable to legally dangerous goods which may be liable to cause delay or detention: *the Darya Radhe* [2009] EWHC 845; [2009] 2 Lloyd's Rep 175.

[69] *The Giannis NK* [1998] AC 605; [1998] 1 Lloyd's Rep 337.

[70] Art I(a) of the Rules.

[71] Where delivery takes place at the seller's premises, eg a factory, plant or warehouse.

[72] Where delivery takes place at an agreed destination, eg an agreed port of arrival.

[73] For variations of these contracts, see Chapter 4.

[74] See s 32(2) of the Sale of Goods Act 1979.

In the concept of sales on shipment terms, for the performance of the sale contract, documents are as significant as goods. Following the fulfilment of physical duties, the seller – depending on the type of sale contract – is also often bound to tender to the buyer some documents stipulated in the contract in order to get paid for the goods.[75] At the centre of these documents lies the bill of lading,[76] which performs some important functions under these sales. First, it is a receipt for the goods containing statements in relation to the quantity and quality of the goods. It is also a document of title enabling the holder to obtain constructive possession of the goods and often property in the goods. Most significantly, it also evidences a contract of carriage for the agreed destination in the sale contract. Almost invariably under CIF sales, and often under FOB sales when the buyer has not concluded the carriage contract, the buyer is not privy to the carriage contract with the carrier. Where this is the case, given the doctrine of privity of contract established under English law,[77] the buyer will not be able to sue or be sued under the carriage contract evidenced in the bill of lading that is concluded on his behalf, however firmly linked with it he is.[78] The contractual gap between the buyer and the carrier was first filled by a statutory anti-privity device, the Bills of Lading Act 1855 (the 1855 Act). Due to not having up-to-date trading standards and other deficiencies in it, it was later repealed by the Carriage of Goods by Sea Act 1992[79] (the 1992 Act).[80] English law in terms of contracts of carriage is based on the principle of mutuality, which means that it is not only concerned with the transfer of rights, but also with the imposition of liabilities.[81] This position is also preserved under the 1992 Act, which accordingly enables transfer not only of rights but also liabilities thereunder. This spawns the question of whether the buyer who is not the shipper is immune from liability for dangerous goods. In relation to liability arising from dangerous goods, the transferability of liability is not settled law as of yet under English law.[82] However, if technically transmissible to the buyer, after incurring this liability under the carriage contract tendered by the seller, the buyer as an innocent party who has nothing to do with the shipment of such goods,

[75] Except where the contract is on bare FOB terms. See generally, Chapter 4.

[76] Indeed, the parties may alternatively choose other shipping documents too. See generally, Chapter 5.

[77] *Tweddle & Atkinson* (1861) 1 B & S 393; *The Giannis NK* [1998] AC 605, 616.

[78] *Thompson v Dominy* (1845) 14 M & W 403, 407; 153 ER 532, 534; *Howard v Shepherd* (1850) 9 CB 297, 319; 137 ER 907, 916. See also *Dunlop Pneumatic Tyre Co Ltd v Selfridge & Co Ltd* [1915] AC 847, 853. The bill of lading enables the buyer only to have document of title, which gives constructive possession and may also enable him to obtain the title to the goods if intended. See *Lickbarrow v Mason* (1794) 5 Term Rep 683. See also *Sewell v Burdick* (1884) 10 App Cas 74.

[79] Repealed by s 6(2) of the 1992 Act.

[80] English law, in order to resolve the issue of privity of contract in general contract law, enacted the Contracts (Rights of Third Parties) Act 1999. However the Act expressly is not applicable to contracts of carriage: ss 6(5)(a) and 6(6). The Act also does not affect the liabilities of third parties in general.

[81] *Borealis AB v Stargas Ltd (The Berge Sisar)* [2001] UKHL 17; [2002] AC 205, [31] and [45]. See also Law Commission, *Rights of Suit in Respect of Carriage of Goods by Sea* (Law Com No 196, Scot Law Com No 130, 1991) para 3.22.

[82] *Ministry of Food v Lamport & Holt Line* [1952] 2 Lloyd's Rep 371, 382. But see *The Giannis NK* [1998] AC 605; [1998] 1 Lloyd's Rep. 337.

would first seek to re-allocate it under the sale contract. However, this is not a fully explored area, given that the buyer has actually yet to have such a liability imposed on him. This begs a further intriguing question of whether the law of international sale of goods would respond to enable recovery of the buyer's loss incurred under the bill of lading which is tendered under the sale contract by his seller.

The complex scheme of the law of international trade therefore proves the necessity to discuss the question which forms the main substance of this book: How does liability arising from the shipment of dangerous goods spread to the parties of international trade, namely between the seller and the buyer under CIF and FOB sales? The significance of this question is threefold as it produces three sub-questions: first, the question of who the shipper is under CIF and FOB sales and whether the courts adopt a different approach in determining the identity of the shipper, specifically for the purpose of the allocation of liability for dangerous goods; second, the question of whether this liability is actually transmissible to the buyer; third, the question of whether the law of international sale of goods would provide any assistance in the re-allocation of liability between the buyer and the seller. With these questions in mind, the book explores the allocation of risk and liability for dangerous goods between the seller and the buyer under CIF (cost, insurance and freight) and FOB (free on board) contracts, providing an in-depth study of the issue of carriage of dangerous goods in the context of the law of international trade. Although much of the content stems from the contractual context, the book also provides a non-contractual angle, proposing suggestions under non-contractual mechanisms. As there has not been much discussion on the issues within the scope of the book, a detailed examination of and attempt to answer these questions will therefore contribute to the literature by filling the gap in this respect.

Some limitations should also be worth adding from the outset. Throughout this book it is assumed that the proper law of contracts of sale and carriage is English law.[83] However, it incorporates case law examples from multiple jurisdictions like the Commonwealth countries and to some extent from the US and the Nordic countries in order to draw comparisons. Also, the 1980 United Nations Convention on Contracts for the International Sale of Goods (CISG) will not be part of this book, since the UK has not ratified it. More significantly, the CISG does not describe CIF and FOB sales, nor does it make any reference to bills of lading. Neither does it provide much, if any, assistance in regard to the issues arising in CIF and FOB sales under English law. Moreover, the commercial parties almost invariably exclude its application under these sales.[84] It is also worth noting that not a great deal of space is devoted to the UN Convention on Contracts for the International Carriage of Goods Wholly or Partly by Sea (the Rotterdam Rules),

[83] The applicable law will be determined under the Rome I Regulation on the Law Applicable to Contracts, Regulation (EC) 593/2008. See arts 3 and 4 of the Regulation.

[84] For such an example, see the standard forms of the Grain and Feed Trade Association (GAFTA) 100, clause 29(b).

since it is unlikely that it will become part of English law any time soon. A final point worth highlighting in respect of the book is a language convention. Since almost all the parties in this work are companies, and so have legal personalities, they will not be regarded as 'it'. Purely due to conventional English usage in this field, each party will be referred to as 'he' or 'him'.

II. Structure of the Book

This book, apart from the Introduction (Chapter one) and Conclusion (Chapter ten), is divided into eight main chapters. Chapter two encapsulates the international efforts regulating the maritime transport of dangerous goods in a nutshell. Chapter three provides a general framework of liability for dangerous goods, discussing the nature of the liability and drawing comparisons from multiple shipping jurisdictions, including the Commonwealth and the United States. Chapter four addresses the question of who would attract liability for dangerous goods under CIF and FOB sales at the shipment stage. It also provides a non-contractual angle addressing the proximity between the non-contractual seller and the shipowner at the shipment stage. Chapter five looks into whether the buyer is offered immunity from liability for dangerous goods simply because he is not the shipper, mapping out the question of whether this liability is transmissible from the shipper/seller to the buyer/transferee under the carriage contract by means of the 1992 Act. Following the discussion of transferability under a contractual regime, Chapter six focuses on whether, where there is no contractual nexus between the carrier and the buyer on the other side of the voyage, namely at the delivery stage, the carrier or other victims affected by dangerous goods are entitled to sue the buyer/consignee for damage or losses arising from these goods under the common law actions. Chapter seven addresses the question of whether the law of international sale of goods would provide any assistance in the re-allocation of liability between the buyer and the seller, finding a causal link between the loss inherited by the buyer consequent upon the damage caused by dangerous goods and the breach by the seller under the sale contract. Following this, Chapter eight discusses whether such loss would be recoverable from the seller under the principles of the law of damages applicable in sale of goods. Chapter nine, in seeking a remedy for the buyer (particularly in chain sales) who has no contractual nexus with the seller/shipper, moves away from the contractual regime and explores alternative non-contractual solutions, proposing that the buyer might have an arguable claim directly against the shipper/seller under the Civil Liability (Contribution) Act 1978 and in tort.

2

International Regulations on Dangerous Goods

I. Overview

Goods are carried by sea across the world on board thousands of commercial vessels with the aim of arriving safely at ports of discharge. This is not easy by any means, as vessels must carry out this task in accordance with both comprehensive national and international regulations. Carriage of dangerous goods, however, requires even more comprehensive and scrutinised means for safe carriage, which necessitates the dedication of all the stakeholders involved in shipment and carriage of these goods with appropriate organisation. Otherwise, improper handling or care of dangerous goods could result in catastrophic damage to the environment, the vessel, other goods and lives on board. Thus, international regulations dedicated to the transport of these goods by individualised measures have paramount importance in ensuring safe shipment and carriage. Before delving into the law surrounding dangerous goods, this chapter will therefore seek to encapsulate the international efforts regulating the maritime transport of these goods as well as their effectiveness in a nutshell.

A. Historical Background

There was no concern regarding dangerous goods until the mid-nineteenth century and the phrase 'dangerous goods', in respect of carriage of goods by sea, was first used in the case of *Brass v Maitland* where the cargo of bleaching powder was considered dangerous, as it damaged the other cargo stowed adjacently due to leakage, because the substance called chloride of lime in the cargo was not known to be capable of corroding the casks.[1] In terms of a legislative measure, the term 'dangerous goods' was first used in section 301 (headed 'Dangerous Goods and Carriage of Cattle') of the Merchant Shipping Act 1894.[2] The International

[1] *Brass v Maitland* (1856) 6 E & B 470; 119 ER 940.

[2] It reads '… an emigrant ship shall not clear outwards or proceed to sea, if there is on board – (a) as cargo, any article which is an explosive within the meaning of the … Explosives Act, 1875, or any vitriol, lucifer matches, guano, or green hides, or (b) either as cargo or ballast, any article or number of articles which by reason of the nature, quantity, or mode of stowage thereof are, either singly or

Convention for the Safety of Life at Sea (SOLAS) is arguably considered the most important international maritime treaty on the safety of commercial vessels. As a term in an international instrument, 'dangerous goods' was first used in the earliest version of the Convention (SOLAS 1914),[3] which was adopted in response to the sinking of the *RMS Titanic*. Article 55(1) reads 'the carriage … of goods which by reason of their nature, quantity and mode of stowage are … likely to endanger the lives of the passengers or the safety of the ship, is forbidden.' Article 55(2) stated what goods were to be considered dangerous goods, and the precautions that were to be taken in packing and stowage were left to the contracting states. In the second version of the Convention (SOLAS 1929), there was not much improvement as regards dangerous goods, as the same notion and wording was preserved in article 24 thereof. This is not entirely surprising, as dangerous goods would have composed only a microscopic proportion of the goods carried by sea at the time and the issues arising from these goods were relatively few.

Until almost the mid-twentieth century, the reported dangerous goods cases were only concerned with certain chemical products such as bleaching powder,[4] ferro-silicon,[5] oxygenated water,[6] sodium chlorate[7] and bichromate of potash.[8] As there were no regulatory measures, naturally there was no awareness of the risks associated with these goods and almost no importance was attached to the issue then. As a result, dangerous goods would be shipped, loaded, stowed, and discharged based on general practices used at the time in the carriage of other goods. By the mid-twentieth century, this approach appeared not to be working efficiently, with the increasing number of dangerous goods carried at sea, as they were not handled, packed or stowed having due regard to their nature and characteristics. After the Second World War, the world started becoming more and more industrialised and the increased production of some dangerous goods around the globe – like petroleum products, chemicals, explosives, flammables, acids or gases – gave rise to an increase in the carriage of these goods by sea. With the advancements in technology after the War, the lists of dangerous goods grew vastly, and an immense number of inherently dangerous substances became the subject of sea transport more than ever. Naturally, questions began to emerge as to the handling, packing, care and stowing practices used in the transport of these goods to ensure safety during shipment and transit.[9] As a consequence, in 1948, into the third version of SOLAS, a new chapter IV concerning carriage of grains

collectively, in the opinion of the emigration officer at the port of clearance, likely to endanger the health or lives of the steerage passengers or the safety of the ship …'.

[3] It never came into force given the outbreak of the First World War.

[4] *Brass v Maitland* (1856) 6 E & B 470; 119 ER 940.

[5] *Bamfield v Goole and Sheffield Transport Co Ltd* [1910] 2 KB 94.

[6] *Great Northern Railway Co v LEP Transport & Depository Ltd* [1922] 2 KB 742; (1922) 11 Ll L Rep 133.

[7] *Shaw Savill & Albion Co Ltd v Electric Reduction Co of Canada Ltd and Imperial Chemical Industries of Australia and New Zealand Ltd (The Mahia)* [1955] 1 Lloyd's Rep 264.

[8] *Hoey v Hardie & Another* (1912) 12 SR (NSW) 268.

[9] See generally, 'IMO and Dangerous Goods at Sea' (1996) International Maritime Organization Working Paper.

and dangerous goods was added. However, arguably the most important step was taken by the United Nations Committee of Experts on the Transport of Dangerous Goods, founded by the UN's Economic and Social Council (ECOSOC), when they published a report (the UN Recommendations on the Transport of Dangerous Goods (the 'Orange Book')) setting out the minimum requirements applicable for the transport of dangerous goods, to provide an internationally uniform approach across all modes of transport.[10]

After the mid-twentieth century, containerisation also changed the dynamics in the global shipping industry and the orthodox practices in relation to care, handling and stowage would consequently have to be changed fundamentally. Containers in most cases would be packed and sealed before they were presented for carriage to carriers, without having any marking, labelling or placarding on the outside to warn the carrier. With a wide range of dangerous goods, however, each substance would require different precautions in their sea carriage for safe passage. For instance, while some would require an adequate container, some would require segregation for safe carriage, as they would create danger when communicated with other goods. Some would need to be stowed below deck without getting exposed to direct sunlight, or contrarily some would require stowing on deck in a ventilated area to prevent spontaneous combustion. Indeed, these examples are not exhaustive. However, the basic practices of the time, of crane-lifting and stowing the container packed with dangerous goods randomly on board the vessel would not work without difficulties. Thus, the well-established practices in the nineteenth and the early twentieth centuries for packing, loading, stowing and handling would fall short for the safe carriage of dangerous goods, as even the slightest detail or the smallest margin concerning the nature and characteristics of these goods would play a significant role in the safe handling, stowage and segregation of these goods. Accordingly, the global shipping industry needed to adjust and update itself to be more information-centred on the nature of dangerous goods, as well as needing to adopt more technical practices in terms of handling, loading and stowing these goods, if they were to be carried at sea safely. Also, with the increasing number of claims arising from the shipment of dangerous goods, underwriters would require shippers to inform carriers of the nature of dangerous goods to be shipped and would start raising concerns about the lack of international regulatory measures on the handling and carriage of dangerous goods at sea. All these together triggered an enthusiasm for introducing an international regulatory measure on the issue and it was soon acknowledged that knowledge of the nature and characteristics of dangerous goods is the most important tool in the handling and the safe carriage of these goods at sea. Eventually, in 1965, the fourth version of SOLAS (SOLAS 1960) came into force, in which there was a special chapter (chapter VII) dealing with the transport of dangerous goods. In pursuance of Resolution 56 adopted at the 1960 SOLAS Conference, a recommendation

[10] ibid, 4.

was made on the necessity for a uniform international code concerning the carriage, packing, stowage and handling of dangerous goods so as to supplement the regulations laid down by SOLAS 1960.[11] In the same Resolution, it was also recommended that the works of the UN Committee of Experts on the Transport of Dangerous Goods on classification, description and labelling, on a list of dangerous goods and on shipping documents should be followed by the International Maritime Organisation (IMO).[12] The UN Committee of Experts produced a nine-class substance classification based on their physical or chemical properties for the purposes of identification, packaging, labelling and documentation.[13] In 1961, a Working Group on the Carriage of Dangerous Goods (CDG) was formed by IMO's Maritime Safety Committee (MSC) to prepare a uniform code applicable across the world.[14] Following the collaboration with the UN Committee of Experts on the Transport of Dangerous Goods, CDG Working Group prepared the early version of a code named the International Maritime Dangerous Goods (IMDG) Code.[15] By the end of 1965, to harmonise the safe carriage of dangerous goods, the IMDG Code was produced and adopted by the fourth IMO Assembly as a recommendatory instrument. Under chapter VII of the current version of the Convention (SOLAS 1974) as amended, the IMDG Code has enjoyed mandatory status since 2004.

II. The IMDG Code

A. General

The IMDG Code is a uniform international code that contains a set of detailed provisions listing the goods that are dangerous and describing requirements for the safe carriage of these goods. The first edition of the Code was based on the pioneering work on the matter developed by the United Kingdom in the 1920s and 1930s, called 'the Report of the Standing Advisory Committee on the Carriage of Dangerous Goods in Ships: the "Blue Book"'.[16] However, since the first edition, the Code has been amended and updated many times in response to developments in technology and regulations.[17] In 1996, it was agreed by the MSC that the IMDG Code should be reformatted in accordance with the above-mentioned

[11] ibid, 5.
[12] 'Radioactive Materials Transport the International Safety Regime – An Overview of Safety Regulations and the Organizations Responsible for their Development', *World Nuclear Transport Institute* (Revised July 2006) 71.
[13] ibid, 10.
[14] See Preamble of the IMDG Code.
[15] n 12 above, 70–71.
[16] ibid, 12.
[17] ibid, 72.

'Recommendations on the Transport of Dangerous Goods' (the Orange Book) published by the United Nations Committee of Experts.[18] In 2001 the IMDG Code was reformatted consistently with the format of the UN Model Regulations on the Transport of Dangerous Goods as well as the other model regulations concerning the transport of dangerous goods by air, rail and road, which were also reformatted to align with the UN requirements.[19] With the introduction of its new format in 2001, the Code was divided into two main volumes with a Supplement containing some relevant materials such as the Medical First Aid Guide for Use in Accidents Involving Dangerous Goods (MFAG) and the Irradiated Nuclear Fuel (INF) Code. The IMDG Code, except for some parts, has applied on a mandatory basis since 2004 under chapter VII of SOLAS 1974 as amended, as well as under Annexe III of the 1973 International Convention for the Prevention of Pollution from Ships as amended by the Protocol of 1978 (MARPOL 73/78) which deals with prevention of pollution arising out of the carriage of dangerous goods by sea.

The IMDG Code applies to all ships entitled to fly the flag of a contracting state to SOLAS 1974.[20] It is updated and revised on a regular basis. Every two years the Code is amended and each amendment is valid for three years. Since amendments overlap one another, when a new edition is published it may be applied voluntarily during the transition period. For instance, the previous edition of the Code was the 2018 Edition (Amendment 39-18) published on 1 January 2019. It became mandatory as from 1 January 2020 and applied mandatorily until 31 May 2022, since the validity of this edition was extended.[21] The newest edition, the IMDG Code 2020 (Amendment 40-20) was published on 1 January 2021 and became mandatory as from 1 June 2022.[22] Amendments and revisions are regularly made by the Sub-Committee on Carriage of Cargoes and Containers (CCC), which must get final approval from the MSC, before it is published as a new edition. Given that the Code is based on the Orange Book, the CCC takes amendments of the UN Committee of Experts into account as well as proposals prepared and submitted to IMO by its member states when preparing a new edition.

The IMDG Code lays down some general principles on the safe carriage of dangerous goods by sea. It classifies goods that are considered dangerous and the risks that they might present in transport. It prescribes hazard-warning labels and marks to be used in order to identify dangerous goods as well as the necessary documentation to be used in the carriage of dangerous goods. It also establishes detailed rules and recommendations on how to stow, segregate and handle each substance and where to load these goods on board the vessel for safe carriage. It also provides advice on emergency response action when a danger arises from these goods. The Code now consists of two volumes (Volume 1 and Volume 2) along with

[18] n 14 above.
[19] n 12 above, 72.
[20] SOLAS 1974, chapter I, art II.
[21] www.imo.org/en/publications/Pages/IMDG%20Code.aspx.
[22] ibid.

a supplement containing some relevant materials, such as the Revised Emergency Response Procedures for Ships Carrying Dangerous Goods (EmS Guide), the Medical First Aid Guide for Use in Accidents Involving Dangerous Goods (MFAG) as well as the Irradiated Nuclear Fuel (INF) Code. While Volume 1 is composed of Part 1 (General Provisions, Definitions and Training), Part 2 (Classification), Part 4 (Packing and Tank Provisions), Part 5 (Consignment Procedures), Part 6 (Construction and Testing of Packagings, Intermediate Bulk Containers, Large Packagings, Portable Tanks, Multiple-Element Gas Containers and Road Tank Vehicles) and Part 7 (Transport Operations), Volume 2 contains Part 3 (Dangerous Goods List 'DGL', Special Provisions and Exceptions), Appendices (List of generic and NOS proper shipping names and Glossary of terms) and Index.

B. Classification

The IMDG Code divides dangerous goods into nine classes based on the type of danger that they present in transit:

- Class 1 – Explosives
- Class 2 – Gases
    - 2.1 Flammable gases
    - 2.2 Non-flammable, non-toxic gases
    - 2.3 Toxic gases
- Class 3 – Flammable liquids
- Class 4 – Flammable solids
    - 4.1 Flammable solids
    - 4.2 Substances liable to spontaneous combustion
    - 4.3 Substances which, in contact with water, emit flammable gases
- Class 5 – Oxidising substances and organic peroxides
    - 5.1 Oxidising substances
    - 5.2 Organic peroxides
- Class 6 – Toxic and infectious substances
    - 6.1 Toxic substances
    - 6.2 Infectious substances
- Class 7 – Radioactive material
- Class 8 – Corrosive substances
- Class 9 – Miscellaneous dangerous substances and articles.

By dividing them into different groups, the Code expressly describes what goods are dangerous. The class of each individual substance is therefore easily determined based on this categorisation. Once the class of a substance is ascertained, the hazards that goods may cause in transport are identified under the relevant class so as to ensure that the necessary measures and precautions are taken for safe carriage of the goods in question. Nonetheless it must be borne in mind that some goods may fall within more than one class, if the hazards they present might be linked with multiple classes.

The goods listed in the Code, except for substances of classes 1, 2, 4.1, 5.2, 6.2 and 7 are also divided into groups according to the level of danger they present:

- Packing group I: substances that represent great danger
- Packing group II: substances that represent medium danger
- Packing group I: substances that represent low danger.[23]

The relevant packing group that each substance is designated to is shown in chapter 3.2 of the DGL. As for self-reactive substances (class 4.1) and organic peroxides (class 5.2), both are grouped into seven types by the level of danger they represent. Both self-reactive substances and organic peroxides range from type A to type G. Whilst the former may not be carried in the packaging in which it is tested, the latter type may be subject to relaxations from the provisions that normally apply to class 4.1 and class 5.2. The classification of types B to F is only for purposes of indicating the maximum quantity allowed in one packaging.[24]

Some goods might be known by different names across the world. When this is the case, it may not be easy to ascertain their appropriate class under the Code, as the use of different names for the same goods might lead to misclassification. The end result of a misclassified dangerous cargo could be catastrophic, so, to avoid such unwanted results beforehand, the Code administers a universal single description. The DGL in volume 2, part 3 of the Code, refers to the goods that are listed by four-digit United Nations Numbers (UN Numbers) along with Proper Shipping Names (PSN) ascertained by the UN Committee of Experts on the Transport of Dangerous Goods. The DGL also lists necessary information for each substance, such as subsidiary risks, packing group, segregation and stowage requirements, etc. While each substance is specifically identified by its UN Number, the PSN is the recognised name of the substances, which is used along with the corresponding UN Number (eg, UN 1090 ACETONE). However, not all dangerous goods are uniquely referred to by a PSN, since some goods, especially chemicals, are a mixture or solution of multiple substances. Thus, such goods are referred to as 'Not Otherwise Specified' (NOS) to cover a group of substances of a particular nature (eg, UN 1477 NITRATES NOS or UN 1993 ALCOHOLS NOS).

C. Marking, Labelling and Placarding

Once a particular substance is specified, the goods must be marked, labelled accordingly and placarded when necessary, to ensure that the carrier is enabled to take

[23] The IMDG Code, Volume 1, para 2.0.1.3.
[24] ibid, paras 2.4.2.3.2 and 2.5.3.2.2.

necessary measures and precautions for safe transport. Each package should be marked with a PSN and the corresponding UN Number of the substance carried. Each class is designated a unique diamond-shaped label. Thus, each package must also be labelled with a particular diamond-shaped label corresponding to the class of the substance carried within that package, in order to display all the hazards (primary and subsidiary) presented by that substance. While the upper half of the diamond-shaped label shows the pictorial symbol of the primary hazard, the bottom half indicates the class or sub-division number and the compatibility group letter, except for the sub-divisions 1.4, 1.5 and 1.6. As for sub-divisions 1.4, 1.5 and 1.6, the upper half of the label shows the relevant class or sub-division number, whereas the bottom half shows the compatibility group letter.[25]

Once a dangerous substance is loaded into cargo transport units such as containers, portable tanks or trailers, they shall be labelled with placards (enlarged labels) as well as marked with the PSN and the UN Number of that particular substance. Placards display the class or sub-division and the compatibility group letter so as to ensure a warning that the goods carried within the unit are of a dangerous nature and present risks. Apart from placards, depending on the goods loaded into cargo transport units or other packages, there might be some marks that must be displayed, such as the Fumigation Warning Mark, the Elevated Temperature Mark, the Marine Pollutant Mark, the Limited Quantity Mark or the Excepted Quantity Mark.[26] For instance, substances that are only harmful to the marine environment but not to humans or the vessel are designated as marine pollutants in Class 9.[27] All Class 9 marine pollutants and any other pollutants falling within the other classes due to presenting hazards to the environment as well as to the vessel and humans should be marked with the Marine Pollutant Mark. Cargo transport units carrying substances or articles that are in a liquid state at 100°C or higher temperature, or substances in a solid state at 240°C or higher temperature, must be marked with the Elevated Temperature Mark on each side and on each end. As for the Fumigation Warning Mark, any fumigated cargo transport unit containing dangerous goods must be so marked on an exterior place of the unit where it can be recognised and seen by anyone attempting to enter in.[28]

When a cargo transport unit or a package is loaded with dangerous goods in limited quantities that are unlikely to present serious danger in transit, it shall only be marked with the Limited Quantity Mark on the exterior. The goods that may be carried as excepted quantities shall also be marked only with the Excepted Quantity Mark. It is, however, worth noting that not all dangerous goods can be carried as limited quantities or excepted quantities. The permitted substances or articles designated as limited and excepted quantities are shown in the DGL chapter 3.3 and in columns 7a and 7b of the list in chapter 3.2.

[25] ibid, para 5.2.2.2.
[26] ibid, para 5.3.2.
[27] As a result of MARPOL 73/78 Annex III.
[28] The IMDG Code, Volume 1, para 5.3.2.1.1.

D. Stowage and Segregation

It is of great importance to label, mark and pack dangerous goods correctly. However, whether dangerous goods are shipped in cargo transport units or packages, stowage and segregation play as significant a role as labelling, marking and packing in respect of safety during transport. For stowage and segregation purposes, under the IMDG Code vessels are categorised into two groups: group 1 includes cargo vessels and passenger vessels 'carrying a number of passengers limited to not more than 25 or to 1 passenger per 3 metres of overall length, whichever is the greater number',[29] whereas group 2 contains 'other passenger ships in which the limiting number of passengers transported is exceeded'.[30] For stowage purposes, the Code divides dangerous goods into further categories (A, B, C, D and E)[31] except for explosives (class 1), according to their classification and the dangers they present during carriage:[32]

	Cargo ships	**Passenger ships**
Category A	On deck or below deck	On deck or below deck
Category B	On deck or below deck	On deck only
Category C	On deck only	On deck only
Category D	On deck only	Prohibited
Category E	On deck or below deck	Prohibited

As for class 1 substances and articles, the stowage categories range from 01 to 05, the latter being the most dangerous. The substances falling within categories 01, 02 and 03 may be shipped on deck in a closed cargo transport unit or below deck. The category 04 substances can be shipped on deck or below deck only in closed cargo transport units, but category 05 only on deck in closed cargo transport units.[33] Limited and excepted quantities of class 1 substances fall within category A.[34]

As the name hints, dangerous goods are dangerous on their own, but some may react even more dangerously and cause undue incidents when they interact with one another as a consequence of leak, spillage or any other reason. For this purpose, two or more substances that are considered mutually incompatible must be segregated from one another in accordance with the provisions in chapter 7.2 (segregation) of the IMDG Code, Volume 1. Whilst the general provisions as to segregation are defined in paragraph 7.2.4, special provisions are listed in paragraph 7.2.8. In case of a conflict, special provisions in 7.2.8 prevail over the general ones in 7.2.4. Segregation requirements are displayed in column 16b

[29] ibid, para 7.1.1.
[30] ibid.
[31] See the IMDG Code, Volume 2, chapter 3.2, column 16 for each substance or article.
[32] The IMDG Code, Volume 1, para 7.1.3.2.
[33] ibid, para 7.1.3.1.
[34] See also, ibid, paras 7.1.5 and 7.1.6, where further stowage and handling codes are indicated.

of the DGL and the following terms are used for the segregation purposes: 'away from', 'separated from', 'separated by a complete compartment or hold from' and 'separated longitudinally by an intervening complete compartment or hold from'. Whereas 'away from' indicates at least three metres' separation vertically, 'separated from' means a separation of at least six metres horizontally. 'Separated by a complete compartment or hold from' specifies a segregation of at least 12 metres horizontally, and 'separated longitudinally by an intervening complete compartment or hold from' means separation by at least 24 metres longitudinally. In relation to limited and excepted quantities, they are allowed relaxations from these provisions, as long as they are not known to interact dangerously with one another.

E. Documentation

When dangerous goods are offered for shipment, in accordance with the IMDG Code, a dangerous goods transport document containing all the relevant information and documentation must be tendered to the carrier by the shipper. Such document may be more than one page and could be in any form, as long as it includes all the required information as specified in the Code. A dangerous goods transport document shall include the following information in the exact order for each substance:

- The UN number of the relevant substance
- The PSN of the relevant substance
- The primary hazard class or the division of the substance (when assigned), the compatibility group letter, including for class 1
- The subsidiary hazard class or the division numbers of the substance
- The packing group (where assigned).

Any additional information (if any) must be placed after the list above. Some required additional information might supplement the PSN of that particular substance in question in relation to 'waste, salvage packaging, elevated temperature, marine pollutants, flashpoint, limited quantity or excepted quantity', if applicable. It is also noteworthy that chapter 5.4 of the Code should be consulted (documentation), as there might be some specific additional information required for particular classes or divisions. Also, together with the number and kind of packages, the total quantity of each substance with a different PSN, UN number or packing group must be provided. For class 1 substances, the quantity shall be the net explosive mass.[35]

In addition, a declaration or certification must be duly signed and dated by the shipper of the goods confirming that the goods are in proper condition for

[35] The IMDG Code, Volume 1, para 5.4.1.5.1.

transport, properly packaged, marked and labelled in compliance with the IMDG Code. If the goods are loaded into a container or vehicle, a container/vehicle packing certificate indicating that they are properly packed and secured in a clean, dry and fit container or vehicle must be provided by whoever is responsible for packing and securing the container or vehicle. It is, however, worth adding that such a container/vehicle certificate is not required for portable tanks.[36] There is also documentation required once on board for vessels carrying dangerous goods. Any vessel carrying dangerous goods shall have a special list, a detailed stowage plan displaying the location of all dangerous goods with their class, and a cargo manifest, in compliance with regulation 4.5 of chapter VII of SOLAS 1974 as amended, and with regulation 4(3) of Annex III of MARPOL 73/78.[37] Under particular circumstances, special certificates or other documents might be required as well, eg a weathering certificate, a certificate exempting a substance from the IMDG Code, or a statement by the competent authority of the country of origin of the approved classification and conditions of transport for new self-reactive substances and organic peroxides.[38]

III. Other IMO Instruments

A. The IMSBC Code

The IMDG Code is not the only international instrument that deals with the safe carriage of dangerous goods by sea. There are other international materials produced, one of which is arguably the second most important after the IMDG Code; the International Maritime Solid Bulk Cargoes (IMSBC) Code. The IMSBC Code was adopted in 2008[39] and came into force in 2011. It applies mandatorily under chapter VI of SOLAS 1974, as amended. The Code is amended every two years, to keep up with the changes and developments in relation to solid bulk cargoes. The current version (Amendments 05-19) came into force on 1 January 2021.[40] The Code does not regulate either goods in packaged form covered by the IMDG Code, or grains, which are covered by the International Grain Code (IGC Code).

Solid bulk cargoes carry some serious risks to the ship, lives on board and the environment, such as instability, explosion or capsizing due to cargo liquefaction, improper loading or stowage. The IMSBC Code provides detailed information as to the hazards that different types of solid bulk cargoes may present. Accordingly, it outlines the required precautions to be adopted and instructions to be followed

[36] ibid, para 5.4.2.
[37] ibid, para 5.4.3.
[38] ibid, para 5.4.4.
[39] By resolution MSC.268(85) of the IMO Maritime Safety Committee.
[40] Adopted by resolution MSC.462(101) of the IMO Maritime Safety Committee.

during the shipment of solid bulk cargoes for safe carriage. When the goods to be shipped are solid bulk cargo, the Code outlines a set of obligations ranging from procedures and precautions to be taken in relation to loading, carriage and discharge (section 2), to trimming procedures (section 5). It also prescribes the necessary documentation to be provided by shippers for safe carriage (section 4). As with the IMDG Code, the carrier must be provided with information concerning the cargo to be shipped prior to shipment under the IMSBC Code, such as its Bulk Cargo Shipping Name (BCSN), physical and chemical properties, and its quantity. Also a declaration stating that the information about the cargo in question is correct must be presented to the carrier by the shipper. Section 7 divides solid bulk cargoes into three groups: group A are cargoes which may liquefy; group B are cargoes that possess chemical hazards; and group C are cargoes that are neither liable to liquefy (group A) nor to possess chemical hazards (group B).

Group A cargoes, such as nickel ore, mineral concentrates or even coal[41] may liquefy, despite the fact that they normally appear to be in dry and granular form. Liquefaction occurs as a result of two main factors in combination with each other. Group A cargoes, albeit being in solid form, may contain a particular amount of moisture and small particles. Once these particles and moisture content are triggered or shaken by the vessel's motion, as a consequence of its constant mobility or a running engine's vibration, group A cargoes are liable to liquefy. When a solid cargo liquefies, this may lead to shifting of that particular cargo, causing instability to the vessel, capsizing or even sinking. To prevent or minimise the risk of such incidents, each group A cargo is therefore required to be tested in order to be sure that its actual moisture content is below the Transportable Moisture Limit (TML).[42] The TML signifies the maximum moisture content allowed for safe carriage[43] and if the declaration signed by the shipper states that the actual moisture content present in a cargo is above the TML, that cargo may not be shipped.[44]

So far as group B cargoes are concerned, they can be divided into two subgroups: the first group is goods in solid form in bulk that are classified as dangerous goods under the IMDG Code, whereas the second group is 'Materials hazardous only in bulk' (MHB). The dangerous goods in solid form in bulk are flammable solids (class 4.1), substances liable to spontaneous combustion (class 4.2), substances that, in contact with water, emit flammable gases (class 4.3), oxidising substances (class 5.1), toxic substances (class 6.1), radioactive materials (class 7), corrosive substances (class 8) and miscellaneous dangerous substances and articles (class 9). Each of these goods is assigned a UN number as part of the Bulk Cargoes Shipping Name (BCSN) as well.[45] On the other hand, the MHB goods

[41] Despite commonly being classified as a group B cargo, coal may as well fall within group A, as it may liquefy, if it is in fine form.

[42] The IMSBC Code, s 7.3.1.1.

[43] ibid, s 1.7.

[44] But also see, ibid, ss 7.3.2 and 8.1.

[45] ibid, s 9.

contain chemical substances which fall outside the classification of the IMDG Code but are still liable to present danger when shipped in bulk. These substances are combustible solids, self-heating solids, solids evolving flammable gas when wet, solids evolving toxic gas when wet, toxic solids, corrosive solids and other hazardous solids.[46] They present some common but serious risks, such as fire, explosion, release of toxic gas and corrosion. The most common types are coal, metal sulphide concentrates, direct reduced iron and organic materials. Due to the risks associated with these goods, they are considered incompatible with one another and accordingly they must be stowed and segregated as described under section 9.3 of the IMSBC Code by the carrier. The shipper must also provide the necessary information about the goods and the precautions to be taken when these goods are shipped.

As for Group C, it classifies the goods that do not fall within group A or B, as they are neither liable to liquefy nor possess chemical hazards. The most common types are iron ore and 'high-density cargoes',[47] cement, sand and fine particle materials like silica dust. Group C goods do not carry the risks commonly linked with groups A and B. Nonetheless, this does not necessarily mean that group C goods do not present any danger. For instance, some types of iron ore fines can be classified as group A, as they are liable to liquefy, depending on the moisture content. However, once such iron ore fines are misclassified as non-liquefiers under group C, the carrier will be unlikely to take the appropriate precautions associated with the group A type iron ore concentrates, to keep the cargo dry. Owing to such a misclassification, the improper precautions taken may eventually lead iron ore to liquefy, causing capsizal or even the total loss of the vessel. Another example of misclassification is bauxite cargoes, which used to be classified only under group C, as bauxite had been considered a non-liquefier. In 2015, *Bulk Jupiter*, carrying bauxite, sank with most of its crew, because of the liquefaction of the cargo on board.[48] Following the total loss of *Bulk Jupiter*, a working group assembled by the IMO concluded that the main cause of the incident was the liquefaction of bauxite. As with iron ore, while some types of bauxite are liable to liquefy, some are not. As a result, by IMO Resolution MSC.462 (101) 'bauxite fines' are now classified as group A goods. Amendments 05-19 of the IMSBC Code, which has applied mandatorily since 1 January 2021, sets out a new schedule to be followed for the group A bauxite fines as well as altering the existing provisions on group C bauxite.

B. The International Grain Code

Despite the fact that the IMDG and the IMSBC Codes are arguably the two most important international regulations for the safe carriage of dangerous goods, they

[46] For the MHB goods see the IMSBC Code, s 9.3.2.

[47] A high-density cargo has a stowage factor equal to or less than 0.56 m³ per metric ton (ie the volume per unit weight of the cargo).

[48] The Bahamas Maritime Authority, *MV Bulk Jupiter Report* (Official No 8001956, 2015).

together may still fall short of providing a complete picture in that respect. As mentioned above, the former code covers packaged goods, whereas the latter covers solid bulk cargoes. There are still goods not falling within the ambit of either of these Codes which may pose danger to vessels, their crew and the environment. For instance, neither code regulates the carriage of grains in bulk. Therefore, in order to update the previous chapter VI of SOLAS 1974 as amended, by resolution MSC.23(59), the 1991 International Code for the Safe Carriage of Grain in Bulk (International Grain Code) was adopted under part C of chapter VI on 1 January 1994, which has been in effect since. The International Grain Code covers mandatorily all ships carrying grain in bulk, irrespective of their size and tonnage, and to which part C of SOLAS 1974 chapter VI applies.[49]

The term 'grain' is described widely enough to cover 'wheat, maize, oats, rye, barley, rice, pulses, seeds and processed forms thereof, whose behaviour is similar to that of grain in its natural state'.[50] Despite seeming innocuous, even such goods may present a great deal of hazards. For instance as a result of improper trimming, cargo shifting may occur or holds of the vessel might be found contaminated due to quality or contents of grain. The risk of fire is not uncommon either, as some grains might have a tendency to overheat under certain circumstances. Thus, the Code is aimed at providing an international standard for the safe carriage of grains and eliminating or reducing the risks posed by transporting grain in bulk.

C. The IBC Code

Regulations covering the carriage of chemicals in bulk are set out in chapter VII of SOLAS 1974 as amended, and MARPOL Annex II.[51] Both Conventions make reference to the International Code for the Construction and Equipment of Ships Carrying Dangerous Chemicals in Bulk (IBC Code), requiring tankers carrying chemicals to adhere to the IBC Code. Regardless of their size or tonnage, chemical tankers constructed after 1 July 1986 must comply with the IBC Code.[52] Tankers built before 1 July 1986 are still subject to the Code for the Construction and Equipment of Ships Carrying Dangerous Chemicals in Bulk (BCH Code), which was replaced by the IBC Code.

The aim of the IBC code is to provide an international standard for the safe carriage of chemicals in bulk. In order to prevent or reduce the risks involved in the carriage of chemicals in bulk, the IBC Code sets out rules concerning the design, construction and outfitting standards to be met by vessels and the equipment that vessels should carry, compatible with the nature of the cargoes carried. The Code prescribes the requirements to be satisfied by a vessel, in order for it to be certified as a chemical tanker. It also contains a list of substances, including

[49] www.imo.org/en/OurWork/Safety/Pages/Grain-Code.aspx.
[50] The International Grain Code, s 2.1.
[51] Regulations for the Control of Pollution by Noxious Liquid Substances in Bulk.
[52] As part B of chapter VII of SOLAS 1974.

the hazards presented by them, as well as the vessel type to carry that particular substance in question.[53]

D. The IGC Code

Vessels built after 1 July 1986, regardless of their size or tonnage must comply with the International Code for the Construction and Equipment of Ships Carrying Liquefied Gases in Bulk (IGC Code). The IGC Code was adopted by resolution MSC.5(48) under part C of chapter VII of SOLAS 1974.[54] The Code for the Construction and Equipment of Ships Carrying Liquefied Gases in Bulk (GC Code)[55] or the Code for Existing Ships Carrying Liquefied Gases in Bulk (EGC Code)[56] still applies to vessels built prior to 1 July 1986.

The IGC Code covers liquefied gases with a vapour pressure exceeding 2.8 bar absolute at a temperature of 37.8°C and also certain other substances set out in chapter 19 of the Code. The Code is aimed at providing an international standard for the safe transport of the liquefied gases and other substances falling within its scope. The purpose of the Code is to prevent or minimise the risks that may arise in carriage of liquefied gases, as properties of these products could be toxic, flammable, corrosive and reactive. Thus, the Code sets out the design and construction standards of the vessels engaged in carriage of liquefied gases in bulk and the equipment that they should carry. The layout of the IGC code is in keeping with the IBC Code, allowing gas carriers complying with the IGC Code to carry liquid chemicals listed by the IBC Code as well.[57]

E. The INF Code

The Code for the Safe Carriage of Irradiated Nuclear Fuel, Plutonium and High-Level Radioactive Wastes on Board Ships (INF Code) was produced as a voluntary code by the IMO in 1993, based on Regulations for the Safe Transport of Radioactive Material produced by the International Atomic Energy Agency (IAEA). The INF Code became a mandatory instrument in 2001 under SOLAS 1974 as amended, and was renamed 'the International Code for the Safe Carriage of Packaged Irradiated Nuclear Fuel, Plutonium and High-Level Radioactive Waste on Board Ships'.[58]

[53] See www.imo.org/en/OurWork/Environment/Pages/IBCCode.aspx; www.imo.org/en/OurWork/Environment/Pages/ChemicalPollution-Default.aspx.

[54] The IGC Code was amended by resolution MSC.370(93) which has been in effect since 1 July 2016.

[55] Applies to vessels constructed after 31 December 1976 but before 1 July 1986.

[56] Applies to vessels constructed prior to 31 December 1976.

[57] See www.imo.org/en/OurWork/Safety/Pages/IGC-Code.aspx; www.imo.org/en/OurWork/Environment/Pages/IGCCode.aspx.

[58] The Code was amended since by resolutions MSC.118(74), MSC.135(76), MSC.178(79) and MSC.241(83).

The purpose of the INF Code is to ensure safety for ships carrying radioactive materials by setting out requirements, such as for damage stability (chapter 2), fire safety measures (chapter 3), temperature control of cargo spaces (chapter 4), structural consideration (chapter 5) and cargo securing arrangements (chapter 6). The Code covers packaged irradiated nuclear fuel, plutonium and high-level radioactive wastes carried as cargo in line with class 7 (radioactive material) of the IMDG Code schedule 10, 11, 12 or 13.[59] While irradiated nuclear fuel includes uranium, thorium and/or plutonium isotopes,[60] plutonium means 'the mixture of isotopes of that material extracted from irradiated nuclear fuel from reprocessing'.[61] High-level radioactive waste covers liquid or concentrated wastes extracted during the reprocessing of irradiated nuclear fuel.[62] As the provisions of the IMDG Code concerning the carriage of radioactive material are based on the IAEA's Regulations for the Safe Transport of Radioactive Material,[63] alongside the INF Code, the relevant provisions of the IMDG Code shall apply to the goods covered by the INF Code.[64] The Code also divides vessels into three classes (INF 1, INF 2 and INF 3) based on the level of aggregate (radio)activity of the material carried on board.[65]

IV. Effectiveness of the Codes

A. Inherent Ineffectiveness

The Codes described above are mandatorily applicable international instruments defining their own scope. However, none of them defines potential penalties if their provisions are breached. As the Codes are silent on the matter, that gap appears to be filled by national laws applying them. In particular, the IMDG and IMSBC Codes can be said to have the impact of stand-alone regulations before the courts, to guide them on whether a party is subject to dangerous goods liability, when a cargo falls within the ambit of either of the Codes. In *The Aconcagua*, a cargo of calcium hypochlorite, described as UN 1748 and packed into a container, had an abnormally high thermal instability which made it prone to be explosive at ordinary sea transit temperatures as low as 30°C. As it was stowed in a position in the hold where it was surrounded on three sides by a bunker tank that had been heated during transit, due to being liable to self-ignite around 30°C, the cargo exploded, causing catastrophic damage to the vessel and the other cargoes

[59] The INF Code, s 1.1.1.3.
[60] ibid, s 1.1.1.4.
[61] ibid, s 1.1.1.5.
[62] ibid, s 1.1.1.6.
[63] The IMDG Code Volume 1, para 1.1.3.
[64] The INF Code, s 1.2.2.
[65] ibid, s 1.1.2.

on board.[66] The calcium hypochlorite actually shipped had a materially different nature and characteristics to the calcium hypochlorite described as UN 1748 under the IMDG Code. The cargo was therefore found to be misdeclared under the Code, and accordingly the shippers were in breach of the Code. Under English law, the shipper's liability for shipment of dangerous goods is strict, unless the carrier has consented to the cargo in question with knowledge of its nature and character.[67] The court thus first asked whether the shipper had complied with the Code. The underlying reason for this is that if the shipper was in breach of the Code, he would inevitably be subject to strict liability. In *The Aconcagua*, the shipper was found liable due to misdeclaration under the Code, because the carrier had only consented to carry the substance described as UN 1748.[68] In the American case of *The DG Harmony* where the facts are very similar to *The Aconcagua*, the court held in a similar fashion that the shipper was liable on the ground that the cargo of calcium hypochlorite was misdeclared under the IMDG Code, as it had a materially different dangerous nature to what the carrier had agreed to carry according to the Code.[69] Although there are not many reported cases on the matter, the Codes can be said to be supplementing the liability regimes adopted under domestic laws. Apparently, once the shipper is found in breach of the IMDG Code, he will inevitably be held liable as well under domestic law. Therefore the arguable assumption is that the shipper will not be subject to liability if he has shipped his goods in compliance with the IMDG Code. However, this may not be always be the case. The shipper may have fully complied with the Code, and accordingly may not be in breach of its provisions at all, but still may be found liable under the applicable domestic law.[70] The underlying reasons for this could be misclassification of goods under the Codes, where a certain substance appearing to be described in a certain category may have been shipped in accordance with the Codes but may have unknown characteristics and properties that pose other dangers not associated with those classified in the same category.

In 2015, *Bulk Jupiter* carried 46,400 tonnes of bauxite fines of which the moisture content was around 21 per cent. Before the *Bulk Jupiter* incident, bauxite fines used to be classified in group C under the IMSBC Code, as bauxite cargoes were generally considered to have no risk of liquefaction. At the time of shipment, according to the Bauxite Schedule of the IMSBC Code, the acceptable moisture level had to be below 10 per cent for the cargo to be loaded. However, the schedule

[66] *Compania Sud Americana de Vapores SA v Sinochem Tianjin Import and Export Corporation (The Aconcagua)* [2011] 1 Lloyd's Rep 683. See also *Northern Shipping Co v Deutsche Seereederei GmbH and Others (The Kapitan Sakharov)* [2000] 2 Lloyd's Rep 255.

[67] See generally, Chapter 3 below.

[68] Despite the fact that the carrier was also in breach of the Code by stowing the cargo next to a source of heat, the bunker: *The Aconcagua* [2011] 1 Lloyd's Rep 683, [22].

[69] *Re M/V DG Harmony*, 533 F 3d 83, 2008 AMC 1848 (2d Cir 2008), affirmed in *Re M/V DG Harmony*, 408 F Appx 435 (2d Cir 2011). But see also *Contship Containerlines Ltd v PPG Industries Inc*, 442 F 3d 74, 75, 2006 AMC 686 (2d Cir 2006).

[70] See *J Lauritzen Singapore Pte Ltd v Yara Asia Pte Ltd (The MV Cheshire)* 20-062574ASD-BORG / 03, Borgarting Court of Appeal, 15 November 2021.

showed no 'special hazard' associated with the carriage of bauxite if the amount of moisture in the cargo was in excess of the allowed moisture level in the schedule.[71] Owing to the high moisture content, *Bulk Jupiter*'s cargo of 46,400 tonnes of bauxite fines liquefied, leading to the total loss of *Bulk Jupiter* along with the tragic loss of 18 lives on board.[72] Following the total loss of *Bulk Jupiter*, a working group assembled by the IMO concluded that the main cause of the incident was the liquefaction of bauxite. As a result, by IMO Resolution MSC.462 (101) 'bauxite fines' are now classified as a group A cargo. For group A cargoes, the shipper must provide a certificate showing that the cargo shipped is within the Transportable Moisture Limit (TML), as they are liable to liquefy. At the time *Bulk Jupiter* sank, bauxite fines were described as a group C cargo. Thus, the shipper was not under any sort of responsibility to provide his bauxite fines' TML under the IMSBC Code. Accordingly, he cannot be said to have been in breach of the relevant provisions of the Code applicable to group C cargoes at the time. At first sight, it might seem probable that the shipper would not be subject to any liability, as first, he complied with the provisions of the Code and second, the total loss of *Bulk Jupiter* was said to be attributable to the misclassification of bauxite fines under the Code. However, regardless of the evidence proving that the shipper complied with the IMBSC Code and that he did not know his cargo could liquefy, the shipper would still have been found liable under the strict liability regime adopted in English law.[73] Indeed, shippers can only carry out their duties according to the Codes[74] that are applicable at the time of shipment and when they have done so, it might be thought that they should be immune from liability. As stated above, the Codes do not describe potential penalties when shippers are in breach of provisions of the Codes. Nor does setting out a liability regime for shipment of dangerous goods fall within their scope, as they merely provide guidance to be followed in the shipment and carriage of these goods. Thus, it is arguable that the liability issue is left to be decided by domestic laws. In this regard, in a Norwegian case, the Court of Appeal held that the Codes (the IMSBC Code) are not exhaustive, and accordingly the classification of the Codes is not conclusive on what are considered dangerous goods under the domestic law.[75] Similarly, under English law, dangerous goods are not limited to those listed in the Codes and the shipper will not be relieved of liability for dangerous goods merely on the ground that he proves that he fully complied with the Codes. To find out whether the shipper is subject to liability for dangerous goods, the courts ultimately ask the question of whether the carrier has consented to the shipment of the goods in question with knowledge of their actual nature and character. If the answer to this question found by the court is not affirmative, the shipper will be found liable under the strict liability regime,

[71] See Appendix 1 of the IMSBC Code.

[72] See n 48 above. Bauxite fines are classified within group A cargoes, following Resolution MSC.462 (101).

[73] See generally, Chapter 3 below.

[74] Whether it is the IMDG, IMBSC or any other IMO Code.

[75] See *J Lauritzen Singapore Pte Ltd v Yara Asia Pte Ltd (The MV Cheshire)* 20-062574ASD-BORG / 03.

irrespective of whether he strictly adhered to the Codes or whether he was not aware of the actual character or nature of his own cargo.[76] As the carrier in the *Bulk Jupiter* case did not consent the cargo of bauxite fines with knowledge that it could liquefy, the shipper would have been held liable under English law, irrespective of the facts that first he did not know the cargo was liable to liquefy, and second he followed the schedule provided under the IMSBC Code.

In the above-mentioned Norwegian case concerning the *MV Cheshire*,[77] a cargo of NPK fertiliser classified under the IMSBC code was shipped from Norway to Thailand. The cargo during transit produced heat and toxic gases, as it underwent a chemical process, which led to destruction of most of the cargo as well as total loss of the vessel. The shipper claimed from the carriers for damage to the cargo, whereas the carrier counterclaimed for total loss of the vessel and other costs caused by the cargo. The Court of Appeal, upholding the first instance judgment in favour of the shipper, found that the shipper had provided the carrier with sufficient information about the risks and properties of the cargo in accordance with the IMSBC Code and that the carriers were negligent in carrying the cargo, as they were not in accordance with the clear instructions provided by the cargo owners. At the time of shipment, there was a newly proposed amendment to the IMSBC Code concerning group B NPK fertilisers, and the carriers claimed that they would have taken precautions differently, if they had been given the relevant information in the proposed amendments. In this regard, the court opined that there was no evidence suggesting that the carriers would in fact have done differently.[78] In general, draft schedules to the Codes are proposed by the MSC's Sub-committee on Carriage of Cargoes and Containers (CCC) following extensive and detailed discussions and examination of research reports submitted to the CCC by stakeholders such as the Flag States, insurers, institutions, universities or councils like the European Chemical Industry Council (CEFIC). Whether these draft proposals are accepted as amendments to the Codes by the MSC is another matter but it would probably be safe to assume that they will provide adequate technical information for the intended substances. However, this does not mean that the shipper would be considered in breach of the Codes by courts if he failed to comply with a draft schedule, as it had yet to become part of the existing Codes at the time of shipment. Nonetheless, as liability for dangerous goods is strict under English law and many other major shipping nations' law,[79] as stated above, just because the shipper strictly adheres to the relevant applicable schedule does not necessarily mean that he will always be immune from liability. Indeed it is unknown whether a draft schedule would be accepted as a compulsory amendment, but under the strict liability regime, shippers would arguably be better off giving the carrier the relevant information provided in the draft schedule anyway,

[76] Unless the carrier himself knew or ought to have had the relevant knowledge.
[77] *J Lauritzen Singapore Pte Ltd v Yara Asia Pte Ltd (The MV Cheshire)* 20-062574ASD-BORG / 03.
[78] ibid.
[79] See Chapter 3 below.

if they thought that: first, their cargo would fall within the description of the draft schedule; second, the risks associated with their cargo are considered similar to those described in the draft schedule; and third the proposed precautions in the draft schedule are materially different from the existing ones.

The codes therefore can be deemed as inherently ineffective, where a substance is misclassified or misdescribed under the Codes, as the shipper may be found liable no matter how strictly he adheres to them. However, strict liability is arguably the correct approach for a number of reasons. First, dangerous goods under English law – which will be discussed in Chapter three – are not limited to those goods that are listed in these Codes. Second, the shipper of dangerous goods is better placed to know the properties and specific dangers associated with his own cargo than the carrier to whom these goods are presented.[80] The shipper often is the seller of the goods[81] and as the party who sells the goods, he arguably can be said to have the closest nexus with the goods both physically and contractually prior to carriage.

In terms of physical proximity, loading responsibilities are mostly allocated to the shipper. For instance, when a substance classified as dangerous in the IMDG Code is shipped, his duty does not end as soon as he puts the goods over the ship's rail. The seller, as shipper, not only is bound to provide a dangerous goods transport document containing all the necessary safety information required by the Code, but also undertakes to see that the goods are properly packed, marked and labelled. The seller, at common law, is also bound to deliver the goods properly packed to withstand a normal voyage.[82] So far as his contractual nexus with the goods is concerned, under CIF (cost, insurance, freight) and many FOB (free on board) sales,[83] the seller as shipper, is under a duty to conclude the carriage contract evidenced in the bill of lading on behalf of the buyer on the usual terms[84] in the specific trade concerned by taking all necessary precautions for safe carriage

[80] *Brass v Maitland* (1856) 6 E & B 470; 119 ER 940; *Effort Shipping Co Ltd v Linden Management SA and Others (The Giannis NK)* [1998] AC 605; [1998] 1 Lloyd's Rep 337.

[81] On this, see generally, Chapter 4.

[82] *A Hamson & Son (London) Ltd v S Martin Johnson & Co Ltd* [1953] 1 Lloyd's Rep 553, 554; *George Wills & Sons Ltd v Thomas Brown & Sons* (1922) 12 Ll L Rep 292; *Sime Darby & Co Ltd v Everitt & Co* (1923) 14 Ll L Rep 120. See also s 29(6) of the 1979 Act. The goods should be also in a merchantable state at the time of shipment to endure the voyage see: *Mash & Murrell Ltd v Joseph I Emanuel Ltd* [1961] 1 WLR 862; [1961] 1 Lloyd's Rep 47. Reversed on different grounds in the Court of Appeal [1961] 2 Lloyd's Rep 326. See also A Gelgec, 'Identifying the Shipper under Bills of Lading' Case analysis *MVV Environment Devonport Ltd v NTO Shipping GmbH & Co KG (The MV Nortrader)* [2020] EWHC 1371 (Comm); (2020) 26 *JIML* 229, 237.

[83] This is not the case where the buyer concludes the carriage contract under the bare FOB and sometimes under classic FOB sales. On this see generally, Chapter 4 below. See also Bridge, *Benjamin's Sale of Goods*, 11th edn (London, Sweet & Maxwell, 2020) para 18-515.

[84] *Ceval Alimentos SA v Agrimpex Trading Co Ltd (The Northern Progress) (No 2)* [1996] 2 Lloyd's Rep 319; *Tsakiroglou & Co v Noblee Thorl GmbH* [1961] 2 All ER 179; [1962] AC 93; *Finska Cellulosaforeningen (Finnish Cellulose Union) v Westfield Paper Co Ltd* (1940) 68 Ll L Rep 75; *TW Ranson Ltd v Manufacture d'Engrais et de Produits Industriels Antwerp* (1922) 13 Ll L Rep 205; *Burstall & Co v Grimsdale and Sons* (1906) 11 Com Cas 280.

of the goods[85] and conferring substantial continuous protective rights throughout the voyage.[86,87] Although strict liability might seem harsh where the shipper has complied with the Codes, and damage arising from dangerous goods could be attributable to lack of the relevant provision in the Codes, the strict liability regime could be arguably justified on the ground that he is better placed and that his knowledge is superior to the carrier as discussed above. In supporting this, even the IMSBC Code itself states in section 1.2.1.:

> these schedules are not exhaustive and the properties attributed to the cargoes are given only for guidance. Consequently, before loading, it is essential to obtain current valid information from the shipper on the physical and chemical properties of the cargoes presented for shipment. The shipper shall provide appropriate information about the cargo to be shipped.

Ultimately, it is the shipper that represents his goods, often sold by him, to a party who has no nexus with them whatsoever prior to shipment and that party agrees to carry these goods with the risks associated with them based on only the information provided by the shipper. It is not uncommon that dangerous goods may cause catastrophic incidents resulting in loss of lives, total loss of the vessel and damage to the environment. And if it were not for strict liability, shippers would have been able to avoid liability caused by dangerous goods presented by them for transport and the carrier would have been left without any sort of remedy, once shippers proved that they did not know the nature and character of their own goods. Strict liability for dangerous goods indeed proves that shippers blindly following the Codes are not immune from liability, as the guidance provided in the Codes may not be always accurate and the classifications provided in them are not conclusive as to what are considered dangerous goods under domestic laws. This no doubt raises questions concerning the effectiveness of the Codes which could arguably be considered limited where a substance is misclassified or misdescribed therein. Such inherent ineffectiveness of the Codes is often sought to be remedied by revising the existing rules every two years based on developments in technology and industry as well as following tragic incidents such as the *Bulk Jupiter*.

B. Inadequate or Poor Implementation

Aside from the Codes' own inherent ineffectiveness, inadequate or poor implementation of the Codes by the relevant stakeholders can also be said to render the Codes ineffective. As shown above in this chapter and in Chapter one, it is almost impossible to carry dangerous goods today under the out-dated principles of the

[85] *Texas Instruments Ltd v Nason (Europe) Ltd* [1991] 1 Lloyd's Rep 146; *Gatoil International Inc v Tradax Petroleum Ltd (The Rio Sun)* [1985] 1 Lloyd's Rep 350; *Thomas Young and Sons Ltd v Hobson and Partners* (1949) 65 TLR 365; *BC Fruit Market Ltd v The National Fruit Co* (1921) 59 DLR 87.

[86] *Hansson v Hamel & Horley Ltd* [1922] 2 AC 36.

[87] By virtue of s 32(2) of the 1979 Act. On this see generally, Chapter 7.

nineteenth and the early twentieth centuries without any incidents. As a result of developments in technology and science, the inevitable outcome concerning dangerous goods regulations is that the existing rule-books are far from simplicity and they set out very complex layers of requirements buried in detail. Perhaps these features, to a degree, are an indirect contributory factor to ineffectiveness of the Codes. Indeed, some shippers fraudulently or deliberately misdeclare or non-declare their goods to avoid the extra costs of shipping, administrative restrictions, or the risk that their cargo will be banned from carriage by the carrier. However, the underlying reasons for dangerous goods incidents are not limited to such misdeclarations. The reasons causing incidents such as misdeclarations, improper or poor packing, packaging, handling and stowing due to lack of training, lack of knowledge and resources, mistakes and errors in cargo booking and declaration owing to details required, may all boil down to poor understanding of the Codes, which could be arguably correlated to their complexity and onerousness. This whole issue, as the elephant in the room, probably results in a lack of safety culture as well as lack of awareness of these rules in the industry. Consequently they are not followed and implemented effectively by the stakeholders involved in the transport of dangerous goods, such as shippers, consignors, suppliers, carriers, shore-based personnel and port authorities.

As the Codes are regularly updated and revised, shippers must not only comply with the existing rules but also keep themselves up to date with the amendments to come into force in future. Alongside these Codes, shippers must also follow the national legislation of the place of shipment, which no doubt heats up the existing complexity of dangerous goods regulations, as it adds a further layer on top of the international ones. Insufficient training and having limited knowledge hinder the establishment of a safety culture, which as a result, leads shippers simply to 'tick the box in the checklist' of the requirements set out in the Codes. Lack of safety culture leads shippers to carry out practices related to preparing their cargo for shipment – such as handling, labelling, marking, packing or securing – with low standards. For instance, shippers become more prone to errors or mistakes in cargo booking and declaration. Required documentation is simply carried out to present a façade of compliance with the Codes, which often causes insufficient information or documentation in the declaration list. However, effective implementation and enforcement of the Codes depends on the competence of every stakeholder in the industry, all of whom should take ownership of this process. Therefore, alongside shippers, to increase awareness and safety culture, carriers should also provide their employees, including shore-based personnel engaged in the transport of dangerous goods, with regular training on effective and functional implementation of the Codes in order to keep pace with changes and updates in regulations and practice. In this way they will be able to more effectively identify misdeclarations/non-declarations, poor packing and handling practices of shippers prior to shipment.[88]

[88] 'A white paper by National Cargo Bureau', US National Cargo Bureau, 8: www.natcargo.org/Holistic-Approach-For-Undeclared-Misdeclared-And-Other-Non-compliant-Dangerous-Goods_White-Paper-by-NCB.pdf.

At this point, the role of national governments comes into the equation to increase effective implementation of the Codes. To enhance and promote effective and consistent implementation of the applicable IMO instruments on a national basis, the IMO Member State Audit Scheme (IMSAS) was founded as a voluntary scheme in 2006, which became mandatory in January 2016.[89] Its main objective is to ensure implementation of compulsory instruments of the IMO to a high standard by providing audited Member States with a comprehensive report showing how effective they administer, incorporate and implement these instruments.[90] It aims to assist Member States to improve their capabilities and overall performances in compliance with the requirements of the IMO instruments which they are party to.[91] According to the Fifth Consolidated Audit Summary Report 2021 (CASR) of the IMSAS, some Member State authorities were found to be failing to adequately regulate, control and supervise practices related to handling of dangerous goods.[92] Despite the fact that it is the shipper's duty to present his goods and necessary documentation in compliance with the relevant regulations, the CASR Report proves that increasing paperwork checks, inspections and controls by port authorities and enforcement agencies, via a sufficient and competent number of personnel who have specific training to be able to implement national and international regulations rigorously as their specific job description, would ensure effective implementation of these Codes to a great extent. This would minimise or eliminate the most common reasons for dangerous goods incidents such as poor packing, misdeclarations or non-declarations.

To increase awareness and enhance proper enforcement and implementation of the Codes, other stakeholders in the industry also assist the main parties engaged in the transport of dangerous goods – such as, consignors, carriers, port authorities and agencies – to carry out their obligations effectively as set out in these Codes. Since insurers bear monetary losses, having paid out compensation to the insured under his policy for damage arising from dangerous goods incidents, the world's leading transport insurers are often the flag-bearers amongst those stakeholders, actively working to increase and promote safety culture and awareness, to minimise the number of dangerous goods incidents across the world. For instance, the TT Club together with the UK P&I Club in December 2019 published a useful report to provide a practical guide ('Book it right and pack it tight') for shippers and others engaged in the transport of dangerous goods.[93] It intends to provide an overview of the technical aspects of the IMDG Code as well as the practical responsibilities of the parties engaged in packing dangerous goods into cargo

[89] IMO Member State Audit Scheme: www.imo.org/en/OurWork/MSAS/Pages/Default.aspx.

[90] The audit scheme uses the IMO Instruments Implementation Code (I I I Code) adopted by Resolution A.1070(28).

[91] n 89 above.

[92] See IMO Member State Audit Scheme – Fifth Consolidated Audit Summary Report 2021 (CASR), [339], [348], [355], [357] and [370].

[93] www.ttclub.com/-/media/files/tt-club/birpit/book-it-right-and-pack-it-tight---amendment-39-18.pdf.

transport units under the Code.[94] As one of the leading insurers in the shipping industry, Gard also held a two-day conference in 2019 focusing on container fires recently occurring on container vessels. The conference attracted some key stakeholders in the industry, representing shipowners, charterers, insurers, flag states, classification societies, the IMO, the International Group of P&I Clubs (IGP&I), Cargo Incident Notification Systems (CINS) and BIMCO.[95] Although it was acknowledged at the conference that shippers' misdeclaration and poor packing and securing of dangerous goods lie at the heart of many container fire incidents, it is also unrealistic to presume that the tightest controls would end the problem once and for all, considering the volume of container shipments today.[96] In addressing a practical solution, Gard strongly recommended the improvement of fire detection and fire-fighting on board container vessels, urging regulators and the industry to consider their recommendation on their safety agenda.[97] The Cargo Incident Notification System (CINS) is a shipping line initiative, launched in 2011 to share information on all cargo-related incidents.[98] Its main objective is to increase safety in the shipping industry by emphasising risks presented by certain goods and packing issues. The CINS currently has 16 shipping line members including the likes of MSC, Maersk Line, Cosco and CMA-CGM, representing more than 85 per cent of the global container slot capacity.[99] With the input and contribution of CINS members and its advisory members – consisting of IGP&I, TT Club, Exis Technologies and the US National Cargo Bureau (NCB) – upon analysis of cargo and container incidents, the CINS raises areas of concern and accordingly publishes and presents its recommendations to the IMO and other bodies, such as proposals for changes to the IMDG or other Codes.[100] For instance, two of its recent guidelines are on the carriage of seedcake in containers[101] and the stowage of dangerous goods on container vessels.[102] Also following the recent spate of dangerous goods incidents, the NCB published a White Paper in 2020 calling for the industry to adopt a comprehensive holistic approach to solving the issues arising from the carriage of misdeclared, non-declared and poorly packed dangerous goods.[103]

The stakeholders involved in the transport of dangerous goods do not only publish guidelines or hold conferences to raise awareness, but also seek to establish

[94] ibid, 7–8.

[95] Gard News, 'Gard to host industry conference o tackle container ship fires', 3 October 2019: www.gard.no/web/news/article?p_document_id=28440601; 'Putting out the fires', *Maritime Risk International* (December 2019).

[96] See generally, 'Putting out the fires', *Maritime Risk International* (December 2019).

[97] ibid.

[98] www.cinsnet.com/about-cinsnet.

[99] ibid.

[100] See www.cinsnet.com/wp-content/uploads/2019/11/CINS-DG-Stowage-Considerations-Final.pdf.

[101] www.cinsnet.com/wp-content/uploads/2021/04/CINS-IG-Seed-Cake-Guidelines-Version-3-April-2021.pdf.

[102] www.cinsnet.com/wp-content/uploads/2019/11/CINS-DG-Stowage-Considerations-Final.pdf.

[103] See n 88 above.

a safety culture in the industry. To do so, they also closely collaborate with the relevant IMO bodies to help improve effectiveness and incorporation of the dangerous goods regulations. It is trite that the Codes are regularly revised every two years by the IMO, to keep up with the changes as well as the emerging new risks associated with dangerous goods. However, revisions and amendments are often a reaction to dangerous goods incidents occurring on the high seas. Following an incident, the sub-committees such as the CCC assess and discuss the reports of experts on the relevant incident as well as submissions and reports of the other stakeholders such as insurers, the flag states, P&I clubs, universities, and other institutions or councils like the European Chemical Industry Council (CEFIC). For instance, this is what happened straight after the tragic incident on board *Bulk Jupiter.* Following consideration of the expert findings on the case, first a circular[104] was published by the CCC in 2015 to inform carriers concerning the risks and hazards associated with carriage of bauxite. Also after the findings of a working group assembled by the IMO that the main cause of the incident was the liquefaction of bauxite, by IMO Resolution MSC.462 (101) 'bauxite fines' are now classified as group A goods. Amendments 05-19 of the IMSBC Code which has applied mandatorily since 1 January 2021 sets out a new schedule to be followed for group A bauxite fines as well as altering the existing provisions on group C bauxite. Similarly, after the incident involving the *MV Cheshire,*[105] the CCC evaluated the findings and reports of the CEFIC, and subsequently considered a draft revised schedule on the carriage of ammonium nitrate and ammonium nitrate-based fertiliser cargoes.[106] In 2018, the CCC discussed the assessments of hazards of ammonium nitrate-based fertilisers submitted by INTERCARGO, Germany and Canada.[107] Later in 2019 and 2020, the sub-committee considered the proposals submitted by the UK and the CEFIC in CCC6/5/8, CCC6/5/9 and E&T33/3/2 for a new individual schedule for ammonium nitrate and ammonium nitrate-based fertilisers. Following up the recommendations after the *MV Cheshire* incident, in 2021, the CCC, in their seventh session (CCC7/6/10), agreed the draft amendments to the IMSBC Code concerning the reclassification of ammonium nitrate-based fertiliser as well as a new individual schedule for ammonium nitrate and ammonium nitrate-based fertiliser which is to be submitted to the MSC in its 105th session to be held in April 2022.[108] These examples therefore appear to prove first, the existence of a close collaboration between the IMO and the other stakeholders to improve effectiveness of the Codes; and second, that no radical changes are expected to be seen in the Codes in the next four to five years, as they are intended to be revised gradually on a reactive evolutional basis every two years.

Alongside collaboration, some stakeholders push hard to set an agenda in the industry to raise awareness for relevant issues affecting them. Following an

[104] See CCC1/Circ2; www.imo.org/en/MediaCentre/PressBriefings/Pages/38-bauxite-CCC.aspx.
[105] See n 70 above.
[106] In CCC6/5/8.
[107] In CCC5/INF17.
[108] www.imo.org/en/MediaCentre/MeetingSummaries/Pages/CCC-7th-session.aspx.

alarming number of fire incidents occurring in recent years on containerships such as *Maersk Honam*, *Yantian Express*, and *APL Vancouver*, insurers (given that the cost of claims borne by them under insurance policies due to container fires could be disproportionate) have lobbied to put pressure on the IMO in order to promote their recommendations in this respect. As mentioned, Gard held a two-day conference in 2019 focusing on container fires observed on container vessels and invited the IMO to incorporate their recommendations.[109] Similarly, the International Union of Maritime Insurance (IUMI) in 2017 published a paper[110] in which it warned the industry about issues concerning container fires on containerships and invited the IMO to take further steps to improve safety on containerships.[111] Following this, in the 101st session of the MSC in 2019, the concerns on container fires were once again raised by the IUMI and the International Association of Classification Societies (IACS).[112] In this regard, the IUMI, along with BIMCO, the shipbuilder's association (CESA) and the flag states of Germany and the Bahamas, in the 102nd session of the MSC, submitted their recommendation to amend the SOLAS.[113] To address the issue concerning container fires on container vessels, in the 103rd session, in accordance with the recommendations and proposals on the matter, the MSC eventually acknowledged the need to adopt a holistic approach to revising the relevant regulations to minimise and prevent risks associated with container fires. Accordingly, the MSC agreed to include 'Development of amendments to SOLAS chapter II-2 and the FSS Code concerning detection and control of fires in cargo holds and on the cargo deck of containerships' in the biennial agenda (2022–23) of the Sub-committee on Ship Systems and Equipment (SSE) with an aim to complete it in 2025 in association with the CCC along with the SSE.[114] The new amendments are due to come into force from 1 January 2028.[115] In the same direction, to prevent fires on container vessels and minimise the number of incidents arising from poor packing practices, considerable efforts have been made in recent years to promote the implementation of the 2014 IMO/ILO/UNECE Code of Practice of Cargo Transport Units (CTU Code). The Code is a revised version of the 1997 IMO/ILO/UNECE Guidelines for Packing of Cargo Transport Units and it was endorsed by the IMO, the Inland Transport Committee of the UNECE and the International Labour Organization (ILO).[116] The CTU Code is a non-mandatory instrument of practice setting out guidance on best practice for the handling and packing of cargo transport units for carriage by road and sea. Albeit adding a further layer to the compendium of dangerous goods regulations,

[109] See n 95 above.

[110] 'IUMI Position Paper – Firefighting systems on board container vessels', International Union of Maritime Insurance (2017).

[111] ibid.

[112] www.iumi.com/news/iumi-eye-newsletter-june-2021/new-output-on-container-fire-issues-approved-by-msc-103.

[113] ibid.

[114] www.imo.org/en/MediaCentre/MeetingSummaries/Pages/MSC-103rd-session.aspx.

[115] If they are adopted prior to 1 July 2026.

[116] www.imo.org/en/OurWork/Safety/Pages/CTU-Code.aspx.

it is acknowledged that incorporation of the Code alongside the IMDG Code by the stakeholders involved in the carriage of dangerous goods may greatly help to minimise the number of incidents arising from poor packing practices. However, as it is a non-mandatory code, implementation of it by the stakeholders involved in the transport of dangerous goods is significantly low. In this regard, to raise awareness for greater adherence to the CTU Code in practice, the International Cargo Handling Coordination Association (ICHCA) started an initiative called the Cargo Integrity Group (CIG) together with the Global Shipper's Form (GSF), the TT Club, the World Shipping Council (WSC) and the Container Owners' Association (COA).[117] Recently in 2019 and later in 2020 and 2021, following the spate of container fires, New Zealand, the ICHCA and the WSC submitted their proposal to the CCC concerning revisions to incorporate the CTU Code and to widen the scope of cargo transport unit inspections including cargo transport units not containing dangerous goods in accordance with the relevant MSC circulars on the amendments to the IMDG Code.[118] No doubt greater compliance with the CTU Code would help reduce these incidents.

The IMO appears to be acknowledging the need to improve the existing measures against the emerging issues on dangerous goods and carrying out effective regulatory changes to iron out inherent ineffectiveness of the Codes in a responsive manner. However, as the recent spate of dangerous goods incidents proves, efficacy and effectiveness are two different things, and regulatory efforts can only yield results if implementing actors are up to the task. Thus, effective implementation and incorporation of the Codes will only be ensured, if the focus is on comprehensive training and education with a holistic approach, based on the specific job description of the actors involved in the carriage of dangerous goods, and this can only be achieved if national governments and the stakeholders in the shipping industry shoulder their corresponding responsibilities as discussed above.

[117] For details, see www.ichca.com/cargo-integrity-group.
[118] In CCC6/10/1; CCC7/10; CCC7/10/1.

3

Liability Arising from Dangerous Goods: General Framework

I. General

In Chapter two, the international instruments regulating the maritime transport of dangerous goods are outlined. Before delving into the allocation of the liability arising out of dangerous goods between the seller and the buyer in contracts on shipment terms, in this chapter we shall look into the liability itself. In introducing liability for dangerous goods, first we shall consider what is meant by 'dangerous goods' under English law, including whether such goods are limited to certain contexts or whether there is a more relaxed approach adopted in English law. Following this, the nature of the liability will be discussed, including under what circumstances the shipper attracts the liability and whether he may be relieved of liability. We shall also draw comparisons from multiple shipping jurisdictions, including the Commonwealth and the US, where relevant.

II. Meaning of Dangerous Goods

When there is a contract of sale on shipment terms, namely CIF (contract, insurance, freight) and FOB (free on board) sales involving sea transport, the goods are carried in pursuance of these sale contracts and one of the parties – the seller or the buyer – must contract for carriage of the goods by sea with a third party, the carrier. The parties to a carriage contract customarily negotiate and draft all details of the contract and its terms regarding the arrangements for carriage of the goods. Allocation of the parties' responsibilities for risks that the ship and the goods can be exposed to constitutes a significant part of these arrangements. The description of the goods therefore is of paramount importance for the allocation of these risks between the parties to the carriage contract. When goods that are considered dangerous are the subject of the carriage contract, the parties' responsibilities for risks that the vessel and the goods might be exposed to become more important than ever.

Under English law, when the subject of the carriage contract is dangerous goods, the shipper of the goods has certain obligations to the carrier. Both at common law and under the Hague-Visby Rules, the shipper may become subject to liability to the carrier, when loss or damage is incurred by the carrier due to the dangerous nature or characteristics of the goods. However, neither in the Merchant Shipping Act 1995[1] nor in the Merchant Shipping (Dangerous Goods and Marine Pollutants) Regulations 1997[2] is there a definition of dangerous goods. As shown in Chapter two, although the classification of inherently dangerous goods by the IMDG Code[3] is of value, the case law appears to show that an exhaustive definition may not be necessary. In contrast, a more flexible approach could be preferable; the nature and characteristics of the goods might be only one of the elements posing danger, as dangerousness may lie often within situations and surrounding circumstances rather than simply in the goods themselves.[4] Indeed, there are obvious examples of inherently dangerous goods such as chemicals, gases, gasoil products, radioactive materials, explosives or corrosive substances. However, even goods that appear innocent may pose a danger under particular situations and can be considered dangerous.

The idea that the goods can be dangerous not only because of their inherent nature but also owing to surrounding circumstances was first put forward in *Brass v Maitland*,[5] where a cargo of chloride of lime was held to be dangerous due to improper packing. Even a cargo of cheese may cause damage due to insufficient packing, when stowed next to chocolate.[6] Similarly, a cargo of tallow can be considered dangerous when the other cargo on board is contaminated by it leaking[7] or a cargo of groundnut could be found dangerous due to infestation with insects causing the other cargo on board to have to be dumped at sea.[8] Without posing any physical threat, sometimes the goods can be legally dangerous owing to causing detention of or delay to the vessel.[9] Even a cargo of fishmeal can be held to be dangerous if it does not receive the necessary treatment so as to decrease its risk of ignition.[10]

[1] Merchant Shipping Act 1995, ss 85 and 87.

[2] Merchant Shipping (Dangerous Goods and Marine Pollutants) Regulations 1997 (SI 1997 No 2367). Albeit not complete, reg 2(1) defines dangerous goods as 'goods classified in the IMDG Code or in any other IMO publication referred to in these Regulations as dangerous for carriage by sea, and any other substance or article that the shipper has reasonable cause to believe might meet the criteria for such classification.' Liability of the carrier to third parties is not within the scope of this book. For this, see The International Convention for the Prevention of Pollution from Ships (MARPOL) 1978 Protocol, and the International Convention on Civil Liability for Oil Pollution Damage 1992 (Civil Liability Convention (CLC) 1992) given force by the Merchant Shipping Act 1995 Part VI, Chapter 3, s 152. See also, the International Convention on Liability and Compensation for Damage in Connection with the Carriage of Hazardous and Noxious Substances by Sea, 1996 (Hazardous and Noxious Substances by Sea Convention (HNS) 1996) and HNS Protocol 2010.

[3] The IMDG Code is mandatorily applied under chapter VII of SOLAS 1974 by the contracting states. See the Merchant Shipping Act 1995, ss 85 and 87 and Merchant Shipping (Dangerous Goods and Marine Pollutants) Regulations 1997, reg 2(1).

[4] M Mustill, 'Carriers' Liabilities and Insrance' in K Gronfors (ed), *Damage from Goods* (Klippan, Tullbergs, 1978) 69, 77.

[5] *Brass v Maitland* (1856) 6 E & B 470; 119 ER 940.

[6] *The Thorsa* [1916] P 257.

[7] *The Ministry of Food v Lamport & Holt Line Ltd* [1952] 2 Lloyd's Rep 371.

[8] *Effort Shipping v Linden Management (The Giannis NK)* [1998] AC 605; [1998] 1 Lloyd's Rep 337.

[9] *Mitchell Cotts & Co v Steel Bros & Co Ltd* [1916] 2 KB 610; *The Steamship Domald* (1919) 1 Ll L Rep 621.

[10] *General Feeds Inc v Burnham Shipping Corporation (The Amphion)* [1991] 2 Lloyd's Rep 101.

As well as embracing dangerousness in surrounding circumstances of the shipment, as outlined above, the courts have also refused to adopt a restrictive approach to the meaning of the word 'dangerous'. In *Chandris v Isbrandsten-Moller*,[11] Devlin J declined to qualify the meaning of dangerous by the immediately preceding words (listing particular types of dangerous goods) in an express clause.[12] Similarly, in *The Giannis NK*, the word 'dangerous' in article IV rule 6 of the Hague Rules was not restricted by the preceding words of 'explosive or inflammable' in the provision, and was instead given a broad meaning so as to include any goods that may cause direct or indirect physical danger to other cargo on board or to the vessel.[13] In *The Athanasia Comninos*,[14] which arguably mirrors the general approach taken in English law, Mustill J in discussing whether the cargo of coal was dangerous or not, opined: 'We are here concerned, not with the labelling in the abstract of the goods as "dangerous" or "safe", but with the distribution of risk for the consequences of a dangerous situation arising during the voyage.'[15]

As outlined above, there appears to be no exhaustive definition or class of dangerous goods. Accordingly, goods do not need to be inherently dangerous in their nature or character in order to be considered dangerous. Even the most innocuous goods can become dangerous, when posing a danger owing to surrounding circumstances. Therefore, traders in CIF and FOB sales should not take it for granted that liabilities arising from dangerous goods are restricted only to those certain types of goods that are recognised as inherently dangerous, unless they are eager to find themselves under liability to the carrier even for goods that appear entirely innocuous. Thus, they must bear in mind that any type of goods could be dangerous, when combined with surrounding elements.

III. Liability under Common Law

A. Physically Dangerous Goods

The shipper of dangerous goods is under a duty at common law to warn the carrier of the dangerous nature of the goods so that the carrier may take necessary precautions having regard to the nature and characteristics of the goods. The duty was first established in *Brass v Maitland*[16] where the cargo of chloride of lime in casks was loaded on board the carrier's vessel. Given the inadequate packing prior to loading, the cargo caused damage to the other cargo on board during transit.

[11] *Chandris v Isbrandsten-Moller Co Inc (The Eugenia Chandris)* [1951] 1 KB 240.
[12] ibid.
[13] [1998] 1 Lloyd's Rep 337, 341.
[14] *The Athanasia Comninos* [1990] 1 Lloyd's Rep 277.
[15] ibid, 282.
[16] *Brass v Maitland* (1856) 6 E & B 470; 119 ER 940. For the early principles see also, *Williams v East India Co* (1802) 3 East 192; 102 ER 571.

Although Crompton J dissented,[17] the majority of the court – Lord Campbell and Wrightman J – held that the shipper's obligation was strict rather than fault-based.[18] The majority decision was later followed by Scrutton LJ in *Great Northern Railway Co v LEP Transport & Depository*[19] and in *Bamfield & Goole v Sheffield Transport Co Ltd*,[20] in which, given the improper packing, the cargo of ferro-silicon carried in casks gave off poisonous gases that caused the death of the plaintiff's husband. The House of Lords in *The Giannis NK*, on the issue of whether liability for dangerous goods was strict or not, eventually settled the matter and held that the shipper's liability was strict both at common law and under article IV rule 6 of the Hague/Hague-Visby Rules (the Rules).[21] In that respect, the very same can be said for Canadian law, where the courts embraced the decision in *The Giannis NK*. Irrespective of whether liability stems under common law or the Rules, in any case it is considered strict under Canadian law.[22] As for US law, under the general maritime law, the shipper is under a duty[23] to warn the carrier of the dangerous nature of the cargo and he is subject to strict liability, even if he had no actual or constructive knowledge of the danger in the goods.[24]

Returning to English law, under the duty, the shipper should warn the carrier of the dangerous nature and characteristics of the goods so that necessary precautions can be afforded during transit by the carrier. If the characteristics and nature of the goods are well known or should reasonably be known by the carrier, the shipper's duty will be considered as discharged.[25] That is to say, if the carrier is aware or should reasonably be aware of the nature and character of the goods, the shipper will not be under any duty to warn him of the nature of the goods. In support of this, in the Canadian *Mahia* case, it was further held that the shipper would be discharged of this duty once the carrier was aware or ought to have been

[17] (1856) 6 E & B 470, 493. He opined that the shipper's liability should not be absolute and accordingly he should not be liable for something he does not know. His dissenting judgment found some support in some early cases: *Hutchison v Guion* (1858) 5 CB 149; 141 ER 59; *Farrant v Barnes* (1862) 11 CB 553; 142 ER 912.

[18] (1856) 6 E & B 470, 483.

[19] *Great Northern Railway Co v LEP Transport & Depository* [1922] 2 KB 742.

[20] *Bamfield & Goole v Sheffield Transport Co Ltd* [1910] 2 KB 94.

[21] [1998] AC 605; [1998] 1 Lloyd's Rep 337. On the detailed analysis of the case, see FD Rose, 'Liability for Dangerous Goods (*The Giannis NK*)' (1998) *LMCLQ* 480. Mustill J in *The Athanasia Comninos* also opined that the previous authorities predominantly supported strict liability: [1990] 1 Lloyd's Rep 277, 282.

[22] *Elders Grain Co Ltd v The MV Ralph Misener (The Ralph Misener)* 2003 FC 837, [53], affirmed in *Elders Grain Co Ltd v The MV Ralph Misener* 2005 FCA 139, [51]; *Industries Perlite Inc v The Marina Di Alimuri (The Marina Di Alimuri)* [1995] CanLII 3567; [1996] 2 FC 426, where the contract was not governed by the Rules, having followed *The Giannis NK*, the shipper was held liable, regardless of whether he was aware of the dangerous nature of the cargo or not. The Court followed the first instant decision of *The Giannis NK* which was later affirmed by the House of Lords; [1994] 2 Lloyd's Rep 171. See also, *Oceanex Inc v Praxair Canada Inc* [2014] FC 6, in which *The Marina Di Alimuri* and *The Giannis NK* were followed.

[23] *International Mercantile Marine Co v Fels*, 170 F 275, 277 (2d Cir, 1909).

[24] *Senator Linie GmbH & Co KG v Sunway Line Inc*, 291 F 3d 145 (2d Cir, 2002).

[25] *Brass v Maitland* (1856) 6 E & B 470, 487. A similar rule applies under the US law: *International Mercantile Marine Co v Fels*, 170 F 275, 277 (2d Cir, 1909).

aware of the danger, even if the carriage instructions given by the shipper were inadequate.[26] However, it should be noted that the carrier cannot be deemed to be an expert chemist or be obliged to resort to 'investigation inconsistent with the usual course of commercial business'.[27] A similar notion was applied in an Australian case, *Hoey v Hardie*,[28] where the carrier was only given the name of the substance that was to be loaded; bichromate of potash. It was held that the carrier could not be reasonably deemed to know, on the sole basis of the cargo's name, that such a substance was dangerous at the time. Nonetheless, sometimes there might be an issue arising in practice as to whether the carrier's imputed knowledge having regard to the nature and the characteristics of the goods is sufficient to relieve the shipper of his duty. In *The Atlantic Duchess*,[29] during ballasting operations at the discharge port, an explosion occurred as a result of butane residues left in the tanks of the ship after the discharge of the cargo of crude oil, resulting in loss of life and damage to the vessel. The issue was whether any special notice should have been given the carrier so as to allow him to take special precautions in the carriage of butanised oil. Crude oil was well known to be dangerous at the time in the shipping trade and it would require special precautions for safe carriage during transit. Pearson J decided that the cargo in question did not require any special precautions beyond that required for a usual crude oil cargo, on the ground that butanised crude oil was not more dangerous or prone to explosion than usual crude oil. Thus, it was held that the cargo in question did not create risks different in kind.[30] Similarly, in *The Athanasia Comninos*,[31] where the issue revolved around whether special precautionary measures and, as a consequence, a special notice were required for the carriage of coal. The propensity of coal to emit methane gas was well-known in the shipping trade. Therefore, in order for the carrier to recover against the shipper, the carrier had to prove that the cargo in question had a different nature to a usual cargo of coal, and accordingly that special precautions were needed, which were beyond those involved in the carriage of ordinary coal, were necessary. As the carrier failed to prove this, Mustill J, following the decision in *The Atlantic Duchess*, rejected the carrier's claim.[32] In *The Amphion*,[33] a cargo of 'anti-oxidant treated fishmeal', which is listed in the IMDG Code, was shipped. However, as the cargo in question had not been properly treated, it required more ventilation than a cargo of anti-oxidant treated fishmeal normally would do.

[26] *Shaw Savill & Albion Co Ltd v Electric Reduction Co of Canada Ltd and Imperial Chemical Industries of Australia and New Zealand Ltd (The Mahia)* [1955] 1 Lloyd's Rep 264.

[27] *Brass v Maitland* (1856) 6 E & B 470, 487. In the Exchequer Court of Canada, following *Brass v Maitland*, the same notion applied: *Heath Steele Mines Ltd v The Erwin Schroder (The Erwin Schroder)* [1969] 1 Lloyd's Rep 370.

[28] *Hoey v Hardie & Another* (1912) 12 SR (NSW) 268.

[29] *Atlantic Oil Carriers Ltd v British Petroleum Co Ltd (The Atlantic Duchess)* [1957] 2 Lloyd's Rep 55.

[30] ibid.

[31] [1990] 1 Lloyd's Rep 277.

[32] ibid, 283–84. See also *Mediterranean Freight Services Ltd v BP Oil International Ltd (The Fiona)* [1994] 2 Lloyd's Rep 506.

[33] [1991] 2 Lloyd's Rep 101.

This is because a cargo of fishmeal that does not receive anti-oxidant treatment is more prone to ignition and burning than a treated one. Since the cargo was not given any special ventilation during transit, it ignited during discharge. Evans J, following the decision in *The Athanasia Comninos*, held that as the cargo in question was described as 'anti-oxidant treated' in the carriage contract, the carrier could not have been expected to afford it special precautions beyond those required in the carriage of anti-oxidant treated fishmeal. Accordingly, the shipowner's claim against the shipper was allowed.

B. The Concept of Legally Dangerous Goods

As discussed above, the shipper is under a duty to warn the carrier for goods which are physically dangerous under common law. This duty was extended by way of analogy in *Mitchell Cotts v Steel Brothers*[34] to cover cases where there is no *physical* danger to the vessel or other cargo whatsoever, but where the shipment of goods leads to *legal* obstacles which may cause economic losses resulting from expenses or delay. A cargo of rice was shipped on board *The Kaijo Maru*, which posed no physical danger whatsoever to the vessel or other cargo on board. The destination was Piraeus and the shippers were aware that the cargo could not be discharged without the permission of the British authorities. As the shipper had failed to obtain the permission to unload, the vessel was detained for three weeks. Atkin J held by way of analogy that the shipper's duty extended to cases in which the goods are not at all physically dangerous but they are liable to cause delay to the vessel:

> I think there is no question that a shipment of goods upon an illegal voyage – i.e., upon a voyage that cannot be performed without the violation of the law of the land of the place to which the goods are to be carried – a shipment of goods which might involve the ship in danger of forfeiture or delay – is precisely analogous to the shipment of a dangerous cargo which might cause the destruction of the ship.[35]

By this decision, the shipper under the duty should not only allow the carrier to take necessary measures having regard to the nature of the goods but also provide any necessary information in relation to the legal obstacles which may result from the shipment of the goods, potentially causing delay to the vessel. Indeed, as with physically dangerous goods, if the carrier is aware or should have been aware of those obstacles, the shipper's duty is deemed to be discharged. However, the carrier will not be entitled to recover all economic loss or expense resulting from delay, unless that delay is caused by 'legal obstacles'.[36] Thus, where delay or detention is

[34] *Mitchell Cotts & Co v Steel Brothers & Co Ltd* [1916] 2 KB 610.
[35] ibid, 614.
[36] *Bunge SA v ADM do Brasil Ltda and Others (The Darya Radhe)* [2009] EWHC 845 (Comm); [2009] 2 Lloyd's Rep 175.

merely caused by reason of the nature or the character of the goods, the carrier will not be able to invoke liability of the shipper.[37]

IV. Liability under the Hague-Visby Rules

There is an express provision in article IV rule 6 of the Hague-Visby Rules as to the carriage of dangerous goods:

> Goods of an inflammable, explosive or dangerous nature to the shipment whereof the carrier, master or agent of the carrier has not consented with knowledge of their nature and character, may at any time before discharge be landed at any place, or destroyed or rendered innocuous by the carrier without compensation and the shipper of such goods shall be liable for all damages and expenses directly or indirectly arising out of or resulting from such shipment.[38]

When the Rules apply,[39] the common law duty is superseded in respect of physically dangerous goods.[40] Hence, the common law duty remains intact and still applies to situations where the goods are legally dangerous, even if the contract is governed by the Rules.[41] Unlike the common law duty, which is a contractual undertaking, once the Rules govern the bill of lading, article IV rule 6 operates as a contractual provision of indemnity.[42] In support of this, in *The Fiona*, the Court of Appeal rejected the notion that the shipper is under any obligation to give notice to the carrier of the nature and characteristics of the goods, which the carrier does not know or cannot reasonably be expected to know.[43]

The ambit of article IV rule 6 was extensively reviewed in *The Giannis NK*[44] by the House of Lords. A cargo of groundnut pellets was loaded in one hold of *The Giannis NK*, while in other holds wheat pellets were shipped for carriage to San Juan, (Puerto Rico) and the Dominican Republic. Following the discharge of some of the wheat cargo at San Juan, the vessel sailed to the Dominican Republic to deliver the cargo of groundnut pellets, where the vessel was quarantined because khapra beetle were detected in that cargo. Following two unsuccessful attempts

[37] *Transoceanica Societa Italiana di Navigazione v HS Shipton & Sons* [1923] 1 KB 31. But see also *Rederi Aktiebolaget Transatlantic v Board of Trade* (1924) 20 Ll L Rep 241.

[38] As the Hague Rules also have the identical provision, it is immaterial whether the Hague or the Hague-Visby Rules apply in respect of dangerous goods liability. For the relevant provisions in other conventions which are not applicable in the United Kingdom, see the Hamburg Rules, art 13 and for the United Nations Convention on Contracts for the International Carriage of Goods Wholly or Partially at Sea (The Rotterdam Rules) 2008, art 32.

[39] See art X of the Hague-Visby Rules and the Carriage of Goods by Sea Act 1971, s 1(1) and (6).

[40] *The Fiona* [1993] 1 Lloyd's Rep 257, 267–68, affirmed in [1994] 2 Lloyd's Rep 506. The application of the provision is restricted to physically dangerous: *The Darya Radhe* [2009] 2 Lloyd's Rep 175.

[41] *The Fiona* [1993] 1 Lloyd's Rep 257, 267–68.

[42] *The Fiona* [1994] 2 Lloyd's Rep 506, 518.

[43] ibid, 512. Indeed, if there is a notice given by the shipper, the carrier can be deemed to have consented to the shipment of the goods in question.

[44] *The Giannis NK* [1998] AC 605; [1998] 1 Lloyd's Rep 337.

at fumigation, the vessel returned to San Juan where it was ordered by the US Department of Agriculture to return the cargo to its origin or dump it at sea. The carrier opted for the latter option and dumped the entire cargo at sea, along with the remainder of the wheat pellets in the other holds, despite the fact that they were in no danger of beetle infestation. Following this, an extensive fumigation was carried out on board the vessel so as to render her ready for future shipments.

Under the bills of lading, the carrier claimed recovery from the shipper for his loss and expenses arising out of dangerous goods by reason of infestation in the groundnut pellets, as per article IV rule 6. On the meaning of the word 'dangerous' in the provision, the House of Lords held that it was not restricted by the preceding words 'inflammable, explosive'. Thus, 'dangerous' was given a broad meaning including goods which are dangerous even in the indirect sense of being liable to give rise to physical harm to other cargo on board and the vessel.[45] In addition, just as it is under the common law duty, the shipper's liability under article IV rule 6 is considered strict, and the fact that the shipper and his agent are unaware that the goods are dangerous does not relieve the shipper of liability under the Rules.[46] Therefore, article IV rule 6 is deemed to be a free-standing provision and is not qualified by article IV rule 3 under which the shipper is discharged of liability in general when loss or damage is incurred by the carrier resulting or arising from any cause without the act, fault or neglect of the shipper or his agents.[47]

So far as the carrier's heads of loss are concerned, he is entitled to claim for 'all damages and expenses', as long as a causal link is established between dangerous goods and the damage and expenses sustained by him, as normal rules of remoteness of damage may not apply to the provision.[48] Under article IV rule 6, the carrier can be entitled to claim for loss of or damage to the vessel,[49] for damage to other cargo on board,[50] for loss of life,[51] for costs of decontamination[52] or fumigation,[53] or for loss of time and bunker expenses.[54]

Considering the major Commonwealth jurisdictions, the Hague or Hague-Visby Rules are in effect in their corresponding legislation, and the interpretation of article IV rule 6 in many of these jurisdictions could be said to be in line with English law, as the decision in *The Giannis NK* was embraced by these jurisdictions.

[45] [1998] AC 605, 613. On the same view see also *The Darya Radhe* [2009] 2 Lloyd's Rep 175.

[46] ibid.

[47] ibid.

[48] *The Fiona* [1994] 2 Lloyd's Rep 506, 522. See also J Cooke, J Kimball et al, *Voyage Charters*, 4th edn (London, Informa, 2014), para 85.448; R Aikens, R Lord and MD Bools, *Bills of lading*, 3rd edn (London, Informa, 2020), para 11.376.

[49] *The Fiona* [1994] 2 Lloyd's Rep 506.

[50] *The Giannis NK* [1998] AC 605.

[51] *Northern Shipping Co v Deutsche Seereederei GmbH (The Kapitan Sakharov)* [2000] 2 Lloyd's Rep 255; *The Fiona* [1994] 2 Lloyd's Rep 506.

[52] *Sig Bergesen DY & Co and Others v Mobil Shipping and Transportation Co (The Berge Sund)* [1993] 2 Lloyd's Rep 453; Nonetheless, the need for ordinary cleaning after a voyage may not render the goods dangerous: *Splosna Pilobna of Piran v Agrelak Steamship Co (The Bela Krajina)* [1975] 1 Lloyd's Rep 139.

[53] *The Giannis NK* [1998] AC 605.

[54] ibid.

Under Canadian law, the application and interpretation of the provision appears to be substantially the same as English law. In *The Ralph Misener*, having discussed *The Giannis NK*, it was held that the shipper was subject to strict liability under article IV rule 6 and the provision was not qualified by article IV rule 3.[55] The court went on to rely on *The Giannis NK* in giving the word 'dangerous' broad meaning, holding that it should not be restrictively interpreted by reason of the preceding words 'inflammable' or 'explosive'.[56] Similarly, the application and interpretation of the provision in *The Giannis NK* by the House of Lords had a substantial impact in the other major Commonwealth jurisdictions, like Australia,[57] South Africa[58] and Malaysia,[59] and the approach adopted on the matter by these countries is substantially the same as the English approach. So far as the Nordic countries – Norway,[60] Denmark,[61] Sweden and Finland – are concerned, all of which also incorporate article IV rule 6 of the Hague/Hague-Visby Rules into their corresponding domestic legislation, in respect of the shipper's strict liability, the approach taken in these countries is substantially the same as the English approach.[62] The main difference, however, lies within the meaning of 'dangerous'. Unlike the English courts, the Nordic courts appear to be interpreting 'dangerous' in a restrictive manner and confining it to the inherent nature and characteristics of the goods.[63] As for US law, in *Senator Linie v Sunway Line Inc*, having discussed both the US and English jurisprudence extensively, it was held that under section 4(6) of the US COGSA (corresponding to article IV rule 6 of the Hague Rules), the shipper was subject to strict liability, even if he had no actual or constructive knowledge of dangerous nature of the goods.[64] Considering the meaning of 'dangerous', the approach taken by the US courts, however, differs from the English approach, as the word is

[55] *Elders Grain Co Ltd v The MV Ralph Misener (The Ralph Misener)* 2003 FC 837, [47]–[53], affirmed in the Court of Appeal: *Elders Grain Co Ltd v The MV Ralph Misener (The Ralph Misener)* 2005 FCA 139, [51].

[56] *Elders Grain Co Ltd v The MV Ralph Misener (The Ralph Misener)* 2005 FCA 139, [38]. For the same view, see also *Oceanex Inc v Praxair Canada Inc* [2014] FC 6.

[57] *Rail Equipment Leasing Pty Ltd v CV Scheepvaartonderneming Emmagracht* [2008] NSWSC 850, [60].

[58] *The MV Recife: Safbank Line Ltd v Control Chemicals (Pty) Ltd* 1997 (4) SA 852, reversed on other grounds in *The MV Recife: Control Chemicals (Pty) Ltd v Safbank Line Ltd* [2000] ZASCA 12.

[59] *Ing Hua Fu Marine Line Sdn Bhd v Vitachem (M) Sdn Bhd* [2013] 9 MLJ 825, reversed on other grounds in *Vitachem (M) Sdn Bhd v Ing Hua Fu Marine Line Sdn Bhd* [2014] 6 MLJ 566.

[60] ND 1954.377 Florentine and ND 1954.364 Florø. See also *Yara Asia Pte Ltd v J Lauritzen Singapore Pte Ltd* TOSLO-2017-180657-2 (17-180657TVI-OTIR / 01), affirmed in *J Lauritzen Singapore Pte Ltd v Yara Asia Pte Ltd (The MV Cheshire)* 20-062574ASD-BORG / 03. For the English transcript of the cases, see www.cmlcmidatabase.org/yara-asia-pte-ltd-v-j-lauritzen-singapore-pte-ltd-0 and www.cmlcmidatabase.org/j-lauritzen-singapore-pte-ltd-v-yara-asia-pte-ltd.

[61] ND 1941.353 Else; ND 1998.167 Leopold. See also, *Nørrejyllands Gensidige Søforsikringsforening v HJ Hansen Genvindingsindustri A/S* FED 2014.64. For the English transcript of the case, see www.cmlcmidatabase.org/n%C3%B8rrejyllands-gensidige-s%C3%B8forsikringsforening-v-hj-hansen-genvindingsindustri.

[62] Josephine Thörnroos, 'The Contracting Shipper's Strict Liability in the Carriage of Dangerous Goods by Sea' (Master's thesis, University of Helsinki 2019), 3.

[63] For a detailed analysis of the dangerous goods liability in Nordic countries, see generally, ibid.

[64] *Senator Linie GmbH & Co KG v Sunway Line Inc*, 291 F 3d 145 (2d Cir, 2002). See also *In re M/V MSC Flaminia No* 12-CV-8892 (KBF) (SD NY 2018).

confined to goods of an inflammable and explosive nature or their like by the US courts.[65]

As with the common law duty, if the carrier has consented to the carriage of the goods with knowledge of their nature and characteristics, the carrier will not be entitled to claim for damages or expenses from the shipper under the provision.[66] However, sometimes an issue may arise over whether the carrier has genuinely consented to shipment of the goods with actual or imputed knowledge. Nevertheless, in that respect, the position under article IV rule 6 is substantially the same as the common law position; the carrier cannot, under article IV rule 6, be deemed to be an expert chemist or possess the same knowledge as the manufacturer of the goods.[67] In *The Fiona*,[68] due to having methane bubbles, the cargo of fuel oil was found to be different in kind to the usual type in the trade and it was considered exceptionally volatile. The carrier was not aware of the high level of volatility in the fuel oil. Thus, he did not take the necessary measures associated with the cargo in question. The Court of Appeal held that as the fuel oil in question was different in kind and created more danger than the usual type, the carrier had not consented to the shipment of the fuel oil in question but only to the usual type in the shipping trade. Similarly, in *The Aconcagua*,[69] a cargo of calcium hypochlorite, which was known to be explosive at temperatures over 60°C, was loaded into a container. The goods shipped in fact had a lower explosive level, which was around 30°C, than the usual kind would have. It was held that unless he was a specialist carrier, the carrier could not be expected to have knowledge of the particular characteristics of the goods in question, which were more prone to explosion than the usual calcium hypochlorite.[70] Therefore, the carrier's claim was allowed. On the other hand, under US law, albeit that liability is strict, once the carrier has some degree of knowledge about the risks associated with the goods, the shipper may not be found liable. In the *Contship* case,[71] the carriers were aware of the general risks involved in the carriage of calcium hypochlorite, but they did not consent to the carriage of the calcium hypochlorite in question in the knowledge of its particular characteristics and nature, as the risks associated with the cargo in question were beyond those involved in the carriage of normal calcium hypochlorite. It was nonetheless held that although the precise characteristics were not available to the carrier, the degree of his actual or constructive knowledge of calcium hypochlorite

[65] See *Stainless Sales Inc v Evergreen America Corporation*, 2006 WL 1328845 (ED Mich 2006); *Pemeno Shipping Co Ltd v Louis Dreyfus Corp*, 238 Fed App'x 6 (5th Cir 2007). See also Cooke, *Voyage Charters*, n 48 above, para 85A.56.

[66] The carrier will be entitled to dispose of the goods without liability except to general average, if any, under the second paragraph of art IV r 6.

[67] *Compania Sud Americana de Vapores SA v Sinochem Tianjin Import and Export Corporation (The Aconcagua)* [2010] 1 Lloyd's Rep 1.

[68] *The Fiona* [1994] 2 Lloyd's Rep 506 (CA).

[69] *The Aconcagua* [2010] 1 Lloyd's Rep 1.

[70] ibid, [60]–[62].

[71] *Contship Containerlines Ltd v PPG Industries Inc*, 442 F 3d 74, 75, 2006 AMC 686 (2d Cir 2006).

was enough to relieve the shipper of strict liability.[72] The carrier was therefore deprived of recovery from the shipper, despite the fact that he could not be reasonably expected to know the specific risks beyond those associated with the carriage of the usual calcium hypochlorite. It is submitted that the decision in the *Contship* case undermines the shipper's strict liability, as it limits the carrier's reliance on strict liability of the shipper, creating a grey zone to impute actual or constructive knowledge on the carrier in relation to the goods.

V. Fault of the Carrier

The carrier is under a duty 'before and at the beginning of the voyage to exercise due diligence to make the vessel seaworthy' under article III rule 1 of the Rules.[73] Where he is in breach of this provision, it is trite law that it has an overriding effect and accordingly he is not entitled to rely on article IV rule 6 for liability arising from dangerous goods against the shipper.[74] In *The Fiona*,[75] the cargo of fuel oil was unusually volatile, due to it containing methane bubbles. The tanks of the vessel had not been properly cleaned before the shipment and there were residues from the cargo of fuel oil carried previously, which together with the fuel generated explosive gases. On arrival, an explosion occurred, causing damage to the vessel and loss of lives. HH Diamond QC said that the carrier had not consented to shipment of the fuel oil in question with knowledge of its particular nature, and also held that the carrier was in breach of article III rule 1 for failing to exercise due diligence to make the vessel seaworthy before the shipment, given the residues of the previous cargo. As a consequence, the vessel had not been fit for carriage.[76] Ultimately, the carrier's claim against the shipper failed on the ground that the dominant cause of the explosion was the carrier's breach of article III rule 1. In approving the judgment of Diamond QC as to the overriding effect of article III rule 1, the Court of Appeal further held that unless otherwise stated, the party that is negligent cannot invoke indemnity clauses on the general rule of construction.[77] This is the case, even if the carrier's breach is not the dominant but just one of the effective causes.[78] In *The Kapitan Sakharov*,[79] undisclosed dangerous goods, which were not known by the carrier before shipment, were shipped in a container on deck. In addition, an inflammable, highly volatile chemical had

[72] ibid. See also *Re M/V DG Harmony*, 533 F 3d 83, 2008 AMC 1848 (2d Cir 2008); *In re M/V Rickmers Genoa Litigation*, 622 F Supp 2d 56 (SDNY 2009).
[73] Art III r 1 (a). See also art III r 1 (b) and (c).
[74] *The Fiona* [1993] 1 Lloyd's Rep 257, 286.
[75] ibid.
[76] ibid, 286.
[77] [1994] 2 Lloyd's Rep 506, 522.
[78] [2000] 2 Lloyd's Rep 255.
[79] ibid.

mistakenly been stowed by the carrier in an unventilated compartment below deck, which rendered the vessel unseaworthy under article III rule 1, because the cargo in question required strong ventilation. The undisclosed goods stowed on deck ignited during transit and the fire spread to the highly volatile cargo stowed below deck, which eventually led to the entire loss of the vessel. It was held that even though the carrier's breach of article III rule 1 was not the dominant cause of the explosion, the carrier was only entitled to claim against the shipper of the undisclosed goods to the extent of the damage arising from the on-deck containers. The carrier's claim for the sinking of the vessel and the other containers failed on the basis that these losses resulted from the combination of the breach of article III rule 1 and the shipment of undeclared goods by the shipper.

Although there is no direct authority, once the carrier's breach of article III rule 2 (by which he is to properly and carefully load, handle, stow and look after the goods), is found to be one of the effective causes, it appears that the carrier is not entitled to claim from the shipper under article IV rule 6.[80] It is arguable that this is also consistent with the general rules of construction that a negligent party cannot invoke indemnity clauses, unless otherwise stated.

When the bill of lading is not governed by the Rules, common law will take effect and the common law position on the matter is less clear than the position held under the Rules. The courts may, however, look into whether the carrier's breach is an intervening act, which breaks the causal link between the shipper's breach and the loss arising from the dangerous goods.[81] Some support can be also found in the Canadian *Oceanex* case, where the Rules did not apply to the contract, the carrier claimed recovery for the damage caused to his vessel's deck and shell plating as a result of the leakage of liquid oxygen from a tank container. The shipper counterclaimed from the carrier for damage to the container. Eventually, the shipper was found liable for the damage sustained, owing to the insufficient packing of the container. The court went on to hold that the shipper was not entitled to claim recovery from the carrier, when the damage was occasioned by his negligence.[82] There is no reason why the same cannot apply to the carrier when the intervening act is his own breach. Alternatively, it might be possible to apply apportionment under the Law Reform (Contributory Negligence) Act 1945, which enables the court to apportion liability between the tortfeasor and a person who was partly in fault. The carrier's breach of its duty to make the vessel seaworthy or its duty of care for the goods may well be classified as fault. Nevertheless, it is not entirely plausible to classify the shipper's breach of the duty concerning the shipment of dangerous

[80] *The Aconcagua* [2010] 1 Lloyd's Rep 1, [337]–[374] (High Ct), approved in [2011] 1 Lloyd's Rep 683 (CA). See also *The Fiona* [1993] 1 Lloyd's Rep 257, 288. Nevertheless, an excepted peril, like an error in the management in the vessel, will not on its own prevent the carrier from claiming his loss from the shipper under art IV r 6: *The Aconcagua* [2010] 1 Lloyd's Rep 1, [372]–[373].

[81] *The Kapitan Sakharov* [2000] 2 Lloyd's Rep 255, 270–71.

[82] *Oceanex Inc v Praxair Canada Inc* [2014] FC 6, [95], applying *Barbour v South Eastern Railway Co* (1876) 34 LT 67.

goods as fault, given that his breach is not restricted to fault under article IV rule 6 or under common law.[83]

VI. Conclusion

Under English law, be it common law or the Rules, it appears that the word 'dangerous' is not restricted to inherently dangerous goods and dangerousness is conceptually taken into account as the combination of the surrounding circumstances with the nature of the goods. The case law predominantly suggests that even the most innocuous goods are potentially capable of being dangerous, unless necessary measures are taken for carriage. In that respect, we have seen that the approach adopted by the English courts has been profoundly influential within the major Commonwealth countries.

So far as damage or expenses arising out of these goods are concerned, regardless of whether they arise under the Rules or common law, the shipper comes under strict liability to the carrier, even if he bears no fault at all regarding the shipment. In this regard, in the shipping countries making use of the Hague/Hague-Visby Rules, like the US and the Nordic countries, the application of article IV rule 6 is similar to the English approach, although there are some differences in other aspects. As for the Commonwealth countries, the English case law can be said to have been vastly influential. As a result, the interpretation of the provision is substantially the same as the English interpretation. The case law also appears to show that the shipper may actually find himself liable for total loss of or damage to the vessel, other cargoes on board or even for loss of life. This proves that liabilities arising out of such goods can be disproportionate and substantial, as the shipper is not statutorily classified within the group of people entitled to limit his liability to the carrier.[84] This follows that money highly turns on this issue. By the same token, traders – sellers and buyers – negotiating sale contracts on shipment terms should give utmost importance to the allocation of liability for dangerous goods, given that whoever the shipper will be – either the seller or the buyer – they may be subject to substantial liabilities to the carrier under the carriage contract.

[83] See generally, S Girvin, 'Shipper's Liability for the Carriage of Dangerous Cargoes by Sea' (1996) *LMCLQ* 487, 499; Cooke, *Voyage Charters*, n 48 above, para 85.462 ff.

[84] Neither in art IV r 5 of the Rules nor under the Merchant Shipping Act 1995, Schedule 7, art 1(2).

4

The Shipper and His Liability under CIF and FOB Contracts

I. General

As shown in Chapter three, at common law, the shipper is under an implied duty to inform the carrier of the nature and character of dangerous goods in order to enable him to take necessary precautions for carriage of the goods concerned.[1] In case of non-declaration or misdeclaration, the carrier will seek redress from the shipper for damage or losses occasioned by the shipment of dangerous goods. Where the Rules are applicable, the common law duty is supplanted.[2] However, similarly to the common law duty, under the Rules, the shipper, by virtue of article IV rule 6, becomes liable for damage and losses arising from dangerous goods, when the carrier has not consented to the shipment of such goods with knowledge of the nature and character of the goods concerned.[3]

Liability for dangerous goods is allocated to the shipper under both common law and the Rules. However, a question arises at this point over the identity of the shipper. For the purpose of the allocation of rights and obligations under the carriage contract, the shipper is the party that enters into a carriage contract with the carrier under the bills of lading.[4] Thus, the common answer to this question is that the party named as the shipper in the bills of lading becomes subject to this liability. Yet, this still does not appear to unveil the real identity of the shipper. The answer to this question may lie within the sale contract rather than under the contract of carriage for the goods.[5] When the sale contract

[1] *Brass v Maitland* (1856) 6 E & B 470; 119 ER 940; *Bamfield v Goole & Sheffield Transport Co Ltd* [1910] 2 KB 94; *Great Northern Railway Co v LEP Transport* [1922] 2 KB 742; (1922) 11 Ll L Rep 133.

[2] *Mediterranean Freight Services Ltd v BP Oil International Ltd (The Fiona)* [1993] 1 Lloyd's Rep 257, affirmed in [1994] 2 Lloyd's Rep 506. The common law duty is superseded in respect of physically dangerous goods. The common law obligation arising from legally dangerous goods is not supplanted by the Rules. See *The Darya Radhe* [2009] EWHC 845; [2009] 2 Lloyd's Rep 175; *Mitchell Cotts & Co Ltd v Steel Brothers & Co Ltd* [1916] 2 KB 610.

[3] *Effort Shipping Co Ltd v Linden Management SA (The Giannis NK)* [1998] AC 605; [1998] 1 Lloyd's Rep 337.

[4] Art I(a) of the Rules.

[5] *East West Corp v Dampskibsselskabet AF, 1912, Aktieselskab (DKBS 1912)* [2003] EWCA Civ 83; [2003] QB 1509, [34].

is on CIF or FOB terms,[6] one of the parties is required to conclude transport arrangements as a result of the stipulation in the sale contract about who is to make the carriage contract for the carriage of the goods.[7] Depending on the terms of the sale contract, which will be discussed below, it could be either the seller or the buyer who concludes the carriage contract and who is named in the bills of lading as the shipper.[8] Nevertheless, this does not necessarily always mean that the bills of lading evidence a contract between the carrier and the named shipper. Sometimes, for instance, the seller can conclude the carriage contract and be named in the bills as the shipper acting as agent on behalf of the buyer, and accordingly the buyer can be considered the shipper.[9] In such cases, the seller may not be original shipper at all. That being the case, this may affect the allocation of liability arising from the shipment of dangerous goods between the seller and the buyer vis-à-vis the carrier.

The need to identify the original shipper (whether the seller or the buyer) under the bills of lading is hence crucial to determine who is subject to liability for damage and losses arising from the shipment of dangerous goods. Therefore for the purpose of the allocation of liability between the seller and the buyer, this chapter will seek to address the question of who the shipper is under CIF and FOB sales and whether the courts follow a different approach in determining the identity of the shipper, when considering liability for dangerous goods.[10] While doing so, we shall also look into how satisfactory English law is on the allocation of the liability, when the real identity of the shipper is unveiled between the seller and the buyer under such sales. This chapter, shall also look into the question of whether, when there is no direct contractual nexus with the carrier, liability can be imposed on the relevant party for dangerous goods under other mechanisms, such as in tort and implied contract.

[6] They are the most common transactions used in commodity sales for well over two centuries. *Ross T Smyth and Co Ltd v TD Bailey, Son and Co* [1940] 3 All ER 60.
DM Sassoon, 'The Origin of F.O.B. and C.I.F. Terms and the Factors Influencing Their Choice' [1967] *JBL* 32, 32.

[7] This is attributable to the centrality of the sale contract in international trade. See F Lorenzon, *C.I.F. and F.O.B. Contracts*, 6th edn (London, Sweet & Maxwell, 2017) 3.

[8] A classic FOB seller is also under a duty to tender shipping documents (bills of lading), as is under CIF contracts. See *Concordia Trading BV v Richo International Ltd* [1991] 1 Lloyd's Rep 475. See also, *Hansson v Hamel and Horley Ltd* [1922] 2 AC 36.

[9] *Borealis AB v Stargas Ltd and Others (The Berge Sisar)* [2001] UKHL 17; [2002] AC 205; *Cho Yang Shipping Co Ltd v Coral (UK) Ltd* [1997] 2 Lloyd's Rep 641. See also, *Texas Instruments Ltd v Nason (Europe) Ltd* [1991] 1 Lloyd's Rep 146. For the usual position under CIF sales, see *Domett v Beckford* (1883) 5 B & Ald 521; *Customs and Excise Commissioners v Aps Samex* [1983] 1 All ER 1042.

[10] For an earlier and raw version of this chapter, see A Gelgec, 'Who Attracts the Dangerous Goods Liability under CIF and FOB Contracts?' in S Zunarelli and M Musi (eds), *Current Issues in Maritime and Transport Law* (Bologna, Bonomo, 2016) 29.

II. The Nature of CIF and FOB Contracts

In the early days of international trade, it was the FOB[11] term that was used first and it was assumed that the CIF term was derived from FOB.[12] In those days, there were no regular shipping lines. Basically, the buyer would have chartered a vessel to call at foreign ports. Then the seller, as a mere duty, would have shipped the goods on board for the account of the buyer.[13] As international trade developed, CIF contracts emerged as a popular alternative to FOB contracts. They shifted greater responsibility onto the seller, relegating the carrier's obligation to one of providing cargo space for the goods.[14] Due to technological advances and commercialisation, the obligations of the parties have become more muddled as judicial interpretation has transformed standard terms into flexible instruments.[15] In the early authorities, the FOB buyer was considered the shipper.[16] By the twenty-first century, the result was that the identity of the shipper was considered flexible and it was difficult to predict from the outset whether the buyer or the seller could be considered to be the shipper.[17]

Today it is not always necessarily the case that the party making the contract of carriage is the party who ships the goods, or vice versa. The buyer of the goods, for instance, could sometimes be considered the shipper, even though in fact it was the seller who physically shipped the goods.[18] Yet, it is also possible that the seller might be exposed or bound by an implied contract under the bills of lading, just because he physically shipped the goods, even though he was not a party to the main contract of carriage and was not even designated as the shipper in the bill of lading either.[19]

For the sake of clarity, it is therefore useful to distinguish two types of shippers in this chapter: (1) the wet shipper, namely the party who physically ships the goods; and (2) the dry shipper, namely the party who concludes the

[11] The very first cases that mentioned FOB terms are *Wackerbarth v Masson* (1812) 3 Camp 270; 170 ER 1378; *Craven & Another v Ryder* (1816) 6 Taunt 433. For the term c.i.f., see *Tregelles v Sewell* (1862) 7 H & N 574; 158 ER 600; *Ireland v Livingston* (1871–72) LR 5 HL 395.

[12] For the historical evolution of FOB and CIF sales, see generally Sassoon, n 6 above; DM Sassoon, 'Application of FOB and CIF Sales in Common Law Countries' (1981) 16 *European Transport Law* 50.

[13] Sassoon, n 6 above, 33.

[14] *Tregelles v Sewell* (1862) 7 H & N 574; *Ireland v Livingston* (1871–72) LR 5 HL 395.

[15] Especially FOB contracts; where Devlin J stated in *Pyrene Co Ltd v Scindia Steam Navigation Co* [1954] 2 QB 402, 424: 'The f.o.b. contract has become a flexible instrument.' See also, the statement of Roskill LJ in *Concord Petroleum Corp v Gosford Marine Panama SA (The Albazero)* [1975] 3 WLR 491; [1975] 2 Lloyd's Rep 295, 302, although the House of Lords reversed the decision, this part of judgment was not affected: [1977] AC 774.

[16] *Cowas-Jee v Thompson and Kebbel* (1845) 5 Moore 165; 13 ER 454.

[17] *The Athanasia Comninos and Georges Chr Lemos* [1990] 1 Lloyd's Rep 277, 280; *Evergreen Marine Corp v Aldgate Warehouse (Wholesale) Ltd* [2003] 2 Lloyd's Rep 597, [29]; *East West Corp v DKBS 1912* [2003] QB 1509, [34]; *AP Moller-Maersk A/S (t/a Maersk Line) v Somiac Villas Cen Sad Fadoul* [2010] EWHC 355 (Comm), [46].

[18] *Pyrene v Scindia* [1954] 2 QB 402.

[19] ibid.

contract of carriage. Such a distinction can be particularly suitable, where a party (wet shipper) other than the dry shipper may be exposed to liabilities under bills of lading. Also acknowledging two classes of shippers can be of some assistance in highlighting the key issue that must be resolved adequately in allocating liability for dangerous goods at the shipment stage between the buyer and the seller.

A. The Shipper under CIF Contracts

CIF and FOB contracts are the two most commonly used standard forms in the sale of goods. While they share many characteristics, there are important differences[20] which distinguish one from the other. One such distinction is to whom they allocate the responsibility to make the contract of carriage under the contract of sale. 'C.i.f.'[21] stands for 'cost, insurance and freight'.[22] It is essentially '… a contract for the sale of goods to be performed by the delivery of documents.'[23] There are some other variants of CIF sales. One of the most common of them is 'c&f' (or CFR)[24] which includes no additional duty to arrange insurance.[25] Therefore, c&f (or CFR) does not differ from normal CIF sales in the sense of the duty to make a contract of carriage, nor do other variants such as CIFE,[26] CIFC,[27] CIFCI[28] and CIFFO.[29]

[20] See *The Parchim; NV Veendammer Kunstmesthandel v HM Procurator-General* [1918] AC 157; *Manbre Saccharin Co v Corn Products Co* [1919] 1 KB 198; *Comptoir d'Achat et de Vente du Boerenbond v Luis de Ridder Limitada (The Julia)* [1949] AC 293; *Kwei Tek Chao v British Traders* [1954] 2 QB 459; *Pyrene v Scindia* [1954] 2 QB 402; *Margarine Union GmbH v Cambay Prince Co Ltd (The Wear Breeze)* [1967] 3 All ER 775; *Scottish & Newcastle Int'l Ltd v Othon Ghalanos Ltd* [2008] UKHL 11; [2008] 1 Lloyd's Rep 462.

[21] Labelling the contract with CIF would not suffice to make it a genuine CIF contract. The contract named as such might in fact be on different terms: *The Julia* [1949] AC 293; *The Parchim* [1918] AC 157. Or where the contract is on CIF terms, this could force the courts to strike down the clauses repugnant to a contract on CIF terms: *Law and Bonar Ltd v British American Tobacco Ltd* (1916) 115 LT 612.

[22] *Biddell Brothers v E Clemens Horst Co* [1911] 1 KB 214. The initials were in different order in the earliest authorities that mentioned CIF sales though: *Tregelles v Sewell* (1862) 7 H&N 574; *Ireland v Livingston* (1871–72) LR 5 HL 395.

[23] *Arnhold Karberg & Co v Blythe, Green, Jourdain & Co* [1916] 1 KB 495, 510. See also, *Gardano and Giampieri v Greek Petroleum George Mamidakis & Co* [1962] 1 WLR 40; *Tricerri Ltd v Crosfields and Calshop Ltd* [1958] 1 Lloyd's Rep 236; *Congimex Compania Geral SARL v Tradax Export SA* [1983] 1 Lloyd's Rep 250; *Margarine Union GmbH v Cambay Prince Steamship Co* [1967] 2 Lloyd's Rep 315; *Berger & Co Inc v Gill and Duffus SA* [1984] AC 382; *Manbre Saccharine Co v Corn Products Co* [1919] 1 KB 198.

[24] This abbreviation has been used by ICC since 1990. See Incoterms 2020 Rules CFR.

[25] *The Pantanassa* [1970] 1 All ER 848, 855.

[26] Cost, insurance, freight and exchange: *National Mutual Life Association of Australasia Ltd v Att-Gen for New Zealand* [1956] AC 369.

[27] Cost, insurance, freight and commission.

[28] Cost, insurance, freight, commission and interest.

[29] Cost, insurance, freight and free out: *Etablissements Soules et Cie v Intertradex SA (The Handy Mariner)* [1991] 1 Lloyd's Rep 378.

To avoid confusion, since this chapter's main subject is the allocation of the shipper's dangerous goods liability between the seller and the buyer, it must also be emphasised that the present focus is on whose duty it is to conclude the *contract of carriage* under the CIF contract rather than the parties' entire obligations which fall on the seller rather than the buyer under CIF contracts.[30] There are various essential judicial statements on the definition of CIF sales indicating the seller's duty to conclude the carriage contract. One of the first most-regularly cited judicial statements on the matter was by Blackburn J in *Ireland v Livingston*:

> … and giving him credit for the amount of the freight which he will have to pay to the shipowner on actual delivery, and for the balance a draft is drawn on the consignee which he is bound to accept (if the shipment be in conformity with his contract) on having handed to him the charterparty, bill of lading, and policy of insurance.[31]

Where Hamilton J numerically described the duties of the seller in *Biddell Brothers*, the very first two related to shipment and contract of carriage: 'A seller under a contract of sale containing such terms has firstly to ship at the port of shipment goods of the description contained in the contract; secondly to procure a contract of affreightment'.[32] In the House of Lords in *Johnson v Taylor Bros* one of the most up-to-date CIF contract definitions was given by Lord Atkinson:

> I think, that when a vendor and purchaser of goods situated as they were in this case enter into a c.i.f. contract, such as that entered into in the present case, the vendor in the absence of any special provision to the contrary is bound by his contract to do six things. First, to make out an invoice of the goods sold. Second, to ship at the port of shipment goods of the description contained in the contract. Third, to procure a contract of affreightment …[33]

Another House of Lords decision describes the seller's duty on shipment and contracting for carriage under a CIF contract:

> The essential characteristics of this contract have often been described. The seller has to ship or acquire after that shipment the contract goods, as to which if unascertained he is generally required to give a notice of appropriation. On or after shipment he has to obtain proper bills of lading and proper policies of insurance.[34]

(i) Where the Seller is Both the Wet and the Dry Shipper

From the cases cited above, the conclusion can be drawn that in general terms, under CIF contracts, the seller is to make the physical delivery of the goods to

[30] The rights and duties arising out of this contract are only transferred from the seller to the buyer by virtue of Carriage of Goods by Sea Act 1992 (the 1992 Act).

[31] (1871–72) LR 5 HL 395, 406.

[32] [1911] 1 KB 214, 220.

[33] *Johnson v Taylor Bros & Co Ltd* [1920] AC 144, 155–56. See also *The Gabbiano* [1940] P 166, 174.

[34] Lord Wright in *Ross T Smyth & Co Ltd v TD Bailey, Son & Co* [1940] 67 Lloyd's Rep 147, 156.

the vessel and undertakes to conclude a contract of carriage for the goods.[35] He is almost invariably named as the shipper in the bills of lading and will be the original party to it.[36] Thus, the CIF seller prima facie undertakes the roles of both dry and wet shipper.[37] Indeed, there might be antithetical factors indicating that the seller in fact acted as agent of the buyer in contracting for carriage. This may rebut prima facie evidence of bills of lading that the contract arises between the carrier and the seller/named shipper. However, it is very unlikely that the seller, in concluding the carriage contract, is deemed to act as agent of the buyer under ordinary CIF sales. So far as sale of goods afloat (ie a sale concluded once the goods are already on board) is concerned, where the seller/named shipper concludes the contract of carriage, he would most likely be in a desperate position to know the identity of a future buyer. Accordingly, he would not be considered an agent of a prospective buyer in making the carriage contract.[38]

There could, however, be other situations calling for discussion. The seller, for example, can be aware of the identity of the buyer and the buyer can sometimes be named as consignee in the bill. The inference therefore is that if the property in the goods is held by the buyer/consignee at the time the carriage contract is concluded, the seller/named shipper can be regarded as agent of the buyer in making the carriage contract.[39] This inference however, is unlikely to be applicable to CIF sales, since the property in most situations passes *after* shipment; often when the documents are tendered against the price under CIF sales.[40] On the other hand, under CIF sales, the buyer will not be considered the shipper merely on the ground that he is designated as the consignee in the bill.[41] A supporting authority for this argument can be found in *TICC Ltd v Cosco (UK) Ltd*,[42] in which, Rix LJ contended that it would be a very unusual situation under CIF contracts for a seller to be acting as agent for his buyer/consignee in making the contract of carriage.[43] He further opined that under CIF sales, the ordinary rule is that the

[35] Despite the variations of CIF contracts mentioned above, this duty still remains with the seller.

[36] *Domett v Beckford* (1883) 5 B & Ald 521.

[37] If the goods are sold afloat or in string sales, the shipper will have been the initial seller.

[38] GH Treitel and FMB Reynolds, *Carver on Bills of Lading*, 4th edn (London, Sweet & Maxwell, 2017) para 4-004; MG Bridge, *Benjamin's Sale of Goods*, 11th edn (London, Sweet & Maxwell 2020) para 19-145.

[39] *Texas Instruments Ltd v Nason (Europe) Ltd* [1991] 1 Lloyd's Rep 146; where the seller is regarded acting as agent for the buyer in concluding the carriage contract, although the bill of lading names the seller as shipper. See *The Berge Sisar* [2002] AC 205, 220; *Enichem Anic SpA and Others v Ampelos Shipping Co Ltd (The Delfini)* [1988] 2 Lloyd's Rep 599, later affirmed in [1990] 1 Lloyd's Rep 252; *Dickenson v Lano* (1860) 2 F&F 188; *Cowas-Jee v Thompson and Kebbel* (1845) 5 Moore 165; 13 ER 454; *Anderson v Clark* (1824) 2 Bing 20; *Fragano v Long* (1825) 4 B & C 219.

[40] Bridge, *Benjamin's Sale of Goods*, n 38 above, para 19-160 ff. Where the seller/consignor acted as agent for the buyer/consignee in making the contract of carriage, see *Texas Instruments Ltd v Nason (Europe) Ltd* [1991] 1 Lloyd's Rep 146. This was in fact a CMR case.

[41] *TICC Ltd v Cosco (UK) Ltd* [2001] EWCA Civ 1862; [2002] CLC 347, [17]; *Fortis Bank SA/NV v Indian Overseas Bank* [2011] EWHC 538, [62]–[67].

[42] [2002] CLC 347; [2001] EWCA Civ 1862.

[43] [2002] CLC 347, 349–50.

seller acts as principal in concluding the contract of carriage.[44] The learned judge went on to hold that even if the seller had acted as agent for the buyer in concluding the carriage contract, this would not have relieved the seller of taking on the liabilities of the shipper.[45]

The only conclusion that can be drawn from this is that under CIF contracts it is almost invariably the seller who concludes the carriage contract with the carrier (as principal) and who is named as the shipper under the bills of lading. Thus, it would be very safe to note that in CIF sales where the seller is named as the shipper under bills of lading, it is to be him that will bear the shipper's dangerous goods liability. Even if it is accepted that the CIF seller acted as agent of the buyer in making the carriage contract, this would be unlikely to prevent him from undertaking liability, on the ground of the decision by Rix LJ in *TICC v Cosco (UK) Ltd*. It could be nevertheless argued – not without some hesitation – that in such an exceptional situation, both the seller and the buyer would possibly become liable vis-à-vis the carrier.[46]

(ii) Where the Seller is the Wet But Not the Dry Shipper

Albeit highly unlikely today, in certain situations the seller may in the past have shipped the goods but might not be identified as the shipper in the bills of lading. In *Hansson v Hamel & Horley Ltd*,[47] even though the CIF seller shipped the goods on board the vessel, the bill of lading designated the buyer as the shipper 'in accordance with a stipulation they had made'.[48] Nominating the buyer as the shipper in the bills of lading could serve two purposes back then.[49] First, it would negate the risk of being deprived of an entitlement right to goods under the contract by virtue of the complex and problematic scheme of the Bills of Lading 1855 Act,[50] which required the property in the goods to be passed upon or by the time the bill of lading was transferred by the seller. The buyer might have sought to circumvent this problem by being an original party to the contract of carriage. The second motivation may have been to deprive the seller of the right to redirect the goods, although the effectiveness of this tactic is far from certain,[51] given that Lord Sumner in the case found that the intention to reserve the *jus disponendi* to

[44] ibid. This is also the position where the bank is named in the bill of lading as consignee and the seller as shipper: *Fortis Bank SA/NV v Indian Overseas Bank* [2011] EWHC 538; [2011] 2 Lloyd's Rep 190.

[45] *TICC Ltd v Cosco (UK) Ltd* [2002] CLC 347, 350. See also, *Perishables Transport Co Ltd v N Spyropoulos (London) Ltd* [1964] 2 Lloyd's Rep 379.

[46] See text below at section II.B(v). See also *The Athanasia Comninos* [1990] 1 Lloyd's Rep 277.

[47] [1922] 2 AC 36.

[48] ibid, 43.

[49] See generally, Treitel and Reynolds, *Carver on Bills of Lading*, n 38 above, para 4-006.

[50] The 1855 Act is no longer in force. It was superseded by the COGSA 1992 Act.

[51] Treitel and Reynolds, *Carver on Bills of Lading*, n 38 above, para 4-006.

the seller was not negated by the mere insertion of the buyer's name in the bill.[52] On the other hand, neither does the first reasoning of the buyer appear valid today. The 1855 Act was superseded by the Carriage of Goods by Sea Act 1992 (the 1992 Act).[53] The introduction of the 1992 Act has eliminated the requirement for property to pass upon consignment or endorsement in transferring such rights under contract and the 1992 Act transfers rights much easier than its predecessor.[54] *Hansson v Hamel & Horley* left no doubt that it was the CIF buyer who was regarded as the shipper at that time under these circumstances. Therefore, he would be liable for damages arising from dangerous goods. However, it is very rare for the buyer to be named as the shipper in the bill under CIF sales, given that there appears no practical reason for this today. In support of this argument, there appears to be no other reported case illustrating this practice.

However, let us assume that such an exceptional case occurred and the carrier suffered damage due to dangerous goods. Suppose also that the carrier sought to bring his claim both against the seller and the buyer/shipper. The question is therefore whether such a CIF seller who was not the shipper could be subject to liability for dangerous goods. At common law, the bailor of the goods can be held liable in respect of dangerous goods to the carrier.[55] At first sight, it might be thought that in such a case the seller is the bailor of the goods, since he made the actual delivery of the goods to the carrier. However, this does not appear to be arguable when the bill names the buyer as the shipper, given that it will then only be considered as a receipt from the buyer. In such a case, the buyer would be regarded as the bailor.[56] Another possibility is the one that Rix LJ contended in *TICC v Cosco*: under CIF sales, even if the seller makes the contract of carriage as agent of the buyer, he might still incur liability along with the buyer/named shipper.[57] However, it is submitted that this may not be plausible either, unless the seller is designated as a participant with his consent. In such unusual situations, the courts may be reluctant to impose on the seller the obligation which explicitly falls on the buyer/named shipper, unless the seller is at fault so as to have caused the damage. Indeed, the carrier may seek redress from the seller under other mechanisms, such as in tort or by an implied contract. Given that these possibilities mostly arise under FOB contracts, they will be discussed below.[58]

[52] [1922] 2 AC 36, 43. His Lordship referred to a similar case in which the buyer's name was inserted as consignee though; *The Kronprinsessan Margareta, The Parana and Other ships* [1921] 1 AC 486. See also the Sale of Goods Act 1979, s 18 r 5; Treitel and Reynolds, *Carver on Bills of Lading*, n 38 above, para 4-006; Bridge, *Benjamin's Sale of Goods*, n 38 above, para 19-149.

[53] Section 6(2) of the 1992 Act.

[54] On this see generally, Chapter 5. See also s 2 of the 1992 Act.

[55] Bridge, *Benjamin's Sale of Goods*, n 38 above, para 18-171, fn 787; Treitel and Reynolds, *Carver on Bills of Lading*, n 38 above, para 6-012, fn 89; GH Treitel, 'Bills of Lading: Liabilities of Transferee' (2001) *LMCLQ* 344, 353, fn 79. The bailor can also be liable for damages arising out of unsafety or defect of the goods; *Blakemore* (1858) 8 E&B 1035; *Coughlin v Gillison* (1899) 1 QB 145.

[56] *The Aliakmon* [1986] AC 785, 818. For discussion on the buyer/consignee's liability under bailment see generally, Chapter 6.

[57] [2002] CLC 346, 350.

[58] See section II.B.(i) below.

(iii) Where the Seller is Neither the Wet Nor the Dry Shipper

Although the CIF seller normally undertakes both to ship the goods and make the carriage contract, this is not invariably the case. CIF sales are commonly traded in string sales. A buyer in one sale hence may be a sub-seller of a subsequent transaction, or vice versa. Alternatively, an FOB buyer may sell his goods, which might have already been shipped, on CIF terms, to his subsequent buyer who later may become a CIF seller of the same goods, once he sells them to his sub-buyer.[59] Or a CIF seller/shipper sells the goods to his buyer, and if this buyer re-sells them again further down the chain, he will subsequently become the intermediate CIF seller who did not personally make the arrangements for the shipment.[60] The intermediate CIF seller does not breach his contractual responsibilities just because he did not personally ship and contract with the carrier. Since the shipment of the goods and procurement of the carriage contract are performed by the preceding seller,[61] intermediate CIF sellers are thereby regarded as relieved from those obligations under string sales.[62] The intermediate party neither makes carriage arrangements nor ships the goods himself or through his agents. Therefore, where he is neither a wet nor a dry shipper, if liability arises from the shipment of dangerous goods, the carrier will not be entitled to sue him in respect of the damage or losses.

B. The Shipper under FOB Contracts

Unlike CIF contracts,[63] FOB contracts[64] are not defined in rigid terms but conversely have evolved into flexible instruments[65] over time. In the past, it was the buyer that was considered the shipper of the goods.[66] However in modern

[59] *Norsk Bjerningskompagnie A/S v Owners of the Pantanassa (The Pantanassa)* [1970] P 187; *Esteve Trading Corp v Agropec International (The Golden Rio)* [1990] 2 Lloyd's Rep 273; *Glencore Grain Rotterdam BV v Lebanese Organisation for International Commerce* [1997] 4 All ER 514.

[60] *Vantol (JH) Ltd v Fairclough Dodd & Jones Ltd* [1955] 1 WLR 642, 646.

[61] *Shipton Anderson & Co v Weston (John) & Co* (1922) 10 Ll L Rep 762, 763; *Bowden Bros and Co Ltd v Little* (1907) 4 CLR 1364.

[62] *Biddell Brothers v Clemens Horst (E) Co* [1911] 1 KB 214; *Johnson v Taylor Bros & Co Ltd* [1920] AC 144; *Scottish & Newcastle International Ltd v Othon Ghalanos Ltd* [2008] 1 Lloyd's Rep 462; [2008] UKHL 11. The only duty on his shoulders in relation to this is to tender the bills of lading evidencing the contract of carriage and the shipment of the goods to their buyers: *Hindley & Co Ltd v East Indian Produce Co Ltd* [1973] 2 Lloyd's Rep 515.

[63] *Wackerbarth v Masson* (1812) 3 Camp 270; 170 ER 1378; *Craven & Another v Ryder* (1816) 6 Taunt 433. See generally on the point, Sassoon, n 6 above, 33.

[64] There are other kinds of FOB contracts in Canada and the United States, which may not carry maritime element at all or may be on destination terms rather than shipment terms.

[65] *Pyrene v Scindia* [1954] 2 QB 402, 424: 'The f.o.b. contract has become a flexible instrument.'

[66] In *Cowas-Jee v Thompson and Kebbel* (1845) 5 Moore 165, 173, Lord Brougham stated: 'It is proved beyond all doubt, indeed it is not denied, that when goods are sold in London 'free on board' the cost of shipping then falls on the seller, but the buyer is considered as the shipper.' See also Sassoon, n 6 above, 33.

times, FOB contracts have been subjected to changes. These changes have not only affected the distribution of roles between the seller and buyer, but also created various types of FOB contracts. The contention that the buyer is the shipper under FOB sales may therefore not cover all types of FOB contracts as of today.

The courts have also kept step with the practical changes and embraced the flexibility[67] of FOB contracts.[68] Just three years after the statement by Devlin J in *Pyrene v Scindia*[69] on the flexibility of FOB contracts, in *NV Handel My J Smits Import-Export v English Exporters (London) Ltd*, it was held that the seller's agreement to secure shipping space did not prevent the sale contract from being on FOB terms;[70] and in another case nor did the seller's payment of freight and insurance change the fact that the contract was on FOB terms.[71] Also Diplock J (who later became Lord Diplock) stated; 'there are probably as many exceptions to the rule as there are examples of it'.[72] Despite their flexible nature, FOB contracts remain characterised by certain common features identified by the courts. In particular, the seller must put the goods on board and bear all the costs and expenses until the goods pass over the ship's rail. Subsequently, the risk is transferred to the buyer on shipment.[73] However, what makes an FOB sale different from another is the allocation of some duties between the seller and the buyer, particularly the duty to nominate the vessel and conclude the contract of carriage.

The first comprehensive categorisation of FOB contracts, which was not only later endorsed by both the Court of Appeal[74] and the House of Lords,[75] but also recognised and applied in Commonwealth countries such as Australia,[76] Canada,[77]

[67] For an example of a flexible FOB contract, see *ERG Raffinerie Mediterranee SpA v Chevron USA Inc* [2007] EWCA Civ 494; [2007] 2 Lloyd's Rep 542.

[68] F Wooldridge, 'The Kinds of F.O.B. Contracts' in F Fabricius (ed), *Law and International Trade Recht und Internationaler Handel* (Frankfurt, Athenaum Verlag, 1973) 388. See also LCB Gower, 'F.O.B. Contracts' (1956) 19 *MLR* 417; P Devlin, 'The Relation between Commercial Law and Commercial Practice' (1951) 14 *MLR* 249.

[69] [1954] 2 QB 402.

[70] *NV Handel My J Smits Import-Export v English Exporters (London) Ltd* [1957] 1 Lloyd's Rep 517, 521.

[71] *Carlos Federspiel & Co SA v Charles Twigg & Co Ltd* [1957] 1 Lloyd's Rep 240. Also the House of Lords decided, in parallel with those decisions, that there was no invariable rule that it was the buyer who would secure any export licence: *AV Pound & Co Inc v MW Hard & Co Inc* [1956] AC 588.

[72] *Ian Stach Ltd v Baker Bosely Ltd* [1958] 1 Lloyd's Rep 127, 132, 137 and 139.

[73] *Stock v Inglis* (1884) 12 QBD 564, 573; affirmed by the House of Lords (1885) 10 App Cas 263; *J Raymond Wilson & Co Ltd v N Scratchard Ltd* (1943–44) 77 Ll L Rep 373, 374.

[74] *The El Amria and The El Minia* [1982] 2 Lloyd's Rep 28.

[75] *Scottish & Newcastle Int'l Ltd v Othon Ghalanos Ltd* [2008] UKHL 11; [2008] 1 Lloyd's Rep 462. This does not necessarily mean that this classification is exhaustive. FOB contracts are still open to evolution.

[76] *McKay Massey Harris Proprietary Ltd v Imperial Chemical Industries of Australia & New Zealand Ltd and United Stevedoring Proprietary Ltd (The Mahia No 2)* [1960] 1 Lloyd's Rep 191; *Glencore Coal Assets Australia Pty Ltd v Australian Competition Tribunal* [2020] FCAFC 145.

[77] *Industries Perlite Inc v The Marina di Alimuri (The Marina di Alimuri)* [1995] CanLII 3567; [1996] 2 FC 426; *AK Steel Corp v Acelormittal Mines Canada Inc* [2014] FCJ No 124.

and New Zealand,[78] can be found in *Pyrene v Scindia.*[79] Devlin J stated that there were three main types of FOB contracts. These contracts were distinguished based upon whether the buyer or the seller nominated the vessel and concluded the carriage contract. The three main FOB contracts are to be named in this work as 'bare', 'classic' and 'FOB with additional services'.[80] Since this categorisation is not just a matter of labelling, and the contracting party for contract of carriage may vary one from another under FOB sales, it is therefore followed below in order to ascertain who attracts the shipper's dangerous goods liability between the seller and buyer under each type.

(i) Bare FOB

Although it is the third type of FOB contract described in *Pyrene v Scindia*, the bare FOB is the oldest used in practice.[81] When compared to other types, bare FOB contracts impose the least number of duties on the seller.[82] They provide the easiest basis on which to illustrate the distinction between the wet and the dry shipper. Under bare FOB sales, the buyer nominates the vessel,[83] and he or his agent as dry shipper makes the arrangements for the carriage of the goods. The only duty of the seller as wet shipper is to put the goods on board the nominated vessel and hand the mate's receipt to the buyer or his forwarding agent. The seller is not responsible for procuring bills of lading from the carrier or paying the freight.[84] Thus, he never holds the bill, or becomes party to it.[85] The buyer or his agent obtains the bills of

[78] *Commissioner of Inland Revenue v International Importing Limited* [1972] NZLR 1095. See also in Hong Kong where the classification of FOB sales in the *Pyrene* case was cited: *Simple Symbol Limited v MCS Limited* [2001] HKCU 1229.

[79] In *Wimble v Rosenberg & Sons* [1913] 3 KB 743 only the 'classic' FOB was described, as it is the buyer's duty to nominate the vessel, and the seller is to put the goods on board for account of the buyer. For another classic FOB definition, see *Concordia Trading BV v Richco International Ltd* [1991] 1 Lloyd's Rep 475.

[80] Terminology on the point may vary from one commentator to another; in Lorenzon, *C.I.F. and F.O.B. Contracts*, they are labelled as 'bare', 'classic' and 'with additional carriage services'. In CM Schmitthoff, *The Law and Practice of International Trade*, 12th edn (London, Sweet & Maxwell, 2012), the types are referred to as 'simple', 'strict' or 'classic' and 'additional services'. In C Debattista and F Hornyold-Strickland, *Debattista on Bills of Lading in Commodities Trade*, 4th edn (London, Bloomsbury Publishing, 2021), they are named as 'straight', 'classic' and 'extended', para 1.16. See also, where they are called as 'real', 'unreal' and 'extended' in J Lebhun, 'Practicing CIF and FOB Today' (1981) 1 *European Transport Law* 24.

[81] Wooldridge, 'The Kinds of F.O.B. Contracts', n 68 above, 391.

[82] This type (bare) was interestingly described as 'classic' in *The Al Hofuf* [1981] 1 Lloyd's Rep 81, 84. See also *Saffron v Société Minière Cafrika* (1958) 32 ALJR 286.

[83] *Wackerbarth v Mason* (1812) 3 Camp 270; 170 ER 1378; *Armitage v Insole* (1850) 14 QB 728; 117 ER 280; *Sutherland v Allhusen* (1866) 14 LT 666; *Cohen & Co v Ockerby & Co Ltd* (1917) 24 CLR 288; *Brandt (HO) & Co v Morris (HN) & Co Ltd* [1917] 2 KB 784; *Maine Shipping Co v Sutcliffe & Co* (1917) 87 LJKB 382; *Burch & Co Ltd v Corry & Co* [1920] NZLR 69; *Cunningham v Monro* (1922) 28 Com Cas 42.

[84] *Green v Sichel* (1860) 7 CB (NS) 747.

[85] See Rix J's statement in *Sunrise Maritime Inc v Uvisco Ltd (The Hector)* [1998] 2 Lloyd's Rep 287, 299.

lading in the buyer's name from the carrier. In the classification by Devlin J in *Pyrene v Scindia*, the learned judge described this type as follows:

> Sometimes the buyer engages his own forwarding agent at the port of loading to book space and to procure the bill of lading; if freight has to be paid in advance this method may be the most convenient. In such a case the seller discharges his duty by putting the goods on board, getting the mate's receipt and handing it to the forwarding agent to enable him to obtain the bill of lading.[86]

The bare FOB was also defined by Donaldson J, in *The El Amria and The El Minia*:

> The third is where the seller puts the goods on board, takes a mate's receipt and gives this to the buyer or his agent who then takes a bill of lading. In this latter type the buyer is a party to the contract of carriage ab initio.[87]

The House of Lords in *Scottish & Newcastle Int'l Ltd v Othon Ghalanos Ltd*, however, laid the matter to rest and bare FOB[88] was described in parallel with the previous cases: '... (c) cases where the buyer arranges and nominates the ship, and the seller ships but the buyer is named in the bill as consignor'.[89]

The consensus hence is that under bare FOB the buyer is named as the shipper in the bills of lading and is the original party to the relevant contract of carriage. There is no doubt that the buyer, as dry shipper, could be liable to the carrier for damage caused by a shipment of dangerous goods, since he is considered the shipper under a bare FOB contract. However, the question that arises at this point is whether the carrier is entitled to sue the seller along with the buyer/shipper for damage arising from dangerous goods under this type.

(a) Seller's Position under Bare FOB

Unlike the buyer, the seller's position is less straightforward than the buyer's under bare FOB sales. He is not party to the contract of carriage concluded between the buyer and carrier, nor can he be privy to the rights and responsibilities assigned by its terms. Yet, as wet shipper, the seller may be bound by the terms of a separate implied contract between himself and the carrier, premised

[86] [1954] 2 QB 402, 424.

[87] [1982] 2 Lloyd's Rep 28, 32.

[88] Indeed the courts were not the only sources for the definitions of FOB contracts. Several organisations and institutions offered detailed definitions on FOB contracts. See 'Revised American Foreign Trade Definitions – 1941', produced by the Joint Committee representing the Chamber of Commerce of the United States, the National Council of American Importers, and the National Foreign Trade Council in the United States; and 'F.O.B. Vessel' (1971), produced by the British Association of Chambers of Commerce in the United Kingdom. According to the Institute of Export, the suggested FOB contract would indicate a contract where the seller puts the goods on board and the buyer nominates the ship and secures the shipping space, namely bare FOB: 'Proposed Definition of the Term F.O.B.' (1951) 14 *Export* 211, [19]. Also in the Incoterms 2020 Rules, under the proposed FOB contract, it is the buyer's duty to make a contract of carriage and the seller's is to deliver the goods on board the vessel nominated by the buyer: Incoterms 2020 Rules FOB A3 and A4.

[89] [2008] 1 Lloyd's Rep 462; [2008] UKHL 11, [34].

upon the same bill of lading. In *Pyrene v Scindia*, the seller sold a fire engine on bare FOB terms. The buyer/dry shipper concluded the carriage contract with the carrier through his agents. The seller/wet shipper was under a duty to ship the goods. When the fire engine was lifted by the vessel's tackle, it was dropped and damaged before passing the ship's rail as a result of the admitted negligence of the carrier.[90] The bill of lading had not yet been issued at the time the fire engine was damaged. When produced, it did not even evidence the shipment of the damaged tender. As the seller was not party to the carriage contract between the buyer and the carrier, he tried to sue the carrier in tort for the actual value of the engine (£966). Conversely, the carrier sought protection under the limitation of liability figures of the Hague Rules, which prescribed a maximum of £200 per unit at the time.[91] Nonetheless, the problem with the carrier seeking limitation under the Hague Rules was that the Rules only governed the contract of carriage concluded between him and the buyer. Therefore, the issue was whether the seller was subject to the contract of carriage concluded between the buyer and the carrier and whether he was bound by its limitation terms pursuant to the Hague Rules. Eventually, Devlin J held that despite the fact that the buyer was considered the shipper of the goods, the carrier was entitled to limit his liability to the seller to £200 under the Rules. The learned judge first considered the applicability of the agency principle[92] to the case before him on the basis that the buyer might have contracted with the carrier as well as on behalf of the seller as an undisclosed principal, but he explained his decision on 'wider principle' grounds instead:

> If it were intended that he [the seller] should be a party to the whole of the contract his position would be that of an undisclosed principal and the ordinary law of agency would apply. But that is obviously not intended; he could not, for example, be sued for the freight. This is the sort of situation that is covered by the wider principle; the third party takes those benefits of the contract which appertain to his interest therein, but takes them, of course, subject to whatever qualifications with regard to them the contract imposes.[93]

Nevertheless, Devlin J's reasoning on grounds of 'wider principle' is not applicable today, since participation in a contract by a third party was laid to rest by

[90] [1954] 2 QB 402. For an interesting case on similar facts, see *Thermo Engineers Ltd v Ferrymasters Ltd* [1981] 1 Lloyd's Rep 200.

[91] According to the British Maritime Law Association's Agreement of 1 August 1950. This limit is not applicable currently under the Hague-Visby Rules.

[92] See GH Treitel, 'Exemption Clauses and Third Parties' (1955) 18 *MLR* 172, 176. See also FE Dowrick, 'A Jus Quaestium Tertio by Way of Contract in English Law' (1956) 19 *MLR* 374.

[93] [1954] 2 QB 402, 426. The learned judge had two underlying reasons for reaching this conclusion. He contended that the seller would be in breach of the sale contract without any 'redress against the ship', if the vessel left the port without loading his goods. Additionally, he also reasoned that the seller would be able to sue for conversion, if the carrier handled the cargo. But see *Carver on Bills of Lading*, n 38 above, para 4-019; P Todd, *Cases and Materials on International Trade Law* (London, Sweet & Maxwell, 2003), 543. See also *Glencore Energy UK Ltd v Transworld Oil Ltd* [2010] EWHC 141 (Comm).

the House of Lords in *Scruttons Ltd v Midland Silicones Ltd*,[94] specifically by Viscount Simonds on the basis of the doctrine of privity under English law. The learned judge criticised the potential breach of the doctrine of privity created by *Pyrene v Scindia* as well as some other cases[95] and put cement on a potential participation in a contract by a third party. In this regard, Devlin J's decision was also criticised in other cases. In the Court of Appeal in *The Kapitan Markos*, Mustill LJ was also reluctant to accept the first ratio decidendi of Devlin J in *Pyrene v Scindia*, namely the 'wider principle'. Accordingly, the learned judge questioned 'whether the first ground [wider principle] of decision in *Pyrene v Scindia* can now be regarded as good law'.[96] It is therefore probable that the first ratio decidendi of Devlin J, namely a *jus quaesitum tertio*, is no longer applicable under English law.

Devlin J, however, had an alternative ratio decidendi for the same conclusion. He inferred an implied contract between the seller and the carrier from the conduct of the parties whereby the seller 'by delivering the goods alongside … implicitly invited the shipowner to load and the shipowner implicitly accepted that invitation'.[97] Therefore, the question of whether this second ground – namely the 'implied contract' – is alive, and if so, whether the seller can attract dangerous goods liability thereunder, call for discussion.

(b) The Implied Contract

There is no difficulty in arguing that for liability for dangerous goods, the carrier has *locus standi* against the buyer, as he is considered the shipper under bare FOB contracts. The difficulty arises if the carrier wishes to sue the seller with whom he normally has no contractual nexus for such liability.[98] In order to see whether the bare FOB. seller could be held liable for dangerous goods, a number of questions will be discussed below. The first question is whether this type of implied contract[99] survives in the light of subsequent common law cases.[100]

[94] *Scruttons Ltd v Midland Silicones Ltd* [1962] AC 446, 471.

[95] *Adler v Dickson* [1955] 1 QB 158; [1954] 3 WLR 696; [1954] 3 All ER 397 (CA). See also *Elder Dempster & Co Ltd v Paterson Zochonis & Co Ltd* [1924] AC 522; [1924] 40 TLR 464 (HL).

[96] *The Kapetan Markos (No 2)* [1987] 2 Lloyd's Rep 321, 331.

[97] ibid, 426.

[98] In such a case, the seller is not considered the bailor of the goods just because he has made the actual delivery of the goods to the carrier. As the bill of lading names the buyer as the shipper under bare FOB sales, it will be regarded only as a receipt from the buyer and accordingly, the buyer would be regarded the bailor. Thus, the seller will not be subject to liability under bailment: *The Aliakmon* [1986] AC 785, 818.

[99] It should be stated from the outset that the Contract (Rights of Third Parties) Act 1999 would not provide any assistance to the carrier, since it does not apply to contracts for the carriage of goods by sea and only gives rights to third parties by s 6(5).

[100] For a different analogy with the *Pyrene*-type contract on a different problem, see generally, A Gelgec, 'Challenging the Impact of FIOST Clauses on Cargo Interests' (2021) 6(1) *University of Bologna Law Review* 29, 39 ff.

(aa) Is it Alive?

Since its inception, the doctrine of privity of contract has been the subject of much debate in English law.[101] The decisions had been split as to whether a third party could enforce a contract[102] or not[103] until the issue was conclusively settled by the House of Lords in several cases in favour of privity of contract.[104] Devlin J in *Pyrene*, by his second ratio decidendi (implied contract), must have sought to circumvent the potential interference of the doctrine of privity of contract with his 'wider principle':

> If this conclusion is wrong, there is an alternative way by which, on the facts of this case, the same result would be achieved. By delivering the goods alongside the seller impliedly invited the shipowner to load them, and the shipowner by lifting the goods impliedly accepted that invitation. The implied contract so created …[105]

While the first part of the reasoning (wider principle) was overruled in the *Midland Silicones* case, the second part appears to have survived. In the *Midland Silicones* case, Viscount Simmons did not entirely overrule Devlin J's decision, and explained it on the implication of a contract, which was the second rationale of Devlin J. His words appear to prove this: 'Devlin J.'s decision … can be supported only upon the facts of the case, which may well have justified the implication of a contract between the parties.'[106] It can be inferred from this passage that the House of Lords did not want to disregard the *Pyrene* case completely, but expressed its survival on the implied contract. Nor did Mustill LJ, in *The Kapetan Markos*, overrule the implied contract of Devlin. When considering the judgment of Devlin J, he only referred to the 'wider principle': 'I doubt with all respect to a very learned judge whether the first ground [wider principle] of decision in *Pyrene v Scindia* can now be regarded as good law'.[107]

On the present state of these authorities, it is submitted that the implied contract of Devlin J can be regarded as alive. However, there is the question of on what grounds this implied contract could be supported. Devlin J was not the first to imply a contract; there were indeed earlier cases.[108] Most notably, in *Brandt v Liverpool, Brazil & River Plate Steam Navigation Co*[109] a contract was

[101] On this point, see generally HG Beale, *Chitty on Contracts*, 33rd edn (London, Sweet & Maxwell, 2021) ch 18; E Peel, *Treitel on the Law of Contract*, 15th edn (London, Sweet & Maxwell, 2020) ch 14.

[102] *Dutton v Poole* (1677) 2 Lev 210; *Martyn v Hind* (1776) 2 Cowp 437; *Marchington v Vernon* (1787) 1 B & P 101; *Smith & Snipes Hall Farm LD v River Douglas Catchment Board* [1949] 2 KB 500; *Drive Yourself Hire Co (London) LD v Strutt* [1954] 1 QB 158; *Adler v Dickson* [1955] 1 QB 158.

[103] *Bourne v Mason* (1668) 1 Ventris 6; *Crow v Rogers* (1726) 1 Stra 592; *Price v Easton* (1883) 4 B & Ad.

[104] *Tweddle v Atkinson* (1861) 1 B & S 393; *Midland Silicones* [1962] AC 446; *Beswick v Beswick* [1968] AC 58.

[105] [1954] 2 QB 424, 426. For similar views of Devlin J, see *Heskell v Continental Express Ltd* [1950] 1 All ER 1033, 1041.

[106] [1962] AC 446, 471.

[107] *The Kapetan Markos (No 2)* [1987] 2 Lloyd's Rep 321, 331.

[108] *Cock v Taylor* (1811) 13 East 399; 104 ER 424; *Sanders v Vanzeller* (1843) 4 QB 260; *Stindt v Roberts* (1848) 17 LJ QB 166; *Young v Moeller* (1855) 5 E&B 755; *Allen v Coltart* (1883) 11 QBD 782; *White & Co v Furness, Withy & Co Ltd* [1895] AC 40.

[109] *Brandt v Liverpool, Brazil & River Plate Steam Navigation Co* [1924] 1 KB 575.

implied between a consignee and the carrier. Devlin J's contract was deemed analogous to the *Brandt v Liverpool* contract, despite the fact that the former was concluded between the seller and the carrier.[110] The contract in *Brandt v Liverpool* was implied on the grounds that the consignee surrendered the bill of lading and paid the freight, whilst the carrier in return delivered the goods against the bill of lading.[111] On the other hand, the contract in *Pyrene v Scindia* was implied, when the seller offered his goods to the carrier and the goods were accepted for loading by the carrier.[112] The relevance of these two implied contracts in respect of liability arising from dangerous goods will be discussed below.[113]

(bb) Formation of the Implied Contract

Devlin J did not explain the underlying reasons of his implied contract, save for by way of offer and acceptance by the parties. However, in order for a contract to arise, the ordinary contractual requirements are offer, acceptance, contractual intention and consideration.[114]

Offer, acceptance and intention

As Devlin J stated, the implied contract between the seller and carrier arose by the conduct of the parties, namely the delivery of the goods to the carrier by the seller (offer) and the loading of such goods on board by the carrier (acceptance).[115] It is no doubt possible under English law for a contract to be formed as a result of the parties' conduct,[116] where it would amount to offer and acceptance. These acts are not, however, sufficient to infer a contract. In addition to these, a contract can only be implied if contractual intention can be found.

The seller's intention is to be protected against non-payment by the buyer, and for that reason he may want to retain the right of disposal over the goods, even though he is not named as the shipper in the bill.[117] In the case of non-payment,

[110] Treitel and Reynolds, *Carver on Bills of Lading*, n 38 above, para 7-010.

[111] For the limitations of the *Brandt v Liverpool* type contract, see *The Owners of Cargo Lately Laden on Board the Ship Aramis v Aramis Maritime Corp (The Aramis)* [1989] 1 Lloyd's Rep 213; *Mitsui & Co Ltd v Novorossiysk Shipping Co (The Gudermes)* [1993] 1 Lloyd's Rep 311. See also *The Aliakmon* [1986] 2 WLR 902.

[112] Indeed, there are other types of implied contract created between the FOB seller and the carrier at the loading operation, which appear to have survived to date. See *President of India v Metcalfe Shipping Company (The Dunelmia)* [1969] 2 Lloyd's Rep 476, 480. This is considered below at section II.B.(ii) below.

[113] See section II.B.(i)(c) below.

[114] *The Aramis* [1989] 1 Lloyd's Rep 213, 224 per Bingham LJ. On the point see generally, Beale, *Chitty on Contracts*, n 101 above, ch 2; Peel, *Treitel on the Law of Contract*, n 101 above, ch 2, 3 and 4.

[115] [1954] 2 QB 402, 426.

[116] *Hart v Mills* (1846) 15 LJ Ex 200; *Steven v Bromley & Son* [1919] 2 KB 722; *Greenmast Shipping Co SA v Jean Lion et Cie SA (The Saronikos)* [1986] 2 Lloyd's Rep 277; *Confetti Records v Warner Music UK Ltd* [2003] EWHC 1274 [2003] EMLR 35.

[117] *Hansson v Hamel & Horley Ltd* [1922] 2 AC 36. See the 1979 Act, s 18 r 5. The seller may retain the title, even if the bill of lading is to the order of the consignee: see *The Kronprinsessan Margareta (The Parana)* [1921] 1 AC 486.

the seller would want to re-sell his goods to another party. In such a situation, a bare FOB seller would be in an unsecure position, since the bill names the buyer as the shipper. From the perspective of the carrier, by being party to the contract with the seller contained or evidenced in the bill of lading, he would have the benefit of being protected by the provisions of the Hague/Hague-Visby Rules, such as article III rule 1 or package limitation figures of the Rules, instead of being sued in tort on an unlimited basis, as was the case in the *Pyrene* case.

Consideration

Apart from offer, acceptance and intention, there must also be consideration moving from one party to another to form a contract. In bare FOB cases, the consideration moving from the seller could be the delivery of his goods to the carrier's vessel. On the other hand, it might be difficult to identify the consideration moving from the carrier to the seller in such cases. However, to form a contract between the seller and the carrier, the carrier's consideration does not have to move to the seller. It could also be a benefit to a third party.[118] Under a bare FOB contract, the carrier is already under a duty to deliver the goods to the buyer, given the carriage contract between him and the buyer. However, at common law, the very same consideration arising under a contract can be the consideration for another contract as well. To put it differently, the existence of a duty to deliver the goods owed to the buyer does not prevent the same delivery (to the buyer) from being consideration from the carrier for the bare FOB seller's promise.[119]

(cc) Terms of Implied Contract

In the light of the general requirements to form a contract, when goods are presented for shipment and accepted by the carrier, it may not be easy to explain the inference of an implied contract within the rigid structure of the law of contract, but the courts – namely in the *Midland Silicones* case as well as *The Kapetan Markos* – appear to have pragmatically accepted the existence of such an implied contract so as to satisfy commercial expectations.[120] However, there is the question of what are the terms of such a contract. In the *Pyrene* case, Devlin J opined: '[t]he implied contract so created must incorporate the shipowner's usual terms …'.[121] Evidently, this raises the question as to what constitutes the 'usual terms' that should be incorporated.[122] These include those 'they enter into …

[118] *Scotson v Pegg* (1861) 6 H & N 295. Approved by the Privy Council in *the Eurymedon* [1975] AC 154.

[119] *Scotson v Pegg* (1861) 6 H & N 295.

[120] There are few cases drilling the rigid structure of the law of contract. See *The Satanita* [1895] P 248; *Clarke v Dunraven* [1897] AC 59; *The Eurymedon* [1975] AC 154. See also *Butler Machine Tool Co Ltd v Ex-Cell-O Corp (England) Ltd* [1979] 1 WLR 401.

[121] [1954] 2 QB 402, 426.

[122] For an accurate criticism of a different type of implied contract, see Treitel and Reynolds, *Carver on Bills of lading*, n 38 above, paras 7-010 ff. See also *Elder Dempster* [1924] AC 522.

which they know or expect the bill of lading to contain.'[123] As the Rules almost invariably govern the bills of lading, by way of a 'paramount clause'[124] incorporated into the bills of lading, the Rules which were also considered 'usual in the trade'[125] by Devlin J in the *Pyrene* case can be said to satisfy the usual terms 'which they know or expect the bill of lading to contain'. The implied contract in the *Pyrene* case was on the same terms as the contract between the buyer and the carrier under the bills of lading in respect of the Hague Rules.[126] Thus, the carrier was entitled to trigger the package limitation provisions of article IV rule 5 of the Rules against the seller. Therefore, on these grounds, it is submitted that the Rules may govern the implied contract once incorporated.

(c) Bare FOB Seller's Liability under Implied Contract

So far, in general terms, it is safe to contend that the implied contract between the seller and the carrier is alive[127] and incorporates the usual terms by reference to the carriage contract between the buyer and carrier.[128] However, it is not entirely clear whether the bare FOB seller could attract dangerous goods liability under the implied contract, as it is attached to the shipper/the buyer in the case of bare FOB contracts.[129]

First, it must be remembered that an implied contract not only confers rights on the parties but also imposes liabilities thereunder.[130] In the *Pyrene* case, the seller was entitled to sue under the implied contract in which the Hague Rules

[123] [1954] 2 QB 402, 419.

[124] Provided that the Rules *are* incorporated by a paramount clause in the bills of lading. If there is no paramount clause in the bills of lading or if there is, but Art X of the Rules cannot be triggered, the Rules will not apply to the contract between the buyer/shipper and the carrier by virtue of the Carriage of Goods by Sea Act 1971 (the 1971 Act). See A Gelgec, 'Clause Paramount and Its Impact on Package Limitation Figures' in M Musi (ed), *New Challenges in Maritime Law* (Bologna, Bonomo, 2015) 147. If the implied contract is not subject to the Hague or Hague-Visby Rules, it would not be arguable to say that it may also be capable of containing the common law duty to inform the carrier of the dangerous content of his goods, since he would not be regarded the shipper.

[125] [1954] 2 QB 402, 426.

[126] Treitel and Reynolds, *Carver on Bills of Lading*, n 38 above, para 4-019.

[127] See GH Treitel, 'Bills of Lading and Implied Contracts' (1989) *LMCLQ* 162, 171; Debattista and Hornyold-Strickland, *Debattista on Bills of Lading in Commodities Trade*, n 80 above, para 1.20; Lorenzon, *C.I.F. and F.O.B. Contracts*, para 10.052.

[128] Treitel and Reynolds, *Carver on Bills of Lading*, n 38 above, para 4-019.

[129] However, the bare FOB seller would not be liable for freight: *Pyrene v Scindia* [1954] 2 QB 402, 426. The carriage is reward for the payment of freight. Although the named shipper normally is under a duty to pay the freight (*Domett v Beckford* (1833) 5 B & Ad 521), unlike liability for dangerous goods, this duty will not necessarily be implied. It is possible that this duty may fall on a party other than the shipper named in the bill, since the carrier may have had contractual relations with others, such as charterers, which may affect the position: see *Cho Yang Shipping Co Ltd v Coral (UK) Ltd* [1997] 2 Lloyd's Rep 641, 643. The Rotterdam Rules adopt an approach for the position of the bare FOB seller in art 1(9) that the documentary shipper is a person agreeing to be named as the shipper alongside the original shipper and he becomes subject to the obligations and the liabilities imposed on the shipper: art 33.

[130] *Tweddle v Atkinson* (1861) 1 B & S 393, 398.

were applicable. It is therefore probable that the seller could also be sued under such an implied contract and be bound by the provisions of the Hague/Hague-Visby Rules, where applicable. Second, in order for the bare FOB seller to be held liable for dangerous goods under the Rules, he must fall within the meaning of the term 'shipper' in article IV rule 6, given that it imposes the liability on 'the shipper of such goods ….'[131] The question arising at this point is whether the bare FOB seller would be considered the shipper within the meaning of the Rules. Indeed, under bare FOB sales, it is the buyer who is considered the shipper, as the party to the main contract, whilst the seller as wet shipper is regarded as the consignor. The term 'shipper', however, is not referred to rigidly in the Rules. The 'shipper' is mentioned in article I(a) in which it prescribes the '"carrier" … who enters into a contract of carriage with a shipper.' On the other hand, in article III rule 3 by the use of 'shipper', the intended reference must have been to the consignor who ships his goods, not to the contracting party: 'After receiving the goods into his charge the carrier or the master or agent of the carrier shall, on demand of the shipper, issue to the shipper a bill of lading showing among other things …'[132] Therefore, the shipper under the Rules can be interpreted both as wet shipper, as per article III rule 3, and dry shipper, as per article I(a), depending on the circumstances.

It is submitted that the bare FOB seller may fall within the meaning of the 'shipper' under article IV rule 6 for several reasons. First, once it is accepted that the Rules are applicable to the implied contract, it is not easy to accommodate its terms with the parties under the strict interpretation of the Rules. Therefore, there would be no harm in applying some verbal manipulation to give proper effect to the Rules thereunder. In this regard, the bare FOB seller can be said to have satisfied the term 'shipper' within article I(a), as he enters into a carriage contract – albeit implied – with the carrier. Second, it has already been said that he no doubt also falls within 'the shipper' in article III rule 3, as the consignor who ships the goods. More significantly, the Rules are only applicable *either* between the shipper and the carrier *or* between the holder of the bill of lading and the carrier.[133] That is to say, in order to apply the Rules to the implied contract, the seller should be considered either the shipper or the bill holder thereunder. It would not logically be accurate to consider the bare FOB seller to be the holder of the bill of lading under the contract implied on shipment, since he never holds the bill.[134] Therefore, once the Rules are employed to govern the implied contract, it is suggested that the bare FOB seller as both wet shipper, as per article III rule 3, and dry shipper – albeit under implied contract – may fall within the meaning of the 'shipper' in article IV rule 6, with some allowance for verbal manipulation.

[131] See art IV r 6 of the Hague/Hague-Visby Rules.

[132] R Aikens et al, *Bills of lading*, 3rd edn (London, Informa, 2020), para 7.82; S Baughen, 'The Legal Status of the Non-contracting Shipper' [2000] 1 *IJOSL* 21, 21.

[133] See art I (a) and (b) of the Rules.

[134] Unless the bill of lading is later transferred to him further down in a chain sale.

The courts may be reluctant to apply this provision to the bare FOB seller under an implied contract, since it is the buyer/shipper who expressly undertakes the obligation under the contract. However, since article IV rule 6 is an indemnity clause, and more significantly the shipper does not owe any sort of duty to warn the carrier of the dangerous nature of the goods thereunder,[135] the courts may show some readiness to apply it under the implied contract, particularly where the seller's fault causes the damage or loss. As mentioned above, the contract is implied in order to satisfy the commercial expectations. In the *Pyrene* case, it was implied so as to satisfy particularly the carrier's expectations in limiting his liability against the seller. If the buyer/shipper is not within reach or his assets are not enough to cover the loss, in order not to deny the carrier's right to redress his loss, the courts may show some willingness to allow his claim against the seller under the implied contract, provided that the seller's fault has caused the damage or loss. This would be more arguable particularly if the bill of lading contained a 'Merchant' clause imposing liabilities on various parties including the consignor.[136]

On the other hand, even if the bare FOB seller can be said to have satisfied the meaning of the shipper in the Rules, one may still contrarily argue that the bare FOB seller is not subject to liability arising from dangerous goods. In *The Athanasia Comninos*, Mustill J held (obiter) that where the contract is implied between the consignee and the carrier, the consignee will only be subject to the rights and liabilities, which 'concern the carriage and delivery of the goods and the payment therefor'[137] under this contract. According to his decision, liabilities of the consignee will not be extended to embrace liability for dangerous goods under the implied contract, given that it is directly related to the shipment of these goods. However, this decision may not have a direct impact on the implied contract created in the *Pyrene* case. First of all, unlike in the *Pyrene* case, the relationship cited by Mustill J in *The Athanasia Comninos* is between the consignee and the carrier at the other end of the voyage, namely at the delivery stage, when the carrier delivers the goods against the bill presented for taking delivery of the goods along with payment of freight and other charges. That is to say, the implied contract created between them is derived from the implied contract commonly known as a '*Brandt v Liverpool* contract' which is explained on the different analysis of offer, acceptance and intention.[138] The *Pyrene*-type contract, however, is created between the seller/wet shipper and the carrier on

[135] *The Fiona* [1994] 2 Lloyd's Rep 506, 512, 518, 521. See also *Total Transport Corp v Arcadia Petroleum Ltd (The Eurus)* [1996] CLC 1084, 1098.

[136] Examples of such clause can be found in some bill of lading forms such as Combiconbill, 'K' Line bill, Conlinebill, P&O Nedlloyd Bill.

[137] [1990] 1 Lloyd's Rep 277.

[138] For the *Brandt v Liverpool* type contract see generally, Bridge, *Benjamin's Sale of Goods*, n 38 above, para 18-347 ff.

different grounds, as explained above.[139] Most significantly, as stated by Mustill J, his reasoning covers only the position of the consignee: 'There is to my mind no reason to assume … that the parties intended the consignee to be made subject to a retrospective liability for acts with which he had nothing to do.'[140] It is therefore submitted that his obiter decision is only applicable to the implied contract arising at delivery stage, which has expressly nothing to do with the shipment part of the voyage and the parties to the implied contract created therein.

In contrast to the consignee, the bare FOB seller as wet shipper may indeed have something to do with the goods prior to shipment. He, as wet shipper, at least is under an obligation to deliver the goods over the ship's rail.[141] So far as bare FOB sales are concerned, where the buyer only concludes a carriage contract through his agent, it is not uncommon that due to the parties' agreement in the contract, the seller would fulfil some duties directly in relation to physical shipment of the goods, like packing, stowing or stuffing them to be seaworthy in transit. For instance, when goods which are expressly classified as dangerous in the IMDG Code are shipped, a copy of a dangerous goods note containing all necessary information required by the IMDG Code – like UN Number of the goods, the Proper Shipping Name (PSN), or a declaration stating that the goods are properly packed, marked and labelled – should be provided to the carrier by the shipper. Sometimes under FOB sales, the seller may handle these duties on behalf of the buyer/shipper. Even if there is no such stipulation in the contract with regard to the shipment, the FOB seller is under a duty to ship the goods carefully and skilfully.[142] Thus, it would be difficult to argue that Mustill J's reasoning on the position of the consignee/buyer is applicable also to the seller/wet shipper.

Moreover, a contra-inference supportive of liability in the FOB seller can be interpreted from Mustill J's words themselves. The learned judge opined that the consignee would be subject to the rights and liabilities under the implied contract, which only 'concern the carriage and delivery of the goods'.[143] If a consignee under an implied contract created at the delivery stage assumes responsibility for the carriage and 'delivery' of the goods, according to the reasoning of Mustill J, it can also be suggested that a consignor – the bare FOB seller – under the implied

[139] The editors of *Benjamin's Sale of Goods*, n 39 above, also suggest that the *Pyrene* type implied contract is different from the *Brandt v Liverpool* type: Bridge, *Benjamin's Sale of Goods*, n 38 above, para 18-358.

[140] [1990] 1 Lloyd's Rep 277, 281.

[141] *Stock v Inglis* (1883–84) 12 QBD 564, 573; affirmed by the House of Lords (1884–85) 10 App Cas 263; *J Raymond Wilson & Co Ltd v N Scratchard Ltd* (1943–44) 77 Ll L Rep 373, 374.

[142] *A Hamson & Son (London) Ltd v S Martin Johnson & Co Ltd* [1953] 1 Lloyd's Rep 553, 554; *George Wills & Sons Ltd v Thomas Brown & Sons* (1922) 12 Ll LR 292; *Sime Darby & Co Ltd v Everitt & Co* (1923) 14 Ll LR 120. See s 29(6) of the 1979 Act. The goods should also be in a merchantable state at the time of shipment to endure the voyage: see *Mash & Murrell Ltd v Joseph I Emanuel Ltd* [1961] 1 WLR 862; [1961] 1 Lloyd's Rep 47; reversed on different grounds in the Court of Appeal [1961] 2 Lloyd's Rep 326.

[143] [1990] 1 Lloyd's Rep 277.

contract created at the shipment stage may assume responsibilities which concern the carriage and 'shipment' of the goods. This – it is suggested – clearly includes shipment of dangerous goods.

(d) Bare FOB Seller's Liability in Tort

Regardless of whether the carrier's claim under the implied contract is valid or not, he might be able to sue the bare FOB seller in tort. In *The Orjula*,[144] the supplier supplied drums of hydrochloric acid to the seller/shipper for shipment. The supplier 'stuffed' (loaded) the drums into the containers provided by the carrier,[145] whereas the seller shipped them. Due to defective packing and staging, the drums of acid leaked and caused damage to the vessel and the containers. The carrier made claims for cleaning up the vessel, decontamination and re-stuffing of the containers, along with the cost of transhipment to the destination. The carrier sued both the shipper/seller, in contract, and the supplier of the goods who stuffed them negligently into the containers, in tort. It was held by Mance J that the defendants owed a duty of care for the damage to the containers and the vessel. Accordingly, the carrier would be entitled to claim in tort against the supplier for the alleged negligence in the stowage of the containers, for the cost of cleaning up the vessel.[146] Mance J also opined that the expenses of decontamination and re-stuffing of the containers could be claimed, either on the basis of loss consequential upon physical damage or as loss incurred in mitigation of the damage. However, as for the cost of transhipment, the learned judge rejected the claim on the ground that it was purely economic.

Indeed, it was the supplier, not the bare FOB seller, who became liable in tort to the carrier. However, as was the case with the supplier in *The Orjula*, given the physical nexus of the seller with the goods prior to shipment, the seller can arguably be said to owe a duty of care to the carrier and for that reason, his negligent act may have caused or triggered the damage or loss arising from shipment of dangerous goods. Regardless of the type, under all FOB sales, the seller is under a duty to make safe delivery of the goods over the ship's rail.[147] He is also under a duty to ship them skilfully and carefully.[148] As mentioned before, FOB sales are flexible instruments. It is not uncommon for the parties to agree on express stipulations as to how the goods should be delivered by the seller in respect of packing, stowing

[144] *Losinjska Plovidba v Transco Overseas Ltd (The Orjula)* [1995] 2 Lloyd's Rep 395, 403. On this see generally, A Tettenborn, 'Tort Liability and environmental responsibility' [1996] 1 *LMCLQ* 8.

[145] The bareboat charterers.

[146] *The Orjula* [1995] 2 Lloyd's Rep 395, 403. For a speech supportive of a claim in tort for dangerous goods, see *The Fiona* [1994] 2 Lloyd's Rep 506, 521–22 (per Lord Hoffmann). For where the shipper owed a duty of care to the charterer in tort, see *Virgo Steamship Co SA v Skaarup Shipping Corp (The Kapetan Georgis)* [1988] 1 Lloyd's Rep 352.

[147] *Stock v Inglis* (1883–84) 12 QBD 564, 573; affirmed by the House of Lords (1884–85) 10 App Cas 263; *J Raymond Wilson & Co Ltd v N Scratchard Ltd* (1943–44) 77 Ll L Rep 373, 374.

[148] See n 142 above.

or stacking on board. Due to the mechanics of the contract, the seller, as wet shipper, would handle those duties better than the buyer/dry shipper, who may only have engaged his forwarding agent at the port of shipment to book space and to procure the bill of lading. Since the bare FOB seller may have fulfilled any of those duties prior to loading to provide safe shipment on board, if his negligent acts – for instance, the declaration note required by the IMDG Code states that the goods are properly packed, but the seller has not done so – have caused the damage or loss resulting from dangerous goods, it is submitted that there is no reason why the seller should not be subject to liability arising from dangerous goods in the tort of negligence, as was the case in *The Orjula.*[149] However, it is worth highlighting that such a claim in tort could be disadvantageous for the carrier. Unlike in a contractual claim, he may be unable to recover losses that are purely economic and that are not linked to any claim for physical damage, like liability for legally dangerous goods[150] or the cost of transhipment, as was the case in *The Orjula*. Therefore, his claims against the seller in tort can be limited to physical damage or loss consequential upon physical damage.

(e) Conclusion on the Bare FOB Seller's Liability

In respect of implied contract, for the reasons given above, it appears to be arguable that the seller, technically, can be subject to liability arising from dangerous goods. However, the courts may feel reluctant to hold him liable, since it is expressly the buyer, as the shipper under bare FOB, who undertakes the obligation in relation to the shipment of dangerous goods. That was probably why Mustill J in *The Athanasia Comninos* refused to render the consignee who had nothing to do with the goods prior to shipment, liable under the implied contract created at the delivery stage. However, in case of a *'Pyrene'*-type implied contract established at the shipment stage, the courts may perhaps show some readiness to imply this contract and hold the seller liable, particularly when he is at fault or negligent in some of his duties in relation to the shipment which causes or triggers damage or loss resulting from dangerous goods.

It is also arguable that while the buyer/shipper is strictly liable under the contract – whether he is at fault or not – the seller, when the damage arises from his act or fault, should also be held liable, as the source of damage, under the implied contract. This also seems more plausible if the buyer/shipper is not worth suing. He may, for instance, be insolvent or may not have valuable assets within reach. However, under the implied contract, the carrier may not be able to claim his loss arising from *legally* dangerous goods, as article IV rule 6 is not applicable to those

[149] This analogy is also applicable to the c.i.f. seller/wet shipper who does not have contractual nexus with the carrier.

[150] In *Mitchell Cotts & Co Ltd v Steel Brothers & Co Ltd* [1916] 2 KB 610, where the shipper was liable for the purely economic loss of the carrier resulting from the detention of the vessel.

goods which only cause delay or detention.[151] Moreover, even if such a contract is not implied, the seller can be still subject to liability for dangerous goods in tort, when his negligent actions caused the damage. Nonetheless, the carrier may not be able to claim in tort purely economic losses which cannot be linked to any physical damage.[152]

(ii) Classic FOB

Devlin J, despite the fact that the sale contract before him was on bare FOB terms in *Pyrene v Scindia*, went on to classify three main varieties of FOB contracts. Under his definition of classic FOB, the seller shoulders a heavier legal burden, when compared to bare FOB. sales. The learned judge, with reference to *Wimble, Sons & Co Ltd v Rosenberg & Sons*,[153] defined a classic FOB contract as one in which the buyer nominates the vessel and the seller puts the goods on board for the account of the buyer and obtains bills of lading.[154] This differs from the bare FOB, as the seller here procures bills of lading; and he becomes 'directly party to the contract of carriage at least until he takes out the bill of lading in the buyer's name.'[155] According to Devlin J, in a classic FOB it is assumed that the seller arranges a carriage contract with the carrier and is party to this contract as principal 'at least until' the bill of lading names the buyer as the shipper.[156] Once the bill designates the buyer as the shipper, the seller is assumed to discontinue being party to this antecedent contract,[157] and for that reason, it will be the buyer who is privy to the contract contained in or evidenced by the bills of lading.

However, the position of the seller and the buyer under a classic FOB contract is not inflexible.[158] In *The El Amria and The El Minia*, the Court of Appeal approved the classification of Devlin J in line with commercial practice. It was also recognised in the case that the classic FOB seller could be named in the bill of lading,

[151] *The Darya Radhe* [2009] EWHC 845 (Comm); [2009] 2 Lloyd's Rep 175; *the Giannis NK* [1994] 2 Lloyd's Rep 171; [1996] 1 Lloyd's Rep 577.

[152] *The Orjula* [1995] 2 Lloyd's Rep 395.

[153] It was the first case that defined the classic FOB sales; [1913] 3 KB 743.

[154] [1954] 2 QB 402, 424.

[155] ibid.

[156] However, this does not necessarily mean that the seller can be subject to liability as being party to that antecedent contract, where damage arises from dangerous goods before the bill is issued. It was held by Devlin J in *Pyrene v Scindia* that it was material whether the issue of the bill was envisaged and not whether the bill was actually issued. Thus, for instance, when damage occurs after the shipment operations start but before the issue of the bill, such a case will be covered by the bill of lading, as if it had been issued before the damage occurred. See *Pyrene v Scindia* [1954] 2 QB 402, 419.

[157] The learned judge, however, did not explain how this antecedent contract between the seller and the carrier was converted into a bill of lading contract between the buyer and the carrier, or the terms of this antecedent contract. See Treitel and Reynolds, *Carver on Bills of Lading*, n 38 above, para 3-002. See also *Leduc & Co v Ward* (1888) LR 20 QBD 475; *Owners of Cargo Lately Laden on Board the Ardennes v Owners of the Ardennes (The Ardennes)* [1951] 1 KB 55.

[158] As McNair J contended in *NV Handel My J Smits Import-Export v English Exporters (London) Ltd* [1957] 1 Lloyd's Rep 517, 521, there is nothing inconsistent in the seller securing shipping space under an FOB contract.

and accordingly be the shipper as principal, instead of the buyer.[159] In addition to this, in the Australian case of *Saffron v Société Minière Cafrika*, where Devlin J's classification of FOB contracts was considered, the classic FOB was described as follows: 'in what has been called the "classic" type of f.o.b. contract it is the duty of the seller both to put the goods on board and to procure a bill of lading.'[160] Furthermore, on the flexibility of the classic FOB, Evans J in *Concordia Trading BV v Richo International Ltd* stated on the classic FOB:

> In the normal case, although the goods have been shipped on a vessel nominated by the buyer, the seller for his own protection will have reserved the right of disposing of the goods, as unpaid seller, and the bill of lading will require delivery to him or to his order.[161]

The case law appears to show that in classic FOB cases, it is often the seller who makes arrangements for the carriage contract.[162] There is, however, available judicial support for a different view that under a classic FOB contract, it is the buyer who makes arrangements for shipment. In *Ian Stach Ltd v Baker Bosley Ltd*, Diplock J (who later became Lord Diplock) unlike the above definitions, stated that under a classic FOB it is the buyer's duty to nominate the vessel and to make the arrangements for carriage.[163] Devlin's definition does not necessarily invalidate Diplock J's view, or vice versa. The two different judicial definitions only attest to the flexible nature of FOB contracts, as both forms are commonly used in commercial practice. This shows that there is no invariable rule under classic FOB sales. Thus, either of the parties could conclude the contract of carriage and be named as the shipper under the bill of lading, depending on the facts.

(a) Modern Classic FOB

As outlined above, Devlin J's definition of classic FOB in the *Pyrene* case may not be entirely reflective of commercial practice. The seller may not always be in a position to reserve space for the goods. Moreover, the buyer might have chartered a vessel for various reasons, or might have reserved space in advance. On the other hand, even in such cases where it is the buyer who makes arrangements for shipment, the seller could be willing to take out the bills of lading in his own name, given that he may have an interest in the performance of the contract of carriage.[164] By doing so, he would retain control over the goods and protect himself against

[159] [1982] 2 Lloyd's Rep 28, 32.
[160] (1958) 100 CLR 231, 241.
[161] [1991] 1 Lloyd's Rep 475, 478–79.
[162] For examples of this type, see *Brandt (HO) & Co v HN Morris & Co Ltd* [1917] 2 KB 784 and *Lusograin Comercio Internacional de Cereas Ltda v Bunge AG* [1986] 2 Lloyd's Rep 654.
[163] *Ian Stach Ltd v Baker Bosley Ltd* [1958] 2 QB 130, 139. A 'special freight agreement' between the FOB buyer and the carrier was not considered a carriage contract in *Evergreen v Aldgate Warehouse* [2003] 2 Lloyd's Rep 597.
[164] See generally A Gelgec, 'Identifying the Shipper under Bills of Lading' (2020) 26 *JIML* 229.

non-payment for the goods from the buyer.[165] In case of non-payment, he could seek to redirect the goods to another buyer.[166] Due to such factors, under the classic FOB, the seller is not necessarily obliged to take out the bill of lading in the buyer's name.[167] By contrast, the seller will not breach the sale contract simply because he asks the carrier to issue a bill of lading in which his own name is put as the shipper.[168]

The proper terminology reflecting commercial practice for this type would be the 'modern' classic FOB contract,[169] since it was considered within classic FOB by the House of Lords in *Scottish & Newcastle v Othon Ghalanos*.[170] While endorsing Devlin J's definition of the classic FOB contract, the House of Lords in *Scottish & Newcastle* also modernised the definition to make it consistent with commercial practice by describing it as 'cases where the buyer arranges and nominates the ship but the seller ships and takes the bill of lading in his own name as consignor …'.[171] In such cases, the buyer often charters the vessel, but it is the seller who is named as the shipper under the bill of lading, once the goods are shipped on board.[172] As was illustrated in *Scottish & Newcastle*, there are examples of both ways where the seller acts as agent[173] or principal[174] by doing so.

The description of such a complex contractual scheme can be found in the statement by Lord Denning MR in *The Dunelmia*, where the Master of the Rolls described four different contracts concluded under international sales. In the case, under a classic FOB contract, which was assumed to be the first contract, the buyer had made the arrangements for carriage and had a charterparty with the carrier.[175] The charterparty was the only contract (second) described by Lord Denning in which the buyer was the original party with the carrier. Although there was no express contractual agreement between the seller and carrier,

[165] Such security problems of the seller were also highlighted even in *Cowas-Jee v Thompson and Kebbel* (1845) 5 Moore 165; 13 ER 454.

[166] *Mitchell v Ede* (1840) 1 Ad & El 888.

[167] Bridge, *Benjamin's Sale of Goods*, n 38 above, para 20-010.

[168] *Browne v Hare* (1853) 3 H & N 484; (1859) 4 H & N 822.

[169] It is called the 'fourth' type of FOB contract in *Benjamin's Sale of Goods*, n 38 above, para 20-142; *Carver on Bills of Lading*, n 38 above, para 4-025.

[170] [2008] UKHL 11; [2008] 1 Lloyd's Rep 462.

[171] [2008] UKHL 11, [34]. In this case, the contract could be assumed to be a classic FOB contract. While the buyer selected the shipping line and agreed to pay the freight, the seller was left to choose the vessel and make the contract of carriage. Although it was not stated in the report, it was assumed that – regardless of who was named in the bills of lading (seaway bills) as the shipper – it was the seller who acted as the agent of the buyer in making the carriage contract. See [2008] UKHL 11, [45].

[172] *KSAS Seateam & Co v Iraq National Oil Co (The Sevonia Team)* [1983] 2 Lloyd's Rep 640; *The Dunelmia* [1969] 2 Lloyd's Rep 476; *Pacific Molasses Co and United Molasses Trading Co v Entre Rios Compania Naviera SA (The San Nicholas)* [1976] 1 Lloyd's Rep 8; *The Athanasia Comninos* [1990] 1 Lloyd's Rep 277; *The Seven Pioneer* [2001] 2 Lloyd's Rep 57 (NZ High Court); *Trafigura Beheer BV v Mediterranean Shipping Co SA (The MSC Amsterdam)* [2007] EWHC 944.

[173] *The MSC Amsterdam* [2007] EWHC 944.

[174] *The Sevonia Team* [1983] 2 Lloyd's Rep 640.

[175] The sale contract was classified as the first contract by Lord Denning MR. See *The Dunelmia* [1970] 1 QB 289, 303.

Lord Denning considered a (third) contract concluded between the seller and the carrier in the bill of lading: 'The third contract is the bill of lading of July 11, 1961. The Master signed a bill of lading, which was on a printed form of the sellers.'[176,177] Accordingly, the fourth contract was the one established by the endorsement and delivery of the bill of lading to which the buyer became a party later by such transfer from the seller.[178]

Such (third) contracts were mostly assumed by the courts to be between the classic FOB seller/named shipper and the carrier, where the facts of cases fit, even if there was no express contractual arrangement between them. Where the sale contract was under classic FOB terms – such as in cases like *The Sevonia Team*,[179] *The San Nicholas*,[180] or even in the New Zealand case of *The Seven Pioneer*[181] – despite the fact that the buyers had chartered the vessel and the sellers had no express contractual dealings with the carrier, it was the sellers who were named as the shipper, and consequently they were considered the original party to the carriage contract under the bills of lading.[182] A similar example can also be found in the Canadian case of *AK Steel v Acelormittal*[183] where an FOB seller was designated as the shipper in the bills of lading, despite the fact that he had no contractual dealings with the carrier and that it was the buyer who had a charter-party with the carrier. Having considered the *Pyrene* case, the court held that the seller was the shipper under the bills of lading.[184] Interestingly, the courts appear never to have justified in clear words this implied contract under modern classic FOB except for Lord Denning MR in *The Dunelmia*, but it can be said to have been tacitly applied so far.[185]

[176] [1970] 1 QB 289, 304. For more detailed and supportive analysis on this see generally, S Baughen, 'The legal status of the non-contracting shipper' (2000) 1 *IJOSL* 21.

[177] More than one carriage contract could be in existence together at the same time with regard to the same shipment. See *Cho Yang Shipping Co Ltd v Coral (UK) Ltd* [1997] 2 Lloyd's Rep 641.

[178] [1970] 1 QB 289, 304. Yet it was held in the case that the bill of lading would be considered as a receipt in the hand of the buyer where he has chartered the vessel from the same carrier that issued the bill of lading. Gelgec, 'Identifying the Shipper under Bills of Lading', n 164 above, 232–33.

[179] [1983] 2 Lloyd's Rep 640.

[180] [1976] 1 Lloyd's Rep 8. The existence of such an implied contract is also observed in Aikens et al, *Bills of Lading*, n 132 above, para 7.78.

[181] *The Seven Pioneer* [2001] 2 Lloyd's Rep 57.

[182] Gelgec, 'Identifying the Shipper under Bills of Lading', n 164 above, 233. For a case where the fixture note between the shipper and charterer was superseded by the issue of bill of lading between the shipper and shipowner, see *Chew Hong Edible Oils Ltd v Scindia Steam Navigation Co Ltd (The Jalamohan)* [1988] 1 Lloyd's Rep 443.

[183] *AK Steel Corp v Acelormittal Mines Canada Inc* 2014 FCA 287; (2014) 466 NR 159.

[184] ibid, [10].

[185] A Gelgec, 'Identifying the Shipper under Bills of Lading', n 164 above, 233. Such an implied contract could be most readily justified in cases where the buyer has no contractual relationship with the carrier but only has a sub-charterparty with the head charterer. In such cases, the only contract that the buyer would be party to with the carrier is the contract contained in or evidenced by the bills of lading, in which the seller is named as the shipper. Here, given that the buyer makes the carriage arrangements with the sub-charter, the seller is accordingly not required to make any. That example would charmingly suit the implied contract assumed by Lord Denning in *The Dunelmia*. For a good example of an FOB contract with a complex charterparty relationship between the parties, see *R Pagnan & Fratelli v NGJ Schouten NV (The Filipinas I)* [1973] 1 Lloyd's Rep 349.

(b) Another Implied Contract

At first sight, it may be thought that this type of implied contract and Devlin J's implied contract can be regarded as the same. However, they are slightly different, even though their existence can be explained on the same grounds set out above, namely the seller's delivery of the goods and the carrier's acceptance of them.[186] Under the modern classic FOB, the seller's intention to become party to the carriage contract is more visible than under the bare FOB, as he is the one who is named as the shipper in the bills of lading. More significantly, unlike the implied contract from the *Pyrene* case, the implied contract under the modern FOB contract is not a collateral one. The *Pyrene*-type contract is one of the two contracts existing under the bills of lading terms, where the bare FOB seller is only party to an implied collateral contract, while the *Dunelmia* type is the only contract under the bills of lading where the seller (as agent or principal) is party to the main carriage contract with the carrier.[187]

The presence of such an implied contract under classic FOB sales can be inferred from the House of Lords' decision in *Scottish & Newcastle*, where it was held that an FOB contract:

> embraces (a) cases where the buyer arranges and nominates the ship but the seller ships and takes the bill of lading in his own name as consignor … in cases (a) [classic FOB] … the seller may be either the only party to the bill of lading or acting as agent for the buyers as a (more or less undisclosed principal).[188]

Under such a classic FOB where the seller makes no contractual arrangements, this begs the question in what sense could the seller act as agent or principal under the bills of lading?[189] The answer to this question would be the acceptance of an implied contract between the seller and the carrier, once the seller is designated as the shipper, as Lord Denning expressly assumed in *The Dunelmia*.[190] Otherwise, there would have been no contract under which the seller could act as principal or agent.

[186] See section II.B(i)(b) above.

[187] Debattista classifies this (modern classic) FOB as 'straight' (bare). See Debattista and Hornyold-Strickland, *Debattista on Bills of Lading in Commodities Trade*, n 80 above, paras 1.19–1.20. It is nevertheless difficult to regard this type as a bare FOB after the decision of *Scottish & Newcastle v Othon Ghalanos*. It is the seller under this type (either as principal or agent) who becomes the party to the carriage contract, and is named as the shipper in the bills of lading. Unlike the modern classic type, the bare FOB seller assumes only one duty, namely delivery of the goods on board the nominated vessel. He is neither named in the bill nor becomes a party to the original carriage contract thereunder.

[188] [2008] UKHL 11, [34].

[189] For a case where both the FOB seller and the buyer were named in the bill as the shippers, see *AP Moller-Maersk v Sonaec Villas Cen Sad Fadoul & Ors (The Maersk Line)* [2010] EWHC 355, [2012] 1 CLC 798.

[190] Such an implied contract could be restricted on the basis of the decisions in *The Aramis* [1989] 1 Lloyd's Rep 213 and *The Gudermes* [1993] 1 Lloyd's Rep 311. However, the restrictions established in these cases are mostly related to the conduct of the buyer and the carrier on discharge.

(c) Conclusion on Classic FOB Sales

For the reasons given above, it is submitted that under classic FOB sales there are two different applications in practice, namely the old and the modern one. It depends on the facts whether it is the seller or the buyer who makes the carriage contract and becomes the shipper under the bills of lading. If there is no space reserved or vessel chartered by the buyer, the seller could conclude a carriage contract between himself and the carrier and ask the carrier to issue a bill of lading naming either himself or the buyer. If it were the buyer named in the bill as the shipper, the buyer would be regarded as the original party to the carriage contract. By the same token, the seller as wet shipper would not be subject to any liability under the main contract.[191] On the other hand, under the modern type, where the buyer reserved space in advance or chartered a vessel, and the seller was named in the bill as the shipper, it would be the seller becoming party to the carriage contract, either as principal or agent of the buyer, depending on the facts. The question of who would be subject to the liabilities of the shipper – including that arising from dangerous goods – under such a contract will be discussed below.[192]

(iii) FOB Contract with Additional Duties

As with all FOB contracts, under this type, the seller/wet shipper (or through his agents) is under a duty to deliver the goods over the ship's rail. The seller as both wet and dry shipper, when compared to the other types of contract, undertakes the maximum number of duties towards the buyer under this type. Unlike in bare and classic FOB contracts where it is the buyer who nominates the vessel, the seller under this type undertakes to fulfil the additional duties,[193] namely of both nominating the vessel and concluding the carriage contract.[194] As McNair J contended in *NV Handel My J Smits v English Exporters*, unless otherwise stated, it is the buyer's duty to nominate the vessel.[195] However, the same judge also held

[191] However, likewise under the bare FOB, it is submitted that the seller as wet shipper can be subject to liability under the implied contract or in tort. See sections II.B.(i)(c) and (d) above.

[192] See section II.B(iv) below.

[193] These additional duties of the seller under this type are not exhaustive. The seller could also prepay the freight and insure the goods for the account of the buyer. See *Carlos Federspiel & Co SA v Charles Twigg & Co Ltd* [1957] 1 Lloyd's Rep 240.

[194] The underlying reasons of this type may vary. In terms of international sales, the buyer could possibly be abroad and accordingly he might have had no commercial practice or business link at the place of loading. Or even if he had, he might have no knowledge on the type of vessel on which the goods are to be carried. More significantly, the seller might have been in a better position to nominate the suitable vessel and make the shipping arrangements for the goods that he sells. Additionally, the required shipping space could be small, and therefore the seller rather than the buyer could more easily reserve the required space, as was the case in *DH Bain v Field & Co Fruit Merchants Ltd* (1920) 3 Ll LR 26. Alternatively, the seller might have booked the shipping space well before the shipment of the goods. See *Scandinavian Trading Co A/B v Zodiac Petroleum SA (The Al Hofuf)* [1981] 1 Lloyd's Rep 81. All aside, the buyer might just have requested the seller to do so. For such reasons, these duties could be shifted from the buyer to the seller under this type of contract.

[195] [1957] 1 Lloyd's Rep 517, 519.

that there is nothing to prevent the allocation of this responsibility to the seller.[196] Such shifting of both duties does not prevent a sale contract from being under FOB terms, as contended by Diplock J in *Ian Stach Ltd v Baker Bosley*:

> it may be a matter of doubt as to whose was to be the responsibility for finding shipping space and for determining shipping port and shipping date. Prima facie, under an f.o.b. contract that is the duty and responsibility of the buyer; but there are probably as many exceptions to the rule as there are examples of it.[197]

As was the case with other FOB contract types, the first judicial recognition of this type was made in the *Pyrene* case by Devlin J: 'Sometimes the seller is asked to make the necessary arrangements; and the contract may then provide for his taking the bill of lading in his own name and obtaining payment against the transfer, as in a c.i.f. contract.'[198] The position of the seller under this type of contract is also recognised in the statement of Lord Mance from *Scottish & Newcastle v Othon Ghalanos* in the House of Lords; '(b) cases [FOB with additional duties] where the seller arranges shipment and takes the bill in his own name as consignor ….'[199]

Given that all the required shipping arrangements, including being named in the bill of lading as the shipper, are made by the seller under this type of contract, this type of FOB may resemble CIF contracts in many aspects.[200] However, unlike in CIF contracts, the seller does not invariably perform them as principal. He may act either as principal or agent of the buyer both in making the carriage contract and being named in the bill of lading as the shipper, as stated by Lord Mance in *Scottish v Newcastle* in the House of Lords.[201] Therefore, it might be crucial to determine who the principal is for the purpose of imposing liabilities on the shipper including that arising from dangerous goods.

[196] ibid. In the case, the seller's undertaking was not considered an absolute obligation but a qualified one.

[197] [1958] 2 QB 130, 138.

[198] [1954] 2 QB 402, 424. In *The El Amria and The El Minia* [1982] 2 Lloyd's Rep 28, the sale contract was classified as FOB with additional duties. In the case, this type of contract was also accepted as the variant of classic FOB by Donaldson J: [1982] 2 Lloyd's Rep 28, 32. This was mostly because the duties of the seller are nearly identical in the two types, except that here the seller nominates the ship and is named in the bill of lading as the shipper. For instance, even though the classic FOB contract was first described in *Wimble v Rosenberg* [1913] 3 KB 743, the FOB contract in that case was mostly recognised as this type (FOB with additional duties). It was the seller who chose the vessel, made the carriage contract, and paid the freight. However, it was not entirely clear whether the seller was acting principal in doing so and should be considered as the shipper.

[199] [2008] UKHL 11, [34].

[200] The difference is that under a FOB contract with additional duties, the buyer undertakes to pay the freight and insurance, if any, since the invoices for these services are separate from the sale contract's invoice. Unlike CIF contracts, here it would be the buyer who bears the risk of fluctuation in the freight rates, even if it were prepaid by the seller. See *The Parchim* [1918] AC 157, 163–64. The differences between FOB and CIF contracts were also considered in *Scottish & Newcastle v Othon Ghalanos* [2008] UKHL 11; [2008] 1 Lloyd's Rep 462.

[201] [2008] UKHL 11, [34].

(iv) Who Attracts the Shipper's Liability under FOB Contracts?

It has been discussed above that under FOB contracts it may be either the buyer or the seller who concludes the carriage contract with the carrier and is named in the bill of lading as the shipper. Under bare FOB and classic FOB sales, when the buyer is named in the bill of lading, it is clear that the buyer is considered the original party as the shipper. On the other hand, the seller can also be named as the shipper in the bill under both classic FOB and FOB with additional duties.[202] However, it does not necessarily follow that the bill evidences a contract between the carrier and the named shipper. Sometimes, under FOB sales, the contract evidenced in the bill of lading can be between the carrier and the buyer, rather than the seller/named shipper.[203] This may lead to the inference that the seller/named shipper concluded the carriage contract as agent of the buyer.[204] It is also clear from the decision by the House of Lords in *Scottish & Newcastle* that when the seller takes out the bill of lading in his own name, he could be doing so either as principal or agent of the buyer.[205] At this point, the question arises as to who would be subject to the liabilities of the shipper including that arising from dangerous goods under such FOB sales. The answer to this question may depend upon whether the seller made the carriage contract as agent of the buyer or as principal.

A solution to the tension between the seller and the buyer in such cases may not be apparent from the bill of lading, but may depend on the examination of the sale contract between the seller and the buyer along with the intention of the parties.[206] To ascertain whether an FOB seller designated in the bill of lading as the shipper is the original party requires an examination of whether he has any commercial interest in being an original party to the carriage contract after shipment.[207] If the seller thus wanted to retain the right of disposal and title in the goods after shipment for security against the non-payment from the buyer, it would strongly follow that he would have an interest in being an original party to the carriage contract.[208] Put differently, if the property has not passed to the buyer on shipment – often in consequence of non-payment from the buyer – the seller named in the bill as the shipper is prima facie regarded as the principal party to the carriage contract.[209] Therefore the inference is that the crucial issue is whether

[202] *Browne v Hare* (1853) 3 H & N 484; (1859) 4 H & N 822.

[203] *The Berge Sisar* [2001] UKHL 17; [2002] AC 205, [19].

[204] *East West Corp v DKBS 1912* [2003] EWCA Civ 83; [2003] QB 1509, [34]; *the Delfini* [1988] 2 Lloyd's Rep 599, 605, affirmed in the Court of Appeal [1990] 1 Lloyd's Rep 252; *Dickenson v Lano* (1860) 2 F&F 188; *Cowas-Jee v Thompson and Kebbel* (1845) 5 Moore 165; 13 ER 454; *Anderson v Clark* (1824) 2 Bing 20; *Fragano v Long* (1825) 4 B & C 219.

[205] [2008] UKHL 11, [34]. Gelgec, 'Identifying the Shipper under Bills of Lading', n 164 above, 235.

[206] *East West Corp v DKBS 1912* [2003] EWCA Civ 83; [2003] QB 1509, [35]; *Cho Yang v Coral* [1997] 2 Lloyd's Rep 641, 643.

[207] [2008] UKHL 11, [15], [17], [37], [44]–[47].

[208] Bridge, *Benjamin's Sale of Goods*, n 38 above, para 20-014 ff.

[209] *Evergreen v Aldgate Warehouse* [2003] EWHC 667; [2003] 2 Lloyd's Rep 597, 604. For a similar view in Hong Kong, see *Central Optical (Hong Kong) Ltd v Jardine Transport Services Ltd* [2001] 2 Lloyd's Rep 678.

the seller has any interest in being the original party to the carriage contract on shipment. It follows that if the property passes at a time after shipment, then it is safe to contend that the seller preserves his interest in the performance of the contract and accordingly acts as principal.[210] The way in which the bill of lading is issued may be of some assistance in resolving whether the seller concluded the carriage contract as agent of the buyer or principal.

(a) Where the Bill is Issued to the Order of the Seller

Where the bill has been issued to the order of the seller, it may not be difficult to ascertain whether the seller has an interest and is a principal party to the carriage contract under the bill of lading. Pursuant to section 19(2) of the Sale of Goods Act 1979, the presumption is that the seller retains the right of disposal once the bill of lading is issued to his order.[211] It is also the position in the case law that the seller prima facie retains the property in the goods if the bill is made out to his order.[212] The seller will retain his interest both in the goods and in bills of lading and thereby, as the named shipper, he will be assumed to be an original party to the carriage contract.[213]

(b) Where the Bill is Issued to the Order of a Party Other than the Seller or the Buyer

Where the bill of lading designates the seller as the shipper, but it is issued to the order of a party other than the seller or the buyer, the considerations can be different. In *Evergreen v Aldgate Warehouse*,[214] the goods were sold on classic FOB. terms. Although the buyer had a special freight agreement with the carrier, the manufacturer of the seller was named as the shipper in the bills of lading.[215]

[210] Gelgec, 'Identifying the Shipper under Bills of Lading', n 164 above, 235–36.

[211] This section is no doubt applicable to FOB contracts. See *Mitsui & Co Ltd and Another v Flota Mercante Grancolombiana SA, The Cuidad de Pasto, The Cuidad de Nevia (The Cuidad de Pasto)* [1989] 1 All ER 951, 956, 959 and 960.

[212] *Jenkyns v Brown* (1849) 14 QB 496; *Ross T Smyth & Co Ltd v TD Bailey, Son & Co* [1940] 3 All ER 60. Indeed, this inference can be rebuttable: see *The Albazero* [1975] 2 Lloyd's Rep 295 (CA).

[213] In *Trafigura Beheer BV and Another v Mediterranean Shipping Company SA (The MSC Amsterdam)* [2007] EWHC 944, the sale contract was on FOB terms, and the buyer made the shipping arrangements. However, it was the seller who was named as the shipper in the bill of lading and the bill was 'to order' of the seller. Even though the seller retained the bill of lading until the payment, it was interestingly held that not the seller, but the buyer was the shipper. This decision is not without some difficulties in this regard, as the buyer should not have been regarded as the shipper. There was nothing to contradict the presumption that the seller was the true shipper when the bill was made out to the order of the seller. He had a reasonable interest in the goods, since the goods were not paid for, and for that reason he only endorsed the bill that was issued to his order after payment. Therefore the only logical explanation is that the buyer became party to the contract under the bill by endorsement. See Treitel and Reynolds, *Carver on Bills of Lading*, n 38 above, para 4-029.

[214] [2003] EWHC 667; [2003] 2 Lloyd's Rep 597.

[215] Because of the local regulations that mandatorily required the manufacturers to be named in the bills as the shipper rather than the seller, whether the seller was named as the shipper in the bill was

One of the bills was made to the order of a bank, as the payment was made through a letter of credit, whilst the second bill was 'to the order'[216] without indicating any name next to it. The payment under the second bill was cash against documents. The issue was whether the seller's manufacturer or the buyer was the shipper of the goods. It was held that the seller's manufacturer was the true shipper of two bills, since the seller retained the right of disposal over the goods until the payment.[217] No doubt the seller had retained his interest in the performance of the contract, given that the payments were through letter of credit[218] and cash against documents.[219]

Supporting authority can be found in the *East West Corp v DKBS 1912*[220] case, in which the facts of the case were similar to those of the *Evergreen* case. The bills of lading were taken out in the name of the seller and made out to the order of the banks. It was held that the seller named in the bill as the shipper did not act as agent of the banks simply on the ground that the bill was issued to the order of the banks as consignees. Conversely, it was found that the banks were acting as agents of the sellers in order to clear the payments, and thus the sellers were held to be the true shippers. Therefore, the mere fact that the bills of lading are made out to the order of a party other than the buyer or the seller does not necessarily mean that the sellers did not conclude the carriage contract as principals. In such cases, the seller/named shipper is prima facie considered the original party to the carriage contract.

(c) Where the Bill is Issued to the Order of the Buyer

In the last of the situations, where the bill is made out to the order of the buyer, but names the seller as the shipper, there is some authority for the proposition that 'where there is a named consignee it may be inferred that the contracting party is the consignee not the shipper.'[221] However, this notion is unlikely to be sustainable in unqualified form. So far as the 1979 Act is concerned, unlike for the seller's right of disposal under section 19(2), there is no section in the 1979 Act supportive of the proposition that the buyer retains a right of disposal, once the bill is issued to

immaterial. The bill of lading could also have named an agent for either the seller or the buyer or both. In *Maersk Line*, the bill was taken out in the name of the company acting as the agent of the buyer and the seller. However, although the evidence before the court was limited, it was held that the seller was considered the original party, since the seller was not paid by the buyer, and accordingly he might have interest in being the party to carriage contract: see *AP Moller-Maersk A/S (t/a Maersk Line) v Sonaec Villas Cen Sad Fadoul* [2010] EWHC 355 (Comm); [2010] 2 All ER 1159. For where the agent acted both on behalf of the buyer and seller, see *The Tromp* [1921] P 337.

216 It equates to 'to the shipper's order'.

217 [2003] 2 Lloyd's Rep 597, [33], [40].

218 See *The Cuidad de Pasto* [1989] 1 All ER 951.

219 See *The Miramichi* [1915] P 71.

220 [2003] EWCA Civ 83, [65].

221 *The Berge Sisar* [2001] UKHL 11; [2002] AC 205, 220. See also *Cho Yang Shipping Co Ltd v Coral (UK) Ltd* [1997] 2 Lloyd's Rep 641, 643.

his order. Additionally, the case law appears to indicate the opposite. In a Privy Council case, it was held that the title in the goods did not pass until a certain point after shipment, namely the moment of payment, despite the fact that the bill was issued to the order of the buyer.[222] Thus, the mere fact that the bill of lading is made out to the order of the buyer does not alter the fact that the seller can still retain his interest in being party to the bill of lading. To put it differently, making the goods deliverable to the order of the buyer does not automatically pass the property to the buyer from the seller on shipment. The seller could have an interest in the performance of the carriage contract even after shipment, even though the bill is made out to the buyer's order. In such cases, in unqualified form, there is no reason to suggest otherwise than that the seller is the shipper as principal rather than agent of the buyer.

However, in the *East West Corp* case, Lord Mance contended that the seller/named shipper could be regarded as agent of the buyer who is named as the consignee in the bill of lading.[223] However, he supported this inference only on the grounds of Brandon J's categorisation of the shipper's position in *The Albazero*.[224] Brandon J in the High Court in *The Albazero*, identified three different categories of shippers.[225] In the first category, the shipper was regarded as agent of the consignee in making the carriage contract, where the property passed before or on shipment. In the second, the shipper was regarded as principal where the property did not pass until after shipment.[226] This categorisation was also followed by the House of Lords in *Scottish v Newcastle* later, in order to determine the original party to the carriage contract.[227] What can be inferred from Lord Mance's reference to Brandon J's categorisation is that issuing a bill of lading to the order of the buyer does not in itself suffice to indicate that the seller acts as agent of the buyer in being named in the bill of lading as the shipper. Such a proposition could only be supported in qualified form, where the seller has no interest in the performance of the carriage contract; namely, if the property passes before or upon shipment.[228]

[222] *The Kronprinsessan Margareta, The Parana and Other ships* [1921] 1 AC 486. For a supporting authority, albeit obiter dicta, see *Arnold Karberg & Co v Blythe Green Jourdain & Co* [1915] 2 KB 379; *The Julia* [1949] AC 293; *The Lycaon* [1983] 2 Lloyd's Rep 548.

[223] [2003] QB 1509, 1533.

[224] [1975] 3 WLR 491. This categorisation was made in relation to the bailment terms. In the House of Lords this categorisation was affirmed by all members of the House, including Lord Diplock: [1977] AC 774, 842.

[225] Only the first two are relevant here.

[226] [1975] 3 WLR 491, 501.

[227] [2008] UKHL 11, [42].

[228] Gelgec, 'Identifying the Shipper under Bills of Lading', n 164 above, 236. However the property in the context of CIF and FOB sales is highly unlikely to pass before shipment. *Carlos Federspiel v Twigg* [1957] 1 Lloyd's Rep 240; *Steel Co of Canada Inc v Canada* [1955] SCR 161 (CA). An opposite example can be given from the context of carriage of goods by road where the property passed before shipment; *Texas Instruments Ltd v Nason (Europe) Ltd* [1991] 1 Lloyd's Rep 146.

In *Scottish & Newcastle*, it was held that the seller had no interest in the performance of the carriage contract.[229] The bill of lading named the buyer as the consignee[230] and it was to be sent to the buyer directly after shipment, with the payment due 90 days from arrival.[231] Upon these facts, the House of Lords held that since the seller secured the price from the buyers, the property passed on shipment. As a result of this, the House of Lords went on to hold that the seller had no interest in the bill of lading, and accordingly he was not the original party to the carriage contract but the agent of the buyer. In a recent case of *The Magellan Spirit*,[232] the approach taken in general by the courts to determine the original party was followed. In that case, where the sale contract was on FOB terms, the contract of carriage was found to be between the buyer/consignee and the carrier, only on the basis that the seller/named shipper had no interest in the carriage contract, as the property in the goods passed on shipment. Therefore, the proposition that the seller/named shipper acts as agent of the buyer, when the bill of lading is made out to the order of the buyer, can be supported only on the ground that the seller does not have any interest in being a principal party to the carriage contract on shipment.[233]

The conclusion is that it may not be easy to find an inflexible rule to ascertain whether the FOB seller/named shipper acts as principal or agent of the buyer in being named as the shipper in the carriage contract, as it mostly depends on the terms of the sale contract and the parties' intentions.[234] As long as the seller has an interest in being party to the carriage contract on shipment, then it is plausible to regard him as the original party to the carriage contract. It would follow that the seller/named shipper and not the buyer is subject to liability to the carrier for dangerous goods. On the other hand, where the property passes on shipment as a result of security of payment, the seller will likely be regarded as having no interest, and for that reason the buyer will be considered the original shipper under the bill of lading.

(v) Who Attracts the Liability for Dangerous Goods?

It has been shown that as a result of the approach adopted by the courts, the buyer can be regarded as principal, when the seller/named shipper has no interest in being party to the carriage contract on shipment. It would normally follow that the seller/named shipper, as agent of the buyer, should not be responsible for liabilities, which are instead imposed on the buyer/principal shipper. However,

[229] [2008] UKHL 11, [15], [17] and [37].

[230] It was a non-negotiable bill of lading which omits 'to the order' next to the name of the consignee. It was also not clear whether the seller or buyer was named in the bill as the shipper.

[231] [2008] UKHL 11, [37].

[232] *Magellan Spirit Aps v Vitol Sa (The Magellan Spirit)* [2016] EWHC 454, [38].

[233] Gelgec, 'Identifying the Shipper under Bills of Lading', n 164 above, 236

[234] *East West Corp v DKBS 1912* [2003] EWCA Civ 83, [35].

in considering liabilities arising from dangerous goods, this may not always be the case, and the general approach taken by the courts in determining the principal may have been set aside, and the seller as principal may find himself under liability.

In *The Athanasia Comninos*,[235] the seller sold coal to the buyer under a sale contract on FOB terms. Even though it was the buyer who made all the carriage arrangements and sub-chartered the vessel from the time charterers, it was the seller who was named in the bills of lading as the shipper. On the other hand, the buyer was named as the consignee in the bill. The cargo of coal caused damage to the vessel and the carrier sued both the buyer and the seller under the carriage contract for his loss resulting from the shipment of coal. The issue was whether it was the seller or the buyer who should have dangerous goods liability imposed on him as the shipper.[236] The defendant seller's argument was that he was only named as the shipper in the bill of lading as agent of the buyer. Mustill J, in rejecting this argument, held that the seller was principal, even though the property passed on shipment. His justification was that the buyer did not need to be party to another contract under the bills of lading, since he already had a contract of carriage in the form of a charterparty.[237] Mustill J ultimately held that the seller was considered the original party and thereby he should attract liability for dangerous goods, if any.[238] He also found that the seller would not have been relieved of liability even if he had acted as the agent of the buyer:[239]

> As regards Devco [sellers], there is in my view no room for doubt. They were shippers of the goods, and were named as such in the bill of lading, without qualification. It was argued on their behalf that it was in fact C.E.G.B. who were the participants in the contract of carriage. To my mind the position of C.E.G.B. has no bearing on the potential liability of Devco. To show that C.E.G.B. were principals would not relieve Devco from liability, but would entail that both parties were principals vis a vis the plaintiffs.[240]

(a) Is the Law Ideal?

The decision of Mustill J is not without some difficulties, as the seller should have been held to be agent of the buyer rather than principal, on the basis of the general

[235] [1990] 1 Lloyd's Rep 277.

[236] Gelgec, 'Identifying the Shipper under Bills of Lading', n 164 above, 234, 236.

[237] [1990] 1 Lloyd's Rep 277, 280–81.

[238] The seller/shipper was not held liable, given that the carrier could not prove that the shipper was in breach of his duty against him: [1990] 1 Lloyd's Rep 277, 280.

[239] Gelgec, 'Identifying the Shipper under Bills of Lading', n 164 above, 236–37.

[240] [1990] 1 Lloyd's Rep 277, 280. Sometimes both the agent and the principal can be subject to the same liability under the contract. See *International Ry Co v Niagara Parks Commission* [1941] AC 328; *Teheran-Europe Co v Belton* [1968] 2 QB 53 and *TICC v COSCO (UK) Ltd* [2002] CLC 346. See also, generally, Beale, *Chitty on Contracts*, n 101 above, para 31-084; P Watts, *Bowstead and Reynolds on Agency*, 21st edn (London, Sweet & Maxwell, 2017) art 98, para 9-004 ff. Especially where the bills of lading contain a 'Merchant Clause' in which agents are also classified as merchants.

approach discussed above. First, on the basis of the House of Lords' decision in *Scottish & Newcastle*, the sale contract in *The Athanasia Comninos* clearly falls within the modern classic FOB definition rather than a bare FOB contract, as it was the buyer who made the shipping arrangements but the seller was named in the bill as the shipper.[241] Under classic FOB sales where the seller is named as the shipper, as discussed above, the approach adopted by the courts is that he should not be considered the principal where he has no interest in the performance of the carriage contract on shipment. In *The Athanasia Comninos*, the property passed on shipment. On this ground, the seller may not be said to have had any interest in being an original party to the carriage contract. However, Mustill J held that the seller was the shipper, although he interestingly indicated an opposing proposition to his judgment:

> Under many forms of f.o.b. contract it can be inferred that the property of the goods passes on shipment, that the entire carriage is performed on behalf of the buyer as owner of the goods, and that the seller participates in the contract primarily (if not exclusively) as agent for the buyer.[242]

In this regard, his decision appears to contradict his own speech as well as the authorities cited above as to determining the principal party of the carriage contract. The learned judge justified his decision on the basis that the buyer already had a contract of carriage and did not need another.[243] Indeed, the buyer had a contract of carriage in the form of a charterparty, but this contract, as he stated, was with the time charterers of the vessel,[244] not with the shipowner/carrier who in fact had sued for the damages. Therefore, contrary tothe learned judge's suggestion, the bills of lading would not be mere receipts in the hands of the buyer but a contract of carriage, since the buyer did not have any contractual privity with the shipowners.[245] As such in contrast to his view, the buyer would need a binding contract contained in the bill of lading against the shipowners.

A contradicting view can be found in the Canadian case of *The Roseline*.[246] In that case, the sale contract was on FOB terms and the bill of lading was issued to the order of the buyer's bank, whilst the bill named the seller as the shipper. The cargo of sulphur caused damage to the vessel. The issue revolved around whether the seller/named shipper or the buyer/named consignee was the original party to the carriage contract under the bill of lading so as to allocate liability for dangerous goods to the true shippers. It was held by the court that the buyer was the true

[241] The contract between the carrier/shipowner and the seller can only be explained on the grounds of the implied contract of Lord Denning from *The Dunelmia* in which he explicitly accepted the existence of implied contract between the FOB seller/named shipper and carrier in the form of bills of lading, where the buyer had a charterparty with the carrier. See *The Dunelmia* [1970] 1 QB 289, 304.

[242] [1990] 1 Lloyd's rep 277, 280.

[243] ibid, 281.

[244] ibid, 277.

[245] See *The Dunelmia* [1970] 1 QB 289.

[246] *Union Industrielle et Maritime v Petrosul International Ltd (The Roseline)* [1987] 1 Lloyd's Rep 18.

shipper merely on the ground that the bill of lading was made out to his order. By the same token, the seller was found to have no interest in being the original party to it. This judgment is not without its difficulties. The fact that the bill is to the order of the buyer does not itself suffice to support that the buyer is the true shipper in unqualified form. Prima facie, it is the named shipper who is the original party to the contract under the bill of lading. In this case, there were no facts proving that the seller/named shipper had no commercial interest in the performance of the bill of lading contract. Nor was there any evidence indicating that the title to the goods passed on shipment to the buyer. For these reasons it is submitted that such a notion, in unqualified form, is highly unlikely to apply under English law. In support of this, the judgment in *The Roseline* was criticised in this regard by the House of Lords, where Lord Goff stated: 'There is doubt whether a similar conclusion [to *The Roseline*] would be reached in English law.'.[247] Lord Goff, having declined to apply *The Roseline* the case before him, considered an unreported case at the time (which was later reported): *The Athanasia Comninos.*[248]

Returning to *The Athanasia Comninos*, although the facts of the case appear to prove that the seller should have been regarded as agent in the present state of the authorities discussed above, when considering the question of on whom (the seller or the buyer) should liability arising from dangerous goods be imposed, it is submitted that the general approach taken by the courts should be set aside and Mustill J's decision should prevail. Therefore, the seller, as both wet and dry shipper, should assume responsibility. There is also a very recent case leaning towards the view that the named shipper may not be the true shipper under the bills of lading.[249] In *The MV Nortrader*,[250] there was a contract closely akin to an ex-works sale contract for a waste product known as 'unprocessed incinerator bottom ash' (UIBA) between the named shipper and the consignee in the bills of lading. Under the terms of the contract, the risk in and title to the goods passed to the consignee as soon as it was loaded onto his vehicles at the shipper's premises. The consignee was responsible for storing the cargo prior to shipment and for making the shipment arrangements. In the 33 bills of lading drawn up by the consignee's agent, the claimant was designated as the shipper. On each occasion, the consignee's agent would send a copy of the bills of lading to the named shipper who at no time objected to being described as the shipper. While the cargo was on board *The MV Nortrader*, an explosion occurred resulting in damage to the vessel. The carrier commenced arbitration proceedings to claim his losses from the named shipper. In denying the carrier's claims, the named shipper challenged the tribunal's jurisdiction, stating that he was not a party to the contract of carriage and he had been wrongly identified as the shipper in the bills of lading. However, the tribunal concluded that it had jurisdiction. Following this, the claimant/named

[247] *Spiliada Maritime Corporation v Cansulex Ltd (The Spiliada)* [1987] 1 Lloyd's Rep 1, 5.
[248] ibid, 5. See also Treitel and Reynolds, *Carver on Bills of Lading*, n 38 above, para 4-025.
[249] See generally, Gelgec, 'Identifying the Shipper under Bills of Lading', n 164 above.
[250] *MVV Environment Devonport Ltd v NTO Shipping GmbH & Co KG (The MV Nortrader)* [2020] EWHC 1371 (Comm).

shipper then applied to the Commercial Court for an order to set aside the tribunal's award. The court eventually held that neither the consignee nor his agent was expressly or impliedly authorised by the claimant/named shipper to enter into a contract of carriage. Thus, it was found that the claimant was not the true shipper under the bills of lading.[251]

As was the case in *The Athanasia Comninos*, the claimant/named shipper had not objected to being so designated in the bills of lading in *The MV Nortrader*. Having said that, *The MV Nortrader* should be distinguished on grounds of the unusual facts of the case. The contract in the case was closely akin to an ex-works contract, which has entirely different characteristics and features concerning duties related to shipment when compared to CIF and FOB sales. The named shipper was not under any duty to ship the goods on board the vessel. Neither did he undertake to make any necessary arrangements for shipment, as, contractually, it was the consignee that was responsible for arranging the shipments of the UIBA from the claimant's plant to the final destination, including chartering a vessel. Thus, from the moment that the UIBA was loaded onto the consignee's vehicles, it was under his control and all responsibilities in relation to loading on the vessel fell on the shoulders of the consignee and his agent. The named shipper took no part in shipment, nor did he instigate it beforehand. He had no nexus with the goods as soon as the UIBA was loaded onto the consignee's lorries. He also lost the title to the goods well before the shipment on board the vessel, namely at his own plant. Therefore, it was the consignee who bailed the cargo to the carrier. In this respect, *The MV Nortrader* should be distinguished from CIF and FOB cases, as the claimant had nothing to do with the goods prior to or during shipment, in contrast to CIF and FOB sellers' position at the shipment stage.[252]

Under CIF and many FOB sales,[253] the seller is under a duty to conclude the carriage contract evidenced in the bill of lading on behalf of the buyer on the usual terms[254] in the specific trade concerned, by providing all necessary precautions for safe carriage of the goods[255] and conferring substantial continuous protective rights throughout the voyage.[256,257] Under FOB contracts, as discussed above, the

[251] Gelgec, 'Identifying the Shipper under Bills of Lading', n 164 above, 229–30.

[252] ibid, 237–38.

[253] This is not the case where the buyer concludes the carriage contract under the bare FOB and sometimes under classic FOB sales. See sections II.B.(i) and (ii) above. See also Bridge, *Benjamin's Sale of Goods*, n 38 above, para 18-515.

[254] *Ceval Alimentos SA v Agrimpex Trading Co Ltd (The Northern Progress)* [1996] 2 Lloyd's Rep 319; *Tsakiroglou & Co v Noblee Thorl GmbH* [1961] 2 All ER 179; [1962] AC 93; *Finska Cellulosaforeningen (Finnish Cellulose Union) v Westfield Paper Co Ltd* (1940) 68 Ll L Rep 75; *TW Ranson Ltd v Manufacture d'Engrais et de Produits Industriels Antwerp* (1922) 13 Ll L Rep 205; *Burstall & Co v Grimsdale and Sons* (1906) 11 Com Cas 280.

[255] *Texas Instruments Ltd v Nason (Europe) Ltd* [1991] 1 Lloyd's Rep 146; *Gatoil International Inc v Tradax Petroleum Ltd (The Rio Sun)* [1985] 1 Lloyd's Rep 350; *Thomas Young and Sons Ltd v Hobson and Partners* (1949) 65 TLR 365; *BC Fruit Market Ltd v The National Fruit Co* (1921) 59 DLR 87.

[256] *Hansson v Hamel & Horley Ltd* [1922] 2 AC 36.

[257] By virtue of s 32(2) of the 1979 Act. For detailed analysis of s 32(2), see F Lorenzon, 'When is a CIF seller's Carriage Contract Unreasonable?' (2007) 13 *JIML* 241.

seller may take out the bill either in his own or the buyer's name. When the seller is named as the shipper with his consent and choice, then it would follow that the seller, as dry shipper, agrees to undertake all the necessary arrangements and obligations under the carriage contract in relation to shipment arrangements for the goods, including enabling the carrier to take all necessary precautions having regard to the nature and character of dangerous goods, even if he acts as agent of the buyer.[258] Also, as wet shipper, loading responsibilities are mostly allocated to the seller rather than the buyer. For instance, when the goods classified as dangerous in the IMDG Code are shipped, his duty does not end as soon as he puts the goods over the ship's rail. The seller, as the named shipper, not only is bound to provide a dangerous goods transport document containing all the necessary safety information required by the Code, but also undertakes to see that the goods are properly packed, marked and labelled. For instance, even if there is no express term in relation to shipment in the sale contract, the seller is bound to deliver the goods properly packed to withstand a normal voyage.[259] Before the goods are placed on board, he should also see to it that the costs in regard to customs duties prior to loading and harbour dues are cleared.[260]

This appears to prove that when the seller is both the wet and dry shipper, he becomes the leading actor of the shipment who has a direct nexus with the goods both physical and contractual. It would also follow that his knowledge in regard to the goods is superior to anyone else's, including the buyer of the goods. Whether it arises under the common law duty or the Rules, so far as dangerous goods are concerned, the carrier should be allowed to take all necessary precautions against the dangerous nature and character of the goods prior to shipment. This can be said to be directly related to the physical and contractual actions of the shipper. It should also follow that as both wet and dry shipper, the seller, when designated as the shipper in the bill, can be said to undertake to fulfil his duty to the carrier both physically and contractually, even if he acts as agent for the buyer. Therefore, despite the fact that the property has passed on shipment, it is submitted that the buyer/consignee – unless he takes part on or before shipment – as undisclosed principal (who is likely abroad somewhere else from the loading port), is unlikely to see the bill of lading until endorsement and delivery and neither ships nor sees

[258] Gelgec, 'Identifying the Shipper under Bills of Lading', n 164 above, 237.

[259] *A Hamson & Son (London) Ltd v S Martin Johnson & Co Ltd* [1953] 1 Lloyd's Rep 553, 554; *George Wills & Sons Ltd v Thomas Brown & Sons* (1922) 12 Ll LR 292; *Sime Darby & Co Ltd v Everitt & Co* (1923) 14 Ll LR 120. See also s 29(6) of the 1979 Act. The goods should be also in a merchantable state at the time of shipment to endure the voyage, see: *Mash & Murrell Ltd v Joseph I Emanuel Ltd* [1961] 1 WLR 862; [1961] 1 Lloyd's Rep 47; reversed on different grounds in the Court of Appeal [1961] 2 Lloyd's Rep 326. See also A Gelgec, 'Identifying the Shipper under Bills of Lading', n 164 above, 237.

[260] *Port of Brisbane Authority v Santos Ltd* [1988] 1 Qd R 645. Indeed, under FOB sales, such responsibilities can be allocated onto the buyer as well: *Attorney-General v Walford (Leopold) Ltd* (1923) 14 Ll L Rep 359.

the goods, and thus should not become liable for damage and loss resulting from the acts or faults of the seller who is both the wet and dry shipper.[261]

Put differently, the seller/named shipper, as the source of the defect, should not be allowed to escape liability resulting from his actions just because he has lost his interest in being party to the contract on shipment in consequence of the passage of property. Given that liability for dangerous goods originates from the contract, and not from the proprietary interest of the shipper in the goods, even if the facts prove that the seller acts as agent for the buyer, the decision of Mustill J imposing liability for dangerous goods on the seller/named shipper rather than the buyer should be followed and preferred on the grounds discussed above.

III. Conclusion

The purpose of this chapter has been to discuss the questions of whether it is the seller or the buyer as the shipper who attracts liability arising from dangerous goods under FOB and CIF sales, and whether the law as it stands is ideal. Although the discussion has shown that it is not entirely possible to find a single rule under CIF and FOB contracts, it is submitted that in most situations, liability for dangerous is associated more with the seller than the buyer. So far as CIF sales are concerned, there is no difficulty in generalising that it is almost invariably the seller, as both wet and dry shipper, who is subject to this liability vis-à-vis the carrier. Even if he is regarded as agent of the buyer in making the carriage contract, which would be a very exceptional case under CIF sales, this will not relieve him of liability to the carrier. Unlike in CIF sales, it is very difficult to conclude a single inflexible result under FOB contracts. Under bare and classic FOB sales, where the buyer concludes the contract and is named as the shipper in the bill, there is no doubt that the buyer becomes subject to liability under the contract. The non-contracting seller under FOB sales can be party to a separate implied contract with the carrier. Indeed, the courts may feel reluctant to impose dangerous goods liability on the seller under this contract, but it is suggested that the seller should not be allowed to avoid liability, particularly where his actions are the source of damage and loss and the buyer is not worth suing. In such cases, the courts should show some readiness to hold him liable under the implied contract. At any rate, even if the carrier does not appear to have fully grasped the potential tort claims for damages arising from dangerous goods, the case law shows that the non-contracting seller can have this liability imposed on him where he is the source of the fault or negligence. Carriers should be encouraged and should not be denied redress against the seller in tort, when necessary.

[261] Gelgec, 'Identifying the Shipper under Bills of Lading', n 164 above, 237.

Under both classic and FOB. 'with additional duties' contracts, where the seller makes the carriage contract and is named as the shipper in the bill, when the seller has no interest in being party to the carriage contract on shipment, the courts appear to have adopted an approach that the seller may have been named as the shipper in the contract as agent of the buyer, and accordingly the bill of lading can be said to evidence a contract only between the buyer and the carrier. However, when considering liability arising from dangerous goods, this approach may have been justifiably set aside and the courts would appear to be inclined to deem the seller/named shipper liable as principal rather than the buyer, even if the facts of the case prove otherwise.

5

Transfer of Liability from the Seller to the Buyer under the Contract

I. General

In Chapter four, it was discussed that in all CIF sales and variations thereon, almost invariably the contract of carriage is concluded by the seller, and liability arising from dangerous goods is imposed on him accordingly. It is also often the case that under f.o.b. sales – except in bare f.o.b. and some classic type f.o.b. sales – the seller, not the buyer is designated as the shipper in the contract of carriage, and attracts liability as the shipper of the goods thereunder.[1] At first sight, it might be presumed that the buyer who is not the shipper of the goods would not be liable for such goods, since he is not party to that carriage contract. However, this may not be always the case.

When parties contract on shipment terms, the sale contract is not the only agreement that traders become party to. As shown in Chapter four, one of the parties under the sale contract must also conclude a contract of carriage, which forms a crucial part of the functioning of CIF and FOB sales. Under CIF and often FOB sales, alongside performing his physical obligations, the seller performs his duty to make a reasonable carriage contract on behalf of the buyer[2] and subsequently tenders the bill of lading evidencing this contract to the buyer. Then, he becomes entitled to payment from the buyer. Thereafter, the seller is unlikely to harbour any interest in keeping the carriage contract. The risk in the goods remains with the buyer while the goods are in transit.[3] All the practical interest in being party to that carriage contract therefore lies with the buyer after that moment. Similarly, carriers may wish to have contractual rights against the buyer/cargo owners. However, given the doctrine of privity of contract established

[1] *Pyrene & Co. v Scindia Steam Navigation Co* [1954] 2 QB 402; *Wimble v Rosenberg & Sons* [1913] 3 KB 743; *The El Amria and The El Minia* [1982] 2 Lloyd's Rep 28; *Concordia Trading BV v Richco International Ltd* [1991] 1 Lloyd's Rep 475; *Scottish & Newcastle Int'l Ltd v Othon Ghalanos Ltd* [2008] UKHL 11; [2008] 1 Lloyd's Rep 462.

[2] The Sale of Goods Act 1979, s 32(2).

[3] *The Julia* [1949] AC 293; *Pyrene Co Ltd v Scindia Steam Shipping Co* [1954] 2 QB 402; *Scottish & Newcastle Int'l Ltd v Othon Ghalanos Ltd* [2008] UKHL 11; [2008] 1 Lloyd's Rep 462. This is also the case for the buyer to whom the goods are sold afloat in string sales before arrival.

under English law,[4] the buyer will not be able to sue or be sued under the carriage contract that has been concluded on his behalf, however firmly linked with it he is.[5] The contractual gap between the buyer and the carrier was first bridged statutorily by the Bills of Lading Act 1855 (the 1855 Act), which was repealed by the 1992 Act,[6] because the former did not meet up-to-date trading conditions and contained deficiencies.[7] The 1992 Act statutorily makes it possible for the buyer who is not the shipper to become party to the carriage contract. English law, in terms of the contract of carriage, is based on the principle of mutuality which is not only concerned with the transfer of rights, but also with the imposition of contractual liabilities.[8] This position is also preserved under the 1992 Act, which accordingly not only enables the transfer of rights but also liabilities thereunder from the shipper to the transferee. The practical question calling for a detailed discussion that will form the main substance of this chapter is whether liability arising from dangerous goods is transmissible from the shipper/seller to the buyer/transferee under the carriage contract by means of the 1992 Act and, if so, whether the proposition can be justified.[9] We shall also look into how the imposition mechanism operates under the 1992 Act, particularly in relation to liability for dangerous goods, and whether the buyer can be divested of liability – or there could be irreversible dead ends for the buyer – when imposed.

[4] *Tweddle & Atkinson* (1861) 1 B & S 393; *Effort Shipping Co Ltd v Linden Management SA (The Giannis NK)* [1998] AC 605, 616.

[5] *Thompson v Dominy* (1845) 14 M & W 403, 407; 153 ER 532, 534; *Howard v Shepherd* (1850) 9 CB 297, 319; 137 ER 907, 916. See also *Dunlop Pneumatic Tyre Co Ltd v Selfridge & Co Ltd* [1915] AC 847, 853. The transfer of the bill of lading enables the buyer to have the document of title, which gives constructive possession and may also enable him to obtain the title to the goods, if intended. See *Lickbarrow v Mason* (1794) 5 Term Rep 683. See also *Sewell v Burdick* (1884) 10 App Cas 74.

[6] Repealed by s 6(2) of the Carriage of Goods by Sea Act 1992. Although this is outside the scope of this book, for the defects and the solutions created under the 1855 Act, see generally: *Sewell v Burdick* (1884) 10 App Cas 74; *The San Nicholas* [1976] 1 Lloyd's Rep 8; *The Sevonia Team* [1983] 2 Lloyd's Rep 640; *Enichem Anic SpA and Others v Ampelos Shipping Co Ltd (The Delfini)* [1990] 1 Lloyd's Rep 252; *The Aramis* [1989] 1 Lloyd's Rep 213; *Brandt v Liverpool, Brazil & River Plate Steam Navigation Co Ltd* [1924] 1 KB 575; *Cremer v General Carriers (The Dona Mari)* [1974] 1 WLR 341; *The Aliakmon* [1986] AC 785; *Compania Portorafti Commerciale SA v Ultramar Panama Inc (The Captain Gregos) (No 2)* [1990] 2 Lloyd's Rep 395; *Mitsui & Co Ltd v Novorossiysk Shipping Co (The Gudermes)* [1993] 1 Lloyd's Rep 311; *Concord Petroleum Corp v Gosford Marine Panama SA (The Albazero)* [1977] AC 774 (HL); *Margarine Union GmbH v Cambay Prince Steam Ship Co Ltd (The Wear Breeze)* [1967] 2 Lloyd's Rep 219; [1969] 1 QB 219; *Compania Continental del Peru SA v Evelpis Shipping Corporation (The Agia Skepi)* [1992] 2 Lloyd's Rep 467.

[7] In order to resolve the issue as to privity of contract in general contract law, the Contracts (Rights of Third Parties) Act 1999 was enacted. However, the Act makes clear that it is not applicable to contracts of carriage: ss 6(5)(a) and 6(6). The Act also does not affect *liabilities* of third parties in general.

[8] *Borealis AB v Stargas Ltd and Others (The Berge Sisar)* [2001] UKHL 17; [2002] AC 205, [31] and [45]. See also Law Commission, *Rights of Suit in Respect of Carriage of Goods by Sea* (Law Com No 196, Scot Law Com No 130, 1991) para 3.22.

[9] As the 1992 Act only deals with the imposition of *contractual* liabilities, the seller's potential dangerous goods liability in *tort* is not transmissible from the seller to the buyer under the 1992 Act. For a discussion of the potential common law actions against the buyer outside of the contract, with regard to liability for dangerous goods, see generally, Chapter 6.

The enactment of the 1992 Act has also led the other major Commonwealth countries to consider reforming their corresponding domestic legislation. Singapore,[10] New Zealand[11] and Hong Kong[12] adopted the 1992 Act verbatim. In Australia, the Australian States enacted the 1992 Act using different techniques either verbatim or by way of incorporation into their domestic legislation.[13] On the other hand, while the 1992 Act inspired the South African legislators in reforming their domestic legislation, the 1992 Act is substantially different from its South African counterpart, though some similarities exist.[14] As for Canada, it is the only major Commonwealth country that still makes use of the 1855 Act in its domestic legislation. So far as the imposition of liability for dangerous goods is concerned in these countries, there appears to be no reported case that has ever tested this under their corresponding domestic legislation as of yet.[15] Therefore, it is impossible to draw comparisons from these countries with English law. Having been inspired by the 1992 Act, it is, however, probable that much of the content in English law on the point could prove influential on the approach to be adopted in these jurisdictions, when (if ever) a case comes before their courts.

II. Contractual Transfer of Liability

A. Carriage of Goods by Sea Act 1992

Unlike in the 1855 Act, liabilities are not automatically imposed at the same time as rights are acquired under the 1992 Act.[16] The 1992 Act is composed of six sections and applies to a broad range of shipping documents; namely, sea waybills, delivery orders and bills of lading.[17] However, since the focus of this chapter is

[10] By virtue of the Application of English Law Act 1994.

[11] By virtue of the Mercantile Law Amendment Act 1994. The exception is s 4 of the 1992 Act.

[12] By virtue of the Bills of Lading and Analogous Shipping Document Ordinance 1993.

[13] Sea-Carriage Documents Act 1996 (Qld); Sea-Carriage Documents Act 1997 (NSW); Sea-Carriage Documents Act 1997 (Tas); Sea-Carriage Documents Act 1997 (WA); Sea-Carriage Documents Act 1998 (SA); Sea-Carriage Documents Act 1998 (Vic). On this, see generally S Girvin, 'Carriage by Sea: the Sea Transport Documents Act 2000 in Historical and Comparative Perspective' (2002) 119 *South African Law Journal* 317, 339–40.

[14] Sea Transport Documents Act No 65 of 2000. For a detailed analysis on this, see generally S Girvin, 'Carriage by Sea: the Sea Transport Documents Act 2000 in Historical and Comparative Perspective' (2002) 119 *South African Law Journal* 317.

[15] In Australia, the New South Wales Court of Appeal considered that so far as rights of suit and imposition of liabilities are concerned, the Sea-Carriage Documents Act 1997 (NSW) is substantially the same as the 1992 Act: *Cro Travel Pty Ltd v Australia Capital Financial Management Pty Ltd* [2018] NSWCA 19, [52].

[16] See ss 2 and 3 of the 1992 Act.

[17] The 1855 Act would only apply to shipped bills of lading. It was not entirely evident whether the 1855 Act would have applied also to the received bill. There were also contradictory views from the courts on whether the received bills are documents of title. See *The Marlborough Hill* [1921] AC 444

only on the transfer of dangerous goods liability from the seller to buyer, only the sections relevant to that will be discussed here.[18] Section 3 prescribes the imposition mechanism for contractual liabilities, in which it expressly imposes those liabilities on 'the person in whom rights are vested by virtue of' section 2.[19] This explicitly makes section 2 a preliminary condition of the imposition of liabilities under the Act. Therefore, before discussing whether this liability is transmissible from the seller to the buyer under section 3, the preliminary discussion in this part will deal with section 2 to see under what circumstances the buyer can be the person 'in whom rights are vested'.

B. The Buyer 'In Whom Rights are Vested'

Section 1(1) of the 1992 Act states the shipping documents that the Act applies to, which are any bill of lading, any sea waybill and any ship's delivery order.[20] Bills of lading predominantly take the central role in the documents required under FOB and CIF contracts.[21] Sea waybills and delivery orders are important, but are only secondary to bills of lading, because they are acceptable documents under these sales only if they are so stipulated in the sale contract. Even though these documents are exhaustively listed in the 1992 Act, it is no doubt more generous than

and *Diamond Alkali Export Corp v Fl Bourgeois* [1921] 3 KB 443. Apparently, the 1855 Act did not apply to straight bills of lading either. See the Law Commission Report, n 8 above, paras 5.8 and 5.10. But see also *The Rafaela S* [2005] 2 AC 423. Although, a bill of lading is not defined in the Act, it is not entirely clear whether a multimodal transport document covering a non-sea element can be regarded as a bill of lading. See also D Faber, 'The Problems Arising from Multimodal Transport' (1996) *LMCLQ* 503, 515.

[18] A complete analysis of the 1992 Act is outside the scope of this book. For a detailed analysis of the 1992 Act with its predecessor, see generally: J Beatson and JJ Cooper, 'Rights of Suit in Respect of Carriage of Goods by Sea' (1991) *LMCLQ* 196; FMB Reynolds, 'The Carriage of Goods by Sea Act 1992' (1993) *LMCLQ* 436; N Curwen, 'The Problems of Transferring Carriage Rights: an Equitable Solution' [1992] *JBL* 245; T Howard, 'The Carriage of Goods by Sea Act 1992' (1993) 24 *JMLC* 181; G Humphreys and A Higgs, 'An Overview of the Implications of the Carriage of Goods by Sea Act 1992' [1993] *JBL* 61; R Bradgate and F White, 'The Carriage of Goods by Sea Act 1992' (1993) 56 *MLR* 188; B Reynolds, 'Further Thoughts on the Carriage of Goods by Sea Act 1992 (UK)' (1994) 25 *JMLC* 143; C Ferris, 'The Carriage of Goods by Sea Act 1992' (1992) 3 *ICCLR* 432; J Bassindale, 'Title to Sue under Bills of Lading: the Carriage of Goods by Sea Act 1992' (1992) *JIBL* 414; B Davenport, 'Reform to Bill of Lading Law – Some Implications for Banks' (1992) *JIBFL* 305. For a detailed analysis of the 1992 Act by the House of Lords, see *The Berge Sisar* [2001] UKHL 17, [28].

[19] See s 3(1) of the 1992 Act.

[20] An earlier version of this part of the chapter was published in A Gelgec, 'Separation of Actual and Physical Possession of Bills of Lading under English Law' in F Berlingieri and M Musi (eds), *Maritime, Port and Transport Law: Current Scenarios and Emerging Issues* (Bologna, Bonomo, 2017) 1.

[21] In respect of 'electronic bills of lading', s 1(5) of the 1992 Act shows that in the absence of legislative change, the Act does not normally apply to such bills of lading, given that it is not easy to apply the concepts like 'delivery', 'endorsement' or 'possession' to them. However, for electronic seaway bills and delivery orders, the very same problem may not arise, as they normally would not require delivery of the document to transfer contractual rights under the 1992 Act. See MG Bridge, *Benjamin's Sale of Goods*, 11th edn (London, Sweet & Maxwell, 2020) para 18-458. See also *Glencore International AG v MSC Mediterranean Shipping Co* [2017] EWCA Civ 365; [2017] 2 Lloyd's Rep 186.

its predecessor in this sense. The majority of the shipping documents commonly used under CIF and FOB sales are thus covered by the 1992 Act, although there are still some documents which may fall outside the scope of the Act such as mate's receipts[22] and merchant delivery orders[23] which are sometimes – albeit rarely – used in practice. For any document outside the ones listed by the Act, the 1992 Act will not provide any assistance.[24] Thus, a buyer holding a merchant delivery order will not fall within the application of the Act, and accordingly will not be open to incur liabilities under the 1992 Act, even if section 3 is triggered.

As stated before, by virtue of section 3(1), the imposition of this liability depends preliminarily upon whether the buyer acquired rights under these shipping documents. That is to say, unless rights within the scope of section 2 are transferred to the buyer, he would not have this liability imposed, on the basis that he would not become the person 'in whom rights are vested' for the purposes of section 3, even if such a buyer is considered as having triggered section 3(1) in a manner that makes him subject to liability for dangerous goods.

(i) *The Buyer Holding Bills of Lading*

The first of the three listed documents in section 1(1)(a) is 'any bill of lading'.[25] Although there is no complete definition[26] of bills of lading in the Act, it cannot be a document 'incapable of transfer either by endorsement or, as a bearer bill, by delivery without indorsement' for the purpose of the Act.[27] Thus, non-transferable bills such as straight bills of lading fall outside this restrictive definition.[28] On the other hand, received bills of lading are regarded as bills of lading in the statutory sense.[29]

Section 2(1)(a) prescribes statutory assignment of contractual rights:

> the lawful holder of a bill of lading … shall (by virtue of becoming the holder of the bill or, as the case may be, the person to whom delivery is to be made) have transferred to and vested in him all rights of suit under the contract of carriage as if he had been a party to that contract.[30]

[22] For an example of use of a mate's receipt, see *Kum v Wah Tat Bank Ltd* [1971] 1 Lloyd's Rep 439.

[23] Ship's delivery order is prescribed in s 1(4).

[24] For those documents, the common law actions, such as under the *Brandt v Liverpool* contract will be available though.

[25] Section 1(1)(a).

[26] It was discussed in the Law Commission Report that a complete definition could have been counter-productive. See Law Commission Report, n 8 above, para 2.50.

[27] Section 1(2)(a).

[28] Although straight bills fall within the sea waybill definition of the Act, which will be discussed below, straight bills are considered bills of lading for the purpose of the Hague & Hague-Visby Rules. See *The Rafaela S* [2005] 1 Lloyd's Rep 347.

[29] Section 1(2)(b). See also the Law Commission Report, n 8 above, para 2.48.

[30] Once the lawful holder obtains rights under the bill of lading contract, he also becomes party to the arbitration agreement incorporated into the bill, regardless of its separate and independent existence from the matrix contract contained in the bill of lading; *Sea Master Shipping Inc v Arab Bank (Switzerland)* [2018] EWHC 1902; [2019] 1 Lloyd's Rep 101. On the case, see generally, A Gelgec, 'Banks' Liability for Demurrage' (2018) 18 *Lloyd's Shipping & Trade Law* 5.

To become assignee, the buyer should thus become a 'lawful holder' for the purpose of the Act.[31] However, there appears to be no assistance in the wording of the section on what 'the lawful holder' is. The interpretations are provided by the Act in section 5(2):

> (a) a person with possession of the bill who, by virtue of being the person identified in the bill, is the consignee of the goods to which the bill relates;
> (b) a person with possession of the bill as a result of the completion, by delivery of the bill, of any indorsement of the bill or, in the case of a bearer bill, of any other transfer of the bill;
> (c) a person with possession of the bill as a result of any transaction by virtue of which he would have become a holder falling within paragraph (a) or (b) above had not the transaction been effected at a time when possession of the bill no longer gave a right (as against the carrier) to possession of the goods to which the bill relates;
>
> and a person shall be regarded for the purposes of this Act as having become the lawful holder of a bill of lading wherever he has become the holder of the bill in good faith.

It would be convenient to summarise the positions described in these sub-sections. Paragraph (a) defines the consignee in possession of an order bill.[32] Paragraph (b) covers both endorsee and bearer in possession, whilst (c) refers to a particular class of holders of a spent bill of lading[33] who would normally have fallen within (a) or (b). All these paragraphs start with 'a person with possession of the bill'. Thus, the inference is that to be a 'holder' within the statutory sense, the holder must also have possession of the bill.

(a) Relationship between the Holder and Possession

In the first of the situations above, which is defined in (a), there is no difficulty in ascertaining who is the holder of a bill of lading. Once the bill of lading is transferred to the buyer who is named as consignee in the bill, he will become the lawful holder within the meaning of the Act.[34] He will not be considered to be in possession of the bill until the moment of obtaining the bill.[35] Unlike under paragraph (a),

[31] Such an assignment covers the rights that existed even before being lawful holder: *Monarch Steamship Co Ltd v A/B Karlshamns Oljefabriker* [1949] AC 196, 218. See also Sir Bernard Eder et al, *Scrutton on Charterparties and Bills of Lading*, 24th edn (London, Sweet & Maxwell, 2019) para 3-015.

[32] It is to be assumed that this is the consignee of an order bill; otherwise it would not fall within the category of 'any bills of lading'.

[33] Section 5(2)(c) also covers the particular situations in which the goods become total loss. See below, and *Primetrade AG v Ythan Ltd (The Ythan)* [2005] EWHC 2399 (Comm); [2006] 1 All ER 367, [71].

[34] This is the case even if the buyer receives the bill from parties other than the original party to the bill: *UCO Bank v Golden Shore Transportation Pte Ltd* [2005] 2 SLR 735; affirmed in [2005] SGCA 42 (Singapore). *East West Corp v DKBS AF 1912 A/S* [2003] EWCA Civ 83; [2003] QB 1509. The consignee was the lawful holder for the purpose of the Act, despite the fact that the consignee was acting as agent of the shipper.

[35] *Gulf Interstate Oil Corporation LLC and the Coral Oil Co Ltd v Ant Trade and Transport Ltd of Malta (The Giovanna)* [1999] 1 Lloyd's Rep 867. Rix J, however, held that an endorsee or consignee could be holder from the moment of the endorser or shipper's disengagement from the bill. Thus,

merely obtaining possession of the bill may not be sufficient to be considered the holder under section 5(2)(b). A person becomes holder of the bill under paragraph (b) 'as a result of the completion, by delivery of the bill, of any indorsement of the bill or, in the case of a bearer bill, of any other transfer of the bill'.[36] There are two groups of holders under this paragraph. The first group encompasses bills 'made out to order'. A person can be a holder only if the bill is endorsed to that person and that bill is delivered to him. Alternatively, that order bill may have been later endorsed in blank,[37] in which case further endorsement is not necessarily required. Mere delivery would suffice to make the person in possession of the bill the 'holder' for the purpose of the paragraph. In the second group, the bill of lading could also be a bearer bill where endorsement is not required, as with order bills endorsed in blank. In this respect, a person becomes a holder once the bill is transferred to him. However, in a Singaporean case it was held that when a bill endorsed in blank is later filled with the name of a consignee by the holder, further endorsement is required by that designated consignee of the bill, if the bill is transferred to another subsequent party.[38]

On the other hand, mere physical custody of the bill may not be sufficient to consider the possessor as the holder for the purpose of the Act. In *The Aegean Sea*,[39] A sold goods to B who in turn sold them to C, which was the associate company of B. The bill of lading was made out to the order of A. A, instead of endorsing the bill to B's order, mistakenly endorsed it to C and delivered it to B who later forwarded the bill to C. Nevertheless, C did not accept the bill and returned it to A for re-endorsement.[40] Thomas J held that C did not become the holder under section 5(2)(b), on the basis that C did not have the possession of the bill 'as a result of completion of an endorsement by delivery'. The first rationale given by Thomas J was that there was no acceptance of delivery of the bill on the part of C. This proves that the requisite intent should not only be on the part of the transferor (A), but the transferee (C) should also have the requisite intent to become

once the endorser or the shipper gives the bill to an independent courier for dispatch, the consignee or endorsee may be considered to be in possession of the bill. There is rightful criticism over this view. Where the shipper or endorser is in a position to cancel delivery despite disengagement from the bill, it is difficult to construe that the consignee or endorsee will be in possession of the bill. See N Gaskell, R Asariotis and Y Baatz, *Bills of Lading: Law and Contracts* (London, LLP, 2000), para 4.22.

[36] Indeed the passing of property is not an element of the requirements to transfer rights of suit under the new Act: *East West Corp v DKBS 1912* [2003] EWCA Civ 83; *Pace Shipping Co Ltd v Churchgate Nigeria Ltd (The Pace)* [2010] 1 Lloyd's Rep 183.

[37] As was the case in *The Aramis* [1989] 1 Lloyd's Rep 213.

[38] *Keppel Tattel Bank Ltd v Bandung Shipping Private Ltd* [2003] 1 Lloyd's Rep 619.

[39] *The Aegean Sea* [1998] CLC 1090; [1998] 2 Lloyd's Rep 39.

[40] No re-endorsement was necessary by C, since he was not the holder for the purpose of the Act: [1998] 2 Lloyd's Rep 39, 61. Re-endorsement is necessary only where a previous holder is redelivered the bill by a subsequent lawful holder. Otherwise he will not be the holder for the purposes of the Act. See *East West Corp v DKBS 1912* [2003] QB 1509, [19].

the holder of the bill.[41] The second rationale, which was the error made by A in endorsement, suggests that the chain of endorsement should match the chain of sale contracts. In this case, the sale chain was in a row of A–B–C, whereas the endorsement omitted B. However, endorsement of the bill should have mirrored the chain of sales, which was A–B–C respectively. This is to say, it should have been endorsed by A to B instead of directly to C. A question that arises at this point is whether C would incur liability under the 1992 Act, if he had accepted such delivery of the bill, once section 3(1) was triggered. The mirroring between the chain of sale and endorsement suggests that he would not. This is because such acceptance would not be enough on its own to make C the holder within the meaning of the Act, given the non-fulfilment of the condition: 'as a result of the completion of an endorsement by delivery'.[42]

Section 5(2)(b) is best illustrated with examples. Assume that a chain of sale is A–B–C in a row. A endorses the bill to the order of B, but B only delivers the bill to C without further endorsement.[43] C accepts the delivery of the bill and somehow triggers section 3(1). There is the question of whether C would be subject to liability. The answer would be the same as in the previous example; despite existence of the requisite intent to be the holder, no liability would be imposed on C, given the lack of 'completion of an endorsement by delivery'. The bill should have been endorsed to him either in blank or to his order. Another important question calls for discussion. Suppose that there is a chain of sale A–B–C in a row. Without delivering it to B, A directly delivers a bearer bill or a bill, which was endorsed in blank to C. C accepts the bill and somehow triggers section 3(1). Would C incur liability under section 3(1) in this scenario? The proposition is that in the case of a bearer bill, it is not necessarily required that B should deliver the bill to C in order to fulfil section 5(2)(b). Accordingly A's direct delivery to C might suffice.[44] The inference is that since delivery of a bearer bill would suffice to make C the holder notwithstanding a further endorsement, A can deliver such a bill directly to C, omitting B.

Such a proposition is not without difficulties. Although there is no requirement of endorsement in the case of bearer bills, B may have had valid grounds to keep the bill against C. It is not uncommon under CIF and FOB sales that the seller wishes to retain the bill of lading until payment. In the example above, B could be a sub-seller, whereas C in return could become his buyer. C may not have paid B against the goods. For that reason, B would most likely wish to retain symbolic

[41] [1998] 2 Lloyd's Rep 39, 59–60.

[42] ibid.

[43] For a similar case, see *Compania Portorafti Commerciale SA v Ultramar Panama Inc (The Captain Gregos) (No 2)* [1990] 2 Lloyd's Rep 395.

[44] GH Treitel and FMB Reynolds, *Carver on Bills of Lading*, 4th edn (London, Sweet & Maxwell, 2017) para 5-022. In the case of a consignee, it is immaterial whether the bill is delivered by an original party or anyone else. See *Standard Chartered Bank v Dorchester LNG Ltd (The Erin Schulte)* [2014] EWCA Civ 1382, [16]. See also R Aikens, R Lord, MD Bools, *Bills of Lading*, 3rd edn (London, Informa, 2020) para 9.50 and *UCO Bank v Golden Shore* [2005] 2 SLR 735; affirmed in [2005] SGCA 42.

possession of the goods through the bill for security against C and, by way of keeping the bill, would also want to keep the title to the goods until payment.[45] In such a case, A's direct delivery to C might cause the loss of B's rights against C. Therefore, without proof of any agency relationship between A and B or requisite consent of B for delivery from A to C, A's direct delivery to C may not suffice to make C the holder for purposes of section 5(2)(b). Therefore, without being the party 'in whom rights are vested', it is unlikely that C would have liability under section 3 imposed on him.

Returning to the first part of Thomas J's reasoning in *The Aegean Sea*, even if there is a complete endorsement, acceptance of the bill into physical custody may not be sufficient to be holder, given that the transferee/buyer could lack the requisite intent to become holder. Once this is the case, the buyer may not be regarded as holder within the meaning of the Act from the moment of acceptance of physical custody of the bill. In *The Erin Schulte*,[46] the bills of lading endorsed to the name of a bank were delivered to it pursuant to a letter of credit. Although the bills were initially rejected by the bank due to some discrepancies, they were eventually held in the custody of the bank until further settlement. Following the settlement, the bank paid out pursuant to the letter of credit. The issue revolved around whether the bank had title to sue and it was significant whether it became lawful holder at the time of the bills' initial tender or after the settlement.[47] In the Court of Appeal, it was held that mere physical custody of the bills was not sufficient to become holder pursuant to the Act. Because the bank, due to discrepancies, at the time of initial tender, merely held the bills in its physical custody and, for the purpose of the Act, the endorser remained the holder until the moment of settlement, the bank could only be said to have had the requisite intent to be holder, following the settlement.[48]

The Erin Schulte may appear to qualify the concept of 'acceptance' of bills of lading. At first sight, it might seem that it complicates being a holder under the Act. However, it is arguable that a party cannot be forced to accept transfer of rights against his will.[49] *The Erin Schulte* proves that there might be a gap between the moment of having physical custody of the bill and the moment of forming the requisite intention, which could be crucial to determining whether the rights are transferred in pursuance of section 2. This gap could prove important to determine whether liability could be imposed on the buyer under section 3(1). Assume that A delivered to B an order or a bearer bill. As was the case in *The Erin Schulte*, due to some discrepancies, that bill was retained by B but B did not have

[45] *Scottish & Newcastle* [2008] UKHL 11, [20].

[46] *The Erin Schulte* [2014] EWCA Civ 1382. For the detailed analysis of the case both at first instance and in the Court of Appeal, see P Todd, 'Bank As Holder Under Carriage of Goods by Sea Act 1992' (2013) *LMCLQ* 275 and P Todd, 'Bank As Holder Under Carriage of Goods by Sea Act 1992' (2015) *LMCLQ* 155.

[47] The issue in relation to s 2(2)(a) is discussed below. See Section II.B.(i)(c).

[48] [2014] EWCA Civ 1382, [52].

[49] [2014] EWCA Civ 1382, [17].

any intent to become its holder. B, before becoming lawful holder within section 2, but while having physical custody of the bill, somehow triggered section 3 for dangerous goods liability. Would B be subject to liability under the 1992 Act? He would not have any liability imposed on him under section 3(1), since he would not be considered the person 'in whom rights are vested' for the purpose of section 2 at the moment when section 3 was triggered. A would still be considered the lawful holder for the sake of the 1992 Act, due to lack of requisite intent on the part of B.

(b) Separation of Actual and Physical Possession

It is not uncommon in international trade for one party to hold the bill for another, particularly considering the complex transaction schemes involving multiple parties. Freight forwarders, for example, may often claim delivery of the goods from the carrier on behalf of buyers, or insurers may obtain the bill of lading from the buyer to settle their claims. However, not every physical possessor of bills will always be considered a holder under the Act. Therefore, the question of whether the physical possessor of the bill or the buyer is the holder for the purpose of the Act could be vitally significant to ascertain whether liability can be imposed on the buyer under section 3(1), while somebody else holds the bill of lading.

The first determining factor is the way the bill of lading is issued or endorsed. In *The Aliakmon*,[50] which was a case under the 1855 Act, although the bill of lading named the buyer as consignee and it was in the physical custody of the buyer, no rights of suit were transferred to the buyer under the 1855 Act. This was because the buyer was held as agent of the seller in holding the bill, due to further agreement between them. The position, however, could be different under the 1992 Act. In one subsequent House of Lords case, it was found that the buyer in *The Aliakmon* would have had rights of suit under the 1992 Act had that legislation been in force at the time.[51] Some support for this can be found in *East West Corp*,[52] where the issue revolved around whether the seller/shipper had rights of suit under the 1992 Act. The bills were issued to the order of the consignee bank, which was regarded as agent of the sellers in holding the bills. However, at the Court of Appeal, which approved the judgment at first instance, it was held that the rights of suit under the bill of lading contract had been transferred to the consignee bank, even though the bank held the bills as agent for the seller. Therefore, the shipper/seller was held to have been divested of contractual rights pursuant to section 2(1).[53]

[50] [1986] AC 785.

[51] *White v Jones* [1995] 2 AC 207, 265. See also Bridge, *Benjamin's Sale of Goods*, n 21 above, para 18-271; *Carver on Bills of Lading*, n 44 above, para 5-023.

[52] *East West Corp v DKBS 1912* [2003] QB 1509.

[53] At first instance, Thomas J, in a holding that indicated the underlying reason of this decision was the simplification of the transferral of contractual rights by the 1992 Act. See [2002] 2 Lloyd's Rep 182, [22]; the case was approved at the Court of Appeal; *East West Corp v DKBS 1912* [2003] QB 1509. In the Law Commission Report, n 8 above, which led to the passing of this Act, such simplification was also suggested. See paras 2.24–2.27.

Unlike under the 1855 Act, it is therefore probable that a named consignee/buyer, despite holding the bill as agent for another party, would acquire rights of suit under the 1992 Act. The position would likely be the same where the buyer was not a consignee but an endorsee. Therefore, since he would be regarded as holder under section 2(1), where the bill of lading is consigned or endorsed to the order of his own name, holding the bill as agent of another party would be unlikely to prevent the buyer from incurring liability once section 3(1) is triggered. The position, however, could be less straightforward where the bill of lading is a bearer bill or endorsed in blank but held by someone else. This position was left untouched by the Court of Appeal in the *East West Corp* case.[54] In the case of a bearer bill or a bill endorsed in blank, the suggestion is that it is the buyer who is the holder for the purposes of the Act, if the agent holding the bill acts in a purely ministerial capacity.[55] If not, it would be the agent who could be the holder for the purpose of the Act. However, the position is less clear where a bearer bill or a bill endorsed in blank is handed over to an independent contractor of the buyer.[56] The proposition is that physical possession and actual possession can be divorced where the bill of lading is endorsed in blank or it is a bearer bill, since in the Act, there is no definition of possession.[57] This proposition was rejected by Mance LJ in *East West Corp* in the Court of Appeal.[58] Nonetheless, Mance LJ's decision concerned a bill that was directly consigned to the order of an agent. Indeed, actual and physical possession of the bill that is consigned or endorsed to the name of an agent would be unlikely to be divorced. However, it is submitted that in the case of a bearer bill or a bill indorsed in blank, this proposition may survive in the light of *The Erin Schulte*. There the bank retained the bill and it was the endorser not the bank who was the holder within the meaning of the Act until the moment of settlement, since the latter was not holding the bill with the intent of being holder within the meaning of the Act. This is to say, although it was the bank that had the physical possession of the bill, it was the endorser who had actual possession for the purpose of the 1992 Act.

In *The Erin Schulte*, at first instance, Teare J observed that delivery 'is a bilateral act not a unilateral act'.[59] Also, the Court of Appeal gave importance to the necessary intent of both parties. In support of this, in the Singaporean case of *The Dolphina*, where there was an element of fraud in the endorsement of the bill of lading prior to delivery, it was held that endorsements should be valid for the purpose of the wording 'any endorsement' in section 5(2)(b).[60] It is therefore

[54] [2003] EWCA Civ 83, [16].

[55] Treitel and Reynolds, *Carver on Bills of Lading*, n 44 above, para 5-027.

[56] ibid.

[57] ibid.

[58] *East West Corp* [2003] EWCA Civ 83.

[59] *Standard Chartered Bank v Dorchester LNG (2) Ltd (The Erin Schulte)* [2013] EWHC 808 (Comm); [2013] 2 Lloyd's Rep 388, 34.

[60] *The Dolphina* [2011] SGHC 273; [2012] 1 Lloyd's Rep 304.

submitted that a similar intent is also needed on the part of the possessor of the bill of lading when transferring the bill to a prospective holder. That said, it does not always appear to be easy to ascertain whether the holder for the purpose of the Act is the buyer or an independent contractor who may hold the bill in such cases.[61] In *The Ythan*, the facts are complex but the relevant parts are as follows. The holder bank, after the sinking of the vessel, delivered the bearer bills to the buyers' insurance brokers. The bills were in the physical custody of the brokers in order to settle the claim of the buyers under the bills. Aikens J held that the brokers were holding the bills on behalf of the buyers and it was the buyers, not the brokers, who would be the holders for the purpose of the Act.[62] Although the insurers were independent contractors, they had physical possession of the bill only in order to settle the claim of the buyers. Under these circumstances, it can be sometimes difficult to find the required intent on the part of independent contractors to become holders within the meaning of the Act, especially where personal endorsement is lacking. Both *The Ythan* and *The Erin Schulte* show that separation of actual and physical possession appears to be possible under the 1992 Act. Accordingly, the buyer can be regarded as the holder for the purpose of the Act, even if somebody else has physical possession of the bills of lading.

A practical issue may arise at this point. It is not uncommon in trade practice for the buyer to hand over the bill to freight forwarders to claim delivery. Assume that the freight forwarder somehow triggers section 3(1) while claiming delivery on behalf of the buyer. Would the buyer be found liable under the Act? The answer to this question depends upon whether it is the freight forwarder or the buyer who is considered the holder for the purpose of the Act. Indeed, this assumption can be rebuttable depending on the facts of each case, but where the freight forwarder holds a bill which is a bearer one or endorsed in blank, it would be prima facie difficult to find requisite intent on the part of the forwarder to become holder, while his only duty is to claim the delivery of the goods on behalf of the buyer. Under such circumstances, the buyer prima facie can be considered holder under section 2(1) and for that reason incur liability under section 3(1). The position would be different if the bill was endorsed to the name of the forwarder. In the light of the *East West Corp* case, the freight forwarder would be likely to be exposed to liability according to section 3(1), even if he acted as agent of the buyer, since it would be him who became the holder for the purposes of the Act.[63] However, the position would be more straightforward where the bill is endorsed to the buyer's

[61] See *The Aramis* [1989] 1 Lloyd's Rep 213.

[62] *The Ythan* [2006] 1 Lloyd's Rep 457; [2005] EWHC 2399 (Comm). Eventually, the buyers were not held to be the holders for other reasons. See II.B.(i)(c) below.

[63] However the buyer would probably become liable alongside his agent. Albeit not strong, there might be some support in the authorities. In *East West Corp*, at first instance, Thomas J observed that even if the agent acquires rights of suit under the Act, those rights could be exercised by the principal as well: [2002] EWHC 83; [2002] 2 Lloyd's Rep 182, 193. See also Treitel and Reynolds, *Carver on Bills of Lading*, n 44 above, para 5-023 and Aikens et al, *Bills of Lading*, n 44 above, para 9.42. Therefore, if the buyer exercises those rights under the Act alongside his agent, he would fall within s 2(1), and accordingly might fall within the ambit of s 3 as well.

name but delivered to his agent forwarder.[64] In such a case, it would be the buyer who would attract the liability under section 3(1), on the ground that he would most likely preserve his position as the holder for the purpose of the Act.

(c) Spent Bills of Lading

The 1992 Act enables transfer of rights of suit under spent bills pursuant to section 2(2)(a) despite the fact that possession of the bill:

> no longer gives a right (as against the carrier) to possession of the goods to which the bill relates …
>
> (a) by virtue of a transaction effected in pursuance of any contractual or other arrangements made before the time when such a right to possession ceased to attach to possession of the bill …[65]

The question of what is a spent bill can be answered in two contexts. The first prescribes the bill of lading as a document of title, which gives constructive possession of the goods to its holder.[66] When it becomes spent, it ceases to operate as a document of title. The second concerns only the continuity of contractual rights of action. The 1992 Act only addresses the latter scenario; the transfer of contractual rights when the bill is spent.[67] The most obvious example of a spent bill is the delivery of the goods against surrender of the bill of lading to a party entitled to it. Section 2(2)(a) prescribes an exceptional situation in which to become the lawful holder of a spent bill. For instance, it is not uncommon in practice, especially in the oil trade, that in string sales the ultimate buyer may not have obtained the bill of lading before arrival of the vessel carrying his goods.[68] When this is the case, the buyer may claim his goods from the carrier against production of an indemnity letter.[69] As the buyer obtains the bill well after taking delivery of the goods,

[64] See Aikens et al, *Bills of Lading*, n 44 above, para 9.42.

[65] Since s 2(2)(a) prescribes the exception, the rights of suit under spent bills are still transferred by s 2(1) rather than s 2(2)(a).

[66] *Lickbarrow v Mason* (1787) 2 TR 63; (1793) 126 ER 511.

[67] See also *Overseas-Chinese Banking Corp Ltd v Owner and/or Demise Charterer of the Vessel Yue You 902 (The Yue You 902)* [2019] SGHC 106; [2019] 2 Lloyd's Rep 617.

[68] See *A/S Hansen-Tangens Rederi III v Total Transport Corp (The Sagona)* [1984] 1 Lloyd's Rep 194; *Mobil Shipping and Transportation Co v Shell Eastern Petroleum Ltd (The Mobil Courage)* [1987] 2 Lloyd's Rep 655.

[69] It is worth noting that the position of spent bills is a controversial matter under common law. The case law predominantly shows that bills of lading become spent, as the goods are delivered to the person entitled to them, notwithstanding production of the bill to the carrier. See *Barber v Meyerstein* (1870) LR 4 HL 317, 330; *The Delfini* [1990] 1 Lloyd's Rep 252, 269. The bills which were marked as 'accomplished' by the carrier were also held to be spent for the purpose of the Act. See *The David Agmashenebeli* [2002] EWHC 104 (Admlty); [2003] 1 Lloyd's Rep 92; [2002] 2 All ER 806, [204]. There are also counter arguments on the issue indicating that the bill of lading will not be spent until the goods are delivered against the production of the bill to the person entitled to them. Under the 1992 Act, although in *the East West Corp* at first instance, it was first held in favour of the former view, in the Court of Appeal, Diamond QC's view from *The Future Express* was freshened by Moor-Bick LJ in *The Erin Schulte*. The issue is still open to argue on either way. See Diamond QC's decision at first instance

the bill will have already been spent, and normally gives no rights to possession of the goods against the carrier. However, section 2(2)(a) enables such a buyer to obtain contractual rights against the carrier under the spent bill.

Although section 2(2)(a) deals with the exception when a party becomes the lawful holder of a spent bill, section 5(2)(c) interprets a spent bill holder as:

> a person with possession of the bill as a result of any transaction by virtue of which he would have become a holder falling within paragraph (a) or (b) above had not the transaction been effected at a time when possession of the bill no longer gave a right (as against the carrier) to possession of the goods to which the bill relates.

The issue with this paragraph is whether the buyer from a spent bill holder is potentially exposed to liability under section 3(1). Therefore, the scope of section 5(2)(c) calls for a preliminary discussion, before considering the operation of section 2(2)(a).

(aa) The Scope of Section 5(2)(c)

Section 5(2)(c) expands the meaning of lawful holder to spent bill holders who would have been regarded as holders either under paragraph (a) or (b), if they had obtained the bill at a time when possession of the bill would have given the right to possession of the goods to which the bill related. However section 5(2)(c) does not only cover the typical situation described above, where the goods are delivered without production of the bill to someone entitled who later obtains the bill. In *The Ythan*, the goods were lost at sea just after the commencement of the voyage. The court sought to determine whether the loss of goods rendered the bill spent pursuant to section 5(2)(c). Aikens J answered this question in the affirmative, indicating that there could not be any contractual rights under the bill of lading regarding goods that did not exist. In holding that, Aikens J referred to the Law Commission report on the 1992 Act which provided some direct assistance in relation to the scope of the paragraph:

> The words 'possession of the bill no longer gives a right … to possession of the goods' cover, inter alia, the case where delivery of the goods has been made and also the case where the goods are destroyed.[70]

Thus, for the purpose of the Act, pursuant to section 5(2)(c), a spent bill also covers situations where the possession of the bill would give no contractual rights to possession for goods that are lost. In *The Ythan*, the buyer nevertheless was

in *The Future Express* [1992] 2 Lloyd's Rep 79, 96, 100. The case was affirmed on other grounds: [1993] 2 Lloyd's Rep 542. See also *The Delfini* at first instance [1988] 2 Lloyd's Rep 599. See *East West Corp* [2002] 2 Lloyd's Rep 182, [35], [41]. See discussions also in the Court of Appeal [2003] QB 1509, [19]. See also *The Erin Schulte* [2014] EWCA Civ 1382, [53]; *The Ythan* [2006] 1 Lloyd's Rep 457, [67], [71].

[70] *The Ythan* [2005] EWHC 2399 (Comm), [67]. See also the Law Commission Report, n 8 above, 64–65. Aikens J also benefited from the speech of Lord Hobhouse in *The Berge Sisar* ([2001] UKHL 17), where his Lordship held that the Act deals with only the contractual rights: [2005] EWHC 2399 (Comm), [70].

not held to be the holder of the bill as per section 5(2)(c). The cargo of 'metallic HBI fines' was sold on f.o.b. terms but exploded during the course of the voyage due to the dangerous content of the cargo. The payment was under an irrevocable letter of credit. Before the explosion, 'to order' bills, indicating the seller as the shipper, were endorsed in blank by the buyer to the seller's bank. After the explosion occurred, the bills were held by the bank until the payment was made by the buyer. Following the payment, the buyer instructed the bank to deliver the bills to the buyer's insurance brokers so that they could settle the claim from the carrier's P & I Club. The carrier claimed damages arising out of the dangerous cargo from the buyer on the ground that he had triggered section 3(1). However, a preliminary issue before the court was whether the buyer would fall within section 5(2)(b) or (c), since the buyer should have been the person 'in whom rights are vested'. Aikens J held that the bills covering the goods that were lost were regarded as spent for the purpose of the Act. The case therefore fell within section 5(2)(c). The learned judge preliminarily found that the word 'transaction' in section 5(2)(c) only refers to the physical process, namely a transfer of the bill.[71] He went on to introduce a qualification to section 5(2)(c) and opined that the transferral of the bill from the bank to the buyer's insurers would not have occurred in the 'normal course of trading'.[72] In holding this, the learned judge contended that if the goods had not been lost, the bill would have stayed at the bank, and would not have been transferred to the broker. Accordingly, the buyer would not have become the holder pursuant to section 5(2)(b). On this ground, Aikens J eventually decided that the buyer was not the holder pursuant to section 5(2)(c), despite the fact that the learned judge said that the buyer's insurers were holding the bills on his behalf.

The requirement of occurrence in the 'normal course of trading'[73] is not without some difficulties in respect of both commercial practice and law. So far as commercial practice is concerned, it is not easy to explain why such a transaction would not be considered normal in commerce. Under CIF contracts, insurance contracts are an inseparable part of them. Under C&F and FOB contracts, although there is normally no insurance contract sold, the buyer either himself or through his agent may conclude his own insurance contract, as was the case in *The Ythan*. Although such explosions or accidents are not expected to happen under normal circumstances, insurance transactions against such risks should be considered normal in the course of trading, since the allocation of such insurable risks is done frequently in practice. In that respect, if such a qualification is correct, any

[71] *The Ythan* [2005] EWHC 2399 (Comm), [66].

[72] ibid, [80].

[73] See also Treitel and Reynolds, *Carver on Bills of Lading*, n 44 above, para 5-021; Bridge, *Benjamin's Sale of Goods*, n 21 above, para 18-270. See also S Baughen, 'Sue and be Sued? Dangerous Cargo and the Claimant's Dilemma' (2006) 5(4) *STLI* 14; F Reynolds QC, 'Bills of Lading and Voyage Charters' in R Thomas (ed), *The Evolving Law and Practice of Voyage Charterparties* (London, Informa, 2009), 210–11.

transaction could fall outside the 'normal course of trading', since what is normal in trade is liable to differ from one practice to another. For instance, any transaction occurring after loss of goods would indeed differ from what would normally occur if the goods were not lost. For that reason, they may not be regarded as being in the normal course of trading. If that is the correct approach, then section 5(2)(c) would be unlikely to apply to cases where the goods are lost. However, legislator are said to have clearly envisaged such transactions and enabled holders of a spent bill to become holders even in the case of loss of goods.

So far as the 1992 Act is concerned, the introduction of 'normal course of trading' could prove problematic as well. First, nothing in the 1992 Act indicates that such a qualification is required to become holder, nor is there any comment or recommendation on this in the Law Commission report. If section 5(2)(c) is qualified by this requirement, the operation of transfer of rights may involve some difficulties. The contractual rights under the 1992 Act are only transferred; they do not vanish. Section 2(5) clearly illustrates that the transfer of rights described in section 2(1) operates only by way of divestment. In *The Ythan*, first it was the bank that was holder for the purpose of the Act. However, once it lost pledge over the bills upon payment from the buyer, the bank delivered the bill to the buyer's brokers. Aikens J held that the bank was no longer the lawful holder from the moment of delivery of the bill to the brokers.[74] Therefore, contractual rights should have been transferred from the bank to another party, since the bank was held to be divested of its rights, and pursuant to section 2(5), divestment only operates by transfer of rights to a new holder. However, the buyer was not held to be holder due to the requirement of occurrence in the 'normal course of trading'. The buyer's insurers would not have been the holder either, because they retained the bill as agent of the buyer, as the learned judge found.[75] Owing to the requirement of 'normal course of trading', no party was regarded as holder for the purpose of the Act in *The Ythan*, although technically there should have been someone to acquire contractual rights, pursuant to section 2(5).[76] For these reasons, this requirement should be limited to the facts of the case, on the basis that such a restrictive approach to the interpretation of section 5(2)(c) seems to be inconsistent with the purpose of the Act.[77]

(bb) The Scope of Section 2(2)(a)

As stated above, the Act normally does not transfer contractual rights under spent bills save for the exceptions stipulated under section 2(2)(a): 'by virtue of a transaction effected in pursuance of any contractual or other arrangements made before the time when such a right to possession ceased to attach to possession of the bill.'[78]

[74] *The Ythan* [2005] EWHC 2399 (Comm), [77].
[75] ibid, [80].
[76] See S Baughen, 'Sue and be Sued? Dangerous Cargo and the Claimant's Dilemma' (2006) 5(4) *S&TLI* 14.
[77] See also Aikens et al, *Bills of Lading*, n 44 above, para 9.55 ff.
[78] Section 2(2)(b) is not directly relevant to the scope of this book.

When looking into the literal meaning of paragraph (a), it has been already said above that 'transaction' amounts to a physical process, which is the transfer of the bill of lading.[79] On the other hand, 'in pursuance of' provides a causal link between 'transaction' and 'contractual and other arrangements'.[80,81] According to the wording in the paragraph, to become a holder, those 'contractual or other arrangements' for transfer of the bill must have been concluded before the bill becomes spent.[82] Put differently, if those arrangements for transfer of the bill are finalised after the bill becomes spent, section 2(2)(a) will not apply.[83]

In *The Ythan*, Aikens J further held obiter that even if the buyer had fallen within section 5(2)(c), he would not have had rights of suit pursuant to section 2(2)(a). In holding that, the learned judged looked for the 'reason or cause' of the transfer of the bills from the bank to the buyer's insurance brokers due to the fact that there must be a link ('in pursuance of') between the transfer and contractual or other arrangements.[84] He applied 'the immediate reason and proximate cause' test to find the reason for the transaction, and subsequently found that the 'ex gratia' payment regarding the loss of the cargo was the immediatc reason and proximate cause of the transfer.[85] The proposed or actual compromise agreement for this payment was completed well after the loss of the goods. Therefore, the learned judge held obiter that the buyer would not have fallen within section 2(2)(a), on the ground that transfer of the bill was made in pursuance of an agreement that was completed well after the bill became spent for the purpose of the Act.[86]

However, in *The Erin Schulte*, Aikens J's narrow test was not followed by the Court of Appeal. A quantity of gasoil was sold which was on board *Erin Schulte*. Since the payment was under a letter of credit, the seller presented the documents to the confirming bank. The bank did not honour the letter of credit due to discrepancies but did not return the bill either. Prior to the further settlement

[79] Although Aikens J made this ruling on the word 'transaction' from s 5(2)(c), there is no reason why his decision should not cover the word 'transaction' in s 2(2)(a).

[80] There is no definition of 'contractual and other arrangements' in the Act. It is, however, suggested that a 'transaction' can even occur in pursuance of a gift: Treitel and Reynolds, *Carver on Bills of Lading*, n 44 above, para 5-067.

[81] *The Ythan* [2005] EWHC 2399 (Comm); *The Pace* [2010] 1 Lloyd's Rep 183.

[82] The transaction has to be 'called for' by the 'contractual or other arrangements': *The David Agmashenebeli* [2002] EWHC 104 (Admlty); [2003] 1 Lloyd's Rep 92, 118. But for a broader view where it was held that s 2 (2) does not require a prior contractual entitlement, see: *The Pace* [2010] 1 Lloyd's Rep 183, [48].

[83] It would probably not cover situations where the transfer of the bill was made in pursuance of the 'contractual and other arrangements', which were essentially varied and regarded as new contract after the bill of lading becomes spent for the purpose of the Act, even though their original versions were made well before: *The David Agmashenebeli* [2002] EWHC 104 (Admlty); [2003] 1 Lloyd's Rep 92; [2002] 2 All ER 806, [206].

[84] *The Ythan* [2005] EWHC 2399 (Comm), [84].

[85] This test was followed later by Teare J in *The Pace*, although he indicated that s 2(2)(a) should not be confined to cases only where there is particular contractual entitlement: *The Pace* [2010] 1 Lloyd's Rep 183, [48].

[86] ibid, [84]–[85].

of the issue between the seller and bank, the goods were delivered to the buyer pursuant to the instruction of the seller. The bank was held to be holder of the bill not at the time of acceptance of the physical custody of it but upon this further settlement, which was made well after the delivery of the goods.[87] The bank sued the carrier for misdelivery of the goods. The issue therefore revolved around whether the bank had rights of suit under the 1992 Act by virtue of section 2(2)(a). At first instance, Teare J applied a different test, which was broader than Aikens J's. The test was the 'real and effective cause' of the transaction, and he found that the relevant 'contractual or other arrangement' which was the cause of the transfer of the bill was the letter of credit, not the further settlement between the seller and bank.[88] This decision was upheld by the Court of Appeal but on much wider grounds. Moore-Bick LJ did not contend that the concept of 'real and effective cause' provided any assistance on the matter, and subsequently rejected its application. Instead, he preferred '… simply to identify the arrangement, if any, pursuant to which the transfer was made.'[89]

In *The Ythan*, the buyer was sued by the carrier and the issue was whether the buyer could be held liable under the 1992 Act, whilst in *The Erin Schulte* it was the carrier who was sued by the bank. Perhaps Aikens J applied this narrow test to allow the buyer/transferee to avoid liability for dangerous goods[90] but it is submitted that section 2(2)(a) should not be interpreted arbitrarily on the basis of underlying reasons to trigger it. The test should not vary depending on whether the holder is to sue or to be sued. Nothing in the Act or the Law Commission report indicates that section 2(2)(a) should apply more restrictedly to cases where the potential lawful holder can subsequently have liability imposed on him under the 1992 Act than where it would be him suing the carrier. It is arguable that this broader approach should prevail over the narrow test of Aikens J in *The Ythan*.[91] Teare J in *The Pace* indicated that the underlying policy of section 2(2)(a) is to avoid trafficking in bills of lading after the bill becomes spent.[92] However, the test in *The Ythan* does not provide any assistance to prevent trafficking in bills but, on the contrary, restricts the rights of action of spent bill holders provided by the Act.

[87] See section II.B(i)(b) above.

[88] [2013] 2 Lloyd's Rep 338, [68], [68], [74].

[89] [2014] EWCA Civ 1382, [56]; [2015] 1 Lloyd's Rep 97, [56]. Moor-Bick J indicated that the bill did not become spent where the goods are delivered to the party entitled to without production of bill of lading. At first sight, this argument would seem to assist the holders of the bills to become holder without proving to fall within s 2(2)(a). However, this would reduce the effect of s 2(2), since the bill will not become spent except for the fact that the goods are only delivered against production of the bill to the party entitled to them. Within the purpose of s 2(2), which is to avoid trafficking of the bills of lading, the bill of lading should become spent for the purpose of the Act, when the goods are delivered to the party entitled to.

[90] See Treitel and Reynolds, *Carver on Bills of Lading*, n 44 above, para 5-025.

[91] On this see also Baughen, n 76 above; P Todd, 'Bank As Holder Under Carriage of Goods by Sea Act 1992' (2013) *LMCLQ* 275 and P Todd, 'Bank As Holder Under Carriage of Goods by Sea Act 1992' (2015) *LMCLQ* 155.

[92] *The Pace* [2010] 1 Lloyd's Rep 183, [48]. See also the Law Commission Report, n 8 above, para 2.43.

It is also arguable that 'other arrangements' –which connotes a wider range of transactions – is adjacent to 'any contractual or' in section 2(2)(a) in order to interpret broadly the potential reason for the transfer of the bill. In this regard, *The Erin Schulte* provides a better interpretation and application of section 2(2)(a). In any case, Aikens J's reasoning was only obiter on the test of 'immediate reason and proximate cause'. Put differently, so far as his narrow test is concerned, his decision is therefore unlikely to stand in the light of the Court of Appeal's decision concerning the wider test for section 2(2)(a), which was part of the ratio in the judgment.[93]

Following the judgment in *The Erin Schulte*, if a similar case arose today, it is probable that the buyers in *The Ythan* would have been transferred rights of action pursuant to section 2(2)(a). This is because the compromise agreement (open cargo cover) between the buyer and the underwriters, which was completed well before the loss of the goods, would likely have been held as the arrangement which affected the transaction on the basis of the wider test of *The Erin Schulte*.[94] Accordingly, it is arguable that they could have had liability imposed on them, if they had triggered section 3(1).

(d) 'Lawful' Holder

Section 2(1) prescribes that a person can only be a 'lawful' holder in order to acquire rights of suit under the contract of carriage. According to section 5(2), a holder becomes a 'lawful' holder only 'wherever he has become the holder of the bill in good faith.'[95] Despite the fact that the word 'lawful' is only depicted as being in good faith, there is no further definition of good faith given in the Act. Nor is there any description given in the Law Commission report, except for the examples of who cannot become a lawful holder as a result of some actions such as theft, fraud and violence.[96]

There have so far been only a small number of cases dealing with the interpretation of 'good faith' to become a lawful holder. In *The Aegean Sea*,[97] Thomas J did not consider that the broad concept of good faith would be the correct interpretation for the purpose of the Act. On the contrary, he opined that 'good faith' simply signifies honest conduct, not a broader concept.[98] In a recent Singaporean case, Thomas J's interpretation in *The Aegean Sea* was also

[93] In the High Court of Singapore, the wider test approach adopted in *The Erin Schulte* was followed: *The Yue You 902 and Another Matter* [2019] SGHC 106; [2019] 2 Lloyd's Rep 617, [95].

[94] In *The Ythan*, Aikens J had referred to a similar wider test as well. See [2005] 2 CLC 911, [85].

[95] This is also consistent with the approach taken under the Sale of Goods Act 1979, s 61(3): 'A thing is deemed to be done in good faith within the meaning of this Act when it is in fact done honestly …'.

[96] The Law Commission Report, n 8 above, para 2.21.

[97] [1998] 2 Lloyd's Rep 39.

[98] It does not cover a broader concept, such as 'the observance of reasonable commercial standards of fair dealing in the conclusion and performance of the transaction concerned'. See *The Aegean Sea* [1998] CLC 1090; [1998] 2 Lloyd's Rep 39, 60.

followed when interpreting 'good faith'.[99] The relevant time at which to evaluate conduct of the party is at the time of his becoming holder. After that moment, any subsequent conduct of the holder, whether it is honest or not, will not alter his position under the Act.[100] 'Good faith' may prove important in respect of the allocation of liability for dangerous goods to intermediate holders. This is considered below.[101]

(ii) Sea Waybills

So far as sea waybills are concerned, as with bills of lading, the transfer of rights is the preliminary condition to impose liabilities on the buyer according to section 3. Sea waybills may often be used instead of bills of lading under CIF or FOB sales – commonly in bulk trades – when the buyer has no intention to re-sell the goods during transit. Unlike bills of lading, they only designate a party as consignee, omitting 'to order' or any similar indication.[102] This is to say, unlike order or bearer bills of lading, they are not transferable.[103] Pursuant to section 1(3), a sea waybill is a document 'which is not a bill of lading', but a receipt for the goods and evidence of the contract.[104,105]

Pursuant to section 2(1)(b), rights of suit are transferred to the buyer 'to whom delivery of the goods to which a sea waybill relates is to be made by the carrier in accordance with that contract'.[106] Unlike for bills of lading, the concept of 'holder' plays no part in determining the transfer of rights under sea waybills. The buyer is transferred rights of suit as soon as the sea waybill is issued.[107] The buyer does not necessarily obtain the sea waybill from the shipper in order to have rights of suit. Thus, the named buyer as consignee in the sea waybill is entitled to delivery of the goods only upon proof of identity.[108] On the other hand, although straight bills are regarded as a bill of lading or a similar document of title in respect of the Hague

[99] *The Yue You 902 and Another Matter* [2019] SGHC 106; [2019] 2 Lloyd's Rep 617, [111].
[100] Aikens et al, *Bills of Lading*, n 44 above, para 9.62.
[101] See section II.V below.
[102] For an example of this, see the Maersk Line 'Non-negotiable sea waybill'. Alternatively, it may expressly state 'not to order'. See the Combiconwaybill and the Linewaybill. The consignee does not have to be named in the bill of lading. It could be identified by description as well as designation under s 5(3).
[103] It omits 'to order' or similar words indicating transferability of the documents. See *The Chitral* [2000] 1 Lloyd's Rep 529, where instead of 'to order' in the consignee box, there was 'if order state notify party' and no notify party was named. Therefore, the bill was held to be a sea waybill.
[104] Section 1(3)(a).
[105] Section 1(1)(b). The 1855 Act would probably not have applied to sea waybills.
[106] Section 2(1)(b).
[107] Unlike bills of lading, for the purpose of s 2(5), the shipper of a sea waybill is not divested of rights of suit. Both the shipper and the consignee will have rights of suit against the carrier.
[108] Delivery is to be made upon acceptable proof of identity. See the Law Commission Report, n 8 above, para 5.7. Nevertheless although straight bills are treated as sea waybills for the purpose of the Act, there are some dicta indicating that they should be produced to obtain the delivery at common law: *The Rafaela S* [2005] 2 AC 423.

or Hague-Visby Rules,[109] as they are 'incapable of transfer … by indorsement', they are considered sea waybills for the purpose of the 1992 Act.[110,111] However, in contrast to their position under the 1992 Act, they may need to be presented for delivery of the goods at common law.[112] This may give rise to some difficulties in terms of satisfying the conditions required by section 3(1) to impose liabilities, which will be discussed below.[113]

Unlike the rights of the shipper of bills of lading, the rights of the sea waybill shipper are preserved pursuant to section 2(5), including his right to redirect the goods under a new contract of carriage, where the rights have been transferred to the buyer/consignee under section 2(1)(b).[114] Preservation of the right to redirect the goods of the original party may also give rise to difficulties in terms of divestment of liability, which will be discussed below as well.[115]

(iii) Delivery Orders

The third and last type of document that the 1992 Act applies to is delivery orders.[116] Here the seller ships the goods in bulk, only obtains one bill of lading from the carrier for the entire goods, and subsequently sells them partially to several buyers. He does not tender the bill of lading to the buyers but instead delivery orders entitling them to delivery of a relevant parcel of the goods from the carrier.[117]

Delivery orders are defined in the Act as 'an undertaking by the carrier to a person identified in the document to deliver the goods to which the document

[109] *The Rafaela S* [2005] 2 AC 423, [20], [26], [46], [79].

[110] The Law Commission Report, n 8 above, para 5.7. However, in *The Rafaela S* it was held that straight bills are regarded as a 'bill or lading or similar document of title' for the purpose of the Hague-Visby Rules: [2005] 2 AC 423, [22] and [50].

[111] However, unless otherwise stated in the contract, the shipper retains his right to redirect the goods under sea waybills. Therefore, he may instruct the carrier to deliver to a party rather than the named consignee. See the Law Commission Report, n 8 above, paras 5.13, 5.25. See also *AP Moller-Maersk A/S (t/a Maersk Line) v Sonaec Villas Cen Sad Fadoul* [2010] EWHC 355 (Comm); [2010] 2 All ER 1159. The initial consignee loses his rights of suit under s 2(5)(b), once the subsequent consignee is transferred rights of suit under the Act. The exception to this rule is where straight bills are held by the consignee. Although straight bills are treated as sea waybills under the 1992 Act, the buyers, in most of the situations would want to hold on to the straight bills in order to obtain delivery of the goods from the carrier. Once the buyer has possession of the straight bill, the shipper loses his right to redirect the goods. See Eder et al, *Scrutton on Charterparties and Bills of Lading*, n 31 above, para 3-027.

[112] *The Rafaela S* [2005] 2 AC 423, [20], [45].

[113] See section II.D below.

[114] *AP Moller-Maersk A/S (trading as Maersk Line) v Sonaec Villas Cen Sad Fadoul* [2010] EWHC 355 (Comm); [2010] 2 All ER 1159. See also the Law Commission Report, n 8 above, para 5.23.

[115] See section II.V below.

[116] Section 1(4).

[117] *Colin & Shields v Weddel & Co Ltd* [1952] 2 Lloyd's Rep 9, 19; *Margarine Union GmbH v Cambay Prince Steam Ship Co Ltd (The Wear Breeze)* [1967] 2 Lloyd's Rep 315, 322; *Siat di dal Ferro v Tradax Overseas SA* [1978] 2 Lloyd's Rep 470, 493. Delivery orders are acceptable documents if the sale contract explicitly so stipulates. Merchant delivery orders were held not to be acceptable. See *The Julia* [1949] AC 293. See also *Cremer v General Carriers SA (The Dona Mari)* [1974] 1 WLR 341.

relates to that person.'[118] The definition leaves merchant orders, which are issued by the bill of lading holder,[119] outside the Act on the ground that the undertaking must be given only by the carrier.[120] Similarly to sea waybills, the rights are transferred to the named person in the order, as soon as it is issued by the carrier according to section 2(1)(c).[121] The buyer acquires the rights only in relation to the goods that the order relates to.[122] The party identified in the order is prima facie entitled to delivery upon proof of identity.[123] Similarly to sea waybills, rights of the shipper or the holder of the bill of lading will be preserved by section 2(5), when rights are transferred to the person identified in the delivery order. It is also probable that, pursuant to section 5(3), the person identified in the order to whom delivery is to be made can be changed after the issue of the order. These may give rise to difficulties in terms of imposition and divestment of liabilities, which will be discussed below.[124]

C. Transfer of Liability

Before discussing how the mechanism of section 3(1) operates to impose liabilities on the transferee/buyer, the most important question calling for discussion is whether the wording of section 3(1) – 'subject to the same liabilities under that contract as if he had been a party to that contract'[125] – is wide enough to embrace the transfer of liability for dangerous goods to the buyer/transferee. Although the matter has not been decisively settled under English law as of yet, it is submitted that it is transmissible from the seller/shipper to the buyer/transferee.

[118] It is negatively defined by s 1(4), which states it is neither a bill of lading nor a sea waybill. But, see the Law Commission Report, n 8 above, para 5.26.

[119] See the Law Commission Report, n 8 above, para 5.30. Tort actions or the doctrine of implied contract (the *Brandt v Liverpool* contract) are still open to the buyer.

[120] It may be attorned to by the carrier. Difficulties may arise in relation to the identity of the carrier. The Act does not define who the carrier is. Where the bill of lading is a shipowner's bill (in which the shipowner is the carrier), the undertaking has to be given by the shipowner. The charterer's undertaking therefore will not suffice. See *The Rewia* [1991] 2 Lloyd's Rep 69 and *The Ines* [1995] 2 Lloyd's Rep 144. On the other hand, if the bill of lading is a charterer's bill (where the charterer is the carrier), it is plausible to argue that the undertaking given by either the charterer or the shipowner will suffice, since the shipowner can be regarded as a non-contractual carrier under the bailment relationship. See *Homburg Houtimport BV v Agrosin Private Ltd (The Starsin)* [2003] UKHL 12; [2004] 1 AC 715. See also Treitel and Reynolds, *Carver on Bills of Lading*, n 44 above, para 5-092. In contrast, see Gaskell et al, *Bills of Lading: Law and Contracts*, n 35 above, para 4.73.

[121] Like sea waybills, the identification by description will suffice under s 5(3).

[122] Sections 2(3)(b) and 5(4).

[123] This rule is subject to s 2(3)(a) by which rights 'shall be so vested subject to the terms of the order.' By virtue of s 5(3), delivery orders can be made out 'to order' or 'bearer' and when they are issued in that way, the terms of the order may prescribe that the carrier will deliver the goods only against production of the order. Once this is the case, the rights can only be acquired, as is the case in bills of lading. See Bridge, *Benjamin's Sale of Goods*, n 21 above, para 18-410.

[124] See section II.E below.

[125] Section 3(1).

(i) Case Law and the Influence of the Law Commission Report

So far as the case law under the 1855 Act is concerned, there appears to be no reported case decided on the actual transfer of liability for dangerous goods to the transferee. Neither was there a case indicating to the contrary.[126] The first case establishing the strict liability of the shipper in relation to dangerous goods was reported in 1856, which was after the enactment of the 1855 Act.[127] It was therefore technically impossible for legislators of the 1855 Act to anticipate the transfer of this liability, well before the establishment of such liability. However, although there is no direct authority on the actual transfer, in the House of Lords (*The Giannis NK*) it was held obiter that the shipper's liabilities, including for the shipment of dangerous goods, were transmissible under the 1855 Act.[128] One may argue that this decision should not be followed under the 1992 Act, as the 1855 Act was superseded by it. However, where the law remained unchanged, the courts would likely follow the authorities decided under the 1855 Act. For instance, in *The Berge Sisar* (a 1992 Act case), both the Court of Appeal and the House of Lords affirmatively relied on a case heard in 1862 on the matter of divestment of incurred liabilities under the 1855 Act.[129] Both under the 1855 and 1992 Acts, the transferee becomes 'subject to the same liabilities'.[130] Therefore, as long as the relevant law is preserved – or rather strengthened – under the 1992 Act, there is no harm in relying on an authority decided under the 1855 Act. In fact, in the Law Commission report, which led to the passing of the 1992 Act without any amendments, following detailed consideration of the arguments for and against subjecting the transferee to liability for dangerous goods, it was eventually suggested that the transfer of pre-shipment liabilities – including liabilities arising from dangerous goods – should be transferred by the 1992 Act:

> It was also suggested to us that special provision should be made so that the consignee or indorsee should never be liable in respect of loss or damage caused by the shipper's breach of warranty in respect of the shipment of dangerous cargo. This is said to be a particularly unfair example of a retrospective liability in respect of something for which the consignee/indorsee is not responsible. However, we have decided against such a special provision. We do not think that liability in respect of dangerous goods is necessarily more unfair than liability in respect of a range of other matters over which the holder of the bill of lading has no control and for which he is not responsible, as for

[126] *Ministry of Food v Lamport & Holt Line Ltd* [1952] 2 Lloyd's Rep 371, 382. Where the judge indicated that it had never been decided under the 1855 Act whether all liabilities of the original party including pre-shipment ones were transferred under the Act.

[127] *Brass v Maitland* (1856) 6 E & B 470.

[128] *The Giannis NK* [1998] 1 Lloyd's 337, 343, 344, 349.

[129] *Smurthwaite v Wilkins* (1862) 11 CB (NS) 842. It was decided on an outdated policy of the 1855 Act in which the rights and liabilities would be transferred together, while the position is divorced under the 1992 Act. Discussed in detail below. See section II.V.

[130] The 1855 Act, s 1; the 1992 Act, s 3(1).

> instance liability for loadport demurrage and dead freight. Also, it may be unfair to exempt the indorsee from dangerous goods' liability in those cases where he may have been the prime mover behind the shipment. Furthermore, it is unfair that the carrier should be denied redress against the indorsee of the bill of lading who seeks to take the benefit of the contract of carriage without the corresponding burdens.[131]

That being the case, the policy of the 1992 Act favours the transfer of dangerous goods liability. The Law Commission report does not contradict the obiter dicta of *The Giannis NK*, but rather strengthens the position of the case as the relevant authority.[132] On the other hand, the Law Commission report is not a primary legal source. It is, however, submitted that its suggestions cannot be overlooked, since the report led to the passing of the 1992 Act with no amendments. The report itself is not only a perfect aid to applying and interpreting the Act adequately, but also establishes the new policy of the Act. It is probable that the report itself could be influential on the courts. The case law also appears to support this. As of today, all the cases which referred to the Report not only called it in aid to apply the Act, but also affirmatively followed its recommendations when interpreting the Act's sections.[133] More significantly, concerning the transfer of dangerous goods liability, the impact of the report can be seen from the cases relevant to the matter. Since the 1992 Act came into force, only three cases (*The Berge Sisar*, *The Aegean Sea* and *The Ythan*) have dealt with the question of whether liability for dangerous goods is transmissible under the Act.[134] In all these cases, it was held or at least assumed that this liability is transmissible under section 3(1).[135] Particularly in *The Berge Sisar*, where the Act was reviewed in its entirety, the House of Lords, when considering the scope of section 3(1), explicitly opined that this liability is transmissible: 'The liabilities, particularly when alleged dangerous goods are involved, may be disproportionate to the value of the goods; the liabilities may not be covered by insurance; the endorsee may not be fully aware of what the liabilities are.'[136]

[131] The Law Commission Report, n 8 above, paras 3.15–3.22.

[132] *The Giannis NK* was reported in 1998, which was well after the enactment of the 1992 Act. That is to say, the House of Lords were well aware of the new Act. They could have opined to the contrary but in fact ruled consistently with the policy of the 1992 Act.

[133] *The Berge Sisar* [1998] 2 Lloyd's Rep 475; [1999] QB 863, 877, 879, 880, 882, 883 (CA); [2001] UKHL 17, [28], [39] (HL). In *The Ythan*, Aikens J called the Report in the aid to determine the scope of s 5(2)(c). The learned judge explicitly followed the recommendations; [2005] EWHC 2399 (Comm); [2006] 1 All ER 367, [67]–[71]. See section II.B.(i)(c) above. Also for the influence of other similar reports on the courts, see *Factortame Ltd v Secretary of State for Transport* [1990] 2 AC 85; *Pepper v Hart* [1993] 1 All ER 42.

[134] *The Aegean Sea* [1998] 2 Lloyd's Rep 39; *The Berge Sisar* [2001] UKHL 17; *The Ythan* [2005] EWHC 2399 (Comm); [2006] 1 All ER 367. See also Aikens et al, *Bills of Lading*, n 44 above, para 9.102.

[135] *The Aegean Sea* [1998] 2 Lloyd's Rep 39; *The Berge Sisar* [2001] UKHL 17; *The Ythan* [2005] EWHC 2399 (Comm); [2006] 1 All ER 367.

[136] [2001] UKHL 17, [33]. Since Lord Hobhouse did not specifically refer to the common law duty or the Hague/Hague-Visby Rules, both liabilities are said to be transferred under the Act. In *Fowler v Knoop* (1878) 4 QBD 299, the consignee was held liable for delays at discharge as a result of a breach of an implied duty of the shipper. Therefore there is no reason why the liabilities resulting from the common law implied duties which are imposed on the shipper cannot be transferred under the 1992 Act as well. See also S Baughen and N Campbell, 'Apportionment of Risk and The Carriage of Dangerous Cargo' (2001) 1 *Int'l ML* 3, 11.

There appears to be no support, in the reported cases dealing with the point, for the view that this liability should not be transferred under the 1992 Act. On the contrary, all the relevant cases affirmed the transferability as recommended in the Report. In the present state of the authorities, including the House of Lords decisions in *The Giannis NK* and *The Berge Sisar* along with *The Ythan* and *The Aegean Sea*, the predominant view therefore is that liability is transmissible.

(ii) Under the Hague/Hague-Visby Rules

There might be an argument that the wording in section 3(1) only entails that the transferee becomes subject to some liabilities of the shipper but not the ones explicitly attached to 'the shipper'.[137] In *The Aegean Sea*, it was held obiter by Thomas J that the term 'shipper', both in article III rule 5 and article IV rule 3 under the Rules, meant solely the shipper, not on whom liabilities are imposed as a transferee.[138] Accordingly, it might be argued that only liability for dangerous goods arising at common law[139] is transmissible, while liability under article IV rule 6 is not, as it is attached to the 'shipper'.[140] If the proposition that the transferee becomes subject to only those liabilities that are not expressly attached to the shipper is correct, then it is submitted that there is no reason why dangerous goods liability arising at common law should be imposed on the buyer/transferee either. It is trite law that liability arising at common law attaches to the shipper as much as it attaches to the shipper under article IV rule 6.[141] There is no difference between common law and the Rules in this regard.

There might also be an argument that the Law Commission may not have had article IV rule 6 in mind when recommending the transfer of liability for dangerous goods.[142] However, there is no reason to infer that the application of section 3(1) should be restricted to the common law duty. As stated above, following the meticulous consideration of the arguments for and against subjecting the transferee to liability for dangerous goods, the Law Commission can be said to have expressly intended that this liability be transmissible, whether it arises from common law or under the Rules.[143] Nothing in the report indicates

[137] S Baughen, 'Charterparty Bills of Lading Cargo Interests Liabilities to the Shipowner' in R Thomas (ed), *The Evolving Law and Pratice of Voyage Charterparties* (London, Informa, 2009), para 11.65.

[138] See *The Aegean Sea* [1998] 2 Lloyd's Rep 39, 69. See also *The Filikos* [1983] 1 Lloyd's Rep 9.

[139] Where the Hague or the Hague-Visby Rules do not apply or where applicable, the common law duty is still applicable for liability arising from legally dangerous goods. See *The Giannis NK* [1998] 1 Lloyd's Rep 337.

[140] For this view, see Baughen and Campbell, n 136 above, 9–10; S Baughen, 'Obligations of the Shipper to the Carrier' (2008) *JIML* 555, 558; Baughen, n 137 above, para 11.66; Gaskell et al, *Bills of Lading: Law and Contracts*, n 35 above, paras 4.51–4.55. Against, D Mildon and D Scorey, 'Liabilities of Transferees of Bills of Lading' (1999) *IJOSL* 94; Aikens et al, *Bills of Lading*, n 44 above, para 11.380; J Cooke et al, *Voyage Charters*, 4th edn (London, Informa, 2014) para 18.100; Eder et al, *Scrutton on Charterparties and Bills of Lading*, n 31 above, para 14.097.

[141] *Brass v Maitland* (1856) 6 E & B 470.

[142] Gaskell et al, *Bills of Lading: Law and Contracts*, n 35 above, para 4.54.

[143] The Law Commission Report, above n 8, 29–34.

that there is a difference between common law and the Rules in this regard, as there appears to have been no discussion conducted on this. More significantly, the Law Commission was indeed well aware of the problems in relation to the Rules as a whole. This is evident from the part of the report in which the problems caused by article III rule 4 of the Rules was expressly discussed.[144] Additionally, section 5(5) of the 1992 Act provides an express policy not to prejudice the application of the Hague-Visby Rules by the operation of the 1992 Act.[145] It would be therefore improbable that the Law Commission, with its legal experts in this area, and which discussed *in extensio* the transfer of this liability, would have overlooked the fact that dangerous goods liability also arises under article IV rule 6.

So far as article III rule 5[146] and article IV rule 3[147] are concerned, it is also not easy to see how the judgment in *The Aegean Sea* in this regard could prove useful to generate a similar result for article IV rule 6. Unlike with article III rule 5 and article IV rule 3, there appears to be no reported direct or indirect authority indicating that article IV rule 6 should be interpreted in a similar fashion in relation to section 3(1). Each of these provisions prescribes different obligations with different wordings. It is true that the term 'shipper' in article III rule 5, article IV rule 3 and article IV rule 6 should mean simply the shipper. However, difficulties may arise, if the term 'the shipper' in article III rule 5 and article IV rule 3 were replaced with 'the transferee'.

Article III rule 5 deals with the shipper's guarantee in relation to statements on marks, number, quantity and weight in the bills of lading. These statements will be conclusive evidence against the carrier, once the bill is transferred to a third party by virtue of article III rule 4. This is to say, if the term 'shipper' in article III rule 5 were replaced with the transferee, the same party (transferee) would be liable under article III rule 5 for these statements to the carrier as well as entitled to rely on them against the carrier at the same time.[148] More significantly, the last sentence of article III rule 5 proves that the provision should apply solely to the shipper: 'The right of the carrier to such indemnity shall in no way limit his responsibility and liability under the contract of carriage to any person other than the shipper.' The fact that article IV rule 6 lacks a statement equivalent to the final sentence of article III rule 5 appears to suggest that there is no technical obstacle

[144] ibid, 35–38.

[145] Section 5(5): 'The preceding provisions of this Act shall have effect without prejudice to the application, in relation to any case, of the rules (the Hague-Visby Rules) which for the time being have the force of law by virtue of section 1 of the Carriage of Goods by Sea Act 1971.'

[146] 'The shipper shall be deemed to have guaranteed to the carrier the accuracy at the time of shipment of the marks, number, quantity and weight, as furnished by him, and the shipper shall indemnify the carrier against all loss, damages and expenses arising or resulting from inaccuracies in such particulars. The right of the carrier to such indemnity shall in no way limit his responsibility and liability under the contract of carriage to any person other than the shipper.'

[147] 'The shipper shall not be responsible for loss or damage sustained by the carrier or the ship arising or resulting from any cause without the act, fault or neglect of the shipper, his agents or his servants.'

[148] Mildon and Scorey, n 140 above, 97.

to transferral of this liability thereunder.[149] On the other hand, as for article IV rule 3, the same rephrasing may not produce a plausible result either, owing to the same reasons already explained for article III rule 5. The provision prescribes that the shipper will not be responsible for loss or damage sustained by the carrier, if this loss or damage does not arise out of the act, neglect or fault of the shipper. If the term 'shipper' in article IV rule 3 were open to replacement by 'the transferee', it is unlikely that section 3(1) would impose liability on a third party, unless the shipper acted negligently. However, this argument was rejected by Thomas J in *The Aegean Sea* in holding that the shipper in article IV rule 3 means solely the shipper and not a third party on whom the liabilities are imposed by section 3(1).[150] It is therefore unlikely that the argument on article IV rule 3 would have an impact on article IV rule 6. In supporting this, Thomas J declined to rule on article IV rule 6 in a similar fashion as he did for article III rule 5 and article IV rule 3.

Returning to article IV rule 6, there is no final sentence equivalent to the one in article III rule 5 which indicates that liability cannot be transferred. Nor could there be an implausible outcome, as would be the case for article IV rule 3 and article III rule 5, if the provision were rephrased. When the term 'shipper' is substituted for 'the transferee', nothing in the provision renders the reading illogical or incapable of being transferred to the transferee:

> Goods of an inflammable, explosive or dangerous nature to the shipment whereof the carrier, master or agent of the carrier has not consented with knowledge of their nature and character, may at any time before discharge be landed at any place, or destroyed or rendered innocuous by the carrier without compensation and [the transferee] shall be liable for all damages and expenses directly or indirectly arising out of or resulting from such shipment.

It should also be remembered that the Rules do not define the terms 'consignee', 'holder' or 'transferee'. They do not directly deal with the allocation of rights or liabilities to third parties either. As Devlin J opined in *Chandris v Isbrandsten Moller*, the Rules are not a complete code and are only meant to cover certain topics.[151] There is no doubt that the transfer of rights and liabilities is outside their scope, as they only govern the contextual contractual relationship between the parties under the carriage contract. On the other hand, due to the doctrine of privity of contract, prior to the 1855 Act, the buyer/endorsee could not sue the carrier under the bill of lading given that the mere transfer of the bill of lading did not

[149] See also Eder et al, *Scrutton on Charterparties and Bills of Lading*, n 31 above, para 14.097.

[150] *The Aegean Sea* [1998] 2 Lloyd's Rep 39, 69–70.

[151] *Chandris v Isbrandsten-Moller* [1951] 1 KB 240, 247. Unlike the Hague or Hague-Visby Rules, the Rotterdam Rules include a provision directly on the transfer of liabilities and, by virtue of art 58(2), the holder of a transferable shipping document can become subject to liabilities 'to the extent that such liabilities are incorporated in or ascertainable from the negotiable transport document'. This clearly envisages contractual liabilities. However the Rotterdam Rules do not apply to non-negotiable shipping documents like seaway bills or delivery orders which are not considered a 'transport document' within art 1(14). On the other hand, similarly to the 1992 Act, it is a precondition that the holder must exercise his contractual rights in order to incur liabilities under art 58(2). See also art 57.

transfer the contract under it.[152] This was overcome by the anti-privty devices – first the 1855 Act and subsequently the 1992 Act – which fill this gap between the carrier and the transferee and accordingly transfer rights and liabilities. Neither the Rules nor the 1992 Act occupies one another's field. This can be confirmed by section 5(5) of the 1992 Act which states:

> The preceding provisions of this Act shall have effect without prejudice to the application, in relation to any case, of the rules (the Hague-Visby Rules) which for the time being have the force of law by virtue of section 1 of the Carriage of Goods by Sea Act 1971.

A good example of this is the last sentence of article III rule 5, which was discussed above. Nothing in the 1992 Act overrides this last sentence and affects the operation of the provision.[153] However, there is no such sentence or wording in article IV rule 6, which may call for the aid of section 5(5), when section 3(1) applies to article IV rule 6 to transfer the liability. In this respect, there is no reason to infer that the application of the 1992 Act should be restricted by the Rules, while the Rules do not have anything to say on this matter. For these reasons, it is therefore probable that section 3(1) does indeed transfer the liability under article IV rule 6.

Some may also argue that the term 'shipper' in article IV rule 6 may not be read as 'holder' or 'transferee' – given the need for some degree of manipulation – on the grounds of *The Miramar*,[154] where the House of Lords refused to manipulate the wording of a clause from the charterparty indicating that the charterer needed to pay demurrage, which was incorporated in the bill of lading, so as to make the bill of lading holder liable.[155] The decision in *The Miramar* on the incorporation of charterparty clauses into the bills of lading contract may not, however, legitimately apply to the issue in question. First, as Thomas J opined in *The Aegean Sea*, it is not easy to see how the analogy of charterparty cases can apply to bills of lading cases, as they are between the shipowner and the charterer.[156] While a charterparty is a contract that governs the relationship between the shipowner and the charterer for the hire of a vessel, a bill of lading once the cargo is loaded, is not only a receipt for the goods but also prima facie evidence of the contract of carriage, which governs the relationship between the carrier and the shipper. While the latter is a transferable document, which becomes the contract of carriage between the carrier and the holder once transferred, the former is not. Shipowners and charterers, depending on their bargaining strengths are free to negotiate the terms of the charterparty without interference from any statute, so they may agree on additional clauses to suit their own interests. On the other

[152] *Thomson v Dominy* (1845) 14 M & V 403; 153 ER 532.
[153] See Mildon and Scorey, n 140 above.
[154] *The Miramar* [1984] 2 Lloyd's Rep 129.
[155] Baughen and Campbell, n 136 above, 10.
[156] Thomas J opined that it is difficult to see that the analogy of charterparty cases can apply to the bill of lading cases; see *The Aegean Sea* [1998] 2 Lloyd's Rep 39, 65.

hand, unlike in charterparties, the parties to a bill of lading have a rather restricted freedom to negotiate their own terms, since it is mostly governed by international conventions, which may define parties' obligations and rights to a great extent. They are different contracts between different parties, which probably involve different obligations and rights. Therefore, it is not immediately apparent why an analogy with charterparty cases should apply to bill of lading cases. Second, in *The Miramar*[157] the shipowner sought to invoke an incorporated clause to recover demurrage under the charterparty from the bill of lading holder. Although it was held that the charterparty demurrage clause was incorporated into the bill, the problem revolved around whether 'the charterer' in the clause should be replaced by 'the holder'. This analogy may not be plausible on the ground that the issue in question is not related to the incorporation of a clause from one contract to another. The 1992 Act does not operate by incorporating terms from one contract into another. In fact, the Act enables the holder to become party to a bill of lading contract via statute. More significantly, the mechanism of the Act does not substitute the 'holder' for a party such as a 'charterer' from a contract of a different kind, but replaces the parties arising under the same contract with one another; namely, the shipper, with the holder or the transferee. Even if such manipulation is needed, support can be found in the Rules, with article I(b) expressly stating: 'regulates the relations between … a carrier and a holder', once the bill is transferred to a holder. The Rules, therefore, themselves provide some verbal manipulation to read the shipper as holder or transferee. Also, if the analogy of *The Miramar* were correct, then the 1992 Act would fail to give effect to the recommendations of the Law Commission in relation to the transfer of dangerous goods liability. It is also worth adding that there appears to be no reported case in which *The Miramar* was considered so as to apply in a similar fashion to section 3(1).

Moreover, neither in *The Aegean Sea*, nor in *The Ythan* or in *The Berge Sisar* were any arguments put forward or even discussed against subjecting the holder or the transferee to dangerous goods liability. In *The Berge Sisar*, the carrier made a claim against the holder for the liability arising out of dangerous goods under article IV rule 6.[158] No argument against the replacement of the shipper with the transferee or the holder was advanced in the case. Further to that, although the claim was made under article IV rule 6, none of the judges in the House of Lords queried this issue, but expressly assumed that liability for dangerous goods is transmissible under article IV rule 6. In any case, it is arguable that the transfer would be made easier with an express term like the 'Merchant' clause, which imposes liabilities on multiple parties, including the shipper, the holder, the consignee and many others. Many bill of lading forms[159] contain such a clause, which would render the imposition of this liability on the buyer/transferee easier.

[157] [1984] 2 Lloyd's Rep 129.
[158] [2001] UKHL 17; [2001] 1 Lloyd's Rep 663, 667.
[159] Examples of such clauses can be found in some bill of lading forms, such as Combiconbill, 'K' Line bill, Conlinebill, P&O Nedlloyd Bill.

(iii) Justification of the Transfer to the Buyer

At first sight it might appear that transferring dangerous goods liability under section 3(1) is against the policy identified in *Brass v Maitland*.[160,161] In *Brass v Maitland*, Lord Campbell imposed strict liability for shipment of dangerous goods on the shipper, because his Lordship opined that the shipper had better means of knowledge in relation to the nature and character of the goods than the carrier. It is unlikely that this argument would be of any direct assistance in preventing the transfer of liability under the 1992 Act. The policy established by Lord Campbell in *Brass v Maitland* covers the apportionment of liability only between the shipper and the carrier, and liability falls on the shipper rather than the carrier even if the shipper has no knowledge of the dangerous characteristics of the goods to be shipped. This is to say that the rationale behind the policy in *Brass v Maitland* aims for the utmost protection of the carrier against the shipper in cases where the issue of allocation of liability for dangerous goods was solely between the carrier and the shipper. His Lordship gave no opinion on the imposition of liabilities on the buyer/transferee or any other third party, since there was no such dispute regarding the transfer of this liability. It is therefore arguable that the policy in *Brass v Maitland* does not extend to a matter that is not directly relevant to it.

On the other hand, the 1992 Act creates its own policy in relation to the imposition of liabilities to transferees, which does not weaken the policy in *Brass v Maitland* but strengthens the core aim. First, the carrier's position is not weakened by the 1992 Act, as under section 3(3) the shipper's liabilities will not be extinguished by the time the transferee becomes liable under section 3(1). Second, in addition to the shipper, the 1992 Act applies this liability to an additional party when section 3(1) is triggered. The policy of the 1992 Act, therefore, does not appear to be contradicting *Brass v Maitland*, on the basis that the policy of 1992 Act aims at the utmost protection of the carrier at all times – as was also the case in *Brass v Maitland* – not only against the shipper but also the transferee. Even if it is accepted that these two policies do contradict one another, it is still difficult to see why a policy from 1856 should overrule an up-to-date policy that is compatible with modern trade practice. This argument can also be supported by the words of Lord Goff commenting on the 1992 Act in the House of Lords: '[the 1992 Act] will move our law in this area from the middle of the 19th century to well into the 21st'.[162]

Also, the policy of the 1992 Act should not be restricted by *Brass v Maitland*, given that the former expressly widens the contractual nexus between the relevant parties of carriage. Once section 3(1) is triggered, in terms of the imposition of liabilities, the 1992 Act creates a tri-partite relationship between the carrier, the shipper and the transferee. The policy of the 1992 Act requires us to approach

[160] *Brass v Maitland* (1856) 6 E & B 470; 119 ER 940.
[161] Baughen and Campbell, n 136 above, 7; Baughen, n 137 above, para 11.63.
[162] Carriage of Goods by Sea Bill, Deb 4 February 1992, col 234.

such a tri-partite relationship from a different angle. By making the carrier entitled to sue both the shipper/seller and the transferee/buyer for the same liabilities, the policy indicates the rationale behind the principle: the carrier should be protected at all times under the tri-partite relationship, on the basis that he is the most innocent and most remote party from the goods which are the source of the damage or loss to him. This is also arguably true in the context of sale of goods law; the buyer as the transferee may have a more proximate connection to and interest in the goods, which may justify his potential liability under the tri-partite relationship. It is trite law that it is the shipper as the original party who drafts all the details in relation to carriage arrangements for the goods and enables the carrier to take all necessary precautions to carry the goods safely. By virtue of section 32(2) of the 1979 Act, under CIF and many FOB contracts,[163] the seller is under a duty to make or procure a contract of carriage on behalf of the buyer. Section 32(2) expressly indicates that the seller concludes this contract 'on behalf of the buyer',[164] whether he concludes it as principal or agent of the buyer. This is to say, when the seller/shipper – even as the original party – drafts all the details and makes all necessary arrangements to enable the carrier to take necessary precautions to carry the goods, he makes all these for the benefit of the buyer/transferee on his behalf under section 32(2). This proves that the contract of carriage is a contract for the benefit of a third party, namely the buyer. At this point, a question calls for comment: why would a beneficiary party be able to be relieved of his obligations when he seeks to enforce that contract which was evidently concluded on his behalf? The policy of the 1992 Act is grounded on the principle of mutuality.[165] It was expressly stated in the Law Commission report that a party who is willing to exercise this contract should not escape from its corresponding liabilities: 'it is unfair that the carrier should be denied redress against the indorsee of the bill of lading who seeks to take the benefit of the contract of carriage without the corresponding burdens.'[166]

More support can be found in section 32(1) of the 1979 Act which prescribes that delivery of the goods to the carrier is prima facie deemed to be delivery to the buyer.[167] Moreover, by virtue of section 45(1) of the 1979 Act, when delivered to the carrier, goods are deemed to be in the course of transit for the purpose of transmission to the buyer. This is to say, the carrier obtains and carries the goods not only on behalf of the buyer but also for the benefit of the buyer. All these factors appear to prove that the buyer can be regarded as the prime reason behind the shipment. Apart from the contractual nexus of the buyer to the goods, the buyer may also have non-contractual proximity to the goods, which may strengthen his

[163] The exception is bare and some classic f.o.b. contracts. See *Pyrene v Scindia* [1954] 2 QB 402; *Scottish & Newcastle Int'l Ltd v Othon Ghalanos Ltd* [2008] UKHL 11.

[164] Section 32(2) of the 1979 Act.

[165] See the speech of Lord Hobhouse in *The Berge Sisar* [2001] UKHL 17; [2002] 2 AC 205, [31] and [45].

[166] The Law Commission Report, n 8 above, para 3.22.

[167] *Dunlop v Lambert* (1839) 6 Cl & F 600. This position can be rebuttable. See *Scottish & Newcastle* [2008] UKHL 11, [9]–[20].

interest in the goods. For instance, once a transferable bill of lading is tendered to the buyer, he becomes the holder of a document of title, which entitles him to constructive possession of the goods.[168] With the function of document of title, the buyer not only holds something that represents the goods but which also puts the goods symbolically at his disposal.[169] From that moment, the carrier is deemed to carry the goods on behalf of the buyer and he is obliged to deliver the goods only to the buyer, as the holder of the document of title. In addition, the buyer can sometimes be regarded as the bailor of the goods[170] or he may obtain the title to the goods and become the owner during transit. Once the buyer wants to exercise the contract, it is therefore difficult to see why he would be allowed to escape from liability that is caused by the goods in which he may have constructive possession or title and which the carrier is not only obliged to deliver only to him but also owes him a duty of care for their safe delivery.[171] For these reasons, in this tri-partite relationship, the buyer, as the transferee who can be considered the prime reason behind the shipment, has not only a stronger contractual nexus with the goods than the carrier, but also may have a non-contractual connection which arguably justifies the policy of the 1992 Act of subjecting the transferee/buyer to dangerous goods liability as an additional party alongside the seller/shipper, once he wishes to exercise his rights under the carriage contract.

This may derive further support by way of analogy on the grounds of another tri-partite relationship: that between shipowners, charterers and cargo interests. Depending on the charterparty terms, as a result of complying with the charterer's orders or requests, the shipowners may sign bills of lading in the form requested by the charterer. Once the bill is issued or is transferred to the person[172] entitled to it, it becomes a carriage contract between the shipowner and the transferee. As a result of complying with the orders of the charterer to sign the bill as requested, the shipowners may find themselves under liability to the person to whom the bill is transferred. Although the reason for the fault may often lie with the charterer's orders and the shipowner may not be personally at fault, the shipowner may not be relieved of the liability to the cargo interests, given the contractual relationship between him and the cargo interests.[173] It is arguable that a similar analogous

[168] *Lickbarrow v Mason* (1794) 5 TR 683; *Barber v Meyerstein* (1870) LR 4 HL 317; *Sanders v Maclean* (1883) 11 QBD 327.

[169] *Barber v Meyerstein* (1870) LR 4 HL 317, 322; *Sewell v Burdick* (1884) 13 QBD 159, 171.

[170] See *The Albazero* [1977] AC 774; *The Berge Sisar* [2001] UKHL 17; *East West Corp* [2003] QB 1509.

[171] The carrier owes a duty of care to the owner of the goods or party with an immediate right of possession at the time of breach: *Homburg Houtimport BV v Agrosin Private Ltd (The Starsin)* [2003] UKHL 12, [39].

[172] Other than the charterer.

[173] The shipowner may have a claim against the charterer under express or implied indemnity: *Kruger & Co Ltd v Moel Tryvan Ship Company Ltd* [1907] AC 272; *Dawson Line Ltd v Aktiengesellschaft 'Adler' Für Chemische Industrie of Berlin* [1932] 1 KB 433; (1931) 41 Ll L Rep 75; *Larrinaga Steamship Co Ltd v The King* [1945] AC 246, 253; *Royal Greek Government v Minister of Transport (The Ann Stathatos)* (1949) 83 Ll L Rep 228; *Naviera Mogor SA v Societe Metallurgique de Normandie (The Nogar Marin)* [1987] 1 Lloyd's Rep 456; *Triad Shipping Co v Stellar Chartering & Brokerage Inc (The Island Archon)* [1994] 2 Lloyd's Rep 227.

relationship exists between the carrier, the shipper/seller and the transferee/buyer. Although the buyer as transferee is not personally at fault for liability arising from the shipment of dangerous goods, as a result of becoming party to the contract concluded by the shipper/seller who might be in fact at fault, the buyer may have this liability to the carrier imposed on him, provided that he seeks to exercise the carriage contract according to section 3(1).

It might appear at first sight that this liability should not be transferred to a third party who had nothing to do with the goods prior to loading.[174] However, this argument is not without difficulties. First, the Law Commission expressly opined that all liabilities, including pre-shipment ones, which the transferees are unlikely to have something to do with before loading, are transmissible under section 3(1).[175] The Act also provides that the transferee can obtain rights against the carrier in relation to breaches committed even before the transfer of the bill.[176] Indeed, the end buyer, as the transferee, may not have any opportunity to ascertain the nature or characteristics of the goods prior to shipment, owing to the lack of physical nexus between the buyer and the goods. However, this might be the case even where the buyer is the shipper, the original party to contract of carriage. Under some f.o.b. sales, the seller not only agrees to ship the goods but may also draft all the necessary contractual arrangements and conclude the contract of carriage as agent of the buyer.[177] Where this is the case, despite being the original party to the carriage contract, the buyer would still be unlikely to have the opportunity to ascertain the nature of the goods prior to loading. Under such f.o.b. sales, the buyer, where he becomes an original party to the carriage contract as the shipper, still becomes liable despite the fact that he had no means to ascertain the true nature or character of the goods prior to shipment. Indeed, the buyer as the shipper is not regarded as a third party, given the contractual relationship between the carrier and himself, but becomes liable to the carrier irrespective of whether he had the opportunity to inspect the goods prior to shipment. Similarly, the transferee buyer who is practically in the same position – who had nothing to do with the goods prior to loading – as the buyer/original party, is not technically considered a third party, when he has had, pursuant to section 2(1) of the 1992 Act, 'transferred to and vested in him all rights of suit under the contract of carriage as if he had been a party to that contract'. The sole difference between the two buyers above is that while the former becomes party to the carriage contract through his seller, the latter becomes a party via section 2(1) of the 1992 Act. Indeed, the buyer in the former scenario is the

[174] See Baughen and Campbell, n 136 above, 7; Baughen, n 137 above, para 11.63.

[175] The Law Commission Report, n 8 above, paras 3.20–3.22.

[176] *Monarch Steamship Co Ltd v A/B Karlshamns Oljefabriker* [1949] AC 196, 218. See Eder et al, *Scrutton on Charterparties and Bills of Lading*, n 31 above, para 3-015.

[177] *Pyrene v Scindia* [1954] 2 QB 402; *Scottish & Newcastle Int'l Ltd v Othon Ghalanos Ltd* [2008] UKHL 11.

principal party, which strongly supports that he should be liable to the carrier. However, the buyer in the latter scenario has the advantage in terms of avoiding liability, when compared to the buyer in the former scenario. In the former, the buyer as the original party becomes liable to the carrier in any event and cannot deny liability, even if he is not personally at fault. However, in the latter, the buyer does not automatically attract liability but may avoid it, unless he seeks to enforce the contract and triggers one of the conditions under section 3(1). Thus, there is no automatic imposition of liability. That being the case, it is not easy to regard the buyer in the latter scenario as a third party, once he becomes a party to the contract under which he exercises his rights.

(iv) Contractual Transfer of Liability from the Seller to the Buyer

For the reasons given above, it is submitted that both under article IV rule 6 and at common law, dangerous goods liability is transmissible from the seller/shipper to the transferee/buyer under the 1992 Act. Indicating otherwise would amount not only to the failure of the Law Commission, which expressly envisaged the transferability of this liability, but would also go against the policy of the Act. In respect of the contract of carriage, since the enactment of the 1855 Act, English law has been based on the principle of mutuality: if a third party is willing to become a party to a contract concluded by another party and seeks to exercise rights, then he must also take on the burden of the obligations thereunder. With the 1992 Act, the policy has been strengthened and it provides no exception to liabilities including liabilities for dangerous goods. The case law also appears to have embraced this policy and leaned in favour of transferability.

Indeed one may argue that it would be fairer if the carrier only looked for compensation to the shipper/seller who is liable. This argument, however, may not be the correct way to approach the complex relationship of these parties. The Act does not automatically make the transferee/buyer liable, unless he enforces his contractual rights. No one can guarantee that in practice suing only the shipper will always provide the ideal outcome for the carrier. So far as dangerous goods liabilities are concerned, they can be disproportionate; so the shipper, for instance, may not have any or sufficient assets within reach. It should be remembered that rights of third parties are a matter of commercial necessity. Carriage contracts are almost invariably concluded because of CIF and FOB sales in which the parties have the flexibility to draft any terms, including the allocation of risks under the carriage contract. On the other hand, liabilities of third parties are a matter of policy. Concerning dangerous goods, the policy of the Act clearly aims to protect carriers from the risk insolvency by giving a right to redress against the buyer/transferee. In respect of the imposition of liabilities, the Act creates a tri-partite relationship and thereunder protects the carrier (as the most innocent party) against the shipper/seller and against that additional party – the transferee/buyer – who is the prime reason behind the shipment, as those goods are ultimately carried for his benefit.

D. Imposition of Liability

It has been discussed above whether section 3(1) is wide enough to embrace liabilities arising from dangerous goods. In this section we shall look into the ambit of section 3(1) so as to see how the mechanism of the section operates to impose particularly liabilities arising from dangerous goods on the buyer/transferee. It is also worth highlighting that unless otherwise stated, everything discussed on the imposition of liabilities under bills of lading will apply *mutatis mutandis* to sea waybills and delivery orders as well.

Before delving into the discussion, two preliminary situations call for comment. First, it is trite law that where the shipper is the charterer, the bill of lading is not a contract but a receipt in the hands of the shipper.[178] The only contract between the shipper/charterer and the shipowner is therefore the charterparty itself. It is also clear that the 1992 Act does not intend to transfer rights and liabilities under the charterparty.[179] Therefore, a question arises at this point as to how the buyer/transferee could have liability imposed on him under a bill of lading that does not evidence or contain a contract? Prior to the 1992 Act, the issue was settled by 'springing a contract'[180] when the bill was transferred to a subsequent holder who was not the charterer. The Law Commission clearly did not want to alter this position and the law remains unchanged.[181] Hence, in this regard, between the shipowner and the transferee who is not the charterer, the Act transfers rights and liabilities under the bill of lading, which becomes a 'sprung up' contract of carriage in the hands of the transferee.[182] The second issue revolves around the question of what happens when the bill of lading is subsequently transferred to the charterer. The bill of lading, yet again becomes a mere receipt in the hands of the charterer, and the charterparty governs the relationship between the shipowner and the charterer/transferee.[183] Suppose that the charterer/transferee somehow triggered section 3(1) and the charterparty contained an exemption of

[178] *Rodocanachi v Milburn* (1886) 18 QBD 67; *President of India v Metcalfe Shipping Co Ltd (The Dunelmia)* [1970] 1 QB 289.

[179] The Law Commission Report, n 8 above, paras 2.52 and 2.54. See also *The Albazero* [1977] AC 774.

[180] *Hain SS Co v Tate & Lyle* (1936) 41 Com Cas 350, 356; *Rudolph A Oetker v IFA Internationale Frachtagentur AG (The Almak)* [1985] 1 Lloyd's Rep 557, 560; *The Arctic Trader* [1996] 2 Lloyd's Rep 449, 455.

[181] The Law Commission Report, n 8 above, para 2.54.

[182] The wording of section 3(1) can also be of some assistance: 'same liabilities … as if he had been a party to that contract'. This is to say, the transferee would have incurred liabilities if the bill had been originally issued to him. See Mildon and Scorey, n 140 above, 101.

[183] *The Dunelmia* [1970] 1 QB 289. Indeed, the charterer and the shipowner may expressly agree otherwise: *Rodocanachi v Milburn* (1886) 18 QBD 67, 75 and 78.

liability clause in relation to shipment of dangerous goods. Prima facie, their relationship will be governed by the charterparty, and for that reason the charterer will not become subject to the liability under section 3(1). However, this position may vary depending on the purpose of contracting under the charterparty. The prima facie rule is based on the assumption that the buyer/charterer chartered the vessel for the purpose of taking delivery under it.[184] If the charterer did not conclude the charterparty for the purpose of receiving the goods in question and there is no nexus between the charterparty and the proximate cause for the transfer of the bill to the charterer, then the relationship between the charterer/transferee and the carrier is said to be governed by the bill of lading instead, where it becomes 'a separate contract … independent of a charterparty.'[185] Once this is the case, the bill of lading as a contract of carriage can become operative, and liability under section 3(1) can be imposed on the buyer/transferee.[186]

(i) Conditions under Section 3

It has already been said that acquiring rights under the Act does not automatically impose liabilities. The underlying policy is that the liabilities under the contract can only be imposed on the parties that wish to enforce their rights.[187] Section 3 prescribes certain actions which should be fulfilled to impose liabilities on the transferees alongside the original shipper:[188]

> (a) takes or demands delivery from the carrier of any of the goods to which the document relates;
> (b) makes a claim under the contract of carriage against the carrier in respect of any of those goods; or
> (c) is a person who, at a time before those rights were vested in him, took or demanded delivery from the carrier of any of those goods …[189]

The ambit of the section was discussed in detail in a number of cases, particularly by the House of Lords in *The Berge Sisar*, which will be of assistance to see how each paragraph should be interpreted.[190]

[184] *The Dunelmia* [1970] 1 QB 289.

[185] ibid, 306. See also Bridge, *Benjamin's Sale of Goods*, n 21 above, para 18-146; Reynolds (n 73) 204–5.

[186] For such examples, see *Gullischen v Stewart Bros* (1884) 13 QBD 317; *Calcutta SS Co Ltd v Andrew Weir Co* [1910] 1 KB 759.

[187] For the mutuality of contractual relationship, see the speech of Lord Hobhouse from *The Berge Sisar* [2001] UKHL 17; [2002] 2 AC 205, [31] and [45].

[188] The transfer of liabilities to another party does not extinguish the original party's liabilities. Albeit not statutorily, this was already the position under English law even before the 1992 Act came into force: see *The Giannis NK* [1998] 1 Lloyd's Rep 337, 343–44.

[189] Section 3(1).

[190] *The Aegean Sea* [1998] 2 Lloyd's Rep 39; *The Berge Sisar* [2001] UKHL 17; *The Ythan* [2005] EWHC 2399 (Comm); [2006] 1 Lloyd's Rep 457; *P&O Nedlloyd v Arab Metals Co* [2006] EWHC 2433; *Fortis Bank SA/NV v Indian Overseas Bank* [2011] 2 Lloyd's Rep 190.

(a) Taking or Demanding Delivery

By taking or demanding delivery, the buyer can become subject to some liabilities arising from dangerous goods as the original party under the carriage contract. Even though paragraph (c) cites similar actions ('took or demanded delivery') to (a), it expands the situations to those where the buyer could attract liability even before acquiring rights provided that those rights should be vested in him later via section 2(2)(a).[191] However, 'delivery' and 'demand' are not defined by the Act. Given that these actions can make the buyer subject to liabilities, it was held that both actions should involve a choice by way of election, which should illustrate a positive step to enforce contractual rights.[192] Hence, where the buyer cooperates with berthing facilities to discharge the goods, this act will not be considered taking delivery of the goods.[193] Conduct of the buyer should involve an element of relative finality or unequivocal affirmation.[194] Taking delivery of 'any of the goods to which document relates'[195] will normally render the buyer liable according to section 3(1).[196] However, given that the goods can be rejected depending on test results, taking routine samples to test the quality of the goods is not regarded as involving any final or unequivocal conduct to take full possession of the goods, and accordingly it is not considered as an act of delivery under section 3(1).[197]

The earliest time that an act of delivery can start is the commencement of discharge. If the goods are left in the warehouse to the order of the carrier, delivery can only occur once the buyer obtains his goods from the warehouse, not at the time of discharge. In such cases discharge from the vessel will not trigger section 3.[198] Delivery for the purpose of the Act requires voluntary action

[191] Paragraph (c) mostly covers typical cases where the arrival of the bill of lading is late and delivery is against a letter of indemnity. See *The Delfini* [1990] 1 Lloyd's Rep 252 and *The Berge Sisar* [2001] UKHL 17; [2002] 2 AC 205.

[192] These three paragraphs are substantially reviewed per Lord Hobhouse in *The Berge Sisar* [2001] UKHL 17, [32]–[36].

[193] ibid, [36].

[194] ibid, [41].

[195] 'Any of the goods' may cover different situations. Delivery may occur partially or it may be left unfinished due to strike action at the port. Or there might be problems about the delivery machines after delivery has started. Alternatively, the buyer after the commencement of delivery, might notice that the goods are contaminated, and accordingly he may reject them. These situations are not exhaustive, but since they involve an element of finality to take the full possession of the goods, such situations are said to trigger 'taking delivery' or at least it might be assumed that there is a 'demand' according to section 3(1)(a). See *The Berge Sisar* [2001] UKHL 17, 209. Thomas J's obiter view in *The Aegean Sea* is that the delivered goods must be 'commercially as the same goods'. See [1998] 2 Lloyd's Rep 39, 63. However, even if the goods' value is reduced to a certain point, delivery of the goods should trigger section 3 provided that the goods are identifiable as the same goods and not essentially perished to the extent that they cannot be used or tradeable in the market. Thus, the goods which have been fundamentally changed where their identity is destroyed, such as lemons squashed into lemon juice, will not be considered as 'commercially as the same goods'. See Aikens et al, *Bills of lading*, n 44 above, para 9.60. See also *Asfar v Blundell* [1896] 1 QB 123; *The Caspian Sea* [1980] 1 WLR 48.

[196] By virtue of section 3(2), the buyer of delivery order will be liable only to the extent of the goods to which the order relates.

[197] *The Berge Sisar* [2001] UKHL 17, [38].

[198] *Barclays Bank Ltd v Commissioners of Customs & Excise* [1963] 1 Lloyd's Rep 81; *Port Jackson Stevedoring Pty v Salmond and Spraggon Pty (The New York Star)* [1981] 1 WLR 138.

from the buyer/transferee to obtain possession of the goods.[199] Thus, where the salvaged goods are taken by the buyer on the order of the local government, there will be no delivery for the purpose of section 3, as the buyer can be said to have taken the goods against his will.[200] Both paragraphs (a) and (c) require that delivery should be 'from the carrier'.[201] Taking delivery from independent salvors therefore, even if done voluntarily, would not make the buyer liable under section 3.[202] The buyer may seek to circumvent section 3(1)(c) by not obtaining bills of lading at all in order to avoid liability by taking actual delivery of the goods against the letter of indemnity. Where this is the case, the buyer would not become the lawful holder according to section 2(2)(a), and for that reason would not be subject to liability under section 3(1)(c) either. However, this is not without difficulties. When the carrier delivers the goods against a letter of indemnity, depending upon its wording,[203] the carrier might be entitled to claim under that letter of indemnity against the buyer for the loss caused by the dangerous nature of the goods.[204]

The nature of delivery orders, too, might give rise to difficulties in terms of the imposition of liabilities when delivery occurs. It has been said above that the party identified in the order can be changed after the issue of the order by virtue of section 5(3). When the delivery order is made out 'to the order' of B1 or 'bearer', B2 may acquire rights under section 2(1)(c) by way of substitution. The carrier may not be aware of such a substitution. Unlike in the case of bills of lading and sea waybills, the carrier may not receive any notice when those rights are transferred to B2 and for that reason may have delivered the goods to B1, instead of B2. Once this is the case, the carrier will not be able to claim against B1, even if section 3(1) is triggered due to delivery, on the basis that the rights formerly acquired by B1 will be regarded as extinguished under section 2(5)(b). In such

[199] *The Aegean Sea* [1998] 2 Lloyd's Rep 39, 62–63; *The Berge Sisar* [2001] UKHL 17, [32].

[200] *The Aegean Sea* [1998] 2 Lloyd's Rep 39, 62, 63.

[201] Problems may arise on the identity of the carrier, when taking or demanding delivery. Where the shipowner is the carrier, there is no apparent issue. However, where there is a charterer's bill, the carrier is the charterer under the bills of lading. When delivery is made by the shipowner, it is plausible to say that for the purpose of section 3, the shipowner should also be regarded as the carrier alongside the charterer, since the carriage contract is performed on board his vessel. The shipowner should be considered the agent or the sub-bailee of the charterer for the purpose of delivery. See Treitel and Reynolds, *Carver on Bills of lading*, n 44 above, para 5-098. See also Aikens et al, *Bills of lading*, n 44 above, para 9.105.

[202] *The Aegean Sea* [1998] 2 Lloyd's Rep, 39, 62, 63. However, if delivery is made under a varied contract which requires delivery at a different place or stage, such delivery would satisfy section 3(1). See *The Aegean Sea* [1998] 2 Lloyd's Rep 39, 62.

[203] In case of delivery without production of the bill of lading, carriers would be in a better position if the buyer issues an indemnity letter indicating that he shall indemnify the carrier for all his losses that he can incur by virtue of s 3(1) against the buyer. Only such or a similarly worded letter of indemnity may cover the carrier's loss that would normally fall within s 3(1).

[204] See MD Bools, *The Bill of Lading: a Document of Title to the Goods: an Anglo-American Comparison* (London, LLP, 1997), 113.

situations, the carrier would be in a better position if he insisted on production of the order before delivery, when he issues 'to order' or 'bearer' delivery orders.

So far as 'demanding delivery' is concerned, such an act should involve choice or election to enforce contractual rights as well.[205] Demanding delivery of 'any of the goods' suffices to trigger liability in relation to all the goods in accordance with section 3(1), as is the case with delivery.[206] Providing berthing facilities or cooperation for discharge is not regarded as 'demanding delivery' for the purpose of the Act.[207] Neither does taking routine samples amount to demanding delivery.[208] The act of demand should involve formality.[209] Lord Hobhouse in *The Berge Sisar* opined that if the buyer demanded the goods before acquiring rights, such a demand would have no legal basis. By the same token, rejection of such a demand with no legal basis would be regarded as an 'act devoid of legal significance'.[210] In this regard, it is probable that application of paragraph (c) is restricted to the cases only where actual delivery occurs.[211] Therefore, merely producing a letter of indemnity to obtain the goods would not be considered a demand for delivery for the purpose of the Act either. This is because a letter of indemnity does not oblige the carrier to deliver against it. It just gives an option to the carrier on whether to deliver, and indemnifies him for claims that can be made under the bill of lading, when the goods are delivered without production of the bill.[212] Therefore, the only action that can be considered as an example of a formal demand is the production of a bill of lading.[213]

In the case of delivery orders and sea waybills, the buyer/consignee is entitled to demand delivery of the goods without production of the relevant document. Under these documents, since delivery will occur against an identity check, the identity check will be considered to be a 'formal demand' if it involves any election to avail the buyer to enforce contractual rights.[214] However, in that respect, straight bills call for discussion. It has already been said that straight bills are sea waybills for the purpose of the Act.[215] On the other hand, there are some dicta in

[205] Where 'demand' is followed by delivery, there is no need to rely on demand. When a demand for delivery is refused or the goods are demanded but not taken later by the buyer, this is not without difficulties. These problems are discussed below. See section II.E.

[206] Save for delivery orders. By virtue of section 3(2), the buyer of a delivery order will become liable only to the extent of the goods to which the order relates. This is the case even if the buyer has two delivery orders for the same bulk, but demands only the goods to which one of the orders relates.

[207] *The Berge Sisar* [2001] UKHL 17, [32]–[36].

[208] ibid, [38].

[209] ibid, [33].

[210] ibid, [35].

[211] ibid, [35]. But see R Thomas, 'Bills of Lading – The Position of Holders and Intermediate Holders Under the English Carriage of Goods by Sea Act 1992' (2001) 5 *Int'l ML* 165, 169.

[212] *The Aegean Sea* [1998] 2 Lloyd's Rep, 39, 61.

[213] *Fortis Bank SA/NV v Indian Overseas Bank* [2011] 2 Lloyd's Rep 190, [28], where the presentation of the bill was expressly considered to be an act of demand under section 3(1)(a).

[214] See The Law Commission Report, n 8 above, para 5.7.

[215] Section 1(2)(b). The Law Commission Report, n 8 above, paras 2.50, 4.12 and 5.7. See also *The Chitral* [2000] 1 Lloyd's Rep 529, 532; *The Happy Ranger* [2002] EWCA Civ 694, [30]; *The Rafaela S* [2005] UKHL 11, [22], [50]; *AP Moeller-Maersk v Sonaec* [2010] EWHC 355, [13].

The Rafaela S where the issue revolved around whether straight bills were bills of lading or 'a similar document of title' under the Hague-Visby Rules. The House of Lords held that straight bills are bills of lading under common law, and therefore they need to be produced against delivery of the goods.[216] Whether they need to be presented under the common law rule is outside the scope of this book but even if they do, it is submitted that the buyer/consignee need not produce a straight bill to demand delivery for the purpose of the Act. Accordingly, a demand without production of the straight bill of lading should trigger section 3(1).[217] The definitions of the 1992 Act are only applicable within the boundaries of the Act. The Act does not have an impact on other legislation or the common law rules. Straight bills are the best examples of this. The fact that they are treated as sea waybills under the Act does not prevent them from being bills of lading at common law. Therefore, as the 1992 Act treats straight bills as sea waybills, then for the purpose of the Act, demand without production of the straight bill should be considered a formal demand so as to trigger section 3(1).[218]

(b) Making a Claim under the Contract of Carriage

As with taking or demanding delivery, making a claim under the carriage contract as described in paragraph (b) should involve choice by way of election, which should illustrate a positive step to enforce contractual rights.[219] To trigger section 3(1)(b), a claim must be made under the carriage contract. If the claim is based on any other legal basis outside the contract, such as in tort, the claimant buyer will not be regarded as having triggered this paragraph.[220]

[216] *The Rafaela S* [2005] UKHL 11, [20], [45]. In an Australian case, similar to *The Rafaela S*, it was held that straight bills of lading had to be surrendered against delivery of the goods: *Beluga Shipping GmbH & Co v Headway Shipping Ltd* [2008] FCA 1791. For a similar view in Hong Kong, see *Carewins Development (China) Ltd v Bright Fortune Shipping Ltd* [2009] 1 HKLRD 409. See also *The Maheno* [1977] 1 Lloyd's Rep 81 (NZ); *Voss v APL Co Pte Ltd* [2002] 2 Lloyd's Rep 707 (Singapore).

[217] For detailed discussion on the point, see *Carver on Bills of Lading*, n 44 above, para 6-016 ff; Debattista and Hornyold-Strickland, *Debattista on Bills of Lading in Commodities Trade*, 4th edn, (London, Bloomsbury Publishing, 2021) para 2.42 ff; P Todd, 'Bill of Lading as Document of Title' [2005] *JBL* 762; G McMeel, 'Straight Bills of Lading in the House of Lords – the Rafaela S' (2005) *LMCLQ* 273; GH Treitel, 'The Legal Status of Straight Bills of Lading' (2003) *LQR* 608; S Girvin, 'Bills of Lading and Straight Bills of Lading: Principles and Practice' [2006] *JBL* 86; DYH Lee and P Sooksripaisarnkit, 'The Straight Bill of Lading: Past, Present, and Future' (2012) 18 *JIML* 39.

[218] This should be the case even if the straight bill expressly provides for production of the bill. Such express provision gives only the right to reject a demand without production to the carrier. This will not alter the formality of such a demand under the Act.

[219] *The Berge Sisar* [2001] UKHL 17, [33].

[220] However, where claims can also be based on the contract of carriage, such an attempt to circumvent the Act will be precluded by the general principle that a claim in tort will be governed by contract if it is also available under the contract. See Bridge, *Benjamin's Sale of Goods*, n 21 above, para 18-330. See also *Greater Nottingham Co-operative Society Ltd v Cementation Piling & Foundations Ltd* [1989] QB 71; *Red Sea Tankers Ltd v Papachristides (The Hellespont Ardent)* [1997] 2 Lloyd's Rep 547.

Also, section 3(1)(b) is not considered satisfied when the buyer/transferee makes a claim before becoming the 'lawful holder' under the Act.[221] Given that being the lawful holder is not required for sea waybills and delivery orders, buyers of such documents who make a claim after the issue would be exposed to triggering paragraph (b). Like 'demand', 'making a claim' requires formality as well.[222] There must be some legal assertion made to the carrier by way of making a claim. Arrest of a vessel was treated as a good illustration of a formal claim.[223] A question arises at this point: would the buyer be liable as a result of a claim based on an invalid reason? Unlike 'demand' within paragraph (c), whether a claim is based on a legitimate reason or not, such a claim can make the buyer liable to the carrier.[224] A claim, by its nature, is something disputable. Therefore, the Act requires formality of the claim, not the validity of its reason. Assume that the arrest of a vessel was made on an incorrect legal basis, but it was based upon the contract of carriage; in any case, such a claim would fall within the meaning of the Act, since the claim was made in a formal way.

On the other hand, in *The Ythan* a request for security, which is a tacit threat of arrest, was held (obiter) not to be a formal claim.[225] The reason given by the court was that unlike an arrest, a request for security in the form of a letter of undertaking is not a formal claim but a contractual agreement.[226] In the case, the identity of the claimant was not known and it was not impliedly or expressly stated that a request for security was made on behalf of the bill of lading holder.[227] Given that Aikens J's decision on the point was obiter only, a request for security can be arguably treated as a claim within the paragraph, depending on the wording and disclosure of the claimant's identity.[228]

E. Cessation of Liability

String sales are not uncommon in international trade. A buyer acquiring contractual rights under a bill of lading before taking delivery may transfer the bill to a subsequent buyer, and accordingly the rights formerly vested in him become extinct.[229] Although the 1992 Act expressly prescribes divestment of *rights*, there is, however, nothing in the Act indicating the cessation of *liabilities*.[230] In this

[221] *The Ythan* [2005] EWHC 2399 (Comm); [2006] 1 Lloyd's Rep 457.
[222] *The Berge Sisar* [2001] UKHL 17, [33].
[223] *The Ythan* [2005] EWHC 2399 (Comm); [2006] 1 Lloyd's Rep 457, [98], [103]–[111].
[224] *The Berge Sisar* [2001] UKHL 17, [35].
[225] *The Ythan* [2005] EWHC 2399 (Comm), [103].
[226] ibid, [103].
[227] ibid, [103].
[228] Buyers whose identities are specified in the request for security may find themselves subject to liability under s 3(1). See Aikens et al, *Bills of Lading*, n 44 above, para 9.109.
[229] Section 2(5)(a).
[230] Section 3(3) only provides for the continuity of the original party's liability.

section we shall look into whether the liability imposed on the buyer is divested, and if so whether there are exceptions to the rule.

Despite no corresponding provision appearing in the Act, the issue of cessation of the transferred liabilities was resolved to a great extent by the House of Lords in *The Berge Sisar*.[231] In the case, the intermediate buyer who took a routine sample of the goods did not take the delivery, but re-sold the cargo to the ultimate buyer, who took the cargo without production of the bills. Well after the cargo was delivered, the bills eventually arrived, and the intermediate buyer endorsed and forwarded them to the ultimate buyer.[232] The carrier made a claim for damage caused to the vessel by the dangerous nature of the cargo against the intermediate buyer who had only been a holder for a short period of time.[233] Although it was held that liability was not imposed on the intermediate buyer under section 3(1), the House of Lords went on to answer the question as to whether the statutory liability would cease on a further transfer of the bills of lading.[234]

Before the case reached the House of Lords, the issue was discussed extensively in the Court of Appeal where, by a majority, it was held that the intermediate buyer who triggered section 3(1) was automatically relieved of liability once the bills of lading were endorsed to the ultimate buyer.[235] The majority (Neill LJ dissenting) opined that the position of the buyer who incurred liability under section 3(1) was not irrevocable, unless and until taking actual delivery of the goods.[236] Millett LJ contended that liability should be substituted rather than being additional; where the intermediate buyer withdraws his demand or claim and subsequently endorses the bill, liability should not remain with him.[237] In holding this, he relied on a case that was decided under the 1855 Act, *Smurthwaite v Wilkins*,[238] in which the intermediate holder was relieved of liability by way of endorsement.[239] The House of Lords in *The Berge Sisar* upheld the decision of the majority in the Court of Appeal on similar grounds.[240] In addition, the House of Lords held that even if liability had been incurred by the intermediate buyer, he would have been relieved

[231] *The Berge Sisar* [2001] UKHL 17.

[232] Both the intermediate and ultimate buyer become lawful holder according to s 2(2)(a).

[233] By virtue of s 2(2)(a).

[234] Taking routine samples was not regarded demand within the meaning of s 3(1). See section II.D.(i)(a) above.

[235] [1998] 2 Lloyd's Rep 475 (Neill LJ dissenting).

[236] According to Millett J's speech, unless and until taking actual delivery of the cargo, the transferee's position is reversible. In other words, after the actual delivery, it is improbable that the buyer would be divested of liability. See [1998] 2 Lloyd's Rep 475, 486.

[237] [1998] 2 Lloyd's Rep 475, 486.

[238] *Smurthwaite v Wilkins* (1862) 11 CB (NS) 842; 142 ER 1026, considered by the House of Lords in *The Giannis NK* [1998] AC 605.

[239] [1998] 2 Lloyd's Rep 475, 487.

[240] In addition to *Smurthwaite v Wilkins*, the House also relied on several authorities for the principle of mutuality: *Sewell v Burdick* (1886) 10 App Cas 74; *Brandt v Liverpool* [1924] 1 KB 575. See *The Berge Sisar* [2001] UKHL 17, [31].

of it, once the bill was subsequently endorsed.[241] The decision was based on the 'principle of mutuality',[242] which has already been considered above.

It is arguable that this part of the decision is not without difficulties. First, Neill LJ's dissenting judgment in the Court of Appeal is significant in several respects. He opined that once liability was incurred, it should irreversibly attach to the intermediate buyer. In holding this, he relied on the preliminary views of Thomas J in *The Aegean Sea*, where the learned judge also argued in favour of the continuity of liability from the moment of imposition.[243] Second, the majority in both the Court of Appeal and the House of Lords, in arriving at this decision, said that there was no intention in the Act to reverse the decision of *Smurthwaite v Wilkins*.[244] *Smurthwaite v Wilkins* was decided under the 1855 Act, in which the rights and liabilities would be transferred simultaneously. The position is to a great extent different under the 1992 Act, which expressly divorces the transfer of rights and liabilities. It enables rights and liabilities to travel pursuant to different sections (sections 2 and 3) by different mechanisms.[245] Additionally, there appears to be no discussion or suggestion on the divestment of the intermediate buyer's imposed liability to the transferee in the Law Commission report. Nor is there any mention of *Smurthwaite v Wilkins* in the report. Whilst the Act only provides for the divestment of rights by virtue of section 2(5), there appears to be no section in the Act in relation to the divestment of liabilities. Moreover, section 2 states 'transfer' in respect of rights, while section 3 makes a party 'subject to' liabilities.[246] It is probable that the difference in the wording of the relevant sections was done deliberately. It might be that section 3 *sub-silentio* indicates no cessation of the transferred liabilities. For these reasons, it is difficult to see why the operation of the repealed 1855 Act, which transferred rights and liabilities together, should be preserved under the 1992 Act, which expressly deals with them separately under the different provisions. Therefore, particularly on the basis that there is nothing on the divestment of liabilities in the Act, there is no reason to infer that they should cease at the same time upon transfer of the bill.

Although the criticism made above has some valid points, it is submitted that the divestment of liabilities by way of endorsement should prevail on the basis of the principle of mutuality.[247] There should be a link between benefit and burdens.[248] A party should not have liabilities imposed on him under a contract

[241] *The Berge Sisar* [2001] UKHL 17, [44]–[45], per Lord Hobhouse.
[242] *The Berge Sisar* [2001] UKHL 17, [31].
[243] [1998] 2 Lloyd's Rep 475, 484. See also *The Aegean Sea* [1998] 2 Lloyd's Rep 39, 52.
[244] *The Berge Sisar* [2001] UKHL 17, [44]–[45] (HL); [1998] 2 Lloyd's Rep 475, 486; [1999] QB 863 (CA). See also Reynolds, 'The Carriage of Goods by Sea Act 1992 Put to the Test – the Berge Sisar' (1999) *LMCLQ* 161; N Campbell, 'Defining the Frontiers of the Bill of Lading Holder's Liability – the Berge Sisar and the Aegean Sea' [2000] *JBL* 196.
[245] Part III of the Law Commission Report is headed 'Separation of Contractual Rights and Duties'. See the Law Commission Report, above n 8, para 3.15.
[246] Mildon and Scorey, n 140 above, 103.
[247] See also GH Treitel, 'Bills of Lading: Liabilities of Transferee' (2001) *LMCLQ* 344, 351–52.
[248] *The Berge Sisar* [2001] UKHL 17, [45].

in which he does not seek to exercise his rights. The wording of section 3(1) may also support this inference. The imposition of liabilities expressly depends on the possession of rights under section 3(1), which only imposes liabilities on a party 'in whom rights are vested'. When the intermediate buyer endorses the bill, he is to be divested of the rights according to section 2(5) and from that moment he will become a party in whom rights 'were' vested. Therefore, section 3(1) will not be considered satisfied. On the other hand, section 3(3) provides only for the original party's concurrent liability.[249] This may also connote the assumption that any party other than the original shipper may be divested of his liabilities under the Act.

Nevertheless, there is still a situation that calls for discussion. With this decision, as soon as the intermediate buyer endorses the bill, the incurred liability is not automatically transferred to the endorsee but vanishes. There is the question of what happens if the end buyer does not wish to exercise his rights at all. Millett J, in delivering the judgment, indicated several times that the liability should remain with the intermediate buyer (endorser) until the endorsee exercise his contractual rights:

> … that is to say, liable unless and until he [the intermediate buyer] endorses the bill to someone who also fulfils the conditions of liability[250]
>
> … the holder endorses the bill in favour of a third party who becomes liable, the previous holder is exonerated.[251]

It is submitted that this part of the judgment should be reconciled with the approach of Millett J due to the policy of the Act.[252] Otherwise, it may be open to abuse. Assume that the intermediate buyer, who incurred liability only in order to be relieved of it, endorses the bill to a further party or a shell company, which will deliberately avoid exercising its rights under the contract. At first sight, it might seem arguable that the endorsee does not have to enforce the contract. But then a question arises why,if he does not wish to exercise his rights under the contract at all, would he purchase the goods and accept the bill of lading? Therefore, to prevent a potential abuse of the decision on the point, the incurred liability should remain with the intermediate buyer until the next endorsee exercises his rights.

On the other hand, even in the present state, it is probable that liability may not be divested but may remain with the intermediate buyer. Section 5(2) requires that a party becomes a holder in 'good faith'. As discussed above, good faith only means honest conduct under the Act.[253] Thus, if the subsequent endorsee just takes the

[249] Section 3(3), 'so far as it imposes liabilities under any contract on any person, shall be without prejudice to the liabilities under the contract of any person as an original party to the contract.'

[250] [1998] 2 Lloyd's Rep 475, 487.

[251] ibid, 487.

[252] Since liability in the case was not incurred by the intermediate buyer, the decision of the House of Lords on the cessation of liability is obiter.

[253] See section II.B.(i)(d) above.

bill and becomes holder not to enforce the contract but with the intention to enable the intermediate buyer to avoid liability, it is difficult to see why the subsequent endorsee should be considered a holder in good faith for the purpose of the Act. Given the lack of good faith, the endorsee may not become the holder for the purpose of the Act, and for that reason the intermediate buyer may preserve his position of being lawful holder.[254]

Some practical questions may call for discussion at this point. What happens if the buyer fulfils section 3(1) by making a claim or demanding delivery, but subsequently withdraws his claim or demand, or his demands are rejected by the carrier and the buyer subsequently does not endorse the bill? Although the House of Lords approached this in doubt, it is submitted that liability remains with the buyer[255] on the ground of the principle of mutuality. Section 3(1) is expressly worded in the present tense declaring that a party should be someone 'in whom rights are vested'. Despite a claim or demand being withdrawn, unless the bill is endorsed to a further party, the rights are still vested in the buyer. He can only be divested of his rights by way of endorsement according to section 2(5). According to the House of Lords in *The Berge Sisar*, the rule on the point is simple: liabilities cease to exist only when the intermediate buyer endorses the bill to a subsequent holder. Put differently, until the moment of endorsement, the incurred liability under section 3(1) remains with him. The rejection of a formal demand by the carrier or the withdrawal of a claim or demand would be unlikely to divest the buyer of the liability imposed. The second question is whether the liabilities incurred by B1 would be considered divested if B2 rejected the bill, endorsing it back to B1. The answer to this question depends on whether B2 became the lawful holder in good faith. If B2 accepts the bill with the intent to become the holder in good faith and later rejects it by a further endorsement, it is submitted that B1, who incurred the liability previously, will cease to be liable, following the transfer of the bill to B2. Accordingly, once he becomes the holder again with re-endorsement, he will be regarded as a new holder and his previously incurred liability will not revive. However, his position would be different if B2 rejected the bill from the very beginning without having any intent to be the holder. In that case, it is probable that B2 would never be the holder for the purpose of the Act. B1 would remain the holder, and therefore would not be divested of the incurred liability.

(i) Exceptions to the Rule

It has been discussed that liabilities of an intermediate buyer/transferee may cease upon making a further transfer of the bill of lading. Although this may appear to be a means of escape for transferees from their incurred liabilities, the rule is not without difficulties. The incurred liability becomes irreversible, once the actual

[254] Such situations were anticipated by Lord Hobhouse: 'It is possible that the conduct of one or other party may give rise to estoppels …' See *The Berge Sisar* [2001] UKHL 17, [43].

[255] See also Eder et al, *Scrutton on Charterparties and Bills of Lading*, n 31 above, para 3-036.

delivery of the goods is taken, such as to prevent 'any further dealing with the goods'[256] between the carrier and the transferee, since it is 'the final act of contractual performance on the part of the carrier'.[257] Apart from this, even in the case of making a claim or demand, liability can be irreversible if the goods become lost prior to further endorsement. Suppose the transferee/buyer made a formal demand to the carrier but before taking the delivery, the vessel and his cargo became lost due to the dangerous nature of his cargo. Or suppose the transferee/buyer commenced proceedings against the carrier for the loss of his cargo without knowing that it was the dangerous nature of his cargo which caused the damage to the vessel. In both scenarios, even if the buyer made a further transfer of the bill, liability would irrevocably attach to him. For the purpose of the Act, once the goods are lost, the bill of lading becomes spent.[258] In order for a further transfer of the bill to be valid under section 2(2)(a), the ultimate endorsee must become the holder 'by virtue of a transaction effected in pursuance of any contractual arrangements' which should have been concluded before the bill became spent. In the examples above, it would be unlikely that there were any contractual arrangements pre-dating the loss of the cargo, at the time when the intermediate transferee made a claim or demand from the carrier.

It is clear that liabilities can be divested under transferable bills of lading. So far as sea waybills and delivery orders are concerned, any liabilities incurred under these documents may be irreversible. However, there can be exceptions both under sea waybills and delivery orders. In respect of sea waybills, the rights of the sea waybill shipper are preserved pursuant to section 2(5), including his right to redirect the goods under a new contract of carriage, where the rights have been transferred to the buyer/consignee under section 2(1)(b).[259] Thus, where a sea waybill is issued to the shipper/seller which is deliverable to B1, but subsequently the shipper/seller validly redirects the goods to B2, while B2 obtains the rights under the contract of carriage via section 2(1)(b), the rights of B1 in the first sea waybill become extinguished pursuant to section 2(5)(b).[260] Similarly, the rights of shippers or holders of the bills of lading will be preserved by section 2(5), when rights are transferred to the person identified in the delivery order. Where this is the case, as for the bills of lading, it is submitted that the liabilities incurred will cease once a new sea waybill or delivery order is issued on the basis of the principle of mutuality.[261] Indeed, for such a substitution, cooperation is needed with the

[256] *The Berge Sisar* [1998] 2 Lloyd's Rep 475; [1999] QB 863, 864 (CA).

[257] *The Berge Sisar* [2001] UKHL 17, [32].

[258] *The Ythan* [2005] EWHC 2399 (Comm).

[259] *AP Moller-Maersk A/S (t/a Maersk Line) v Sonaec Villas Cen Sad Fadoul* [2010] EWHC 355 (Comm); [2010] 2 All ER 1159. See also the Law Commission Report, n 8 above, para 5.23.

[260] ibid.

[261] However, if the practice adopted requires cancellation and re-issue of the bill of lading to the same consignee to avoid delay and discharge formalities, this may not prevent the consignee being a party who acquired rights under the Act: see *Finmoon v Baltic Reefers* [2012] 2 Lloyd's Rep 388, [43]. In a similar fashion, a switch bill might be issued in order to substitute a new shipper for the shipper in the original bill. The issue of a switch bill might sometimes constitute a novation or variation of the original

carrier, who may not be willing to lose an additional party to sue. As for delivery orders, they can be made out 'to order' or 'bearer'. Once this is the case, liabilities can be divested, as is the case with bills of lading when the rights are acquired under section 2(1)(c) by a further party.

III. Conclusion

For the reasons set out above, liability arising from the shipment of dangerous goods is said to be transmissible from the seller/shipper to the buyer/transferee under the carriage contract. This is justified as follows. First, as a result of the divorce of the transfer of rights from that of liabilities, liability for dangerous goods is not automatically transferred at the time the rights are vested in the buyer. The principle of mutuality, which constitutes the basis of the Act, requires that the transferee will not bear any obligations, unless he wishes to exercise rights under the contract. Second, the transfer of rights is a prerequisite to the imposition of liabilities under the Act. Thus, even if section 3(1) is satisfied by the buyer/transferee, liability will not be incurred unless rights are acquired by him. Third, the courts appear to interpret restrictively the mechanism of section 3(1) in favour of the buyer/transferee. Fourthly, unless an irreversible step is taken, buyers, by trading transferable bills of lading will have an important option which could relieve them of liability, even if it is incurred preliminarily. Nonetheless, in considering liability for dangerous goods, such an option is not without difficulties, and liability may irrevocably attach in exceptional situations, particularly when taking delivery of the goods.

contract in the bill of lading. In a very recent Australian case, it was held that once the switch bills were issued with the intention of the parties not to preserve the original shipper's rights and obligations under the cancelled bills, the original shipper's rights and obligations in the cancelled bills were considered extinguished and the substituted shipper acquired the rights and obligations as the shipper under the switch bills: *Wollongong Coal Ltd v PCL (Shipping) Pte Ltd (The Illawarra Fortune)* [2020] NSWSC 184; [2021] 1 Lloyd's Rep 385. See also *Noble Resources v Cavalier Shipping Corp (The Atlas)* [1996] 1 Lloyd's Rep 642; *Sea Master Shipping Inc v Arab Bank (Switzerland) Ltd (The Sea Master)* [2018] EWHC 1902; [2019] 1 Lloyd's Rep 101.

6

Other Mechanisms for Imposing Liability on the Buyer

I. General

In Chapter five, it was discussed that under a contractual regime, liability for dangerous goods is transmissible from the seller/shipper to the buyer/transferee under the 1992 Act. Since the Act came into force, there has been almost no need to rely on other common law actions outside the contract, given that it has created a comprehensive contractual regime between the carrier and the transferee/buyer who is not the shipper. However, albeit rarely, there may be some residual situations for which there are no contractual actions falling within the scope of the 1992 Act.[1] The Act has not abolished the common law actions and does not govern the law outside the contract. As such, particularly in the absence of a contract, routes under the common law actions for recourse can be significantly relevant.

It has already been discussed earlier, in Chapter four, that at the shipment stage the non-contracting seller may be subject to liability in tort and under an implied contract to the carrier. In this chapter, when there is no contractual nexus between the carrier and the buyer on the other side of the voyage, namely at the delivery stage, we shall look into whether the buyer could be subject to liability for damage or losses arising from dangerous goods under the common law actions. Put differently, we shall see whether the buyer can take advantage of the absence of a contractual regime, and accordingly avoid liability.

II. Liability under the *Brandt v Liverpool* Doctrine

Although in practice problems involving entitlement to sue are resolved by the 1992 Act to a great extent, it did not abolish the well-established common law

[1] Without giving an exhaustive list of examples, the bill of lading may, for instance, not have reached the buyer at all or the shipping document used may not fall within the scope of the 1992 Act. Alternatively, as was the case in the *East West Corp* case, there may not have been a contractual action due to the divestment of rights: [2003] QB 1509.

Brandt v Liverpool[2] doctrine. In that case, a separate contract from the original contract was implied on bill of lading terms between the receiver and the carrier on delivery of the cargo against presentation of the bill of lading.[3] Although the importance of the doctrine was reduced by the 1992 Act, there may still be circumstances where such a contract can be implied. For instance, a document outside the ambit of the 1992 Act may have been used.[4] When this is the case, a contract can be implied between the carrier and the receiver/buyer, depending on whether the facts of the case satisfy the conditions of the doctrine.[5]

At first sight, when a contract is implied, it might appear that the carrier may have a claim against the buyer for damages caused by dangerous goods under the implied contract, given that it is implied on bill of lading terms. However, in *The Athanasia Comninos*, Mustill J held that the dangerous goods obligations were not transferred to the buyer/receiver under the *Brandt v Liverpool* contract, and indicated that the buyer/receiver would only assume rights and liabilities concerning the carriage and delivery of the goods and payment therefor.[6] Therefore, even if the 1992 Act does not apply and a contract is implied between the carrier and the buyer, it seems unlikely that the *Brandt v Liverpool*-type implied contract would give rise to liability for dangerous goods for the buyer.

III. Bailment Action

Where a person delivers his goods into the custody of another party that accepts these goods voluntarily, a relationship of bailment can be established between those parties.[7] In terms of carriage of goods by sea, bailment in most cases arises between the shipper/bailor and the shipowner/bailee, once the goods are shipped. Even though it may have some features in common, a bailment action differs from both contractual and tort actions.[8] It can exist independently of contract but may

[2] *Brandt v Liverpool, Brazil & River Plate Steam Navigation Co Ltd* [1924] 1 KB 575.

[3] In *Cremer v General Carriers (The Dona Mari)* [1974] 1 WLR 341, the contract was implied on the terms of a ship's delivery order.

[4] For such examples, see *Ilyssia Compania Naviera SA v Ahmed Abdul Oawi Bamadoa (The Elli 2)* [1985] 1 Lloyd's Rep 107; *Compania Portorafti Commerciale SA v Ultramar Panama Inc (The Captain Gregos (No 2))* [1990] 2 Lloyd's Rep 395.

[5] The application of the doctrine was restricted by the following cases: *Aramis (cargo owners) v Aramis (owners) (The Aramis)* [1989] 1 Lloyd's Rep 213; *Mitsui & Co Ltd v Novorossiysk Shipping Co (The Gudermes)* [1993] 1 Lloyd's Rep 311.

[6] *The Athanasia Comninos* [1990] 1 Lloyd's Rep 277, 281. See generally, Chapter 4, Section II.B.(i)(c) above.

[7] NE Palmer, *Palmer on Bailment*, 3rd edn (London, Sweet &Maxwell, 2009), 64–71. See also *East West Corp v Dampskibsselskabet AF, 1912, Aktieselskab (DKBS 1912)* [2003] QB 1509; [2003] EWCA Civ 83, [24]; *The Pioneer Container* [1994] 2 AC 324, 341–42; *Morris v CW Martin & Sons* [1966] 1 QB 716.

[8] *East West Corp v DKBS 1912* [2003] EWCA Civ 83; 2003 QB 1509, [24]–[32]; *Yearworth v North Bristol NHS Trust* [2009] EWCA Civ 37; [2010] QB 1, [50]. See also *TRM Copy Centres (UK) Ltd v Lanwall Services Ltd* [2009] 1 WLR 1375.

also co-exist and survive on the contractual terms already made between those parties.[9] Where the parties' relationship is governed by the 1992 Act, bailment will arguably add nothing to the contract. However the scope of the 1992 Act is limited to contract only, and bailment is considered an independent cause of action today.[10] The 1992 Act albeit seldom, may give no right of action,[11] and accordingly parties may seek to rely on a bailment action.

At common law, the bailor of the goods can be held liable to the carrier in respect of dangerous goods.[12] In most cases where the shipper is also the bailor – who is almost invariably the seller in CIF sales[13] but could be either the seller or the buyer under FOB sales, depending on the terms – the carrier will naturally base his claim against the shipper/bailor on contract rather than bailment. However, two questions call for discussion at this point: first, the question of whether the consignee/buyer could be considered the bailor instead of the shipper; and if so, second, the question of whether he could have liability for dangerous goods imposed under bailment.

A. Buyer as Original Bailor

In *The Aliakmon*, Lord Brandon in rejecting the argument that the bailment was between the buyers/consignee and the carrier, held that the 'only bailment was one by the sellers [shipper] to the shipowner'.[14] On the other hand, there appears to be a contradictory angle in *The Berge Sisar* in which Lord Hobhouse opined:

> The bill of lading acknowledges the receipt of the goods from the shipper [seller] for carriage to a destination and delivery there to the consignee. It therefore evidences a bailment with the carrier who has issued the bill of lading as the bailee and the consignee [buyer] as bailor.[15]

[9] *Akts De Danske Sukkerfabriker v Bajamar Cia (The Torenia)* [1983] 2 Lloyd's Rep 210, 216.

[10] See *East West Corp v DKBS 1912* [2003] QB 1533, [45] and *Yearworth* [2009] EWCA Civ 37; [2010] QB 1. Of the same view, see also R Aikens, 'Which Way to Rome for Cargo Claims in Bailment When Goods Are Carried by Sea?' (2011) *LMCLQ* 482, 485. See also the Law Commission, *Rights of Suit in Respect of Carriage of Goods by Sea* (Law Com No 196, Scot Law Com No 130, 1991), paras 2.39, 2.45, 5.24.

[11] As was the case in *East West Corp* [2003] EWCA Civ 83, due to endorsement, the shipper may have been divested of right of suit by s 2(5) of the 1992 Act, but bailment may allow him to put his claim against the shipowner.

[12] MG Bridge, *Benjamin's Sale of Goods*, 11th edn (London, Sweet & Maxwell, 2020), para 18-172, fn 786; GH Treitel and FMB Reynolds, *Carver on Bills of Lading*, 4th edn (London, Sweet & Maxwell, 2017), para 6-012, fn 89; GH Treitel, 'Bills of Lading: Liabilities of Transferee' (2001) *LMCLQ* 344, 353, fn 79. The bailor can also be liable for damages arising out of unsafety or defect of the goods: *Blakemore v Bristol and Exeter Ry Co* (1858) 8 E & B 1035; *Coughlin v Gillison* (1899) 1 QB 145. See Palmer, *Palmer on Bailment*, n 7 above, 636 and 1580; NE Palmer and E McKendrick, *Interests in Goods*, 2nd edn (London, LLP, 1998), 486.

[13] *Leigh & Sillivan Ltd v Aliakmon Shipping Co Ltd (The Aliakmon)* [1986] AC 785, 818.

[14] ibid.

[15] [2001] UKHL 17, [18]. His Lordship supported his view with two cases: *Ryans v Nix* (1839) 4 M & W 775 and *Evans v Nichol* (1841) 3 M & G 614.

If the words of Lord Hobhouse are deemed to be correct, the rule that the shipper is the bailor could be rebuttable; as such, the buyer/consignee can be the bailor of the goods.

Between Lord Brandon's and Lord Hobhouse's propositions, prima facie the former proposition should prevail, as the seller/shipper may often want to retain the title in the goods and the bills of lading as security for payment.[16] It is argued that there is no such presumption merely due to the fact that the bill names the buyer as consignee.[17] Nevertheless, this does not necessarily mean that the two views cannot be reconciled. In *The Albazero*, it was held that the goods could be bailed in three different ways:

> The first category of cases comprises those in which it was held that the consignee rather than the consignor was the proper person to sue. The ground of decision in those cases was that the consignor, in delivering the goods to the carrier, was acting as agent for the consignee, and that the property and risk in the goods were either in the consignee before such delivery or passed to him upon its taking place.
>
> The second category of cases comprises those in which it was held that the consignor rather than the consignee was the proper person to sue. The ground of decision in those cases was that the consignor, in delivering the goods to the carrier, was acting as principal on his own account, and that the property and risk in them remained in him during the carriage.[18]

In *The Aliakmon*, the property did not pass on shipment. It did not even pass subsequently, since the consignee/buyer was not able to pay and they were holding the bills as agent of the seller, given the further agreement between them. Accordingly, the buyer in the case cannot be classified in the first group of *The Albazero*. Therefore, it is the seller who was the bailor, which would fall within the second category. On the other hand, the first category emphasises that the consignee is the bailor if the property passes before or on shipment.[19] Although this is not very common under CIF and FOB sales, the property may pass to the consignee/the buyer on delivery of the goods to the carrier.[20] Further support for such reconciliation between the propositions can be found both in the Court of Appeal[21] and the House of Lords[22] decisions. In *Kum v Wah Tat Bank Ltd*, it was

[16] Treitel and Reynolds, *Carver on Bills of Lading*, n 12 above, para 6-012 ff; Bridge, *Benjamin's Sale of Goods*, n 12 above, para 18-171 ff. See also R Aikens, R Lord, MD Bools, *Bills of Lading*, 3rd edn (London, Informa, 2020), para 10.62.

[17] Treitel and Reynolds, *Carver on Bills of Lading*, n 12 above, para 6-012 ff; Bridge, *Benjamin's Sale of Goods*, n 12 above, para 18-171 ff.

[18] *Concord Petroleum Corp v Gosford Marine Panama SA (The Albazero)* [1977] AC 774, 786 (HL). The third category is not relevant here.

[19] It is very unlikely that the property passes before shipment on sea carriage. See *Texas Instruments Ltd v Nason (Europe) Ltd* [1991] 1 Lloyd's Rep 146.

[20] For such examples, see *Scottish & Newcastle v Othon Ghalanos* [2008] UKHL 11; *The Sevonia Team* [1983] 2 Lloyd's Rep 640; *The San Nicholas* [1976] 1 Lloyd's Rep 8; *The Dunelmia* [1970] 1 QB 289; *The Athanasia Comninos* [1990] 1 Lloyd's Rep 277.

[21] *East West Corp* [2003] QB 1533.

[22] *Scottish & Newcastle Int'l Ltd v Othon Ghalanos Ltd* [2008] UKHL 11.

held by the Privy Council that it was the consignee who was the original bailor, not the shipper, since the property passed on shipment.[23] In *East West Corp*, Mance LJ applied the principles of *The Albazero* to determine who the bailor was in that case.[24] In *Scottish & Newcastle*, yet again Lord Mance, citing *The Albazero*, *The Berge Sisar* and *East West Corp*, was inclined to hold that the consignee/buyer could be the bailor on the grounds discussed above.[25] All these authorities appear to show that the proposition of Lord Hobhouse in *The Berge Sisar* can only be supported, once qualified with the classification established in *The Albazero*.[26] It is therefore probable that if the facts of the case prove that the property passes on shipment, the consignee/buyer will be regarded as the original bailor within the first category of *The Albazero*.[27]

Indeed, it might be argued that where the consignee/buyer is the original bailor, he may also be regarded as the original party to the carriage contract[28] and the carrier may have a claim for damages arising from dangerous goods against that buyer who is considered the original party to the carriage contract.[29] This is no doubt possible under many FOB contracts, as discussed earlier, in Chapter four. However, there are some examples of such FOB sales where the property passed on shipment to the buyer but it was still the seller/shipper who was held to be a principal party to the carriage contract.[30] This was the case in *Kum v Wah Tat Bank Ltd*, where the consignee was regarded as the bailor, and the shipper was a different party.[31] Albeit not very common, it is possible that the shipper and the original bailor can sometimes be different parties. Therefore, if this inference is correct, this makes the FOB buyer/consignee who is considered the original bailor technically exposed to liability for damage arising from dangerous goods.

However, there appears to be no reported case which renders the consignee/bailor liable for dangerous goods, as such a proposition is not without difficulties. First, the prima facie rule that the shipper is the bailor is rarely rebuttable, since title in the goods seldom passes on shipment under CIF and FOB sales.[32] Second, bailment was not properly considered an independent cause of action until the 1960s.[33] By the enactment of the 1992 Act, there is almost no need to

[23] [1971] 1 Lloyd's Rep 439, where the pledge was completed on shipment of the goods.

[24] [2003] QB 1533, [34].

[25] [2008] UKHL 11, [41]–[43].

[26] See also *Sumanu Natural Resources Ltd and SJM Gems International Ltd v Mediterranean Shipping Company SA* [2014] EWHC 2829 (Comm), affirmed in the Court of Appeal [2016] EWCA Civ 34.

[27] It was Brandon J (who later became Lord Brandon) who first defined the three categories at first instance in *The Albazero* [1974] 2 Lloyd's Rep 38. This was later approved by the House of Lords. It was also Lord Brandon who delivered the decision in *The Aliakmon*.

[28] *East West Corp* [2003] QB 1533, [34]. For an example of this where the consignee/buyer was considered the shipper, see *Scottish & Newcastle v Othon Ghalanos* [2008] UKHL 11.

[29] See *The Athanasia Comninos* [1990] 1 Lloyd's Rep 277.

[30] *The Sevonia Team* [1983] 2 Lloyd's Rep 640; *The San Nicholas* [1976] 1 Lloyd's Rep 8; *The Dunelmia* [1970] 1 QB 289; *The Athanasia Comninos* [1990] 1 Lloyd's Rep 277.

[31] [1971] 1 Lloyd's Rep 439, where the pledge was completed on shipment.

[32] *Mitsui & Co. Ltd. v Flota Mercante Grancolombiana SA (The Ciudad de Pasto)* [1988] 1 WLR 1145.

[33] *Morris v Martin* [1966] 1 QB 716; *Building and Civil Engineering Holidays Management Ltd v Post Office* [1966] 1 QB 247.

rely on bailment, since the parties put forward their claim under contract. Indeed, bailment is considered an independent cause of action today.[34] But where a contractual relationship arises under the 1992 Act, the courts arguably feel reluctant to impose dangerous goods liability on the buyer/consignee under bailment, even if he is regarded as the original bailor. This is because once there is a contract between them via the 1992 Act, the consignee/buyer will not be subject to liability unless section 3(1) is triggered. Thus, provided that there is a contractual nexus, the courts would likely defy such an attempt by the shipowner to circumvent the mechanism of section 3(1) in order to render the buyer liable under bailment.

B. Buyer as Attornee

Where the title in the goods passes at a stage after the shipment of the goods, the consignee/buyer will hardly be the original bailor, and accordingly there will not be bailment between the bailee and the buyer. However, it is trite law that if an attornment is established, the consignee/buyer will replace the original bailor as the new bailor/attornee.[35] Attornment is a recognition that the goods are held on behalf of the successor in the title rather than the original bailor and that the former is entitled to delivery of them.[36] An attornment will not usually be established merely on the ground of naming a party in the bill of lading or transferring the bill to the relevant party.[37] If this is correct, then only an actual attornment can be said to establish bailment between the buyer and the bailee.[38] Such an attornment therefore will usually take place on presentation of the bill of lading to demand or take delivery of the goods.[39] However, the mechanism of attornment is not exhaustive. There can be an attornment even in the case of delivery without presentation of the bills of lading.[40]

[34] See *East West Corp* [2003] QB 1533 and *Yearworth* [2009] EWCA Civ 37; [2010] QB 1. See also, R Aikens, 'Which Way to Rome for Cargo Claims in Bailment When Goods Are Carried by Sea?' (2011) *LMCLQ* 482, 485.

[35] *The Aliakmon* [1986] 1 AC 785, 815.

[36] *The Gudermes* [1993] 1 Lloyd's Rep 311, 324.

[37] *The Aliakmon* [1986] 1 AC 785, 818; *The Captain Gregos (No 2)* [1990] 2 Lloyd's Rep 395, 406; *The Future Express* [1993] 2 Lloyd's Rep 542, 550 (CA). See also *The Starsin* [2003] EWCA Civ 174; [2003] 1 Lloyd's Rep 239, [136]. For the authorities against attornment, see *The Kapetan Markos (No 2)* [1987] 2 Lloyd's Rep 321, 340. See also the dictum of Devlin J in *Heskell v Continental Express Ltd* (1949) 83 Ll L Rep 438, 453; and dictum of Lord Hobhouse in *The Berge Sisar* [2001] UKHL 17, [18].

[38] *The Aliakmon* [1986] 1 AC 785, 818.

[39] *The Captain Gregos (No 2)* [1990] 2 Lloyd's Rep 395, 406. Treitel, 'Bills of Lading: Liabilities of Transferee', n 12 above, 354; Aikens, Which Way to Rome?', n 10 above, 492. But see S Baughen, 'Bailment or Conversion? Misdelivery Claims against Non-contractual Carriers' (2010) *LMCLQ* 411, 421, fn 48. A problem may arise where the delivery is made by a sub-bailee. However, Baughen thinks that if the delivery is made on the authority of the head-bailee, the buyer may find himself bound as a result of attornment. See S Baughen 'Bailment's Continuing Role in Cargo Claims' (1999) *LMCLQ* 393, 398.

[40] *The Captain Gregos (No 2)* [1990] 2 Lloyd's Rep 395, 406. Attornment may arise during negotiations between the shipowner and the buyer: see *The Gudermes* [1993] 1 Lloyd's Rep 311. In respect

Thus, once an attornment is established, the question as to whether the buyer/attornee can become liable for losses and damage arising out of dangerous goods calls for discussion. Unlike the original bailor, he cannot be said to owe any duty in relation to shipment of such goods to the bailee. For that reason, he would not have any liability imposed on him under the common law duty. However, where an attornment is established between the bailee and the buyer, the courts are inclined to rule that it would be on the terms of original bailment, which is in most situations on bill of lading terms.[41] This is also the case where there is sub-bailment, which generally arises when the carrier is the time charterer, not the shipowner,[42] or where the initial carrier delivers the cargo to another carrier for transhipment.[43] Although it appears to be unclear whether the bailee can enforce all or some of his rights against the bailor or attornee, it is suggested that the bailee should enforce all of his rights.[44] If this is correct, then since most bills of lading incorporate the Rules, the buyer/attornee will be technically open to incur liability under article IV rule 6 for dangerous goods.[45] Indeed, in most cases there will be a contractual nexus and the carrier will not need to rely on bailment. Nonetheless, this might be an option for the shipowners when there is no contract. At first sight, this may seem implausible where the attornee/buyer has no duty to the bailee in respect of the shipment of dangerous goods. However, the bailee's entitlement to damages arising from dangerous goods can be justified on several grounds. First, attornment has a retrospective effect, and accordingly the attornee will be entitled

of ships' delivery orders, the carrier will attorn to the holder of the order by issuing the order. Such bailment will likely be on bill of lading terms. On the other hand, any delivery order issued by someone other than the carrier will not carry any attornment. See P Todd, *Bills of Lading and Bankers Documentary Credits*, 4th edn (London, Informa, 2007), paras 7.133 and 7.134. However, there will not be attornment at all when the buyer takes delivery of the goods on behalf of the shipper/seller: *The Aliakmon* [1986] AC 785.

[41] *The Aliakmon* [1986] AC 785, 818; *The Captain Gregos (No 2)* [1990] 2 Lloyd's Rep 395. See also *Sumanu v Mediterranean Shipping Company SA* [2014] EWHC 2829, [31]. The terms can be implied: *Glyn Mills Currie & Co v East and West India Dock Co* (1882) 7 App Cas 591, 611–12. Bailment may be on charterparty terms too. This is likely to arise where the shipper is also the charterer, and accordingly the original bailment arises on charterparty terms: *The Gudermes* [1993] 1 Lloyd's Rep 311.

[42] *Elder Dempster & Co Ltd v Paterson Zochonis & Co Ltd* [1924] AC 522. In the case, the shipowner, who was not the carrier under the bill, was entitled to rely on the terms of the charterer's bill against the bailor. However the subsequent authorities rejected such an approach, indicating that in such a case the terms of sub-bailment are rather on the terms of a time charter than the bills of lading. See *Morris v Martin* [1966] 1 QB 716; *The Pioneer Container* [1994] 2 AC 324; *The Forum Craftsman* [1985] 1 Lloyd's Rep 291, 295; *The Starsin* [2004] 1 AC 715, [137]. See also *The Mahkutai* [1996] AC 650. See Aikens et al, *Bills of Lading*, n 16 above, para 10.81.

[43] *The Pioneer Container* [1994] 2 AC 324 (Privy Council). The sub-bailee would be able to rely on all terms of sub-bailment even including non-germane ones such as jurisdiction clauses, provided that the original bailor has expressly or impliedly consented to these terms. However, the courts will most likely find that the original bailor has tacitly consented to be bound by the Hague or Hague-Visby Rules. See Baughen, 'Bailment's Continuing Role in Cargo Claims', n 39 above, 401. See also *Morris v Martin* [1966] 1 QB 716 which was applied in *the Pioneer Container.*

[44] Palmer and Mckendrick, *Interests in Goods*, n 12 above, 1375–76. See also *The Winson* [1982] AC 939, 961.

[45] The courts might be reluctant to manipulate the term 'shipper' though, not to impose liability onto the attornee/buyer. However, if the bill also contains a merchant clause, the liability is more likely to arise.

to rights against the bailee for losses and damage that had already occurred before he became the subsequent bailor/attornee.[46] Thus, it should follow that there would be no injustice, if the bailee were retrospectively entitled to rights against the attornee for the obligations that occurred at an earlier stage. Moreover, while the courts appear to be inclined to enlarge the bailee's liability when the bailment terms are relied upon by the bailor,[47] there is no reason why the terms should be interpreted restrictively, when they are relied upon by the bailee.[48] Third, as discussed above, attornment will often be established on demanding or taking delivery of the goods between the buyer and the bailee. Under a contractual relationship, when there is delivery or demand, section 3(1) will be satisfied and the buyer will become liable under the 1992 Act. However, if there is no contract but bailment on terms, the buyer/attornee may be able to take advantage of this and avoid liability, when he would normally have had liability imposed on him due to a demand or delivery under contract.[49] Transferring rights and liabilities under the 1992 Act is based on the principle of mutuality, which provides that the party who wishes to exercise rights should be burdened with liabilities as well. That being the case, although there is no contract but instead a bailment relationship, the same principle should perhaps apply by analogy to bailment, and for that reason when the buyer/attornee is willing to exercise his rights on terms of bailment by demanding and taking delivery, he should also bear the corresponding burdens thereunder.

IV. Function of the Document of Title

Under CIF and FOB contracts, the seller is required to tender a transferable (or negotiable) shipped bill of lading unless otherwise stipulated in the sale contract.[50] A shipped bill of lading issued as 'to order' or 'bearer' is a transferable document.[51]

[46] *The Gudermes* [1993] 1 Lloyd's Rep 311. See also *Sonicare International Ltd v East Anglia Freight Terminal Ltd* [1997] 2 Lloyd's Rep 48. Palmer suggests that too. See Palmer, *Palmer on Bailment*, n 7 above, 90.

[47] *Sandeman Coprimar v Transitos Integrales* [2003] QB 1270, where the bailee was found liable for loss of the goods which occurred after delivering them to a subsequent bailee.

[48] For a similar view, see Cooke et al, *Voyage Charters*, 4th edn (London, Informa, 2014), para 18.133.

[49] In *East West Corp*, the bailee could not take the advantage of not having a contractual nexus with the shipper but became liable under bailment. See [2003] QB 1509.

[50] In terms of received bills of lading, the authorities are not conclusive. See *The Marlborough Hill* [1921] 1 AC 444; *The Diamond Alkali* [1921] 3 KB 443. A mate's receipt is not a document of title at common law: *Nippon Yusen Kaisha v Ramjiban Serowgee* [1938] AC 429. However, it can be upon proof of custom. See *Kum v Wah Tat Bank* [1971] 1 Lloyd's Rep 439, 443–44.

[51] Although in the very first case where the document of title function was established, the bill of lading was mentioned as 'negotiable and transferable', the bill of lading technically is not a negotiable in the sense that it gives the transferee better title than the transferor: *Lickbarrow v Mason* (1794) 5 TR 683, 685. This is just a popular usage to indicate its transferable feature. See *Gurney v Behrend* (1854) 3 El & Bl 622, 633–34; *Heskell v Continental Express Ltd* (1949–50) 83 Ll LR 438, 453; *Kum v Wah Tat Bank* [1971] 1 Lloyd's Rep 439, 446; *The Future Express* [1993] 2 Lloyd's Rep 542, 547 (CA); *The Rafaela S* [2005] UKHL 11, [37]. For discussions on transferability and negotiability, see also R Negus, 'The Negotiability of bills of lading' (1921) 37 *LQR* 442; C Debattista, *Sale of Goods Carried*

This transferable document is considered a document of title to the goods at common law.[52] Once transferred, the holder of a document of title becomes entitled to constructive possession of the goods.[53] This function is described in the case law in many forms.[54] However, it is best illustrated in the famous dictum of Bowen J from *Sanders v Maclean*:

> A cargo at sea while in the hands of the carrier is necessarily incapable of physical delivery. During this period of transit and voyage, the bill of lading by the law merchant is universally recognised as its symbol, and the indorsement and delivery of the bill of lading operates as a symbolical delivery of the cargo.[55]

Erle CJ in *Meyerstein v Barber* also held: 'the indorsement and delivery of the bill of lading while the ship is at sea operate exactly the same as the delivery of the goods themselves to the assignee after the ship's arrival would do.'[56] The bill of lading as a document of title symbolises the goods, and its delivery is equivalent to delivery of the goods.[57] By the function of constructive possession,[58] the buyer holds something that not only represents the goods but also puts the goods at his disposal.[59] A document of title establishes a special relationship between the actual possessor of the goods (the carrier) and the possessor (the buyer) of the bill of lading. From the moment of transfer, the buyer/holder who has the right to the goods becomes the creditor, while the carrier who owes the duty to deliver against the

by Sea (Dublin, Butterworths, 1990), 19; A Tettenborn, 'Transferable and Negotiable Documents of Title – a Redefinition?' (1991) *LMCLQ* 538; Palmer and McKendrick, *Interests in Goods*, n 12 above, 547–54.

[52] Apart from order and bearer bills, the position of a straight bill of lading is not straightforward. However, the House of Lords held that a straight bill of lading is a document of title for the purpose of the 1971 Act. In the House of Lords, Lord Bingham, agreeing with the reasoning of Rix J from the Court of Appeal, was also inclined to hold that it is a document of title at common law. See *The Rafaela S* [2005] UKHL 11, [20]–[24]. See also P Todd, 'Bill of Lading as Document of Title' [2005] *JBL* 762; G McMeel, 'Straight Bills of Lading in the House of Lords – the Rafaela S' (2005) *LMCLQ* 273; GH Treitel, 'The Legal Status of Straight Bills of Lading' (2003) 119 *LQR* 608; S Girvin, 'Bills of Lading and Straight Bills of Lading: Principles and Practice' [2006] *JBL* 86; DYH Lee and P Sooksripaisarnkit, 'The Straight Bill of Lading: Past, Present, and Future' (2012) 18 *JIML* 39.

[53] *The Delfini* [1990] 1 Lloyd's Rep 252, 268.

[54] In this part, we shall only examine whether the carrier may have rights against the holder of a document of title for damage caused by dangerous goods, not the infinite discussion of document of title generally.

[55] *Sanders v Maclean* (1883) 11 QBD 327, 341.

[56] *Meyerstein v Barber* (1866) LR 2 CP 38, 45.

[57] *Barber v Meyerstein* (1870) LR 4 HL 317, 322; *Sewell v Burdick* (1884) 13 QBD 159, 171; *Clemens Horst Co v Biddell Bros* [1912] AC 18, 22–23. This is also consistent with s 27 of the 1979 Act in which delivery requirement is defined. See also, DM Sassoon, *CIF and FOB Contracts*, 4th edn (London, Sweet & Maxwell 1995) 113.

[58] Constructive possession can be often called as symbolic too. But see AP Bell, *Modern Law of Personal Property in England and Ireland* (Dublin, Butterworths, 1989), ch 3; Bools, *The Bill of Lading: a Document of Title to the Goods: an Anglo-American Comparison* (London, LLP 1997) 184.

[59] *Mitchell Cotts & Co Ltd v Hairco Ltd* (1943) 77 Ll L Rep 106; *C Sharpe & Co Ltd v Nosawa & Co* [1917] 2 KB 814, 818; *NV Veendammer Kunstmesthandel v HM Procurator-General (The Parchim)* [1918] AC 157, 171–72; *Biddell Brothers v E Clemens Horst & Co* [1911] 1 KB 934, 956.

document of title becomes the debtor in this relationship, which has nothing to do with contract but with possessory title.[60]

From the moment of transfer of the bill, the carrier is only obliged to deliver the goods to the holder of the document of title, not to the transferor or original shipper.[61] That is to say, if the carrier delivers the goods to someone other than the buyer/holder or refuses to deliver to the buyer/holder, the buyer will have an alternative course of action to contractual action,[62] in conversion.[63] However, just because the buyer will have a right of action for conversion arising out of the document of title to the goods,[64] does not mean that any liability of the buyer to the carrier will arise. For this reason, the carrier will not have a right of action for loss or damage suffered in consequence of the shipment of dangerous goods against the buyer/holder.

V. Potential Tort Actions against the Buyer

By means of the 1992 Act, the buyer in most cases will have a contractual nexus with the carrier, and accordingly those parties will have an action in contract against each other. Although the problems in relation to contractual actions have largely been resolved by the 1992 Act, there are still some leftover situations not

[60] Unlike in bailment, attornment takes no part to establish relationship between the carrier and the holder in terms of document of title: *The Future Express* [1992] Lloyd's Rep 79, 94 (High Ct) per Diamond J.

[61] The transfer of a document of title does not necessarily also pass the property, unless there is intention of the parties so: *Sanders v Maclean* (1883) 11 QBD 327, 341. The conventional view is that the bill of lading ceases to be a document of title, once the goods are delivered to the person entitled to; *Barber v Meyerstein* (1870) LR 4 HL 317; *Barclays Bank v Commissioners of Customs & Excise* [1963] 1 Lloyd's Rep 81. However it was held obiter by Diamond J in *The Future Express* that the bill of lading does not become stale until the goods are delivered against production of it: [1992] 2 Lloyd's Rep 79, 96. This point was left open in the Court of Appeal: [1993] 2 Lloyd's Rep 542. See also *The Delfini* [1988] 2 Lloyd's Rep 59, 608; *Standard Chartered Bank v Dorchester LNG Ltd (The Erin Schulte)* [2014] EWCA Civ 1382; [2015] 1 Lloyd's Rep 97, [53]. The bill of lading also appears to remain as a document of title, even if the goods are lost: *Manbre Saccharine v Corn Products* [1919] 1 KB 198. See also Cooke et al, *Voyage Charters*, n 48 above, para 18.149.

[62] *Glyn Mills Currie & Co v East and West India Dock Co* (1882) 7 App Cas 592; *The Stettin* (1889) 14 PD 142; *Sze Hai Tong Ltd v Rambler Cycle Co Ltd* [1959] AC 576; *The Sormovskiy* 3068 [1994] 2 Lloyd's Rep 266; *Motis Exports Ltd v Dampskibsselskabet AF 1912, Aktieselskab* [2000] Lloyd's Rep 211; *The Houda* [1994] 2 Lloyd's Rep 541; *Trucks & Spares Ltd v Maritime Agencies Ltd* [1951] 2 All ER 982; *The Happy Ranger* [2002] EWCA Civ 694; *The MSC Amsterdam* [2007] EWCA Civ 794.

[63] *The Sormovskiy* 3068 [1994] 2 Lloyd's Rep 266, 283. See also *Sze Hai Tong Ltd v Rambler Cycle Co Ltd* [1959] AC 576.

[64] An action in conversion seeks to protect possession or the immediate right to possession: *Rogers v Kennay* (1846) 9 QB 594, 596; *International Factors Ltd v Rodriguez* [1979] QB 353. See also P Todd, 'The Bill of Lading and Delivery: the Common Law Actions' (2006) *LMCLQ* 539, 545 ff; Todd, *Bankers Documentary Credits*, n 40 above, paras 7.61–7.66.

covered by the Act.[65] When one of these arises, the claimants will seek to bring an action in tort against the defendants. On this, the case law appears to show that in the shipping law context, most of the tort actions concern claims in negligence by the cargo owners/buyers against the carriers/shipowners.[66] However, this does not necessarily mean that the carriers are not entitled to sue the cargo owners in tort.

A. Actions in Negligence and Vicarious Liability

At this point, the question that arises is whether the carrier or other victims can sue the end buyer/cargo owner in tort for liability arising out of the shipment of dangerous goods. So far as liability for dangerous goods is concerned, there are a number of cases showing that the carrier successfully sued the negligent party for his loss. In *The Orjula*,[67] due to defective packing and staging, the drums of acid leaked and caused damage to the vessel and containers, which were supplied by the carrier. For the damage, the carrier sued (in tort) both the shipper/seller named in the bill of lading and the party who supplied the drums of chemicals to the shippers and also stuffed them in the containers. It was held by Mance J that the defendants owed a duty of care to avoid damage to the containers and the vessel, and for that reason the carrier would be entitled to claim in tort against the supplier for the alleged negligence in the stowage of the containers.[68] Similarly, in *The Kapetan Georgis*, the time charterer, who was sued by the shipowner for damage arising from dangerous goods, in return issued a third party notice against the shipper/seller, who did not have a contractual relationship with the time charterers.[69] The charterers claimed in tort against the shipper/sellers, alleging that the latter owed a duty to take reasonable care that the goods shipped were not dangerous, and that they were liable due to negligent shipment of excessively gaseous goods. It was eventually held that the charterers had a good arguable claim in negligence.[70] In addition, in the Court of Appeal in *The Fiona*, where

[65] For instance, the bill of lading might have been lost before reaching the buyer, or a document which is outside the scope of the Act may have been used, such as a mate's receipt, as was the case in *Kum v Wah Tat Bank Ltd* [1971] 1 Lloyd's Rep 439. Or contractual rights may not have been vested due to the problems in endorsement: *East West Corp v DKSB 1912* [2003] QB 1509.

[66] For such examples, see *Margarine Union GmbH. v Cambay Princes Steam Ship Co (The Wear Breeze)* [1969] 1 QB 219; *The Aliakmon* [1986] AC 785.

[67] *Losinjska Plovidba v Transco Overseas Ltd (The Orjula)* [1995] 2 Lloyd's Rep 395, 403.

[68] ibid, 403. For a speech supportive of a claim in tort for dangerous goods, see *The Fiona* [1994] 2 Lloyd's Rep 506, 521–22 (per Lord Hoffmann). For a case where the shipper owed duty of care against the charterer in tort, see *Virgo Steamship Co SA v Skaarup Shipping Corp (The Kapetan Georgis)* [1988] 1 Lloyd's Rep 352.

[69] *Virgo Steamship Co SA v Skaarup Shipping Corp (The Kapetan Georgis)* [1988] 1 Lloyd's Rep 352.

[70] ibid, 356.

some of the crew lost their lives due to an explosion caused by dangerous goods, Lord Hoffmann opined:

> Their [crew] interests are protected by … the law of tort. If the personal representatives of the victim of this accident were to sue in tort, they would in English law on the Judge's findings recover against BP [the shipper/seller].[71]

These authorities appear to prove that not only the shipowner but also other victims, such as the charterer, crew members or other cargo owners can be entitled to claim in tort for damage[72] caused by dangerous goods against the party responsible, which in all three cases was the shipper/seller whose negligent actions during or before shipment caused the loss or damage. However there appears to be no reported case showing that end buyers may owe any sort of duty of care to the carriers or to other third parties. This seems therefore improbable that such a duty exists, unless they can be said to have taken part before or during shipment in a way to cause the damage. Given that an action in negligence against the end buyer is not an option for the carrier, at first sight it might seem arguable that carriers could sue end buyers in tort for potential vicarious liability.[73] Considering the nature of vicarious liability of the buyer to the carrier in tort, where the employers become liable for the wrongdoings of their employees, such an action would probably fail against the end buyer as well. Some support can be found in the Australian case of *The Mahia (No 2)*, where the shipowner sued the buyer/consignee for the damage caused by an explosion during discharge of the cargo of sodium chlorate, on the ground that the seller acted as agent of the buyer in delivering the goods on board the vessel. The Supreme Court of Victoria, in dismissing the appeal, held that the seller did not act as agent of the buyer in delivering the goods over the ship's rail, on the basis that the property in the goods had not passed to the buyer prior to the shipment.

It is not justifiable that the seller under CIF and FOB sales can be regarded as employees of the buyer.[74] First, particularly under CIF sales where string sales are not uncommon, the initial seller and the end buyer are unlikely to have any contractual relation with one another. Secondly, even if there is a contractual nexus between them, the argument that the seller may have acted as agent for the buyer in delivering the goods over the ship's rail is not arguable[75] on two grounds: first, the seller carries out his physical duties imposed under CIF and FOB sales, not in any capacity other than that of seller. Thus, it is highly unlikely that the seller could be considered an employee of the buyer. Second, the property in the goods

[71] [1994] 2 Lloyd's Rep 506, 521–22.

[72] In such a case, recoverable damages in tort can be more limited than claims made in contract, since pure economic losses which are not linked to physical damage may not be recoverable in tort claims: *The Orjula* [1995] 2 Lloyd's Rep 395, 401.

[73] *McKay Massey Harris Proprietary Ltd v Imperial Chemical Industries of Australia and New Zealand Ltd and United Stevedoring Company Ltd (The Mahia (No 2))* [1960] 1 Lloyd's Rep 191, 224–25.

[74] ibid.

[75] They may have acted as forwarding agents; *The Mahia (No 2)* [1960] 1 Lloyd's Rep 191, 224–25.

hardly ever passes before shipment under CIF and FOB sales.[76] Thus, where the property in the goods lies with the shipper/seller prior to shipment, it is unlikely that the seller acts as agent of the buyer in delivering the goods over the ship's rail. Therefore, given that the seller performs his physical duties in his capacity as seller, he may hardly ever be regarded as an employee of the buyer under CIF and FOB sales. For these reasons, the carrier's action under vicarious liability against end buyers would likely fail, as would be the case with an action in negligence.

B. The Rule in *Rylands v Fletcher*

It has been discussed above that the buyer who has no contractual nexus with the carrier and has taken no part during or prior to shipment in causing any loss or damage may, to a great extent, avoid liability, and claims for shipment of dangerous goods may not be pursued against him in negligence or vicarious liability. However, there might be an alternative option for the carrier in which he may have a valid claim against the buyer in tort by way of analogy under the rule established in *Rylands v Fletcher*,[77] as a defendant does not necessarily need to take part in or commit any sort of legal wrong to be found liable thereunder.

In the case, the defendant had built a reservoir on his land for his water mill. While the independent contractors hired by the defendant were building the water mill, they also noticed that there were several disused shafts on the defendant's land. When the reservoir was filled with water, the water penetrated through and damaged the claimant's mineshafts. Therefore, the question before the court was whether the defendant was liable for damages done to the coalmine, even though the defendant had not known that there were shafts on his land. The decision of the Court of Exchequer Chamber, which was upheld by the House of Lords, was that the defendant was found strictly liable to the claimant.[78]

(i) Conditions of the Rule

The rule in *Rylands v Fletcher* has been applied ever since under English law and reviewed by the modern authorities.[79] In order for a defendant to be held liable, there are some conditions to be satisfied under the formulation of the rule.

[76] *Texas v Nason Europe* [1991] 1 Lloyd's Rep 146; *The Berge Sisar* [2001] UKHL 17, [18].

[77] *Rylands v Fletcher* (1868) LR 3 HL 330.

[78] (1868) LR 3 HL 330, 339–40.

[79] *Cambridge Water Co v Eastern Counties Leather* [1994] 2 AC 264; *Transco Plc v Stockport Metropolitan Borough Council* [2004] 2 AC 1. For detailed analysis on the rule, see generally M Jones, *Clerk & Lindsell on Torts*, 23rd edn (London, Sweet & Maxwell, 2020), para 19–44 ff; W Stallybrass, 'Dangerous Things and the Non-Natural User of Land' (1929) 3 *CLJ* 376; FH Newark, 'Non-Natural User and Rylands v Fletcher' (1961) 24 *MLR* 557; T Weir, '*Rylands v Fletcher* Reconsidered' (1994) *CLJ* 216; DP Nolan, 'The Distinctiveness of Rylands v Fletcher' (2005) 121 *LQR* 421; J Murphy, 'The Merits of Rylands v Fletcher' (2004) 24 *OJLS* 643.

Whether the buyer could be considered as having satisfied those conditions so as to be held liable to the carrier for dangerous goods under the rule will be discussed below by way of analogy.

The very first condition established in the case is that there should be a 'dangerous thing'. Blackburn J opined in *Rylands v Fletcher* that 'anything likely to do mischief'[80] can be regarded as dangerous. In the House of Lords in *Transco Plc v Stockport MBC*, where the rule was reviewed, Lord Bingham thought that whether a thing can be considered dangerous under the rule is dependent on the defendant's use of it. Thus, even water stored in a dam can be regarded as a dangerous thing.[81] In supporting this, the case law appears to prove that anything can be a dangerous thing, such as gas, electricity, oil, explosions, water or even flagpoles[82] or fairground rides.[83] In the context of shipping law, similarly to the rule in *Rylands v Fletcher*, the case law also shows that any goods can be regarded as dangerous, since dangerousness concerns surrounding circumstances rather than merely the nature of the goods.[84] In particular, under the IMDG Code where the dangerous goods are expressly classified, there is no difficulty in satisfying the first condition under the rule.

The second condition is that a dangerous thing is brought or kept on land that should not be naturally there.[85] To put it differently, there should be 'non-natural use of land'. In *Transco v Stockport* where the rule was reviewed, what is meant by 'non-natural use' was examined and it was held that the use of land must be extraordinary and unusual. The House of Lords in *Transco v Stockport* drew a line between usual and extraordinary use in terms of the risk created to the property of a third party, if an escape results from that use.[86] In *Cambridge Water*, Lord Goff (obiter) held that 'storage of substantial quantities of chemicals on industrial premises should be regarded as an almost classic case of non-natural use'.[87] If the storage of chemicals on industrial premises can be regarded as a classic case of 'non-natural use', in the context of shipping law, when goods which are considered dangerous – particularly the goods expressly classified as dangerous under the IMDG Code – are brought onto a vessel, there is no reason why such 'use' on the vessel should not be regarded as 'non-natural use' under the rule, on the ground that in the event of escape of such goods, the risk posed to the vessel and other cargo can be considered unusual or exceptional, in the light of the approach taken in *Transco v Stockport*.

For the purpose of the rule, the third condition is that there should be an escape, from land which the defendant has occupation of or control over, to land

80 (1866) LR 1 Ex 265, 279.

81 *Transco Plc v Stockport Metropolitan Borough Council* [2004] 2 AC 1, [10]–[11].

82 *Shiffman v Order of St John of Jerusalem* [1936] 1 All ER 557.

83 *Hale v Jennings Brothers* [1938] 1 All ER 579.

84 See *The Athanasia Comninos* [1990] 1 Lloyd's Rep 277; *The Giannis NK* [1998] AC 605.

85 *Rylands v Fletcher* (1866) LR 1 Ex 265, 280.

86 *Transco Plc v Stockport Metropolitan Borough Council* [2004] 2 AC 1, [103].

87 *Cambridge Water v Eastern Counties Leather plc* [1994] 2 AC 264, 309.

where he has no occupation.[88] To hold the defendant liable under the rule, the defendant does not necessarily have to be the owner or the tenant of the land from which a thing escapes.[89] In the House of Lords case of *Transco v Stockport*, Lord Bingham opined that being an 'occupier of land' would suffice to be a potential defendant under the rule.[90] In *Rainham v Belvedere*, where the explosives were stored on the premises of a wartime munitions factory, Lord Sumner said that the defendants could not avoid liability under the rule merely on the ground that they had no tenancy or independent occupation.[91] Moreover, the place occupied by the defendant does not have to be independent from the place occupied by the claimant. Thus, the rule can even apply to a case where escape occurs from a theatre to a shop, which forms part of that theatre.[92] Although a vessel is not land, it can be analogously regarded as 'floating land' in the maritime context.[93] Support for this can be found in *Ruck v Hatfield*,[94] where in an FOB sale, the vessel was regarded as the 'floating warehouse' of the buyer, and in a recent case of *VTB Commodities v JSC*,[95] where the vessel was used as floating storage. Where the property in the goods passed to the buyer or where the buyer has constructive possession over the goods through a document of title, the goods will be regarded as in the control and at the disposal of the buyer.[96] Once control over the goods passes to the buyer through a document of title, the carrier can be said to carry the goods of which the buyer holds constructive possession. Accordingly, by way of analogy with *Rainham v Belvedere* and *VTB Commodities v JSC*, from that moment, for the purpose of the rule, it is arguable that the buyer can be regarded as an 'occupier' of the place on the vessel where his goods are stored or loaded. If this analogy is correct, once an escape (such as an explosion or leak) occurs from the place (bulk cargo, container etc) that is occupied by the buyer's goods into the vessel (floating premises), which is outside his occupation, and such an escape causes damage to the vessel, it might be argued that the third condition is also satisfied.[97]

[88] *Read v J Lyons & Company Ltd* [1947] AC 156, 168.

[89] *Eastern & South African Telegraph Co v Cape Town Tramways Co* [1902] AC 381; *West v Bristol Tramways Co* [1908] 2 KB 14; *Charing Cross Electricity Supply Co v Hydraulic Power Co* [1914] 3 KB 772; *Rainham Chemical Works Ltd v Belvedere Fish Guano Ltd* [1921] 2 AC 465; *Shiffman v Order of St John of Jerusalem* [1936] 1 All ER 557.

[90] [2004] 2 AC 1, [11].

[91] *Rainham Chemical Works Ltd v Belvedere Fish Guano Ltd* [1921] 2 AC 465, 479.

[92] *Peters v Prince of Wales Theatre* [1943] KB 73.

[93] The claimant does not have to be the owner. A legally recognised interest in land like a tenancy would suffice. See *Transco v Stockport* [2004] 2 AC 1, [9], [11].

[94] *Ruck v Hatfield* (1822) 5 B & Ald 632; 106 ER 1321.

[95] *VTB Commodities Trading DAC v JSC Antipinsky Refinery and Petraco Oil Co SA* [2020] EWHC 72; [2020] 1 Lloyd's Rep 540.

[96] *Mitchell Cotts & Co Ltd v Hairco Ltd* (1943) 77 Ll L Rep 106; *C Sharpe & Co Ltd v Nosawa & Co* [1917] 2 KB 814, 818; *The Parchim* [1918] AC 157, 171–72; *Biddell Brothers v E Clemens Horst & Co* [1911] 1 KB 934, 956.

[97] Even if this analogy is accepted as feasible, it would probably be inapplicable to legally dangerous goods, since there will be no damage to the vessel as loss will be purely economic.

The last condition, which was added by Lord Goff in the *Cambridge Water* case, is that the damage caused by the escape should be foreseeable.[98] The claimant does not have to show that escape itself is reasonably foreseeable. For the purpose of satisfying the rule, he only has to show that in the event of escape, it was foreseeable that damage would be suffered. This condition is relatively easier to satisfy under the shipping law context. Suppose a cargo of fishmeal is stored in a container and carried on a vessel. Suppose further that the fishmeal caused an explosion and managed to escape, and damaged the vessel. The carrier does not have to show that escape was foreseeable. All the carrier has to prove is that for the purpose of the rule, it was reasonably foreseeable that damage would be suffered in the event of such escape.

(ii) Defences Available to the Buyer

The fact that the defendant does not need to commit any wrong to be found liable under the rule does not necessarily mean that he cannot take advantage of a number of defences. First, if an escape occurs due to the act of a person whom the defendant cannot control, then the defendant will have a defence against the claimant.[99] In the present context, the buyer can be said to have a defence if he argues that the escape resulted from the act of the shipment, which is in most cases carried out by the shipper – whom the buyer cannot have control over – when the shipper contracted with the carrier as principal. Second, the defendant may have a defence available to him, if the claimant consented to the storage of a dangerous thing on board by the defendant, provided the escape did not occur as a result of the defendant's negligence.[100] In the present context, even if the carrier has not consented to the shipment of the goods with the knowledge of their dangerous nature, the carrier would be unlikely to prove the end buyer's negligence, unless he can be said to have taken part during or prior to shipment to cause the relevant loss or damage.

(iii) Conclusion on the Rule

It is not easy to apply a land-based strict liability case analogously to the shipping law cases. Even if it is argued that all the conditions of the rule appear to be satisfied by way of analogy, the buyer may have a number of valid defences available to him against the claim of the carrier for the damage caused by dangerous goods. Accordingly, even if sued by the carrier under the rule, the buyer would be able to

[98] *Cambridge Water v Eastern Counties Leather plc* [1994] 2 AC 264.

[99] *Box v Jubb* (1879) 4 Ex D 76; *Rickards v Lothian* [1913] AC 263; *Perry v Kendricks Transport Ltd* [1956] 1 WLR 85. For other available defences like act of god or fault of the claimant, see *Rylands v Fletcher* (1868) LR 1 Ex 265, 280; *Nichols v Marsland* (1876) 2 Ex D 1; *Greenock Corporation v Caledonian Railway Co* [1917] AC 556.

[100] *Peters v Prince of Wales Theatre* [1943] KB 73.

defeat such a claim by the defences available to him, as would be the case with the other tort claims discussed above.

VI. Conclusion

The question at the beginning of this chapter was whether the buyer could take advantage of the absence of a contract and avoid liability arising out of dangerous goods. Unlike the contractual regime provided by the 1992 Act, the common law actions appear to protect the buyer/consignee against a claim by the carrier/shipowner or other potential victims of dangerous goods, when the buyer, as consignee, is neither at fault nor has any rights to exercise. Once established, under the implied contract, the buyer is unlikely to be at risk of attracting liability. In addition, he will not be in danger of being sued for liability for dangerous goods either, merely because he holds a document of title that gives him constructive possession of the goods. Under the rules of tort, the buyer/consignee, unlike the seller/wet shipper,[101] can be said to be under protection against claims by the carriers and other potential victims of dangerous goods, unless they took part before or during shipment in such a manner to cause damage or loss. This is also true under the rule in *Rylands v Fletcher*, although it does not require the defendant to be involved in any sort of legal wrong to render him liable.

On the other hand, unlike the other common law actions, the buyer, when regarded as the original bailor, technically can be said to become liable under the bailment action. However, the courts may justifiably be reluctant to impose such liability on the buyer/consignee under bailment, given that it is unlikely that the shipowners would be allowed to circumvent the mechanism of section 3(1) of the 1992 Act with the presence of a contractual regime. Where the buyer becomes the bailor as a result of actual attornment established on demanding delivery or taking delivery of the goods, the courts should show more readiness to render the buyer/attornee liable, particularly where the carrier only has a minimal chance of gaining redress from the shipper, due to practical difficulties like having no assets within reach. Given that buyers would normally have been subject to liability under section 3(1) on demanding and taking delivery of the goods, the courts should not allow them to take advantage of the absence of a contract, when they wish to exercise their rights by demanding or taking delivery of the goods under the bailment on terms.

[101] See Chapter 4.

7

Causal Link under the Contract of Sale

I. General

In Chapter five, it was discussed that liability for dangerous goods is transmissible to the buyer who is not the shipper from the shipper/seller under the carriage contract by virtue of the Carriage of Goods by Sea Act 1992 (the 1992 Act). In respect of attracting this liability, it was also shown in chapter six that the buyer appears to be more protected in non-contractual actions than he is under the contract. Once this liability is imposed on the buyer who is not the shipper – which is invariably the case under CIF sales and often under FOB sales[1] – he will seek to recover his loss both in contractual and non-contractual[2] actions from other parties, whichever are available to him. So far as contractual actions are concerned, as a matter of course, he will not be able to recover his loss under the carriage contract, given that the burden of the loss is already allocated to him as transferee thereunder. Therefore, the only potential contractual action available to the buyer will be under the sale contract, as his liability is inherited under the carriage contract tendered by his seller in pursuance of the sale contract.

In order to recover the loss consequent upon the damage caused by the goods, in pursuance of section 51(2) of the 1979 Sale of Goods Act (the 1979 Act), the buyer should first prove a causal link between the loss and the breach by the seller under the sale contract.[3] As such a loss has actually yet to fall on the buyer/transferee, this area – whether there might be a causal link between such loss and the breach by the seller – has not been fully explored under the international sale of goods law. Therefore, in this chapter we shall look into whether it is probable that a causal link will be found between the loss consequent upon the damage caused by the goods and the seller's breach under the sale contract.[4] In doing so, the

[1] Save for the bare f.o.b. and some classic f.o.b. contracts. See generally Chapter 4.

[2] See generally ch 9.

[3] Section 51(2): 'loss directly and naturally resulting … from the seller's breach'. *Monarch Steamship Co Ltd v Karlshamns Oljefabriker (A/B)* [1949] AC 196, 225; *Quinn v Burch Bros (Builders) Ltd* [1966] 2 QB 370; *Sykes v Midland Bank Executor and Trustee Co Ltd* [1971] 1 QB 113.

[4] The courts have refused to apply any formal test for establishing a causal link between the breach and the loss. They have relied on common sense to guide their findings as to whether there is a causal link or not: *Galoo Ltd v Bright Grahame Murray* [1994] 1 WLR 1360; *British Racing Drivers'*

relevant sections of the 1979 Act and the common law principles which could be of some assistance will be discussed in detail. The major Commonwealth jurisdictions adopted either the 1979 Act or its predecessor 1893 Act with little variance. Therefore, in order to draw comparisons with English law, the case law from these countries, if any, will also be referred to.[5]

II. Under the 1979 Act

A. Section 32(2) Reasonable Carriage Contract

By virtue of section 32(2) of the 1979 Act, the seller is under a duty to make a reasonable carriage contract 'on behalf of the buyer'. The sub-section applies whenever sale of goods involves transport of the goods. In terms of CIF and C&F contracts, the seller is already contractually bound to make a carriage contract. However, the sub-section becomes applicable even if the seller is not contractually bound to do so but merely authorised by the buyer.[6] However, under FOB sales, due to their flexibility, section 32(2) applies to certain types of them.[7] It is no doubt applicable to the FOB contract with additional duties, where the seller concludes the contract of carriage either in his own name or as agent of the buyer.[8] It is also applicable to the classic FOB and its variation, the modern classic f.o.b., where the seller is named as the original party in the carriage contract either as principal or agent of the buyer.[9] The only f.o.b. contract to which section 32(2) does not apply is the bare f.o.b., in which the seller plays no part at all in making the carriage contract but where it is concluded by the buyer.[10] Therefore, the bare f.o.b. buyer's

Club Ltd v Hextall Erskine & Co [1996] 3 All ER 667. See also Beale, *Chitty on Contracts*, 33rd edn (London, Sweet & Maxwell 2021), para 26-066.

[5] While Singapore and Hong Kong adopted the 1979 Act almost identically except for a number of different sections, Australia, New Zealand and Canada (save for the province of Quebec) adopted the 1893 Act with little modification.

[6] MG Bridge, *Benjamin's Sale of Goods*, 11th edn (London, Sweet & Maxwell, 2020), para 18-515. *Houlders Bros & Co Ltd v Commisioner of Public Works* [1908] AC 276, 290; *Tsakiroglou & Co v Noblee Thorl GmbH* [1961] 2 All ER 179. Although s 32(2) states 'on behalf of the buyer', this should not restrict the application of the sub-section to CIF sales where the seller concludes the carriage contract as a principal. *Scottish & Newcastle Int'l Ltd v Othan Ghalanos Ltd* [2008] UKHL 11; [2008] 1 CLC 186, [39]. See also MG Bridge, *The International Sale of Goods*, 4th edn (Oxford, OUP, 2017), para 4.08; Debattista and Hornyold-Strickland, *Debattista on Bills of Lading in Commodities Trade*, 4th edn, (London, Bloomsbury Publishing, 2021), para 4.18.

[7] Discussed in Chapter 4. See also; *Pyrene Co Ltd v Scindia Navigation Co Ltd* [1954] 2 QB 402.

[8] Bridge, *Benjamin's Sale of Goods*, n 6 above, para 18-515; Debattista and Hornyold-Strickland, *Debattista on Bills of Lading in Commodities Trade*, n 6 above, para 4.18.

[9] In Bridge, *Benjamin's Sale of Goods*, n 6 above, at para 18-515, it is suggested that s 32(2) even applies where the buyer is named as the shipper and directly party to the carriage contract, which was in fact concluded by the seller. If that is the case, the buyer/named shipper may also have a right to recourse against the seller under s 32(2) for liability falling upon him where the proximate cause of the loss is the seller's fault in concluding carriage contract.

[10] Bridge, *Benjamin's Sale of Goods*, n 6 above, para 18-515; Bridge, *The International Sale of Goods*, n 6 above, para 7.55.

position is practically immaterial here, as he already attracts liability for dangerous goods as the shipper of the goods. Accordingly, section 32(2) will be of no use against his seller.

Leaving aside the bare f.o.b. seller, under the varieties of CIF and other FOB sales, the seller is not relieved of his duties once he makes a reasonable contract of carriage. He is also under a duty to procure and tender a bill of lading, which must contain or evidence this reasonable contract, given that the bill is to govern the contractual relationship between the buyer and the carrier, once transferred to the buyer.[11] Technically speaking, these are separate duties. However, since they are closely connected and almost identical, if the contract is not concluded on reasonable terms, this will also lead to the tender of a shipping document containing an unreasonable contract, thus justifying a breach of the sale contract. As discussed in Chapter five, the buyer as transferee only becomes liable for damage or losses arising from dangerous goods following a breach of the carriage contract evidenced and contained in the bills of lading. As a matter of course, the buyer therefore would initially seek to find a solution under section 32(2), since it is the most directly relevant section to the seller's duty to conclude a contract of carriage:

> Unless otherwise authorised by the buyer, the seller must make such contract with the carrier on behalf of the buyer as may be reasonable having regard to the nature of the goods and the other circumstances of the case; and if the seller omits to do so, and the goods are lost or damaged in course of transit, the buyer may decline to treat the delivery to the carrier as a delivery to himself or may hold the seller responsible in damages.[12]

Section 32(2) provides a general protection for the buyer under the Act 1979, which arises by the implication of law and 'may only be negatived or varied by express agreement'.[13] If the seller fails to do as stated in the sub-section, the buyer will have two available options against the seller. First, he may reject the goods[14] and sue for damages for non-delivery.[15] However, it is unlikely that this would be a viable alternative for the buyer who becomes liable to the carrier. This is because if the buyer rejected the bills of lading and declined to accept the delivery, not only would he be enabled to put the entire risk back on the seller retrospectively, but also avoid liability for dangerous goods, even if he had triggered section 3(1) of the 1992 Act.[16] There would be no loss for the buyer, arising from the transferred

[11] See s 2(1) of the 1992 Act. Indeed the shipping document could be a ship's delivery order or a sea waybill, if the parties agree on this in the sale contract. See s 1(3) and (4) of the 1992 Act.

[12] Section 32(2) of the 1893 Act is substantially the same. Thus, in Australia, New Zealand and Canada, the same section is in effect in their corresponding Acts. Also s 32(2) of the 1979 Act is applicable in Singapore and Hong Kong in the form of their counterpart Acts.

[13] Section 55(1). In addition to this, s 32(2) starts with 'unless authorised by the buyer'. Thus, a clear authorisation is required by the buyer in order to negative or vary the impact of s 32(2). See also *Bigge v Parkinson* (1862) 7 H & N 955.

[14] Indeed he may reject the documents as well, if possible.

[15] Under s 51 of the 1979 Act.

[16] *Borealis AB v Stargas Ltd and Others (The Berge Sisar)* [2001] UKHL 17.

liability, to recover under section 32(2).[17] As for the second option where the buyer does not reject the goods but accepts the delivery, he will be entitled to sue for damage or loss resulting from the seller's failure to make a reasonable carriage contract under section 32(2).

Therefore, the question arising at this point is: What does the seller's duty to make a reasonable carriage contract under this sub-section entail? Although the issue has preserved its position under English law for more than a century, it did only attract very limited judicial examination before the English courts as well as the courts in the other Commonwealth jurisdictions.[18] If the existent authorities regarding the duty of the seller to make a reasonable carriage contract were to be categorised, such a contract could be said to have three different features: it must be 'on usual terms';[19] it must 'give the buyer protective rights against the carrier';[20] and it must be 'appropriate[21] to grant sufficient protection to the goods while in transit'.[22,23] As there has been no reported case in which an actual transfer of liability for dangerous goods from the seller/shipper to the buyer/transferee has occurred, naturally there also appears to be no reported case to have dealt with the buyer's position under section 32(2) in this regard. That being the case, the following section will discuss each of the three aspects of the sub-section to see whether there might be a causal link between the seller's breach under section 32(2) and the buyer's loss consequent upon the damage caused by dangerous goods.

(i) The Contract Must be on 'Usual Terms'

The first aspect of section 32(2) is that the seller is under a duty to enter into a carriage contract on usual terms.[24] Put simply, the buyer would be entitled to

[17] On the other hand, the seller's failure under section 32(2) may not be apparent until the bills of lading are delivered to the buyer, as in practice the buyer may sometimes take the delivery of the goods without production of the bills of lading. In such cases, the buyer cannot be relieved of the liability, even if he later on rejects the bill, given that the buyer's liability under the 1992 Act is irreversible once the actual delivery is taken. See generally Chapter 5 on this.

[18] For a detailed examination of s 32(2), see Lorenzon, *C.I.F. and F.O.B. Contracts*, 6th edn (London, Sweet & Maxwell, 2017), para 2-024 ff; F Lorenzon, 'When is a CIF Seller's Carriage Contract Unreasonable? – Section 32(2) of the Sale of Goods Act 1979' (2007) 13 *JIML* 241.

[19] *Ceval Alimentos SA v Agrimpex Trading Co Ltd (The Northern Progress)* [1996] 2 Lloyd's Rep 319; *Tsakiroglou & Co Ltd v Noblee Thorl GmbH* [1961] 2 All ER 179; [1962] AC 93; *Finska Cellulosaforeningen (Finnish Cellulose Union) v Westfield Paper Co Ltd* (1940) 68 Ll L Rep 75; *TW Ranson Ltd v Manufacture d'Engrais et de Produits Industriels Antwerp* (1922) 13 Ll L Rep 205; *Burstall & Co v Grimsdale and Sons* (1906) 11 Com Cas 280.

[20] *Hansson v Hamel & Horley Ltd* [1922] 2 AC 36.

[21] *Thomas Young and Sons Ltd v Hobson and Partners* (1949) 65 TLR 365; *BC Fruit Market Ltd v The National Fruit Co* (1921) 59 DLR 87.

[22] *Texas Instruments Ltd v Nason (Europe) Ltd* [1991] 1 Lloyd's Rep 146; *Gatoil International Inc v Tradax Petroleum Ltd (The Rio Sun)* [1985] 1 Lloyd's Rep 350.

[23] The categorisation is inspired from Lorenzon, *C.I.F. and F.O.B. Contracts*, n 18 above, para 2-025; Lorenzon, 'When is a CIF seller's carriage contract unreasonable?', n 18 above, 244.

[24] *The Northern Progress* [1996] 2 Lloyd's Rep 319, 328; *Tsakiroglou & Co v Noblee Thorl GmbH* [1962] AC 93, 121–22; [1962] AC 93; *Finska Cellulosaforeningen (Finnish Cellulose Union) v Westfield Paper Co Ltd* (1940) 68 Ll L Rep 75, 81.

sue the seller for a breach of the sale contract, if the carriage contract concluded by the seller is on unusual terms. The terms of the contract should be usual for the trade concerned[25] at the time of shipment.[26] In *Tsakiroglou & Co*,[27] where the usual route was suspended after the sale contract was concluded, it was held by the House of Lords that the route chosen afterwards by the seller at the time of shipment was the usual and customary route albeit being longer than the suspended one. A similar judgment was delivered in an Australian case[28] where the usual route was unavailable at the time the carriage contract was made. Citing with approval two English cases,[29] the Australian High Court held that the carriage contract by the available route, which was unusual in the trade, was reasonable.[30] So far as the word 'usual' is concerned, the answers to the questions of what is 'usual'[31] for the trade concerned and whether it has a broader meaning than reasonable were given in *Tsakiroglou*. When answering the question of 'What is a usual route?' Viscount Simonds opined: 'The answer must depend on the circumstances of each case.'[32] So far as the meaning of 'usual' is concerned, Lord Radcliffe said:

> Various adjectives or phrases are employed to describe the point of reference. I can quote the following from judicial decisions: recognised, current, customary, accustomed, usual, ordinary, proper, common, in accordance with custom or practice or usage, a matter of commercial notoriety: and, of course, reasonable. I put 'reasonable' last because I think that the other phrases are at bottom merely instances of what it is reasonable to imply having regard to the nature and purpose of the contract.[33]

In the sense of what is usual in the 'trade concerned', in the circumstances of the case, the question was whether the goods required any special packing or stowing to withstand the longer route.[34] The House of Lords held there was no evidence of the need to take special precautions for the goods to survive the longer voyage.[35] On the other hand, in terms of what is usual, the passage above also proves that various adjectives can be used to describe 'usual', and the word 'reasonable' no doubt appears to denote a broader meaning than 'usual'. Considering the shipment

[25] Lorenzon, *C.I.F. and F.O.B. Contracts*, n 18 above, para 2-026.

[26] *Finska v Westfield* (1940) 68 Ll L Rep 75; *Tsakiroglou & Co v Noblee Thorl GmbH* [1962] AC 93, 121–22.

[27] *Tsakiroglou & Co v Noblee Thorl GmbH* [1962] AC 93.

[28] *Plaimar Ltd v Water Trading Co Ltd* (1945) 72 CLR 304; [1945] ALR 469.

[29] *Burstall & Co v Grimsdale and Sons* (1906) 11 Com Cas 280 and *NV Arnold Otto Meyer v Aune* [1939] 3 All ER 168.

[30] *Plaimar Ltd v Water Trading Co Ltd* (1945) 72 CLR 304, 316.

[31] What is usual in the trade is regarded as 'mercantilely reasonable'. See *Sanders v MacLean* (1883) 11 QBD 327, 337.

[32] [1962] AC 93, 114.

[33] ibid, 122.

[34] The goods must be in a fit and satisfactory state to reach the agreed destination. See *Mash & Murrell Ltd v Joseph I Emanuel Ltd* [1961] 1 Lloyd's Rep 47, 55. Reversed on different grounds in the Court of Appeal [1961] 2 Lloyd's Rep 326.

[35] [1962] AC 93, 114, 123.

of dangerous goods, if the alternative adjectives stated by Lord Radcliffe above are employed, the question becomes: 'What is the usual / recognised / customary / current / proper thing in the sale of dangerous goods?'. Put differently, in the words of Lord Radcliffe, what is reasonable 'having regard to the nature and purpose of the contract?'. To find out what the usual thing is in the sale of dangerous goods, it is necessary to look into the practice employed in the same line of business in order to make the contract efficacious.

As the contract is for sale of goods involving sea transport from the seller to the buyer, the shipper of dangerous goods is under an absolute obligation to warn the carrier in relation to the nature and characteristics of the goods in order to enable the latter to take reasonable precautions for their safe carriage.[36] The common law implies such a duty in relation to shipment of dangerous goods, not because the contractual parties must have intended to include it, but as a result of a necessary aspect of the relationship.[37] The law no doubt considers this duty more than usual as 'recognised' and 'customary', as being necessary for business efficacy, and accordingly does not leave it to the parties' intention. This is to say, if such a duty, particularly considering its absoluteness, were not regarded at least as 'usual' in the trade of dangerous goods, it would not have been implied by the law into all carriage contracts concerning the shipment of dangerous goods.[38] Moreover, where the Rules apply, the common law obligation is replaced by an express term found in article IV rule 6 of the Rules on the shipment of dangerous goods.[39] Therefore, in the formulation of Lord Radcliffe, in respect of the shipment of dangerous goods, providing the carrier with sufficient instructions to enable him to take necessary precautions for safe carriage of the goods should be considered the 'usual thing', according to the dicta from *Tsakiroglou* above.

A question immediately arises at this stage: When a 'usual thing' is not duly performed under the carriage contract, would the buyer be allowed recovery in damages against the seller for breach of the sale contract? The seller is indeed under a duty to tender a shipping document evidencing a carriage contract on usual terms, but he does not promise due performance of the carriage contract in the manner stipulated. However, if the buyer is concerned about further duties or specific obligations beyond those usual ones in the carriage contract and wants

[36] *Brass v Maitland* (1856) 6 E & B 470; *Bamfield v Goole & Sheffield Transport* [1910] 2 KB 94; *Great Northern Railway v LEP Transport* [1922] 2 KB 742. Indeed, this is a common law obligation and where the Hague-Visby or Hague Rules apply, this obligation is supplanted and art IV r 6 replaces it except for the obligation in relation to legally dangerous goods. However Mr Justice Pearson in *The Atlantic Duchess* said that in relation to dangerous goods, the obligation is substantially the same regardless of arising at common law or under the Rules: *Atlantic Oil Carriers Ltd v British Petroleum Co Ltd (The Atlantic Duchess)* [1957] 2 Lloyd's Rep 55, 121.

[37] Lady Hale SCJ on the implied terms. See *Societe Generale London Branch v Geys* [2012] UKSC 63; [2013] 1 AC 523, [55].

[38] Unless otherwise expressed by the parties.

[39] The common law obligation in relation to legally dangerous goods is not replaced by the Rules. See *The Giannis NK* [1998] AC 605; [1998] 1 Lloyd's Rep 337.

to preserve his rights against the seller as well as the carrier, he should stipulate in the sale contract those terms imposing specific obligations in relation to the carriage.[40] By doing so, the buyer would be able to preserve his rights against the seller, if the latter did not comply with the requirements in the carriage contract. For instance, where the carriage contract provides for direct shipment as a result of a stipulation in the sale contract, shipment by an indirect route would be considered a breach of the sale contract.[41] This, however, begs another question of whether every specific obligation regarding the carriage of goods should be written into the sale contract, in order for the buyer to preserve his rights against the seller.

In the case of CIF and FOB contracts, such sales contain a variety of obligations including those written into the contract itself and those supplied by the implication of law for the business efficacy of the transaction.[42] This is because even though it is considered that the seller performs his duty only by tendering shipping documents evidencing the carriage contract on usual terms, once the 'usual thing' in that business line is not duly performed, the sale contract may be deprived of its business efficacy, given that the carriage contract may not provide any substantial assistance to the buyer. Accordingly, the courts on occasions imply terms in the sale contracts imposing particular obligations on the seller as to the obligations to be included under the carriage contract to preserve business efficacy in the sale contract.[43] In order for the court to imply a term in the sale contract, in *Tsakiroglou*, Lord Radcliffe said:

> It is necessary first to ascertain what is the commercial nature or purpose of the adventure that is the subject of the contract; that ascertained, it has next to be asked what within this scope are the essential terms which, so far as not expressed, must be implied in order to make the contract efficacious as a business instrument. The natural way to answer this question is to find out what is the usual thing in the same line of business.[44]

An example of such an implication can be found in *Ranson v Manufacture d'Engrais*,[45] where 56 tons of ground basic slag was sold under CIF terms. The goods were found to be damaged, when unloaded. The buyers claimed that the goods were damaged in consequence of shipping on a sailing vessel. The sale contract

[40] *Indian Oil Corp Ltd v Vanol Inc* [1991] 2 Lloyd's Rep 634; *Bergerco USA v Vegoil Ltd* [1984] 1 Lloyd's Rep 440.

[41] *Bergerco USA v Vegoil Ltd* [1984] 1 Lloyd's Rep 440.

[42] *Tsakiroglou & Co Ltd v Noblee Thorl GmbH* [1962] AC 93, 120.

[43] *Ranson v Manufacture d'Engrais* (1922) 13 Ll L Rep 205. See also *Finska v Westfield Paper* (1941) 46 Com Cas 87, 91–93. A bill of lading with an invisible defect can be considered invalid tender in the trade: *PT Putrabali Adyamulia v Societe Est Epices Same v Enrico Webb James Snc* (*The Intan 6V 360A SN)* [2003] 2 Lloyd's Rep 700, [26]–[27]. The case was concerned whether the notice of appropriation was valid though.

[44] [1962] AC 93, 122.

[45] (1922) 13 Ll L Rep 205.

was silent on specifying on what kind of vessel the goods were to be shipped. Greer J, in order to give the sale contract business efficacy, sought to find out what was the usual thing in this particular line of business. The court accordingly found that the goods should have been carried on a steamship rather than a sailing one. The seller was found in breach of an implied term in the sale contract that the particular type of goods should have been carried on a steamship. Accordingly, such a bill of lading evidencing a carriage contract for those goods on a sailing vessel was not due performance of the sale contract, and the bill was held to be bad tender. However, since the buyers accepted the goods, they were entitled to recovery in damages under the sale contract, from the seller, for breach of the implied term.[46]

So far as the test of Lord Radcliffe in *Tsakiroglou* for implying a term in the sale contract is concerned, first there is the question of 'what is the commercial nature or purpose of the adventure that is the subject of the contract?'.[47] Considering the nature and purpose of the sale of dangerous goods under c.i.f. and f.o.b. terms, the subject of the contract is sale of goods that require precautions – having regard to their nature and characteristics – for their preservation and safe carriage during transit. As already outlined above, the usual thing in this line of business is that the seller concluding the carriage contract in a c.i.f. or f.o.b. sale should provide the carrier with the information enabling him to take necessary precautions having regard to the nature of the goods. If this duty to the carrier is not duly performed, not only will the goods cause damage to the carrier's property, but also for this reason, they will often be in a damaged state or lost.

In *Ranson v Manufacture d'Engrais*, the court implied a term into a sale contract on CIF terms because the usual thing in forming the carriage contract for that type of goods was to ship them on a steamship. The seller did not duly perform this duty, and accordingly the court found that the implication was necessary to provide business efficacy to the sale contract. Otherwise, if the goods were found to be damaged, the buyer would not have had a right to recovery against the carrier, because the carrier was not under any obligation to carry the goods on a steamship, unless the seller instructed him to do so in the carriage contract. Nor would the buyer have had any remedy against the seller under the sale contract in the absence of an express or implied term in this regard. In such a case, the buyer would be left without having any contractual remedy for his loss. However, the court implied a term to satisfy business efficacy and allowed the buyer to recover from the seller.

Similarly in the case of dangerous goods, if the goods are not afforded the required precautions for their safe carriage, they may not only cause damage to the carrier but also become damaged or lost. CIF and FOB sales are performed by

[46] ibid, 205. See also *Tsakiroglou*, where the claimants asserted the existence of an implied term that the shipment should be by the usual or customary route. However, the House of Lords refused to imply such a term: [1962] AC 93, 114.

[47] [1962] AC 93, 122.

shipping the goods as stipulated in the contract as well as by the tender of documents containing a contract of carriage which imposes some specific obligations regarding the carriage of goods with the ultimate aim of the preservation of the goods during transit. The buyer of the goods pays in exchange for the transport document, providing him the right of suit against the carrier. If the goods are damaged during transit, the transport document normally provides him with substantial rights against the carrier. However, if there is no practical remedy against the carrier under the carriage contract, no matter how reasonable it may be, and if there is also no remedy either against the seller on the sale contract, it is submitted that the sale contract would be deprived as a whole of its business efficacy.

If the 'usual thing' is not duly performed in the trade of dangerous goods, namely that the goods are not afforded the precautions that their nature requires, and if the buyer accepted such goods at the port of discharge, he would not have any recovery against the carrier but in fact would be subject to liability arising from them when exercising his contractual rights under the carriage contract.[48] If no term is implied in the sale contract indicating that the goods should be handled with the necessary precautions for safe carriage, the buyers would be deprived of any substantial remedy under the sale contract as well. This outcome would deprive the sale contract of its business efficacy, unless a term were implied in the contract, as was the case in *Ranson v Manufacture d'Engrais*. Moreover, business efficacy requires that a party should not be deprived of substantially the benefit that the parties intended him to receive under the contract.[49] Something that should not be forgotten is the connection between the international sale of goods and shipping law. As a consequence of this, the nature and purpose of CIF and FOB sales require that the goods are carried in pursuance of these contracts for the benefit of the buyer. It would be therefore difficult to talk about business efficacy, where the buyer had no remedy under the sale contract either against the seller, or against the carrier in the carriage contract.

Indeed, it is also true that the courts may not readily imply terms in the sale contract as to specific obligations under the carriage contract, that are not negotiated between the seller and the buyer when drafting.[50] However, the core of commercial law has been advanced by inferring from the common use of the trade what the unexpressed intention of the parties is. More significantly, section 32(2) starts with 'unless otherwise authorised by the buyer' and if not surrendered by the buyer, the seller is under a duty to conclude a carriage contract on usual terms 'having regard to the nature of the goods and other circumstances of the case'. So far as the duty in the shipment of dangerous goods is concerned, there is no need for the buyer's authorisation or negotiation, as – whether it is

[48] By virtue of s 3(1) of the 1992 Act.

[49] *Hongkong Fir Shipping Co Ltd v Kawasaki Kisen Kaisha* [1962] 2 QB 26, 70.

[50] Debattista and Hornyold-Strickland, *Debattista on Bills of Lading in Commodities Trade*, n 6 above, para 7.12. But see also Lorenzon, 'When is a CIF Seller's Carriage Contract is Unreasonable?', n 18 above, 246, 250.

implied or express – it is already considered 'usual' in the carriage contract. Thus, concluding a carriage contract with such a term is clearly considered to be the unexpressed intention of the parties. In suppor of this, in *The Rio Sun*, Bingham J opined that the seller is bound to have reasonable knowledge of the nature and the characteristics of the goods that he sells and to ensure that the contract of carriage provides for any necessary precautions to preserve the goods during the voyage in question.[51] Implying a term in the sale contract indicating that the goods should be afforded the necessary precautions for their preservation and safe carriage would therefore probably not add an extra obligation on the seller requiring an express detailed negotiation between the seller and the buyer, as traders in this line of business are, a fortiori, well aware of the fact that for the safe carriage and preservation of the goods, these goods should be afforded the precautions they require on shipment.

(ii) The Contract Must be Appropriate to Sufficiently Protect the Goods

The second aspect of a 'reasonable' carriage contract imposes on the seller a duty to conclude a contract granting protection to the goods while in transit.[52] This aspect is related to the physical protection of the goods and may force us to look beyond the terms of the contract, and perhaps require the contract to be reasonable in a wider sense. The case law proves some support in that regard. In *Tsakiroglou*, the longer route was found not to be unreasonable by the House of Lords on the basis that there was no sign that the longer 'voyage would be prejudicial to the condition of the goods or would involve special packing or stowing'[53] or 'could damage the [goods]'.[54] Similarly in *The Rio Sun*,[55] where the cargo of crude oil solidified during discharge, the CIF buyers claimed that the sellers were in breach of section 32(2), since the cargo required heating en route and they had failed to procure a carriage contract specifying this. However, it was found that the contract providing no heating during the voyage was reasonable, on the basis that it was not necessary for the survival of the cargo in question for the contemplated voyage.[56] Although Bingham J found on the facts of the case that heating was unnecessary for the cargo in question, the learned judge, with regard to the duty of the seller to make a reasonable contract opined:

> In considering the cargo, [the sellers] were, in my view, bound to possess reasonable knowledge of the characteristics of the goods they were selling and ensure that their

[51] *The Rio Sun* [1985] 1 Lloyd's Rep 350, 360.

[52] In 1888 Sale of Goods Bill, clause 40(2) Lord Chalmers found the common law implied a duty 'to make the carrier responsible to the buyer for the safe custody and carriage of the goods'.

[53] [1962] 2 AC 93, 123.

[54] ibid, 118.

[55] [1985] 1 Lloyd's Rep 350.

[56] ibid, 360.

> contract of affreightment provided, whether expressly or by virtue of the duty lying on the shipowner, for the taking of any necessary precautions to preserve the goods during the voyage in question.[57]

There is probably no better way to set out the duty of the seller in respect of the second aspect than Bingham J did in *The Rio Sun*, and his words prove that for the preservation of the goods during the voyage, the seller is under such a duty to ensure that the carrier takes any necessary precautions under the carriage contract. Additionally, in *Texas Instruments v Nason*, Tudor Evans J, on section 32(2) said that the seller has a statutory obligation to make an 'appropriate' contract of carriage under the circumstances on behalf of the buyer.[58] The word 'appropriate', it is submitted, must indicate something which involves all aspects of a case to make the contract suitable for the preservation of the particular goods in question. In support of this, Bingham J in *The Rio Sun*, speaking of the seller's duty, also stressed that the seller should conclude an 'appropriate' contract of carriage for the voyage and the goods.[59] Following this, he went on to examine the appropriateness of the contract by discussing all aspects of the case, including the nature of the goods and the necessary precautions required.[60]

When returning to section 32(2), even the literal wording of the sub-section appears to be wide enough to prove that the contract should be appropriate and reasonable from *all* aspects of the case for the preservation and safe carriage of the goods: 'reasonable having regard to the nature of the goods and the other circumstances of the case'. For instance, the nature of the goods may not ordinarily have required taking special precautions but the circumstances of the case may have made it essential to do so. In a Canadian case where the goods in question were cabbages, they were found in a frozen condition on arrival, since the seller failed to make a carriage contract stipulating they were to be carried in heated wagons.[61] In holding that the contract was unreasonable, despite the fact that cabbages did not normally require heating Stuart J said of the carrier:

> … the latter would be bound to protect the cabbages from frost while in transit because that would clearly be the only contract which would be 'reasonable having regard to the nature of the goods and the other circumstances of the case'.[62]

The pre-existing common law cases, which were the origin of section 32(2), may be of some assistance along the same lines, given that the 1979 Act does not exclude

[57] ibid.
[58] *Texas Instruments v Nason* [1991] 1 Lloyd's Rep 146, 149.
[59] [1985] 1 Lloyd's Rep 350, 360.
[60] ibid.
[61] *BC Fruit Market Ltd v National Fruit Co* (1921) 59 DLR 87. For a similar judgment in another Canadian case, see *DM Duncan Machinery Co Ltd v Canadian National Railway Co* [1951] OJ No 487; [1951] OR 578, [9].
[62] ibid, 95.

the common law rules provided they are not inconsistent with its provisions.[63,64] In *Clarke v Hutchins* in describing the duty of the seller, it was held:

> … it was his duty to do whatever was necessary to secure the responsibility of the carriers for the safe delivery of the goods and to put them into such a course of conveyance, as that in the case of a loss the [buyer] might have his indemnity against the carriers.[65]

In *Pointin v Porrier* the same duty of the seller was similarly redefined by Grove J, as existed in *Clarke v Hutchins*: '[the seller] must take reasonable precautions to insure safe delivery and if it does not … it cannot be said to have been a proper delivery.'[66] Similar wording in relation to the seller's duty can also be found in the submission of Lord Chalmers for the first draft of the Sale of Goods Bill: 'the seller must entrust the goods to the carrier on such terms as may be usual for making the carrier responsible to the buyer for the safe custody and carriage of the goods.'[67] All these quotes are said to indicate that the duty of the seller is primarily aimed at the preservation and safe carriage of the goods in a wider sense. It effectively follows that the second aspect strongly focuses on the carriage contract appropriately covering all aspects of the circumstances and nature of the goods that are relevant for their preservation and safe carriage during the voyage. As a matter of principle, the propositions from the cases above, particularly Lord Bingham's from *The Rio Sun*, would extend to any necessary precautions that are related to the survival and preservation of the goods during transit. For instance, certain goods may require some specific measures, ranging from heating, refrigerating and ventilation to special packing for their preservation during transit. If loss of or damage to the goods is the likely result of failing to afford that particular protection they require, such a contract would likely fail to fulfil the second aspect of section 32(2).[68] So far as dangerous goods are concerned, the case law appears to prove that when the contract fails to provide all necessary precautions for the carriage of dangerous goods, the likely result is not only damage to the carrier but also loss of or damage to the goods. For instance, when a cargo of fishmeal is not treated with anti-oxidant, it may require considerable air circulation by means of channels during voyage. The particular nature and characteristics of this type of fishmeal require ventilation during transit to prevent heating of the goods. When the carrier is not instructed about the precaution the cargo of fishmeal requires, it is likely to heat. Thus, combustion of the goods is the likely result of heating, and

[63] Section 62(2).
[64] *Clarke v Hutchins* (1811) 14 East 475; *Cothay v Tute* (1811) 3 Camp 129; *Buckman v Levi* (1813) 3 Camp 414.
Halsbury's Laws of England (2019) vol 91, Sale of Goods and Supply of Serices, para 191; M Mark, *Chalmers' Sale of Goods Act 1979*, 18th edn (London, Butterworths, 1981), 65–66.
[65] *Clarke v Hutchins* (1811) 14 East 475, 476.
[66] *Pointin v Porrier* (1885) 49 JP 199.
[67] Sale of Goods Bill 1888 cl 40(2).
[68] See also Lorenzon, 'When is a CIF seller's Carriage Contract Unreasonable?', n 18 above, 247–48.

this may cause damage to the carrier as well as to the goods.[69] Another good example is gasoil. Some types of gasoil, when the necessary measures are not taken, may produce excessive levels of bacteria.[70] When a certain type of gasoil requires heating during the voyage, and if the cargo is not afforded this, it may produce unacceptable units of bacteria, which may not only render it of unsatisfactory quality, but also cause contamination in the tanks of the vessel.[71]

Container cargoes are also a good example. According to the data collected from the Cargo Incident Notification System (CINS), the majority of incidents in recent years in relation to container shipping were the result of poor or defective packaging.[72] When the cause of damage or loss is attributable to poor or defective packaging, the goods are deemed to have been packed in a way that they cannot be carried safely during the intended voyage. Where this is the case, there is also no difficulty to see that such poor or defective packing would not only cause damage to the carrier but would also be prejudicial to the condition of the goods. In support of this, according to the dicta in *Tsakiroglou*, the goods may require special packing or stowing for the voyage under the circumstances, and failing to give them the protection they require may also fail the test of section 32(2).[73] Another example is a cargo of calcium hypochlorite, which is known to be explosive at 60°C. However, sometimes the nature of the cargo shipped can be different from the ordinary type and it might be potentially explosive at a lower temperature.[74] Where this is the case, for the protection of the goods in question, cooling may be required, as their specific nature demands. Otherwise, due to an abnormal critical ambient temperature, the goods may explode, resulting in both loss of the goods and damage to the carrier as well as to other goods on board.[75] A supporting example can be given from a Canadian case where a cargo of cabbages was, under the sale contract, to be shipped on a heated train car.[76] The bill of lading failed to stipulate that the cabbages were to be so carried, and accordingly they were found to be frozen on arrival. The carriage contract tendered was found to be unreasonable 'having regard to the nature of the goods and the other circumstances of the case',[77] on the ground that it failed to make clear the protection the cabbages required.

[69] *General Feeds Inc v Burnham Shipping Corporation (The Amphion)* [1991] 2 Lloyd's Rep 101.

[70] *Marimpex Mineralöl Handelsgesellschaft mbH v Louis Dreyfus et Cie Mineralöl GmbH* [1995] 1 Lloyd's Rep 167.

[71] ibid.

[72] 'Mis-Declaration in 27 percent of the incidents', *Maritime Risk International* (October 2016). Some analysis suggests 65% of insurance claims for damage to cargo arise from poorly packed, blocked or secured cargo: https://www.maritimeprofessional.com/news/incorrect-container-packing-leads-damaged-301711 (February 2017).

[73] [1962] 2 AC 93, 123.

[74] *The Aconcagua* [2010] 1 Lloyd's Rep 101.

[75] ibid.

[76] *BC Fruit Market Ltd v The National Fruit Co* (1921) 59 DLR 87.

[77] ibid.

Another good example is a cargo of iron ore. As shown in Chapter two, the International Maritime Solid Bulk Cargoes (IMSBC) Code, which is mandatorily applicable under SOLAS 1974, provides guidelines on certain types of solid bulk cargo to ensure they are carried safely. Section 7 of the Code divides solid bulk cargoes into three groups: Group A consists of cargoes which may liquefy, Group B cargoes possess a chemical hazard, and Group C cargoes are neither liable to liquefy (Group A) nor to possess chemical hazards (Group B). Even though iron ore fines normally can fall within Group A, given that they are likely to liquefy, sometimes they might be misclassified as non-liquefiers in Group C. Due to such misclassification, the carrier may not have been allowed to take the necessary precautions which the goods required, such as: 'it should be kept dry at all times, the holds should be inerted and temperature and gas monitoring should be carried out'.[78] Eventually, the cargo could be exposed to moisture, which may lead iron ore to liquefy, causing damage itself or even the sinking of the vessel.

Indeed, examples of dangerous goods cases are by no means exhaustive. However, the examples outlined above are said to show that there is a strong correlation between loss of or damage to the goods and the failure to take the precautions they require for safe carriage. So far as dangerous goods are concerned, when the contract of carriage fails to provide for any necessary precaution for safe carriage, the examples above shows that not only damage to the carrier but loss of or damage to the goods is also the likely result. It would follow that those measures are not only necessary for safe carriage, but ultimately also necessary for the preservation of the goods during transit. This is because failure to take the necessary precautions for safe carriage will not only cause damage to the carrier but also to the goods themselves as illustrated above. Therefore, this makes it necessary for those measures that the goods require to be specified in a reasonable contract. This is because under the second aspect, the contract must grant sufficient protection to the goods during transit. Accordingly, the contracts in the examples outlined above can hardly be said to have granted sufficient protection to the goods, if they are damaged or lost, when they could have been preserved if the goods had been afforded the particular protection they required for safe carriage.

In the dangerous goods cases, if the goods are likely to become lost or damaged as a proximate result of the lack of measures required for safe carriage, these contracts also fail to afford the goods the preservation they require under the second aspect of reasonable carriage contract. Put differently, if the goods become lost or damaged as a result of failing to take the relevant precautions the goods require – which is mostly the case in dangerous goods cases – it is unlikely that

[78] 'Dangerous solid cargoes in bulk. DRI, nickel and iron ores', *A selection of articles previously published by Gard AS* (January 2014): https://www.gard.no/Content/6227919/Dangerous%20solid%20cargoes%20in%20bulk%20June%202011.pdf.

the contract is appropriate for the particular goods and grants sufficient protection to the goods. Had the contract provided for those precautions, the goods would have been afforded with the protection, and accordingly they would have been preserved as well. Otherwise, as in the examples above, the loss of or damage to the goods is the likely result of failing to provide those precautions for safe carriage.

One further example may support this proposition. When a cargo of excessively gaseous coal requiring ventilation is not afforded relevant precautions, not only damage to the carrier but also to the goods is likely to result. When they are not ventilated as required, the goods will not only cause damage to the vessel as a result of burning, but also they are likely to be in a damaged state on arrival. The very purpose of the second aspect of section 32(2) is to grant sufficient protection to the goods appropriate to the surrounding circumstances during transit. The contract of carriage failing to make it clear that ventilation is to be applied, would also fail to afford the goods the protection they require, since they would likely become lost or damaged as a result of this. Put differently, had the contract specified the necessary ventilation to be applied, the goods would not have been lost or damaged and they would not have caused any damage to the carrier either. Thus, a contract that fails to make it clear that ventilation should be applied cannot be said to be reasonable or appropriate to grant sufficient protection to the goods during transit, since the contract lacks that necessary measure and the lack of that measure is the cause of loss or damage to the goods.[79] It follows that ventilation is not only a necessary measure for safe carriage, but also crucial for the preservation of the goods during transit.

Once a particular measure that is required for the safe carriage of dangerous goods is not afforded, the cases outlined above show that it is not plausible to argue that the carriage contract grants sufficient preservation to the goods, as they are likely to become damaged or lost while causing damage to the vessel as well. Therefore, it might be difficult to argue that the contract is reasonable per se in a wider sense and 'appropriate' under the circumstances. Bingham J's words in *The Rio Sun* read that the seller is bound to have reasonable knowledge of the nature and the characteristics of the goods that he sells and ensure that the contract of carriage provides any necessary precautions to preserve the goods during the voyage in question.[80] His proposition adequately fits the dangerous goods cases, where the contract lacks a certain precaution and the lack of that certain precaution is the cause of loss of or damage to the goods as well as the reason of the

[79] Indeed one may argue that s 32(2) may not be triggered, if the goods are not lost or damaged. However, albeit very unlikely in the dangerous goods cases, even if the goods are not damaged or lost, the buyer should be entitled to damages under s 60 of the 1979 Act in which it entitles that rights, duties or liabilities in the Act may be enforced by action. See Bridge, *The International Sale of Goods*, n 6 above, 4.108, fn 502.

[80] [1985] 1 Lloyd's Rep 350, 360. See section II.A.(ii) above.

damage to the carrier.[81] Therefore, the bill of lading tendered which fails to afford the necessary measures to protect the goods during transit would not fulfil the second aspect of section 32(2).

(iii) The Contract Must Confer Substantial Protective Rights

The third aspect of a reasonable carriage contract is that the contract must confer protective rights to the buyer vis-à-vis the carrier.[82] This proposition was introduced in *Hansson v Hamel & Horley Ltd.*[83] At first sight, it might seem arguable that once the buyer obtains title to sue the carrier under the shipping document tendered by the seller by virtue of section 2(1) of the 1992 Act, the seller might be held to be discharged from his duty under the proposition.[84] However, this may not always be true, since the interpretation of this proposition may vary from one case to another depending on the particular facts of each case. In *Hansson v Hamel & Horley*,[85] the goods had to be transshipped, but the tendered bill of lading did not cover the entire voyage from the initial port of loading to the port of destination, but only the second leg of the voyage. It was found by the House of Lords that such a bill of lading tendered by the seller was defective, as the so-called 'through bill of lading' provided no continuous documentary cover from the shipment to destination. It should have given documentary protection to the buyer covering

[81] The goods can be classified as *legally* dangerous goods under the common law principle, if the goods lead to legal obstacles and are thereby liable to cause delay to the vessel. For instance, the goods may fail to comply with customs regulations under the law of the place of discharge: *Mitchell Cotts & Co v Steel Brothers & Co Ltd* [1916] 2 KB 610. See also *The Giannis NK* [1994] 2 Lloyd's Rep 171, 179; *The Darya Radhe* [2009] 2 Lloyd's Rep 175. In *The Rio Sun*, Bingham J held that the contract should not only be appropriate to the goods but also to the voyage in question. Indeed, in the case, his reference to the voyage in question was made in relation to the delay incurred in discharging the cargo due to the conduct of the master. Accordingly, the seller was not held to foresee unusual incidents when making the carriage contract. *The Rio Sun* [1985] 1 Lloyd's Rep 350. However, it is submitted that there is no reason to restrict his reference to the appropriateness of the contract to incidents like delay caused by the conduct of the master. As it should be for the goods, the contract should be 'appropriate' to the voyage in question in all aspects. Accordingly, it is not uncommon for the seller to conclude a carriage contract providing for compliance with the law of the destination. Indeed, when a delay caused is attributable to non-compliance with the formalities of import, the buyer may not argue that the seller is in breach, since the procurement of any import licence is normally the obligation of the buyer under CIF sales. See *Mitchell Cotts & Co (Middle East) Ltd v Hairco Ltd* [1943] 2 All ER 552. In contrast, if the goods are liable to cause delay or detention given that the cargo is not allowed into the country of destination by the local authorities due to its particular characteristics or abnormal condition, the buyer may be able to argue that the goods are not of satisfactory quality. This is discussed elsewhere. See section II.B.(ii)(a) below.

[82] This aspect may be known as 'continuous documentary cover'. See Bridge, *Benjamin's Sale of Goods*, n 6 above, para 19-043; Debattista and Hornyold-Strickland, *Debattista on Bills of Lading in Commodities Trade*, n 6 above, para 7.13.

[83] [1922] 2 AC 36. The House of Lords followed *Landauer & Co v Craven & Speeding Bros* [1912] 2 KB 94 where it was held that the tendered bills of lading did not give continuous documentary cover to the CIF buyer throughout the voyage.

[84] Debattista and Hornyold-Strickland, *Debattista on Bills of Lading in Commodities Trade*, n 6 above, para 7.11. This should be regarded as the minimum requirement for a carriage contract as to s 32(2); Lorenzon, 'When is a CIF Seller's carriage contract is unreasonable?', n 18 above, 246.

[85] [1922] 2 AC 36.

the first leg of the voyage. This is, however, only one side of the rule settled in the case. In fact, the rule established in *Hansson v Hamel & Horley* is that the bill of lading should not only provide continuous documentary cover but also 'substantially confer protective rights throughout': 'When documents are to be taken up the buyer is entitled to documents which substantially confer protective rights throughout. He is not buying a litigation ….'[86]

This passage illustrates that the rule no doubt envisages something beyond providing mere continuous documentary cover. There might be a strong connection between the second and the third aspect of reasonableness. The case law may lend some support in this regard. In *Holland Colombo v Segu and Others*,[87] despite the fact that the bill was a proper through bill of lading, providing continuous documentary cover, the Privy Council found that 'a bill of lading issued by a shipowner who by the transhipment terms in it disclaims all liability in respect of the goods in the event and as from the time of transhipment, gives no such "continuous" cover'.[88] In another case,[89] where the goods were sold on 'c. & f. liner terms Rotterdam', the court held that 'liner terms' meant that the responsibility to discharge the goods upon arrival was on the carrier. In contrast with the sale contract, the bill of lading tendered by the seller placed the responsibility for discharge on the seller (or the buyer with a right to indemnity against the seller). It was therefore held that the bill of lading did not grant any 'documentary protection or rights against the carriers in respect of the discharging operation.'[90] In *Young & Sons v Hobson and Partner*,[91] the electrical engines that were sold on FOR terms[92] were damaged because they were improperly secured by battens. The carriage contract tendered by the seller provided for the goods to be carried at the owner's risk. However, they could have been carried for the same cost at the carrier's risk. The Court of Appeal held that the contract was unreasonable in the circumstances, as it failed to afford sufficient protection to the goods, and accordingly the buyer was not entitled to protective rights to claim indemnity for his loss against the carrier.

Some pre-Act cases that underpinned section 32(2) may also lend some assistance to find a nexus between the two aspects. In *Clarke v Hutchins*,[93] it was held that it was the duty of the seller

> to do whatever was necessary to secure the responsibility of the carriers for the safe delivery of the goods, and to put them into such a course of conveyance, as that in case of a loss the [buyer] might have his indemnity against the carrier.[94]

[86] ibid, 46.
[87] *Holland Colombo Trading Society Ltd v Segu Mohammed Khaja Alawadeen and Others* [1954] 2 Lloyd's Rep 45.
[88] ibid, 53.
[89] *Soon Hua Seng Co Ltd v Glencore Grain Co Ltd* [1996] 1 Lloyd's Rep 398.
[90] ibid, 401.
[91] *Thomas Young & Sons Ltd v Hobson and Partner* (1949) 65 TLR 365.
[92] Free on rail.
[93] (1811) 14 East 475.
[94] ibid, 476.

In *Pointin v Porrier*,[95] where the court followed *Clarke v Hutchins*, it was decided that the contract of carriage must include 'reasonable precautions to insure the safe delivery, and if it does not, and in the case of loss the defendant has no indemnity against the carrier, it cannot be said to have been a proper delivery.'[96] It is clear from the rule established in *Hansson v Hamel & Horley* that the bill of lading must give the buyer substantial protective rights. The cases outlined above show that when the contract fails to afford the goods the protection they require, it also fails to give the buyer any substantial protective rights as against the carrier. Accordingly, any bill of lading that fails to provide substantial protective rights to the buyer should be considered bad tender.[97] For instance, if the goods require heating during shipment for their preservation and the carriage contract fails to make it clear that the goods are to be so carried, the contract will fail to grant sufficient protection to the goods. For this reason, the buyer will also be deprived of any substantial rights against the carrier. The contract tendered would fail to provide for heat to be applied to the goods and the buyer would thus not have indemnity against the carrier for something which is not in the contract. Put differently, had the contract provided that the goods were to be so carried, in case of undue performance of the carrier, the buyer would have had substantial rights against the carrier. It is therefore arguable that once the contract fails the test of the second aspect of reasonableness, it fails the test of the third aspect as well.

In repect of the second aspect (section II.A.(ii) above), it is argued that there is a strong correlation between loss of or damage to dangerous goods and the precautions they require for safe carriage. When the contract of carriage fails to provide for any necessary precaution that their nature requires, loss of or damage to the goods is also likely to result. It is also said on the second aspect that this proves those measures are not only necessary for safe carriage but eventually also crucial for the preservation of the goods during transit. Thus, when ventilation is required for a cargo of excessively gaseous coal, and the contract fails to provide for the application of ventilation, then due to lack of ventilation by the carrier, the goods are likely to be found heated and for this reason, both damage to the goods and to the carrier is the likely result. Where this is the case, the buyer would be to all practical effects deprived of any substantial rights against the carrier, as the contract failed to specify that ventilation should be applied. The buyer would then not be entitled to sue the carrier for failing to ventilate the goods. As a result, a bill tendered which contains such an unreasonable contract will also fail to meet the third aspect of reasonableness, given that it fails to give substantial protective rights against the carrier. More significantly, if the vessel is damaged as a result of this, the buyer may find himself inheriting liability arising from the goods under the bill tendered, by virtue of section 3(1) of the 1992 Act, let alone

[95] *Pointin v Porrier* (1885) 49 JP 199.
[96] ibid.
[97] *Soon Hua Seng Co Ltd v Glencore Grain Co Ltd* [1996] 1 Lloyd's Rep 398, 401.

acquiring substantial protective rights against the carrier.[98] Indeed the buyer will not automatically attract liability, unless he fulfils one of the conditions set out in section 3(1) of the 1992 Act, while exercising his contractual rights against the carrier. When he inspects the goods on arrival, he may promptly reject them if they are in a defective state causing some damage to the vessel. However, this may not always be apparent beforehand, and it could be too late for the buyer, as section 3(1) may already have been triggered. An alternative possibility would be that the buyer might not be aware that the goods are in such a state owing to the seller's failure, but may have thought this was due to the carrier's fault, and accordingly may seek to pursue his claim against the carrier under the carriage contract.

Of course, the seller is not under a duty to tender a bill of lading which ensures the buyer's recovery against the carrier.[99] However, as Lord Sumner opined in *Hansson v Hamel & Horley*, the buyer does not wish to 'buy a litigation', when the documents are tendered to him.[100] The rationale behind section 32(2) is that it grants such a reversing effect, entitling the buyer to a right of redress against the seller, if the contract fails to provide substantial protective rights against the carrier. In the present context, the buyer not only 'buys a litigation' under the bill of lading that fails to give substantial rights, but is also at potential risk of being liable to the carrier therein. Even if the contract *has* stipulated such measures as being necessary to preserve the goods during transit having regard to the nature and the particular circumstances of the case, the buyer would be entitled to substantial rights against the carrier, if the goods were not so afforded during transit. Therefore, it is probable that the bill of lading that fails the second aspect, on the grounds discussed above, would also fail to satisfy the third aspect due to failing to give protective rights against the carrier.

B. Other Potential Causal Links

In this part, we shall look into whether there might be a proximate relation between some breaches – beyond section 32(2) – under the sale contract and the damage caused by dangerous goods. The causal link between breach of some sections under the 1979 Act as well as breach of some common law principles and the damage caused by dangerous goods might be stronger than first thought.

[98] Indeed, at first sight, if the Hague or the Hague-Visby Rules govern the contract, it might be argued that the buyer could assert that the carrier is at fault in ensuring seaworthiness as per art III r 1 or in breach of art III r 2: *Northern Shipping Co v Deutsche Seereederei GmbH (The Kapitan Sakharov)* [2000] CLC 933; [2000] 2 Lloyd's Rep 255; *The Fiona* [1993] 1 Lloyd's Rep 257. However, it would not be plausible to argue this, once the buyer has already become subject to liability under s 3(1) of the 1992 Act as a result of making a claim, if the carrier was not at fault under these provisions.

[99] *Wimble Sons & Co Ltd v Rosenberg & Sons* [1913] 3 KB 743, 757.

[100] [1922] 2 AC 36, 46.

(i) Description of the Goods

Under the 1979 Act, the seller undertakes to deliver the goods in compliance with the sale contract.[101] In particular, under CIF and FOB sales involving sea transport, the seller must ship the contractual goods as agreed in the contract. One aspect of contractual goods as agreed in the contract occurs in the form of the identity of the goods, under a statutorily implied condition laid down in section 13(1): 'Where there is a contract for the sale of goods by description, there is an implied term that the goods will correspond with the description.' The shipped goods should be in conformity with the description in the contract in accordance with section 13, where there is a contract of sale by description.[102] If the goods tendered are different in any aspect from the description agreed in the contract, they would fail the test of section 13. Although the requirement in the section is a very strict one,[103] there is no definition of 'description' given in the 1979 Act. However, a comprehensive definition of 'description' can be found in the following dictum by Lord Diplock in *Ashington Piggeries*:

> The 'description' by which unascertained goods are sold is, in my view, confined to those words in the contract which were intended by the parties to identify the kind of goods which were to be supplied. It is open to the parties to use a description as broad or narrow as they choose. But ultimately the test is whether the buyer could fairly and reasonably refuse to accept the physical goods proffered to him on the ground that their failure to correspond with that part of what was said about them in the contract makes them goods of a different kind from those he had agreed to buy. The key to section 13 is identification.[104]

Each contract revolves on its own terms. Hence, the description of the goods is to be considered in the very words used in each contract, and accordingly may vary from one case to another. Indeed, not every word stated concerning the goods in the contract forms part of the description as per section 13. Contractual terms should be worded in a way to identify the subject matter of the contract, if they are to be considered part of the description.[105] There could be other kinds of statements that identify the subject matter of the contract, which can be considered part of the description, such as stipulations regarding time of shipment.[106] However, they will not be dealt with here, as they are not relevant to the present context.

[101] Section 27 of the 1979 Act.

[102] *Scaliaris v E Ofverberg & Co* (1921) 37 TLR 307.

[103] The buyer is entitled to reject the goods even for minor discrepancies, if the goods are not in conformity with the description in the contract. However, although the strictness of this requirement was questioned by Lord Wilberforce, his lordship also opined that in the description of unascertained goods, 'each detail of the description must be assumed to be vital'. See *Reardon Smith Line Ltd v Hansen-Tangen (The Diana Prosperity)* [1976] 1 WLR 989, 998.

[104] *Ashington Piggeries Ltd v Christopher Hill Ltd* [1972] AC 441, 503–4.

[105] Bridge, *Benjamin's Sale of Goods*, n 6 above, para 18-544.

[106] *Bowes v Shand* (1877) 2 App Cas 455.

It is already stated above that there is no definition of 'description' in the 1979 Act. In this regard, the case law, however, contains a few examples, which may be of some assistance to see the interpretation of section 13. In *Tradax Export v European Grain*,[107] where the contract of sale was for soya bean meal, 'maximum 7.5% fibre' was found to be part of the description used to identify the subject matter of the contract, and thus any percentage above 7.5 per cent was not regarded as acceptable in terms of the description.[108] In *Toepfer v Continental Grain Co*,[109] where the subject of the contract was 'hard amber durum wheat', the word 'hard' was found to be part of the description, given its reference to the quality of the goods. Similarly, in *Toepfer v Warinco AG*,[110] where soya bean meal was described as 'fine-ground', the shipped soya bean meal that was coarse-ground was held not to be in conformity with the description in the contract. When the shipped goods do not conform with the contractual description, the seller is considered in breach of section 13 under the sale contract. Similarly, sometimes liability for dangerous goods may have resulted from the non-compliance of the shipped goods with their description stated in the carriage contract. In *The Amphion*,[111] the goods were described as 'anti-oxidant treated fishmeal' in the charterparty. However, the fishmeal shipped did not conform to the description in the contract, given that it was in fact 'not properly treated'. Evans J held that the charterers were in breach, as the goods did not comply with the description, and the shipowner only agreed to carry goods of a particular description in the carriage contract.[112] *The Amphion* appears to prove that liability for dangerous goods may arise from their non-conformity with the contractual description in the carriage contract. This case may also be of some assistance to illustrate that there might be proximity between the seller's breach of section 13 under the sale contract and the damage caused by dangerous goods. Assume that in the sale contract, the subject matter was described as 'anti-oxidant treated fishmeal'. Also assume that, as was the case in *The Amphion*, the cargo shipped did not comply with the description in the contract, given that it was in fact 'not properly treated'. Also suppose that the seller tendered a bill of lading indicating the goods to be 'antioxidant treated fishmeal' as agreed in the contract, and that the vessel was damaged by the cargo of fishmeal, as a result of being 'not properly treated'. In such a case, it is arguable that the very same reason that causes damage to the vessel is also what makes the goods not conform to the description

[107] *Tradax Export SA v European Grain & Shipping Ltd* [1983] 2 Lloyd's Rep 100, 104–5. For a similar statement, see *Vargas Pena Apezteguia y Cia SAIC v Peter Cremer GmbH* [1987] 1 Lloyd's Rep 394.

[108] But see also, *Tradax Export SA v Goldschmidt SA* [1977] 2 Lloyd's Rep 604.

[109] [1974] 1 Lloyd's Rep 11, 13.

[110] [1978] 2 Lloyd's Rep 569.

[111] *General Feeds Inc v Burnham Shipping Corporation (The Amphion)* [1991] 2 Lloyd's Rep 101.

[112] ibid, 103–5. Evans J followed the test of Mustill J in *The Athanasia Comninos*, where the issue revolved around whether the shipped goods were in conformity with the description in the contract: [1990] 1 Lloyd's Rep 277. Subsequently, the learned judge found that it was unnecessary to consider whether the charterers also breached the implied duty of common law regarding the shipment of dangerous goods, since they were already in breach of the contractual description: *The Amphion* [1991] 2 Lloyd's Rep 101, 105–6.

under the sale contract. This is to say, in a case like this, the reason that renders the goods non-conforming to the description for the purposes of section 13 could be the same reason that renders the goods dangerous. Put differently, the damage caused by the goods would not have occurred, had the goods been in conformity with the contractual description as required by section 13. Where this is the case, it is likely that there is a causal link between the damage caused by the goods and their non-conformity with the description under the sale contract.

A hypothetical example could be of some assistance to see the nexus. Let us suppose that the contract of sale is for 'X' goods with a 'maximum 10% "Y" level' which forms part of the description under the sale contract, as was the case in *Tradax Export v European Grain*.[113,114] Also assume that the 'Y' level is in fact 20 per cent in the goods, which makes the goods non-compliant with the contrast as per section 13. Also suppose that the damage caused to the vessel originated from the high level of 'Y' in the goods. Once the buyer proves that the damage caused to the vessel would not have occurred had the 'Y' level in the goods been below 10 per cent as required by the description, there is nothing to suggest otherwise than that the damage caused by the goods would be a result of the section 13 non-conformity with the description under the contract of sale. In support of this proposition, some assistance can be found in a sale of goods case where the subject of the CIF contract was described as 'normal Russian gasoil'.[115] It was held that the word 'normal' formed part of the description. However, the oil was not considered 'normal', because the bacteria level was not within the limits of 'normal Russian gasoil'. As a result, the vessel's tanks were found to be damaged due to contamination from the high bacteria level, which was also the cause of the breach under section 13.[116] This case and the examples discussed above – depending on the case-by-case analysis where the facts fit – it is submitted, support the proposition advanced above that there might sometimes be a causal link between the damage caused by the goods and the breach of section 13.[117] Accordingly, the damage

[113] [1983] 2 Lloyd's Rep 100, 104–5.

[114] Sometimes such specifications can be classified as stand-alone conditions or warranties or innominate terms of the contract, instead of being part of the description under s 13. This might be immaterial in the present context, since the issue here is not the right to reject the goods but claiming damages resulting from breach of s 51 (non-delivery) or s 53 (breach of warranty) of the 1979 Act. Indeed breach of s 13 gives a right to reject to the buyer but the buyer will no doubt have right to claim damages from the seller, however the term – either warranty or condition – is classified. For such examples, see *Montague L Meyer Ltd v Kivisto* (1930) 142 LT 480; *Tradax Internacional SA v Goldschmidt SA* [1977] 2 Lloyd's Rep 604. See also s 15A.

[115] *Marimpex Mineralöl Handelsgesellschaft mbH v Louis Dreyfus et Cie Mineralöl GmbH* [1995] 1 Lloyd's Rep 167.

[116] Although it was not the issue in the case, it is clear from the report that the charterers accepted liability: [1995] 1 Lloyd's Rep 167, 173.

[117] One may argue against this proposition on the ground that the cause of the loss is the shipper's breach under the carriage contract. However, it is trite law that the breach of contract does not have to be the sole cause of the loss: *Galoo Ltd v Bright Grahame Murray* [1994] 1 WLR 1360, 1374–75. As long as the defendant's breach of contract is one of the two causes which co-operate in causing the loss, the defendant becomes liable to the claimant for that loss: *Monarch Steamship Co Ltd v Karlshamns Oljefabriker (A/B)* [1949] AC 196, 212, 227; *Heskell v Continental Express Ltd* [1950] 1 All ER 1033,

caused by the goods may sometimes flow from the reason that renders the goods non-compliant with the description under the sale contract.[118]

(ii) Satisfactory Quality and Other Common Law Principles

(a) Satisfactory Quality of the Goods

The second statutory condition laid down by the 1979 Act is section 14(2) which obliges the seller to supply goods of a satisfactory quality[119] – which was 'merchantable' quality before an amendment made by the Sale and Supply of Goods Act 1994: 'Where the seller sells goods in the course of a business, there is an implied term that the goods supplied under the contract are of satisfactory quality'. Although there is no definition of satisfactory quality in the Act,[120] some aspects, which could be relevant to the quality of the goods, are prescribed in section 14(2B):

> (2B) For the purposes of this Act, the quality of goods includes their state and condition and the following (among others) are in appropriate cases aspects of the quality of goods—
>
> (a) fitness for all the purposes for which goods of the kind in question are commonly supplied,

1047–48; *Banque Keyser Ullmann SA v Skandia (UK) Insurance Co Ltd* [1990] QB 665, 813–14; *Carlos Soto Sau and Another v AP Moller-Maersk AS (The SFL Hawk)* [2015] EWHC 458, [32]. The claimant does not have to prove that the defendant's breach was the dominant cause as long as it was an effective cause: *County Ltd v Girozentrale Securities* [1996] 3 All ER 834. Thus, the shipper's breach (either implied or express) under the carriage contract does not prevent the buyer from claiming against his seller so long as the seller's breach is an effective cause. In most cases, the bills of lading incorporate the Rules and art IV r 6 does not burden the shipper with a duty to warn the carrier. It is an indemnity provision, and accordingly the shipper does not have to be at fault to be liable to the carrier. Liability under art IV r 6 arises when the carrier has not consented to carry the goods with knowledge of their nature and the characteristics of the goods. This is to say, the carrier's damage under the provision results from the nature and the characteristics of the goods, which are unknown to him. Therefore, as advocated above, as long as the buyer proves that the nature or the characteristics of the goods causing damage to the carrier also render the goods non-conforming to the description as per s 13 (or any other breach), it is submitted that the buyer would be able to prove that the seller's breach is an effective cause of the loss. Under these circumstances, the seller becomes liable for the buyer's loss and the court does not have to choose whichever cause was the dominant or the most effective one: *County Ltd v Girozentrale Securities* [1996] 3 All ER 834.

[118] It is trite law that when the goods do not conform to the contractual description, the seller not only breaches a condition of the contract, but he is also considered as having failed to perform the contract entirely. Thus, where the seller entirely fails to perform the contract due to non-conformity under section 13, he should not also have the advantage of such failure against the buyer. As Lord Abinger stated: 'the contract is to sell peas, and if he sends him anything else in their stead, it is a non-performance of it': *Chanter v Hopkins* (1838) 4 M & W 399, 404. For a similar statement, see also *Bowes v Shand* (1877) LR 2 App Cas 455, 480, per Lord Blackburn. See also Mark, *Chalmers' Sale of Goods Act 1979*, n 64 above, 121.

[119] According to s 14(2A), goods must be of satisfactory quality, 'if they meet the standard a reasonable person would regard as satisfactory', who should be in the position of the buyer: *Bramhill v Edwards* [2004] EWCA Civ 403; [2004] 2 Lloyd's Rep 653, [39].

[120] There was a definition of 'merchantable' quality in the previous version of s 14(6) which was repealed.

(b) appearance and finish,
(c) freedom from minor defects,
(d) safety, and
(e) durability.

When considering whether the goods supplied are of satisfactory quality under those aspects, any description of the goods in the contract[121] and the price paid should be taken into account, if relevant. In other words, if the goods sold under a description do not satisfy one of the aspects stated in section 14(2B) at the time of shipment,[122] they may not be considered of satisfactory quality within section 14(2).

When the goods are of unsatisfactory quality and the reason that renders them unsatisfactory under section 14(2) may sometimes mirror the reason that has induced the damage incurred by the carrier, so far as the shipment of dangerous goods is concerned. Put differently, there might be a causal link between the unsatisfactory quality of the goods and the reason for the damages or expenses incurred by the carrier. *Marimpex v Louis Dreyfus*[123] may be of some assistance to see the relevant proximity. It was a CIF sale by description in which the gasoil was described as 'normal Russian gasoil'. The issue was whether the gasoil was of satisfactory quality under that description. Clarke J held that the gasoil was neither normal Russian gasoil nor of satisfactory quality due to the unacceptable level of bacteria. Accordingly, it was not found fit for any purpose without treatment.[124] It was also clear from the case report that the reason that made the goods unsatisfactory for the purpose of section 14(2) was also the cause of contamination in the tanks, namely the bacteria level in the gasoil.[125] The case therefore appears to support the proposition that the damage incurred by the carrier may sometimes result from the defect that makes the goods unsatisfactory under section 14(2). A cargo of fishmeal is another good example to support this proposition. Under sale of goods law, fishmeal could be of unsatisfactory quality when it contains excessive amounts of oil or fat.[126] On the other hand, under shipping law, a cargo of fishmeal could be considered dangerous, when it undergoes spontaneous heating and combustion owing to the excessive amounts of oil or fat, which is the very

[121] Not only the statements falling within the scope of s 13 but also other statements which may not be considered part of the description within the meaning of s 13 might yet be relevant to the quality of the goods: see *Harlingdon and Leinster v Christopher Hull Fine Arts Ltd* [1991] 1 QB 564, 565, 583, 586.

[122] *Scottish & Newcastle International Ltd v Othon Ghalanos* [2008] UKHL 11, [52]; *Bominflot Bunkergesellschaft für Mineraloele mbH & Co KG v Petroplus Marketing AG (The Mercini Lady)* [2010] EWCA Civ 1145; [2011] 1 Lloyd's Rep 442, [21] and [40].

[123] [1995] 1 Lloyd's Rep 167.

[124] ibid, 178.

[125] For cases where the contamination which required special cleaning was held to be physical damage resulting from dangerous goods, see *The Orjula* [1995] 2 Lloyd's Rep 395; *The Berge Sund* [1993] 2 Lloyd's Rep 453.

[126] *Soproma SpA v Marine & Animal By-Products Corporation* [1966] 1 Lloyd's Rep 367; *Christopher Hill Ltd v Ashington Piggeries Ltd* [1972] AC 441; [1971] 1 Lloyd's Rep 245.

same reason that renders the cargo of unsatisfactory quality.[127] Some reported dangerous goods cases may contain examples supporting the argument above. In *The Agios Nicolas*,[128] the goods shipped were iron ore concentrate and they were held to be dangerous because of the high moisture content, which was not made known to the shipowner. Assuming that such iron ore was sold under a CIF or FOB sale, the high level of moisture in the goods, which made them dangerous, may have also rendered them of unsatisfactory quality under section 14(2). For example, iron ore may liquefy, if the moisture content is above a critical level, which would render it unsatisfactory.[129]

Another example is *The Aconcagua*, where the cargo of calcium hypochlorite, which is normally in danger of exploding at temperatures over 60°C, was held to be dangerous, on the ground that it was abnormally in danger of exploding at temperatures above 40°C. As was the case in *Marimpex v Louis Dreyfus*, if the buyer might be able to prove that the goods are not fit for any purpose with such a low explosive temperature (without any treatment), such goods may also be considered of unsatisfactory quality for the very same reason which caused the damage to the carrier. Nevertheless, even though the goods are of unsatisfactory quality, sometimes the buyer may not be able to trigger section 14(2), if he has examined the goods or the relevant aspect of the goods was specifically drawn to his attention before the contract was made.[130] However, this would be unlikely to occur under some FOB and particularly CIF sales where the buyer usually takes no part in the shipment of the goods.[131] Another suitable example can be found in *The Giannis NK*[132] where the shipped goods were groundnut pellets destined for the Caribbean. The goods were infested with insects, which were the reason for their quarantine by the agricultural authorities of the Dominican Republic. Accordingly, they were ordered to be dumped at sea along with the other cargo on board which, however, did not carry any risk of infestation. The cargo was ultimately found to be dangerous under article IV rule 6 of the Hague-Visby Rules, due to being infested with insects, which gave rise to loss of other cargoes that were dumped at sea. So far as the sale contract is concerned, the cause of damage in *The Giannis NK* could have been the same reason that made the groundnut pellets of unsatisfactory quality, as long as the buyer could prove the goods were not fit any purpose, without treatment, under section 14(2). For instance, the buyer would likely argue that the groundnut pellets would not be fit for human consumption or any other common purposes, as they were not even allowed into the country. If this assumption were

[127] *Islamic Investment Co 1 SA v Transorientshipping Ltd and Alfred C Toepfer International Gmbh (The Nour)* [1999] 1 Lloyd's Rep 1.
[128] *Micada Compania Naviera SA v Texim (The Agios Nicolas)* [1968] 2 Lloyd's Rep 57.
[129] ibid, 60.
[130] Section 14(2C).
[131] The exception could be the bare f.o.b. contract. See *Pyrene Co Ltd v Scindia Navigation Co Ltd* [1954] 2 QB 402.
[132] *The Giannis NK* [1998] AC 605; [1998] 1 Lloyd's Rep 337.

correct, the damage caused by the goods could be considered the same as what rendered the goods unsatisfactory under section 14(2). Nevertheless, the inference above may sometimes prove wrong. For instance, it is probable that elsewhere around the world there may not be such strict regulations, and accordingly entry of such goods into other countries might not be an issue at all. Where this is the case, the goods may not be held to be of unsatisfactory quality under section 14(2). However, the buyer may seek to invoke section 14(3) by which the seller is obliged to supply the goods for the particular purpose which is made known to him by the buyer,[133] if the buyer can prove that he relied on the seller's skill and judgment for the particular purpose that was made known to the seller. In *Phoenix v LB Clarke*,[134] potatoes were the subject of the sale contract for delivery in Poland. As was the case in *The Giannis NK*, the potatoes were not allowed into the country by the Polish authorities on the basis that they were diseased. The buyers sought to invoke both section 14(2) and section 14(3) – which was section 14(1) at that time under the 1893 Act – on the grounds respectively that they were of non-merchantable quality and not fit for their particular purpose (which was their use in Poland). The buyer failed to invoke section 14(3), as he could not prove that there was an express term or warranty on their particular suitability for use in Poland. His claim under section 14(2) also failed, as potatoes of that quality could have been sold elsewhere. When this is the case, even if the disease in question rendered the goods dangerous, the buyer would probably be unable to argue that the cause of disease was the unsatisfactory quality of the goods, since no breach had been committed under section 14(2). However, he would be able to rely on section 14(3) in respect of the disease, if he proved that the particular purpose was made known to the seller.

(b) Implied Duties and Other Contractual Statements

When the buyer is concerned about some aspects in relation to the goods, the contract of sale may often stipulate specifications or quality statements regarding the goods, or additionally there might be some implied duties provided at common law. In addition to the protection provided by section 13 and section 14, for a claim for breach of the contract the buyer might also rely on those specifications or quality statements stipulated in the contract, or those implied duties which avail that the goods are of a non-contractual quality, if relevant. There might be sometimes a causal link between those statements in the contract and implied duties, and the damage caused by the goods to the carrier.

In this regard, an example of contractual specifications and quality statements in the sale contract that might be related to dangerousness of the goods

[133] See *Henry Kendall & Sons v William Lillico & Sons Ltd* [1969] 2 AC 31.

[134] *Phoenix Distributors Ltd v LB Clarke (London) Ltd, Cullen Allen & Co (Third Parties)* [1967] 1 Lloyd's Rep 518.

is *The Berge Sisar*.[135] The buyers purchased from the sellers a cargo of grade propane, which was arguably not up to the contractual quality and was considered defective. As was the case in *Marimpex* outlined above, it was clear from the report that the tanks of the vessel were contaminated due to the non-contractual quality of the propane. Subsequently, the carrier claimed for his loss arising out of the contamination from the buyers as the holders of the bills of lading under the 1992 Act, for breach of the obligation under article IV rule 6. In return, the buyer claimed under the sale contract from the seller in respect of any sum he might be found liable to pay to the carrier for decontamination, as a consequential loss of the breach for the goods non-conforming with the quality statements as agreed in the contract.[136] Although, the buyers were not ultimately found liable to the carrier, since section 3(1) of the 1992 Act was not triggered by the buyer on the facts, the case still can be said to prove that the contamination caused by the propane may have resulted from the defect that rendered the propane of non-contractual quality.

So far as implied duties are concerned, what is advocated for both sections 13 and 14(2) and the contractual statements above may also be put forward for some of the implied duties established by the case law. It is trite law that the goods should be in a merchantable state at the time of shipment[137] to withstand a normal voyage under the implied undertaking established in *Mash & Murrell*.[138,139] Under this common law principle, the goods either may not be visibly in a merchantable state at the time of shipment or may appear to be sound during shipment but there could be a latent defect existing at the time of shipment, which may become apparent later. In either of these situations, the reason rendering the goods unlikely to endure the normal voyage may be the cause of damage incurred by the carrier.[140] Examples are not limited, but for instance, it is not uncommon that the damage caused by dangerous goods could be the result of poor or defective packing.[141,142]

[135] [2001] UKHL 17; [2001] Lloyd's Rep 663.

[136] ibid, [15].

[137] *Scottish & Newcastle International Ltd v Othon Ghalanos* [2008] UKHL 11, [52]; *The Mercini Lady* [2010] EWCA Civ 1145; [2011] 1 Lloyd's Rep 442, [21] and [40].

[138] [1961] 1 WLR 862; [1961] 1 Lloyd's Rep 46, reversed on other grounds; [1962] 1 WLR 16; 2 Lloyd's Rep 1. The implied duty laid down in *Mash & Murrell* was applied in Singapore; *Harrisons & Crosfield (NZ) Ltd v Lian Aik Hang* [1987] SGHC 4; [1987] SLR 216, [38].

[139] It is also arguable that the seller could be held in breach of s 14(2) under 'durability' as well as under the principle of *Mash & Murrell*. See Bridge, *Benjamin's Sale of Goods*, n 6 above, para 18-528.

[140] Similar assumption can be made where the seller is under another implied duty in which he is responsible for skilfully and carefully loading of the goods; *A Hamson & Son (London) Ltd v S Martin Johnson & Co Ltd* [1953] 1 Lloyd's Rep 553. His failure to do so may not only cause loss of the goods, but additionally could be the reason of the damage done to the carrier.

[141] *Brass v Maitland* (1856) 6 E & B 470; *Bamfield v Goole & Sheffield Transport* [1910] 2 KB 94; *Great Northern Railway v LEP Transport* [1922] 2 KB 742. For instance, in the case of sale of radioactive materials, which are classified in class 7 in the IMDG Code, they should be packed in accordance with the provisions stipulated in the Code.

[142] If packing is part of the description, the seller could be held in breach of s 13 as well. See *Re Moore & Co and Landauer & Co* [1921] 2 KB 519.

On the other hand, the goods may sometimes require special packing to preserve their merchantable quality condition during the voyage and for this reason the principle from *Mash & Murrell* can be extended to packaging of the goods.[143] If this assumption is correct and the goods have not been properly packed to endure the intended voyage, it is not only the goods that may be in an unmerchantable state to endure the voyage, failing the test of *Mash & Murrell*, but also the vessel may be damaged as a result of such poor or defective packing.[144]

Similarly, unless the instructions are given by the buyer, the f.o.b. seller is under an implied duty as to the packing of the goods, if the nature of the goods requires packing to preserve them from the risk of deterioration during the intended voyage.[145] As a result of this, the seller may bear the burden of responsibility for loss or damage caused by defective or poor packing.[146] Additionally, sometimes packing can be stipulated as a separate responsibility in the contract. Where the seller breaches his (either express or implied) duty due to improper packing, sometimes such defective or improper packing may not only be the cause of the deterioration of the goods, but also may be the cause of the damage incurred by the carrier, as was the case in the early dangerous goods cases, such as *Brass v Maitland*[147] and *Bamfield v Goole*.[148,149] Put differently, the deterioration of the goods and the damage incurred by the carrier may have resulted from the same fact, namely improper or defective packing. This appears to prove that there could sometimes be a causal link between the cause of the damage done to the carrier and the breach under the sale contract resulting from improper or defective packing.

III. Conclusion

In order to recover the loss consequent upon the damage caused by the dangerous goods, the buyer should first prove a causal link between the loss and the breach by the seller under the sale contract. To start with the causal link between the other potential breaches of the conditions implied by the 1979 Act – like description or satisfactory quality of the goods – and the loss arising from the damage caused by

[143] See Lorenzon, *C.I.F. and F.O.B. Contracts*, n 18 above, para 10-037.

[144] Nevertheless, the seller cannot be found responsible for any deterioration during transit, unless deterioration is due to 'inherent vice'. The same principle applies where there is a 'certificate final on loading' clause as to quality. *The Mercini Lady* [2010] EWCA Civ 1145; [2011] 1 Lloyd's Rep 442.

[145] Lorenzon, *C.I.F. and F.O.B. Contracts*, n 18 above, para 10-037.

[146] *George Wills & Sons Ltd v T Brown & Sons* (1922) 12 Ll L Rep 292; *Sime Darby & Co Ltd v Everitt* (1923) 14 Ll L Rep 120; *Board of Trade v Steel Brothers & Co Ltd* [1952] 1 Lloyd's Rep 87.

[147] *Brass v Maitland* (1865) 6 E & B 470.

[148] *Bamfield v Goole & Sheffield Transport Company Ltd* [1910] 2 KB 94. See also *Great Northern Railway Company v LEP Transport and Depository Ltd* [1922] 2 KB 742.

[149] Indeed, it is the buyer who should prove the causal link between the damage incurred by the carrier and the cause of deterioration of the goods.

the goods to the carrier, depending on the facts of each case, the buyer may not always be able to invoke the particular breach, if the facts do not prove the link. Therefore, the propositions made may not fit every case, and accordingly there may not be one general solution for this.

Having said that, in order to provide a general solution to the buyer, section 32(2) is said to be of some assistance for the buyer to find a causal link between the loss consequent upon the damage caused by dangerous goods and the breach by the seller of the sale contract. Section 32(2) is by no means the most popular section of the 1979 Act and has been dormant for a long while. As shown in Chapter five, the courts often adopt a restrictive approach in transferring liability for dangerous goods to the buyer/transferee under the 1992 Act. However, if liability is actually transferred to him, then perhaps the courts may show more readiness to interpret section 32(2) in accordance with the suggestions made above in favour of the buyer shifting the loss back onto the seller.

8

Recovery of the Loss under the Contract

I. General

It was discussed in Chapter seven that there might be a causal link between the loss inherited by the buyer consequent upon the damage caused by dangerous goods and the seller's breach under the sale contract. However, this does not necessarily mean that all losses are recoverable, despite them flowing from that breach, as it is trite law that the loss should not be considered too remote to recover. In this chapter, in order to determine whether the buyer can recover such loss from his seller under the sale contract, we shall look into the principles in the law of damages for breach of contract to observe the extent of their applicability to sale contracts.[1] As there appears to be no reported case on the recoverability of such loss,[2] the focus will be on whether the law of damages applicable in sale of goods would achieve the recovery of such consequential loss of the buyer from his seller.

In section II below, in relation to the rule of remoteness (consisting of two limbs) established in English law which guides the law of damages, it will first be discussed whether this loss is considered too remote, and if not, under which limb this consequential loss falls. Following this, by drawing comparisons particularly with the consequential losses claimed under CIF and FOB sales, we shall look into whether the courts may allow the recoverability of this loss under the rule of remoteness. In the last part of section II, whether an analogy can be drawn with other sale of goods cases that involve no sea transport will be discussed.

[1] Discussion in this chapter will be limited to the relevant parts of the rules on contractual damages. For detailed examinations of contractual damages on sale of goods law, see generally, J Edelman et al, *McGregor on Damages*, 21st edn (London, Sweet & Maxwell, 2020) ch 25; Beale, *Chitty on Contracts*, 33rd edn (London, Sweet & Maxwell, 2021) ch 44.

[2] See *Borealis AB v Stargas Ltd and others (The Berge Sisar)* [2001] UKHL 17; [2001] 1 Lloyd's Rep 663. The buyer wished to claim against his seller under the sale contract in respect of the consequential loss that he might be adjudged liable to pay the carrier for the latter's loss transferred under the 1992 Act, resulting from dangerous goods. However, as the liability was not actually transferred to the buyer, the issue remained undecided.

II. Damages under the 1979 Act

Under the Sale of Goods Act 1979, depending on the facts, the buyer has several available options to recover his losses in the event of a breach of contract by the seller.[3] Section 51 entitles the buyer to bring an action for damages for non-delivery of the goods where the seller fails to do so. On the other hand, section 53 comes into play for the measure of damages for breach of warranty or breach of condition which technically gives rise to the right to reject but when that right is not exercised by the buyer. Put differently, section 53 becomes relevant when delivery of defective goods is not rejected, but accepted by the buyer.[4] This makes section 53 the most relevant section for the buyer for recovery of such consequential loss, given that upon delivery of the goods, liability for dangerous goods attaches to the buyer irreversibly, as discussed in Chapter five.[5] In addition to sections 51 and 53, the buyer, by virtue of section 54, has a separate right to recover special damages in respect of losses that result from special circumstances known to the seller at the time the contract was made.

A. The Rule of Remoteness

The 1979 Act is not designed to eliminate the common law rules, unless they are inconsistent with the provisions of the Act.[6] That is to say, the buyer's losses would be recoverable under the 1979 Act as well as under the rules of common law. To determine the contractual liability for damages, since 1854, English law has been guided by the rule of remoteness established in *Hadley v Baxendale*:[7]

> the damages which … may fairly and reasonably be considered either arising naturally, ie, according to the usual course of things, from such breach of contract itself, or such as may reasonably be supposed to have been in the contemplation of both parties, at the time they made the contract, as the probable result of the breach of it.[8]

[3] Although the buyer's remedies are prescribed in ss 51, 52, 53 and 54, s 52 is immaterial to the subject of this chapter, since difficulties may arise in applying this section in case of CIF and FOB sales. See Bridge, *Benjamin's Sale of Goods*, 11th edn (London, Sweet & Maxwell 2020) paras 19-359 ff, and 20-222.

[4] This section would apply to all breaches of ss 13, 14 and 15 including breaches of other contractual undertakings with regard to the condition of the goods. See Bridge, *Benjamin's Sale of Goods*, n 3 above, para 17-047; Beale, *Chitty on Contracts*, n 1 above, para 44-411.

[5] In case of rejection, as the buyer rejects the goods before taking the delivery, liability will be unlikely to transfer to the buyer, since such rejection will most likely avert the impact of s 3(1) of the 1992 Act even if there is a formal demand under it. On the other hand, upon rejection of the documents, there will be no liability transferred under the 1992 Act either, unless the goods were delivered to the buyer before the bill of lading was rejected. In such a case, discussion of s 53(2) and the relevant analogous common law principles would be applicable. Although unlikely, even in case of non-delivery, the buyer could possibly be subject to liability under s 3(1)(a) and (b) of the 1992 Act via formal demand or claim under the carriage contract. On this, see generally Chapter 5.

[6] See ss 54 and 62.

[7] *Hadley v Baxendale* (1854) 9 Ex 341.

[8] ibid, 354.

There are two limbs to this rule, and damages that do not fall within either of the limbs are not recoverable. The first limb of the rule prescribes that damages arising in 'the usual course of things' will be recoverable, whilst the second limb requires disclosure of special circumstances to recover damages arising outside 'the usual course of things'. Both limbs can be found in the 1979 Act. The first limb is incorporated into the 1979 Act by sections 51(2) and 53(2)[9] the latter of which prescribes: 'The measure of damages for breach of warranty is the estimated loss directly and naturally resulting, in the ordinary course of events, from the breach of warranty.'[10] Albeit not directly, it is also considered that the second limb is incorporated by section 54.[11] Given the incorporation of these two limbs into the 1979 Act, the interpretation of the rule by the case law can be of assistance in understanding the extent to which those sections can be stretched to apply to such consequential loss.[12]

The rule of remoteness in *Hadley v Baxendale* has been repeatedly depicted by the courts at all levels and it appears that its orthodox approach has mostly been preserved.[13] However, at this point, before discussing the features of the rule in depth, it is worth noting that in *The Achilleas*,[14] concerning losses for late delivery under a time charterparty, the House of Lords introduced a novel dimension to the rule of remoteness. It was held that the loss would not be recovered, even if it fell within the rule of remoteness, unless the defendant was considered to have 'assumed contractual responsibility' for the loss suffered. *The Achilleas* may have an impact on the direction of the rule of remoteness but this has yet to occur in the case law, as the orthodox approach still appears to be preserved by the courts.[15] So far as CIF and FOB sales are concerned, the rule appears to continue to apply to CIF and FOB contracts without being qualified by *The Achilleas*. In a sale of goods

[9] *Parsons (H) (Livestock) Ltd v Uttley Ingham & Co Ltd* [1978] QB 791, 800, 807.

[10] In case of consequential loss arising from non-delivery, what is discussed for s 53(2) would be *mutadis mutandis* applicable to s 51(2), since both sub-sections' wording is almost identical. Section 51(2): 'The measure of damages is the estimated loss directly and naturally resulting, in the ordinary course of events, from the seller's breach of contract.'

[11] *Saipol SA v Inerco Trade SA* [2014] EWHC 2211 (Comm), [14]; *Parsons (H) (Livestock) Ltd v Uttley Ingham & Co Ltd* [1978] QB 791, 807.

[12] *Parsons (H) (Livestock) Ltd v Uttley Ingham & Co Ltd* [1978] QB 791, 807, 809.

[13] In the Court of Appeal, *Victoria Laundry v Newman Industries* [1949] 2 KB 528; *Parsons (H) (Livestock) Ltd v Uttley Ingham & Co Ltd* [1978] QB 791; *John Grimes Partnership Ltd v Gubbins* [2013] EWCA Civ 37. In the House of Lords, *Czarnikow v Koufos (The Heron II)* [1969] 1 AC 350; *Jackson v Royal Bank of Scotland* [2005] UKHL 3.

[14] *Transfield Shipping Inc v Mercator Shipping Inc (The Achilleas)* [2008] UKHL 48; [2009] 1 AC 61; [2008] 2 Lloyd's Rep 275.

[15] See *ASM Shipping Ltd v TTMI Ltd (The Amer Energy)* [2009] 1 Lloyd's Rep 293; *Classic Maritime v Lion Diversified Holdings* [2009] EWHC 1142 (Comm); [2010] 1 Lloyd's Rep 59; *Pindell Ltd v Airasia Bhd* [2010] EWHC 2516 (Comm); *Supershield Ltd v Siemens Building Technologies FE Ltd* [2010] EWCA Civ 7; [2010] 1 CLC 241; *Sylvia Shipping Co Ltd v Progress Bulk Carriers Ltd* [2010] EWHC 542; [2010] 1 CLC 470; *Saipol SA v Inerco Trade SA* [2014] EWHC 2211 (Comm). On the impact of *The Achilleas*, see also M Stiggelbout, 'Contractual Remoteness, Scope of Duty and Intention' (2012) *LMCLQ* 97; P Wee, 'Contractual Interpretation and Remoteness' (2010) *LMCLQ* 150; S Sabapathy, 'Falling Market and Remoteness' (2013) *LMCLQ* 284.

case on FOB terms, *Sapiol v Inerco*,[16] it was argued whether the novel dimension of *The Achilleas* qualified section 53(2) and section 54, namely the rule of remoteness established in *Hadley v Baxendale*. *The Achilleas* was held to be a highly exceptional case and the applicability of the approach taken by *The Achilleas* to sections 51(2), 53(2) and 54 was rejected by the court. In rejecting the application of *The Achilleas*, in *Saipol v Inerco*, Field J also showed the accurate path to follow concerning how a claim for consequential loss under the 1979 Act should be pursued. He considered that not all consequential losses necessarily fall within the second limb of the rule, namely section 54. Depending upon the facts of each case, the learned judge opined that such losses can be claimed under section 53(2) as well as under section 54. He went on to say that the starting point should be section 53(2), to find whether a consequential loss falls within the first limb of *Hadley v Baxendale* following the assessment of the facts of the case.[17] If a loss does not fall within the first limb, he further opined that the buyer should resort to section 54 next.

Prior to discussing the application of the rule of remoteness, it is worth saying a few words on the rules of mitigation.[18] The buyer must comply with these rules, and accordingly he should not be able to recover loss caused by the seller's breach, if he could have avoided or minimised it by taking reasonable steps.[19] Under the 'avoidable loss' rule,[20] the buyer would be barred from recovering any part of his loss which might be owing to his failure to take such steps.[21] However, the rules of mitigation may not be applicable to the loss in question due to the type of loss the buyer is burdened with. The rules of mitigation are almost directly connected to 'market price' rules prescribed in section 50(3) and section 51(3).[22] Nevertheless, the buyer in the present context is faced with a loss consequent upon damage caused by the goods. Under sale of goods law, the rules of mitigation require the buyer to act immediately upon becoming aware of the breach of the seller, and in order to minimise his loss he is required to buy or sell the goods if there is an available market.[23] However, the buyer is not under any kind of *duty* to mitigate.[24] Mitigation is considered as an assumption (for the purposes of calculating damages) that the buyer could have avoided loss by taking reasonable steps and

[16] *Saipol SA v Inerco Trade SA* [2014] EWHC 2211 (Comm).

[17] The decision in *Saipol v Inerco* is also consistent with *Bence Graphics International Ltd v Fasson UK Ltd* [1998] QB 87, in which it was held that s 53(2) was the 'starting point' and the prima facie rule in s 53(3) for the measure of the damages should not apply where the buyer's true loss is higher.

[18] See generally, *Benjamin's Sale of Goods*, n 3 above, 16-054 ff.

[19] *British Westinghouse Electric and Manufacturing Co Ltd v Underground Electric Rys Co of London Ltd* [1912] AC 673; *Darbishire v Warran* [1963] 1 WLR 1067; *The Solholt* [1983] 1 Lloyd's Rep 605.

[20] ibid.

[21] *British Westinghouse Electric and Manufacturing Co Ltd v Underground Electric Rys Co of London Ltd* [1912] AC 673, 689.

[22] Bridge, *Benjamin's Sale of Goods*, n 3 above, para 16-054.

[23] Sections 50(3) and 51(3) of the 1979 Act. See also *Deutsche Bank AG v Total Global Steel Ltd* [2012] EWHC 1201; *Spar Shipping AS v Grand China Logistics Holding (Group) Co Ltd* [2015] EWHC 718.

[24] *Darbishire v Warran* [1963] 1 WLR 1067, 1075; *The Solholt* [1983] 1 Lloyd's Rep 605, 608.

therefore did so (whether or not he in fact did).[25] Under this assumption, whether the buyer took reasonable steps to avoid his loss is a question of fact, depending on the facts of each case.[26] When the goods which arrive conform to the contract, the buyer is reasonably expected to take delivery. However, not all damage caused by the goods is apparent from outside and some may not have been observed until delivery or some time after. Where this is the case, there appear to be no reasonable steps that the buyer could take to avoid his loss, since liability for dangerous goods irreversibly attaches to the buyer/transferee under the 1992 Act, when he takes delivery of the goods.

In the alternative scenario where the goods do not conform to the contract, it is not always easy to anticipate that the goods will not conform due to the seller's breach. As risk generally passes on or as from shipment, the buyer may reasonably choose to accept the goods and claim damages from the carrier under the carriage contract procured by the seller. This is because it may not always be apparent from the goods themselves or from the documents that the seller is in fact in breach and, more significantly, that the goods have caused damage to the carrier. When this is the case, the buyer can be forced to accept the goods, since his rejection can be considered wrongful if he cannot prove that the seller is in breach of the contract. Even if the buyer genuinely thinks that the seller is in breach of the contract before accepting delivery of the goods but after demanding or claiming delivery from the carrier, rejection or re-sale of the goods may not always be a practical solution due to other surrounding circumstances,[27] such as the difficulty in finding a subsequent buyer for the defective goods with a potential liability in a limited time.

For these reasons, it would not be easy for the buyer to comply with the rules of mitigation to minimise his loss consequential upon the damage caused by the goods, which can hardly be said to be due to his neglect to take reasonable steps. In any of the scenarios above, he would probably not be regarded as being aware that he can have liability imposed on him under the 1992 Act before it actually attaches to him. Even if he can be said to have been aware of it, it would be unlikely that the buyer could have avoided the loss, even if he had acted reasonably as illustrated above. Accordingly, he would not be barred from claiming against the seller on the grounds of failure to mitigate.

B. Application of the Rule to the Loss of the Buyer

Once the buyer proves that there is a causal link between the damage caused by dangerous goods and the seller's breach under the sale contract, the starting point

[25] *Thai Airways International Public Co Ltd v KI Holdings Co Ltd* [2015] EWHC 1250, [34].

[26] *Payzu Ltd v Saunders* [1919] 2 KB 581, 588, 589; *Lesters Leather & Skin Co Ltd v Home and Overseas Brokers Ltd* (1948) 64 TLR 569; *The Solholt* [1983] 1 Lloyd's Rep 605.

[27] *Bominflot Bunkergesellschaft fur Mineraloele mbH & Co KG v Petroplus Marketing AG (The Mercini Lady (No 2))* [2012] EWHC 3009 (Comm); [2013] 1 All ER 610.

to pursue a claim for such a loss should be section 53(2).[28] If the loss does not fall within section 53(2), then section 54 should be the next resort for the buyer, as such a loss shows greater proximity to the first limb than the second.

As said above, losses arising naturally in the ordinary course of things are recoverable under the first limb. As to the second limb, it requires disclosure of special circumstances which are outside the usual course of things, as such circumstances might cause unanticipated losses. The underlying logic of the second limb therefore is that the parties should have a chance to discuss and allocate unknown additional risks that may arise from special circumstances outside the ordinary course of things.[29] It follows that if there was an entirely unknown risk, which was not discussed or allocated to the defendant, those risks would not be regarded as recoverable under the rule. Put differently, only the risks that are contemplated by the parties can be recoverable under the contract. The next step is that possession of the relevant knowledge is required, in order for a loss to be assumed to be within the contemplation of the parties. As to the first limb of *Hadley v Baxendale*, knowledge is imputed to the defendant and he is assumed to possess, as a reasonable man, the knowledge of what loss is likely to result from a breach of contract in the usual course of things.[30] On the other hand, once the second limb comes into play and a breach is likely to cause more unanticipated loss than it would in the ordinary course of things, the defendant must possess the actual knowledge of special circumstances.[31] Hence, the categorisation of a fact as basic or special knowledge determines whether the case falls within the first or the second limb.[32] As Lord Wright opined in the *Monarch Steamship* case, the professions of the parties can be of assistance on what kind of knowledge can be imputed to the parties:[33]

> what reasonable business men must be taken to have contemplated as the natural and probable result if the contract was broken. As reasonable business men, each must be taken to understand the ordinary practices and exigencies of the other's trade or business.[34]

This could be best illustrated by *The Mercini Lady (No 2)*[35] in the present context. The FOB buyer concluded a charterparty with the shipowner for the carriage of gasoil. Although, the seller had no direct contractual relation with the shipowner, as the FOB seller, he was assumed to have contemplated that there could

[28] Or s 51(2), depending on the facts.

[29] *Hadley v Baxendale* (1854) 9 Ex 341, 355.

[30] *Hadley v Baxendale* (1854) 9 Ex 341, 355; *Victoria Laundry v Newman Industries* [1949] 2 KB 528, 539.

[31] *Hadley v Baxendale* (1854) 9 Ex 341, 355; *Victoria Laundry v Newman Industries* [1949] 2 KB 528, 539, 540.

[32] *Victoria Laundry v Newman Industries* [1949] 2 KB 528, 539; *Tthe Heron II* [1969] 1 AC 350, 416.

[33] Edelman et al, *McGregor on Damages*, n 1 above, para 8-192.

[34] *Monarch Steamship Co Ltd v Karlshamns Oljefabriker (A/B)* [1949] AC 196, 224. See also *The Heron II* [1969] 1 AC 350, 424.

[35] [2012] EWHC 3009 (Comm); [2013] 1 All ER 610. See section II.C below.

be a demurrage clause in the charterparty concluded between the buyer and the shipowner, since he was supposed to have known the ordinary practices of such contracts when trading in that business. Accordingly, the knowledge of demurrage clauses in the charterparty was imputed to him by the court. Where sale contracts are on FOB or CIF terms, the parties trading in this business are considered to be well aware of the general practices and operation of such contracts involving sea transport. When making the carriage contract, the seller under CIF sales and often under FOB sales,[36] as the shipper of the goods, is already aware that liability arising from the shipment of dangerous goods falls on him. Following the payment from the buyer, once the shipping document is tendered, all the practical interest in being party to that carriage contract lies with the buyer. Accordingly, the seller is said to be familiar with the 1992 Act for regulating the transfer of contractual rights and liabilities under the shipping documents tendered by him. For this reason, he is also assumed to possess knowledge of the fact that the buyer of the goods may attract liability under the 1992 Act, when exercising his contractual rights in the carriage contract evidenced in the bill of lading procured by him. Therefore, for such a loss there is no reason why the knowledge should not be imputed to the seller.

Even if it were assumed that in order to recover damages for such a loss, the actual knowledge of the seller was required, the seller can indeed be said to have possessed the actual knowledge of it. Under the second limb, when the claimant seeks to recover for unusual losses arising from special circumstances, he must prove that the defendant had the actual knowledge of the relevant facts at the time the contract was made.[37] With actual knowledge of a particular fact, the defendant may not be willing to accept the additional risk arising out of it.[38] It is therefore crucial that there should be communication of the special circumstances between the buyer and the seller. In the present context, whilst the – so-called – additional risk would be the loss arising from dangerous goods, the special circumstance would be the undertaking of that loss by the buyer. However, as a matter of course, as outlined above under c.i.f. and often FOB sales, the seller can be said to automatically assume such a risk by being the shipper.[39] When the seller contracts with the carrier, he is familiar with the international conventions regulating such contracts, and the risk of liability arising from dangerous goods is already contractually allocated by common law or the Hague-Visby Rules to him.[40] Thus, this situation does not necessarily create an *additional* risk for the seller. On the contrary, he is well aware that it is something contemplated and allocated by the law to him from the start.

[36] On this see generally, Chapter 4.

[37] *Victoria v Newman* [1949] 2 KB 528, 539. *Jackson v Royal Bank of Scotland* [2005] UKHL 3; [2005] 1 WLR 377, [35]–[36].

[38] *Safet-Huttenes Albertus SpA v Paloma Tercera Shipping Co SA* [1981] 1 Lloyd's Rep 175, 183-184. See also *The Achilleas* [2008] UKHL 48.

[39] *The Athanasia Comninos* [1990] 1 Lloyd's Rep 277, 280.

[40] In string sales, the seller can be an intermediate party who may not conclude the carriage contract personally. For discussion on string sales, see section II.F below.

In addition, it is not plausible to argue that taking on the risk of such a loss by the buyer under the 1992 Act should be considered a special circumstance, given that the seller is well aware that under the shipping document tendered by him, the buyer can have this liability imposed on him, as a matter of law under the 1992 Act. Moreover, actual knowledge of special circumstances is only necessary where the defendant would not have been liable without it.[41] Once the buyer becomes subject to liability under the 1992 Act, the seller/shipper's liability will not extinguish but he will remain liable, as the original party, to the carrier as well.[42] On these grounds, such a loss incurred by the buyer should be recoverable under the first limb rather than the second limb. Even if it is accepted that section 54 (the second limb) comes into play for such a loss, the inference above makes it clear that the seller can be said to have the actual knowledge of the special circumstance and no additional risk is taken on by the seller.

In addition to the possession of imputed or actual knowledge of a fact, in order to render the seller liable under either limb, according to the rule in *Hadley v Baxendale*, he should not ask himself whether, at the time of the breach, the loss caused was foreseeably the result of that breach. Instead he should ask whether, at the time the contract was made, he should, as a reasonable man, have contemplated that the loss in question was likely to result.[43] The rule therefore does not prospectively require the anticipation of a particular loss resulting from a particular breach. In *The Heron II*,[44] where the claimant charterers were sugar merchants, they suffered a loss by reason of a fall in the market price of sugar following late delivery of the goods by the shipowners. Lord Morris held, on the basis of the above formulation:

> I think that such a ship owner must reasonably have contemplated that if he delivered the sugar at Basrah some nine or ten days later than he could and should have delivered it then a loss by reason of a fall in the market price of sugar at Basrah was one that was liable to result or at least was not unlikely to result.[45]

The rule also does not require that the defendant should have contemplated the exact details of the loss and the exact manner of its occurring.[46] More significantly, a loss does not even have to be a *necessary* result of that breach.[47] It is sufficient if, upon the information available to the defendant, as a reasonable man, he could have foreseen that the loss was 'liable to result'. For instance, in the case of sale

[41] Edelman et al, *McGregor on Damages*, n 1 above, para 8-188 ff.

[42] Section 3(3) of the 1992 Act.

[43] *The Heron II* [1969] 1 AC 350, 388, 406, 410, 414, 425; *Victoria Laundry v Newman Industries* [1949] 2 KB 528, 539, 540. See also *Satef-Huttenes Albertus SpA v Paloma Tercera Shipping Co SA (The Pegase)* [1981] 1 Lloyd's Rep 175.

[44] [1969] 1 AC 350.

[45] ibid, 406.

[46] *Christopher Hill Ltd v Ashington Piggeries Ltd* [1969] 3 All ER 1496, 1524. *The Heron II* [1969] 1 AC 350, 417. See also *Brown v KMR Services Ltd* [1995] 4 All ER 598; *Kpohraror v Woolwich Building Society* [1996] 4 All ER 119.

[47] *Victoria Laundry v Newman Industries* [1949] 2 KB 528, 540.

of ferro-silicon, where the seller breaches his duty to pack the goods – either express or implied –, or in the case of fishmeal of unsatisfactory quality, where it contains excessive amounts of oil or fat, the seller does not have to contemplate in what manner such improper packing or unsatisfactory quality of the goods will cause damage to the carrier. It would suffice that when considering his breach, the seller would have concluded that the damage incurred by the carrier was 'liable to result',[48] and accordingly for that loss the buyer could be adjudged liable to the carrier under the 1992 Act when exercising his contractual rights. Furthermore, a loss would not be regarded as too remote merely because the possibility of the event causing the loss would have been less than an even chance.[49] Even an exceptional loss may flow naturally from the breach and satisfy the first limb of the rule. In *The Heron II*, Lord Pearce illustrated such an example when discussing the rule in *Hadley v Baxendale*:

> A thing may be a natural (or even an obvious) result even though the odds are against it. Suppose a contractor was employed to repair the ceiling of one of the Law Courts and did it so negligently that it collapsed on the heads of those in court. I should be inclined to think that any tribunal (including the learned baron himself) would have found as a fact that the damage arose 'naturally, i.e., according to the usual course of things.' Yet if one takes into account the nights, weekends, and vacations, when the ceiling might have collapsed, the odds against it collapsing on top of anybody's head are nearly ten to one.[50]

In *The Achilleas*, Lord Walker opined that liability does not depend upon the question of probability; it is also a 'question of what the contracting parties must be taken to have had in mind, having regard to the nature and object of their business transaction'.[51] Subsequently, his Lordship went on to give a suitable example for the inference:

> If a manufacturer of lightning conductors sells a defective conductor and the customer's house burns down as a result, the manufacturer will not escape liability by proving that only one in a hundred of his customers' buildings had actually been struck by lightning.[52]

When considering 'the nature and object of their business transaction' in c.i.f. and FOB sales, the seller is well aware that the buyer, as transferee, can both be entitled to rights and have liabilities imposed under the shipping document tendered by him, by virtue of the 1992 Act. The seller should not be able to avoid liability vis-à-vis the buyer on the basis that liability for dangerous goods is rarely imposed

[48] For the degree of probability, different phrases were suggested such as 'liable to result', 'not unlikely to occur', 'real danger' or 'serious possibility'. See *The Heron II* [1969] 1 AC 350, 406, 415, 425; *Victoria Laundry v Newman Industries* [1949] 2 KB 528, 540.

[49] *The Heron II* [1969] 1 AC 350, 388.

[50] ibid, 416–17.

[51] *The Achilleas* [2009] 1 AC 61, [78].

[52] ibid.

on the buyer/transferee under the 1992 Act. Support can be found in a case where the loss was not regarded as too remote on the basis that it was within the contractual duty, although it was very unlikely to result.[53] Toulson LJ, in *Supershield v Siemens*,[54] opined that the rule of remoteness cannot be examined without taking into consideration the purpose of the contract and the scope of its obligations.[55] He subsequently held that if the loss could be held to be within the scope of the duty, it could not be considered too remote, even if it would not have happened in ordinary circumstances.[56]

Under CIF and often FOB contracts, once the seller fulfills his physical obligations and ships the goods in conformity with the sale contract, he is under a duty to tender to the buyer a reasonable carriage contract conferring protective rights throughout, thus enabling the carrier to take any necessary precautions for the preservation of the goods during transit. Risk in the goods remains with the buyer while the goods are in transit and he has all the practical interest in that carriage contract against the carrier. If the contract tendered is deemed to be unreasonable, the seller can be said to have failed in his duty to tender a reasonable carriage contract and the buyer of the goods is, to all practical effects, deprived of any substantial rights against the carrier. As discussed in Chapter seven, when the contract fails to afford the goods the protection they require, they may not only be found to arrive in a damaged state but also sometimes cause damage to the carrier.[57] Where this is the case, the contract may fail the test of reasonableness, particularly the second and third aspects of it (see Chapter 7, section II.A.(ii) and (iii)).

Although this is discussed in detail in Chapter seven, there is no harm in illustrating it with an example. In the case of a sale of excessively gaseous coal, extra ventilation may be required for the preservation of the goods during transit. If the contract fails to provide for ventilation, the goods can overheat and may start burning. Once this occurs, it is not only the goods but also the vessel or other cargo on board that can be found to be damaged. For this reason, both damage to the goods and to the carrier would be the result of the contract failing the test of reasonableness. Once the buyer, as transferee, comes under liability for the damage caused by the goods, it is submitted on the basis of Toulson LJ's decision in *Supershield v Siemens* that this loss can be held to be within his duty and should not be considered too remote, given that it is the likely result of the seller's failure of his duty to tender a reasonable carriage contract.

[53] *Supershield Ltd v Siemens Building Technologies FE Ltd* [2010] EWCA Civ 7; [2010] 1 CLC 241.

[54] [2010] EWCA Civ 7; [2010] 1 CLC 241.

[55] ibid, [40], [43]. While Toulson LJ was considering the exclusionary impact of *The Achilleas* on the 'assumption of responsibility', he opined that the same principle could also have inclusionary impact.

[56] ibid, [40], [43].

[57] See generally, Chapter 7.

C. Consequential Losses under CIF and FOB Sales

So far as consequential losses under c.i.f. and f.o.b. sales are concerned, the case law appears to show that the buyer is entitled to recover losses in respect of dead freight, demurrage or damage done to third parties that he may have paid as a result of the seller's breach or in respect of extra costs incurred in order to supply replacement cargoes to execute the existing contracts.[58]

In *The Mercini Lady (No 2)*,[59] in which the contract was on f.o.b. terms for the sale of gasoil, samples were taken from the cargo prior to loading, in order to certify it to be on-specification. The buyer had chartered the vessel for the shipment of the gasoil. By the time of arrival at the discharge port, further samples were taken to test the quality of the goods but this time the cargo was found to be off-specification. Since it was not possible for the buyer to reject it under the circumstances, he had to find a new buyer to whom he could sub-sell the goods. While the tests were being carried out and a new buyer was sought, the buyer incurred not only demurrage costs under the charterparty, but also further costs of freight in order to deliver the cargo to the new buyer. The buyer claimed damages against the seller including for consequential losses from the breach of the implied term under section 14(2) that the cargo was of satisfactory quality. The gasoil was held to be of unsatisfactory quality under section 14(2). Subsequently, the court also found that the buyer was entitled to recover under section 53(2) from his seller, as consequential loss, the sums that he had to pay both for demurrage and extra freight costs, on the basis that the time spent while the tests were carried out and in the search for a new buyer resulted from the unsatisfactory quality of the gasoil.

It has already been discussed above that the rationale behind the rule in the first limb is the tacit allocation of risk. Although there appears to be no discussion in the report, it is probable that the judge must have considered that the risk of demurrage and additional freight costs was within the contemplation of the parties. Accordingly, since the claim of the buyer in *The Mercini Lady (No 2)* was allowed under section 53(2), the knowledge that there can be demurrage clauses under the charterparty between the buyer and the shipowner and the possibility of resale along with the further costs of freight for the delivery to the new buyer must have been imputed to the seller.[60] When comparing the consequential loss to

[58] *J & J Cunningham Ltd v Robert A Munro Ltd* (1922) 28 Com Cas 42; *Trading Society Kwik-Hoo-Tong v Royal Commission on Sugar Supply* (1923) 16 Ll L Rep 343; *Marimpex Mineralöl Handelsgesellschaft mbH v Louis Dreyfus et Cie Mineralöl GmbH* [1995] 1 Lloyd's Rep 167; *Bominflot Bunkergesellschaft fur Mineraloele mbH & Co KG v Petroplus Marketing AG (The Mercini Lady (No 2))* [2012] EWHC 3009 (Comm); [2013] 1 All ER 610. For the seller's recovery of consequential loss in respect of demurrage, see *Vitol SA v Phibro Energy AG (The Mathraki)* [1990] 2 Lloyd's Rep 84.

[59] [2012] EWHC 3009 (Comm); [2013] 1 All ER 610.

[60] Despite the fact that the seller may not quantify a particular time allowance for laytime and demurrage.

the buyer in *The Mercini Lady (No 2)* with the loss that he might have to pay to the carrier in consequence of liability flowing from dangerous goods under the 1992 Act, the latter kind of loss is arguably just as recoverable from the seller as the former, as a consequential loss on a similar basis. In *The Mercini Lady (No 2)*, the buyer's demurrage loss was incurred under the charterparty whose terms he, as the charterer, himself agreed on with the shipowner, including the demurrage terms. Unlike bills of lading, charterparties are not regulated by international conventions, and freedom of contract is fully preserved. The seller therefore can be said to have had no control over, or any knowledge about, the demurrage clauses stipulated in the charterparty or about the additional freight for sub-sale. Even so, the seller in *The Mercini Lady (No 2)* came under liability for the loss that resulted from a demurrage clause under a contract whose terms he may not have had a glimpse of. On the other hand, unlike in the charterparty example above, the seller as the original party to the contract evidenced in the shipping document, is well aware of its terms and knows that the shipping document tendered by him to the buyer is governed by the 1992 Act and the buyer may inherit all contractual liabilities, including liability in respect of dangerous goods therein. When compared to demurrage and additional freight, there is no reason why the risk of the buyer's loss under the 1992 Act should not be considered as being well within the contemplation of the seller.

When applying the rule of remoteness to factual causation between the loss and the breach, the court is 'not concerned with philosophic speculation, but is only concerned with ordinary everyday life and thoughts and expressions'.[61] The courts apply 'common sense' when approaching the remoteness between the breach and the loss. Particularly so far as CIF and FOB cases are concerned, it will be seen that the courts, without elaborating in detail, appear to take only basic common sense into consideration in deciding consequential losses under these contracts.[62] Scrutiny of the decision in *The Mercini Lady (No 2)* shows that the court, without having a detailed discussion on the matter, found that the buyer came under liability for demurrage as a result of the seller's breach because of the unsatisfactory quality of the goods.[63] The consequential loss arose when samples were taken in order to test the quality of the goods – which exposed the unsatisfactory quality of the goods – leading to the need to find a new buyer. By the same token, it was found that the majority of the delay that caused demurrage occurred

[61] *Monarch Steamship Line Co Ltd v Karlshamns Oljefabriker (AB)* [1949] AC 196, 228. See also *ENE Kos I Ltd v Petroleo Brasileiro SA (No 2)* [2012] 2 AC 164 and *The Miss Jay Jay* [1987] 1 Lloyd's Rep 32. See also *Quinn v Burch Bros (Builders) Ltd* [1966] 2 QB 370; *Galoo Ltd v Bright Grahame Murray* [1994] 1 WLR 1360. In *The Athanasia Comninos*, a similar common sense approach was applied to the factual causation between the charterer's orders and loss: [1990] 1 Lloyd's Rep 277, 296.

[62] *J & J Cunningham Ltd v Robert A Munro Ltd* (1922) 28 Com Cas 42; *Trading Society Kwik-Hoo-Tong v Royal Commission on Sugar Supply* (1923) 16 Ll L Rep 343; *Marimpex Mineralöl Handelsgesellschaft mbH v Louis Dreyfus et Cie Mineralöl GmbH* [1995] 1 Lloyd's Rep 167; *The Mercini Lady (No 2)* [2012] EWHC 3009 (Comm); [2013] 1 All ER 610; *Vitol SA v Phibro Energy AG (The Mathraki)* [1990] 2 Lloyd's Rep 84.

[63] [2012] EWHC 3009 (Comm), [69].

as a result of the seller's breach.[64] The court simply accepted that had there been no breach of the seller, the demurrage would not have been incurred by the buyer.[65]

In respect of the rule of remoteness, factual causation between the seller's breach and the buyer's loss under the 1992 Act would be best illustrated by some examples. In the *Marimpex* case, given the abnormal level of bacteria in the gasoil, the cargo was neither of satisfactory quality for the purposes of section 14(2), nor did it conform with the contractual description under section 13(1) of the 1979 Act. For the very same reason, the tank of the vessel was found to be damaged. Had there been no breach by the seller, the gasoil would not have damaged the vessel. Similarly, in *The Berge Sisar*,[66] the cargo caused contamination in the tanks of the vessel due to its non-contractual quality under the sale contract. Had the goods been of contractual quality, there would not have been any contamination. Sometimes defective packing of the goods causes damage to the vessel.[67] For the very same reason, the seller can be held in breach of the sale contract, since the goods can be considered to be defective because of improper packing, which meant they were unable to endure the voyage.[68] Had the goods been adequately packed, they would not have caused any damage to the vessel. Another good example is a cargo of fishmeal. Under sale of goods law, fishmeal can be considered of unsatisfactory quality where it contains excessive amounts of oil or fat.[69] On the other hand, a cargo of fishmeal could be found dangerous, owing to the very same factors which may cause spontaneous heating and combustion.[70] If the goods had not had excessive levels of oil or fat, they would not have spontaneously heated or combusted.

All these examples outlined above are likely to prove that the link between the seller's breach and the loss of the buyer consequent upon the damage caused by the goods to the carrier may vary from one case to another. However, section 32(2) may prove a general solution for the buyer. As shown in detail in Chapter seven, when the contract of carriage fails to provide for any necessary precaution that the nature of the goods requires for safe carriage, it may not only cause damage to the carrier but also loss of or damage to the goods. This also proves that those

[64] ibid.

[65] ibid, [70].

[66] [2001] UKHL 17.

[67] *Brass v Maitland* (1856) 6 E & B 470; *Bamfield v Goole & Sheffield Transport* [1910] 2 KB 94; *Great Northern Railway v LEP Transport* [1922] 2 KB 742.

[68] Provided that he is under a duty to the buyer to pack the goods. See *Re Moore & Co and Landauer & Co* [1921] 2 KB 519; *George Wills & Sons Ltd v T Brown & Sons* (1922) 12 Ll L Rep 292; *Sime Darby & Co Ltd v Everitt* (1923) 14 Ll L Rep 120; *Board of Trade v Steel Brothers & Co Ltd* [1952] 1 Lloyd's Rep 87; *Tsakiroglou & Co Ltd v Noblee Thorl GmbH* [1961] 2 All ER 179; [1962] AC 93. See also Lorenzon, *C.I.F. and F.O.B. Contracts*, 6th edn (London, Sweet & Maxwell, 2017) para 10-037.

[69] *Soproma SpA v Marine & Animal By-Products Corporation* [1966] 1 Lloyd's Rep 367; *Christopher Hill Ltd v Ashington Piggeries Ltd* [1972] AC 441; [1971] 1 Lloyd's Rep 245.

[70] *Islamic Investment Co 1 SA v Transorientshipping Ltd and Alfred C Toepfer International GmbH (The Nour)* [1999] 1 Lloyd's Rep 1.

measures are not only necessary for safe carriage but ultimately also crucial for the preservation and survival of the goods during transit. For instance, if the nature of the goods requires cooling or ventilation to be applied during transit for its safe carriage, and if the contract fails to so provide, once the cargo ignites, both damage to the goods and to the carrier are likely to result. This therefore makes it necessary for their preservation and survival that, in a reasonable contract, such protection as the goods require should be provided. If the contract fails to afford dangerous goods the preservative measures they require, they are likely to be lost or damaged as a proximate result of that failure. If they are to become entirely lost or damaged due to the lack of a necessary measure, it is not arguable that the contract is appropriate for the goods or that it grants the goods the protection they require. In most dangerous goods cases, it follows that such a failure in providing the necessary precaution would also lead to damage to the carrier. This in most cases proves that the loss imposed on the buyer via the 1992 Act, consequent upon the damage caused to the carrier by dangerous goods, is not too remote from the seller's breach of section 32(2). Had the contract afforded the measure(s) that the nature of the goods requires, the goods would not have been damaged or lost, and accordingly no damage would have been caused to the carrier either.

In the light of these examples, such loss of the buyer should not be considered too remote but within the contemplation of the parties. The courts apply a factual causation test, particularly in sale of goods cases, when applying the rule of remoteness between the breach and the loss. In the present context, the examples given above appear to prove the factual causation between the seller's breach and the buyer's loss. The loss imposed on the buyer under the 1992 Act consequent upon the damage caused by dangerous goods would probably satisfy the rule of remoteness applicable to sale of goods cases, and accordingly it can be claimed from the seller on the grounds discussed above.

It is also worth adding that once there is a breach of section 32(2) concerning the content of the contract of carriage, the buyer's loss is recoverable under sections 51(2) and 53(2) as well as under the common law rules of damages.[71] Additionally, unlike other sections in the 1979 Act, section 32(2) explicitly provides its own right to recover damages from the seller, when he is in breach of section 32(2):

> and if the seller omits to do so, and the goods are lost or damaged in course of transit, the buyer may decline to treat the delivery to the carrier as a delivery to himself or may hold the seller responsible in damages.[72]

The phrase plainly ends merely with the word 'damages' without indicating any limitation or qualification. When considering this sub-section, with its autonomous reference to damages which is not found in the other sections of the 1979

[71] Section 62(2) of the 1979 Act.

[72] However, even if the goods are not lost or damaged, the buyer should be entitled to recover damages under s 60; 'Where a right, duty or liability is declared by this Act, it may (unless otherwise provided by this Act) be enforced by action.'

Act, section 32(2) might be interpreted to extend to the recovery of such a loss as a direct loss rather than a consequential one.

D. Analogy with Other Sale of Goods Cases

Recovery of such a loss can also be established on the grounds of analogy with sale of goods cases that involve no transport of the goods. The buyer could be entitled to recover damages for injuries to himself, his family or property caused by the seller's breach, if it was within the contemplation of the parties at the time the contract was made.[73] Thus, for instance, where the goods are sold for human consumption, the buyer is entitled to recover damages for injuries or illness caused by its defective condition.

Assume that a CIF or FOB buyer purchased ordinary fishmeal under a sale contract but due to its high levels of oil and fat, the goods were of unsatisfactory quality. Also suppose that the goods caused damage to the vessel, for the very same reason; namely, their abnormal oil and fat content. Once the buyer becomes subject to liability under the 1992 Act for the damage incurred by the carrier, and subsequently when the carrier seeks to recover his loss from the buyer, the carrier would be subrogated by the buyer by virtue of the 1992 Act and the latter would be put in a position as if the goods had directly injured or damaged him or his property by their unsatisfactory quality. This analogy appears to be even more plausible by virtue of section 32(1), whereby the goods are deemed to be delivered to the buyer, when the seller delivers the goods to the carrier.[74] The buyer would therefore be regarded as having borne the burden of the loss caused to the vessel instead of the carrier, analogically resembling the position of the buyer where his family or his property is directly injured as a result of the seller's breach. Hence, this analogy may support the proposition that the buyer, subrogating the carrier for loss, should be entitled to recovery, as is the buyer in the sale of goods cases involving no sea transport.

Another analogy, arguably a more plausible one, can be established from *Lambert v Lewis*, where it was held that – providing it was within the reasonable contemplation of the parties at the time the contract was made – the buyer may recover compensation he has paid to a third party, from his seller. The following conditions are to be fulfilled: a) the third party or his property is not unlikely to be damaged in consequence of the seller's breach; and b) as a result of this damage,

[73] *Priest v Last* [1903] 2 KB 148; *Wren v Holt* [1903] 1 KB 610; *Frost v Aylesbury Dairy Co Ltd* [1905] 1 KB 608; *Jackson v Watson & Sons* [1909] 2 KB 193; *Square v Model Farm Dairies Ltd* [1939] 2 KB 365; *Grant v Australian Knitting Mills Ltd* [1936] AC 85; *Godley v Perry* [1960] 1 WLR 9; *Darlington Borough Council v Wiltshier Northern Ltd* [1995] 1 WLR 68; *Alfred McAlpine Construction Ltd v Panatown Ltd* [2001] 1 AC 518.

[74] Section 32(1): '… delivery of the goods to a carrier (whether named by the buyer or not) for the purpose of transmission to the buyer is prima facie deemed to be a delivery of the goods to the buyer.'

the buyer would not be unlikely to be found liable to reimburse the third party for damage or loss resulting from the seller's breach.[75] First, there is no difficulty in considering the carrier as a third party, since he is not party to the sale contract. Second, the legal basis of the buyer's liability to the carrier could be under a contract as well as the law of torts.[76] As shown in Chapter seven, damage caused to the carrier may have happened as a consequence of the seller's breach under the sale contract. Once the buyer proved a causal link between the carrier's loss and the seller's breach, as discussed in Chapter seven,[77] then the first condition of *Lambert v Lewis* would be considered fulfilled. So far as the second condition is concerned, it could be deemed to be satisfied, once the buyer finds himself legally[78] liable under the 1992 Act as per section 3(1).

Support for this analogy can be found in a c.i.f. sale case where the buyer was entitled to recover the sum that he had to pay a third party that resulted from the seller's breach. In *Marimpex*,[79] upon arrival, the gasoil was discharged into a shore tank in order for tests to be carried out on the quality of the goods. Following the tests, the gasoil was found to be of unsatisfactory quality under section 14(2) due to an abnormal level of bacteria in it. As a result of this, the shore tank was found to be contaminated. Accordingly, the court allowed the buyer's claim against the seller for consequential loss in respect of the sum that the buyer had to pay to the shore tank owner for the damage resulting from the unsatisfactory quality of the goods. Indeed the principle established in *Lambert v Lewis* was not applied to the case in *Marimpex*, but the facts of the case appear to prove that the two conditions of *Lambert v Lewis* could have been arguably satisfied. It follows that a principle established in a sale of goods case involving no sea transport could well be applicable to CIF and FOB cases by analogous. Therefore, the principle accepted in *Lambert v Lewis* can be plausibly applied to the buyer's payment of damages to the carrier under the 1992 Act in consequence of the seller's breach, and the buyer's claim based on this principle should be allowed.[80]

[75] *Lexmead (Basingstoke) Ltd v Lewis and Others* (*Lambert v Lewis*) [1982] AC 225. Albeit not applied in the relevant case, this principle was approved by the House of Lords. See the previous cases on the principle, *Mowbray v Merryweather* [1895] 2 QB 640; *Scott v Foley, Aikman & Co* (1899) 16 TLR 55. See also, Bridge, *Benjamin's Sale of Goods*, n 3 above, para 17-075; Beale, *Chitty on Contracts*, n 1 above, para 44-431; Edelman et al, *McGregor on Damages*, n 1 above, para 25-085.

[76] *Mowbray v Merryweather* [1895] 2 QB 640; *Scott v Foley, Aikman & Co* (1899) 16 TLR 55. See also Bridge, *Benjamin's Sale of Goods*, n 3 above, para 17-075; Beale, *Chitty on Contracts*, n 1 above, para 44-431.

[77] On this see generally, Chapter 7.

[78] The claim of a third party does not necessarily have to be defended before the court. If the claim is reasonably settled out of court, the buyer may also recover from the seller his loss paid under the settlement. See *Biggin & Co Ltd v Permanite Ltd* [1951] 1 KB 422.

[79] *Marimpex Mineralöl Handelsgesellschaft mbH v Louis Dreyfus et Cie Mineralöl GmbH* [1995] 1 Lloyd's Rep 167.

[80] The buyer additionally may recover costs incurred in defending the carrier's claim: *Scott v Foley* (1899) 16 TLR 55, 56; *Brittannia Hygenic Laundry Co Ltd v John I Thorneycroft Co Ltd* (1925) 41 TLR 667; reversed on other grounds (1926) 42 TLR 198.

E. Intervening Act of the Buyer

It might be argued that the buyer's triggering section 3(1) of the 1992 Act may break the link between his loss and the seller's breach under the sale contract.[81] However, such an act of the buyer should not be treated as an intervening act that breaks the link between the breach and the loss.[82]

In order to break the link between the loss and the breach, first the buyer's act should be considered unreasonable in the circumstances.[83] Under the 1992 Act, the buyer becomes subject to liability only when exercising his contractual rights under the carriage contract, namely demanding or taking delivery of the goods or making a claim under the contract.[84] It would be implausible to suggest that seeking to exercise his contractual rights should be treated as unreasonable conduct. Second, the conduct of the buyer 'must constitute an event of such impact that it obliterates the wrongdoing'[85] of the seller in order to break the causal link. That is to say, the conduct of the buyer must be the true cause of the loss rather than the breach by the seller. The buyer's exercising of his rights under the 1992 Act, it is submitted, cannot be treated as obliterating the wrongdoing of the seller, on the basis that exercising rights under the carriage contract is not the true cause of the buyer's loss. It should be remembered that since risk passes on or as from shipment under FOB and CIF sales, all the practical interest in being party to the carriage contract lies with the buyer. He only becomes party to it by way of statute and it is a contract for the benefit of a third party, namely the buyer (himself). Therefore, exercising contractual rights is the ordinary consequence of this, not the true cause of the loss. Unless the buyer is the shipper – which is not the case in the present context – and has taken part during or prior to shipment, the buyer seeking to perform his rights under the 1992 Act would hardly have the effect of obliterating the wrongdoing of the seller.

Even if such conduct of the buyer was accepted as an intervening event and the loss was said to have resulted from the combined operation of the seller's breach and the conduct of the buyer, this would not relieve the seller of liability. If an intervening event is reasonably expected by the parties at the time the contract was made, it is considered that such an event would not break the link between

[81] *Compania Naviera Maropan SA v Bowaters Lloyd Pulp & Paper Mills Ltd* [1955] 2 QB 68; *Reardon Smith Line Ltd v Australian Wheat Board* [1956] AC 266.

[82] Indeed, in such a case, the burden is on the buyer who must prove that the seller's breach is an effective or dominant cause of the loss. See *Carlos Soto Sau and Another v AP Moller-Maersk AS (The SFL Hawk)* [2015] EWHC 458 (Comm); [2015] 1 Lloyd's Rep 537, [33]. *Borealis AB v Geogas Trading SA* [2010] EWHC 2789 (Comm); [2011] 1 Lloyd's Rep 482, [43]; *Galoo Ltd v Bright Grahame Murray* [1994] 1 WLR 1360, 1374–75. See also *Hi-Lite Electrical Ltd v Wolseley UK Ltd* [2011] EWHC 2153 (TCC), [131]–[135].

[83] *Lambert v Lewis* [1982] AC 225.

[84] Section 3(1).

[85] *Borealis AB v Geogas Trading SA* [2010] EWHC 2789 (Comm), [44]; *Carlos Soto Sau and Another v AP Moller-Maersk AS (The SFL Hawk)* [2015] EWHC 458 (Comm); [2015] 1 Lloyd's Rep 537, [33].

the loss and the breach.[86] In that respect, upon arrival, if the goods appear to conform to the contract, what is reasonably expected from the buyer would be to demand or take delivery of his goods. However, there might be some inherent damage caused by the goods to the carrier, which may not appear until delivery or sometime afterwards. Alternatively, if they do not conform to the contract, since risk generally passes on or as from shipment, the buyer may choose to claim damages from the carrier under the carriage contract procured by his seller. Another scenario could be that if he thinks that the seller is in breach of one of the conditions under the sale contract – whether concerning the goods or documents – the buyer would have two separate rights: rejection of the goods and rejection of the documents. However, rejection may not always be the practical solution, and subsequently the buyer may have elected to accept the goods and claim damages in return from his seller instead. In either of these situations, the buyer may not be aware of the fact that the damage to the carrier resulted from the seller's breach, as the seller's fault would probably not be apparent from the goods or on the face of the bills of lading. Even if at first sight the buyer assumes that the seller could be in breach of the contract, he may not be able to reject the goods or documents, on the basis that his rejections could be considered wrongful, if he cannot prove that the seller is in breach of one of the conditions. This is to say, even if seeking to exercise rights under the 1992 Act is considered an intervening act, it would be unlikely to break the causal link, as the conduct of the buyer in the above scenarios would be reasonably expected in the commercial practice of CIF and FOB sales at the time the contract was made. More significantly, even if it is supposed that the seller's breach and the buyer's conduct are concurrent causes, the link would still be unlikely to be broken. The seller's breach does not necessarily have to be the effective cause of the loss; it is sufficient that his breach was an effective cause of the loss.[87] This is the case, even if the seller's breach and the buyer's conduct are together equally effective to cause the loss.[88] It would therefore suffice for the buyer to prove that the seller's breach is one of the effective causes of the damage incurred by the carrier.

F. String Sales

It is not uncommon for commodities to be sold multiple times before or during transit through a string of contracts. Although this might usually happen

[86] *Monarch Steamship Co Ltd v Karlshamns Oljefabriker (A/B)* [1949] AC 196.

[87] *Borealis v Geogas Trading* [2010] EWHC 2789 (Comm), [44]; *Great Elephant Corp v Trafigura Beheer BV* [2013] EWCA Civ 905, [45]; *Flanagan and Coles v Greenbanks Ltd* [2013] EWCA Civ 1702; *Carlos Soto Sau and Another v AP Moller-Maersk AS (The SFL Hawk)* [2015] EWHC 458 (Comm); [2015] 1 Lloyd's Rep 537, [33].

[88] *Heskell v Continental Express Ltd* [1950] 1 All ER 1033, 1047–48; *Banque Keyser Ullmann SA v Skandia (UK) Insurance Co Ltd* [1990] QB 665, 813–14; *ENE 1 Kos Ltd v Petreleo Brasileiro SA (No 2)* [2012] UKSC 17; [2012] 2 AC 164, [71].

under CIF contracts, an FOB buyer, following the shipment of the goods, may sell them to a sub-buyer on CIF terms as well.[89] While only the initial seller will be responsible for shipment of the goods, other sellers in the string will deal with tender of the documents further down in the chain.[90] No matter how many traders there are in the string, only the ultimate buyer may potentially incur liability vis-à-vis the carrier. Where this is the case, the buyer, given the doctrine of privity of contract, would not be able to sue the initial seller further up the string, but only his seller with whom he is in a contractual relationship.[91]

The 1979 Act provides a system of strict liability for defective goods.[92] That is to say, although a seller may not be personally at fault, he may be liable to his buyer, given the fault of the initial seller.[93] CIF sales are generally considered as sale of goods through performance of the documents.[94] Not being the initial seller will not prevent an intermediate seller from being in breach of his contractual duties towards his buyer.[95] For instance, a CIF seller – and often an FOB seller – is under a duty to conclude a reasonable carriage contract by virtue of section 32(2). The seller is also under an independent duty to tender bills of lading evidencing the carriage contract. Although they are separate duties, once the seller fails to carry out the former duty, the latter in most cases can be said to have been breached as well. It follows that when the initial seller makes an unreasonable carriage contract and tenders the bill of lading containing that contract to his buyer, further down the string an intermediate seller procuring this bill of lading will be considered in breach vis-a-vis his buyer.[96] This means that the end buyer in the string would only be able to pursue his claim against his contractual seller in that respect. Thus, when the ultimate buyer recovers his loss from his seller under the last contract in the

[89] For an example of this, see *Norsk Bjerningskompagnie A/S v Owners of the Panthanassa (The Panthanassa)* [1970] P 187; *Esteve Trading Corp v Agropec International (The Golden Rio)* [1990] 2 Lloyd's Rep 273.

[90] That is the rationale behind why c.i.f. sales are considered to be sale of goods through performance of the documents. See *Gardano & Giampieri v Greek Petroleum George Mamidakis and Co* [1962] 1 WLR 40, 52; *The Gabbiano* [1940] P 166, 173–74; *Smyth (Ross T) v Bailey (TD) Sons & Co* [1940] 3 All ER 60, 68; *Arnhold Karberg & Co v Blythe, Green Jourdain & Co* [1916] 1 KB 495; *Hindley & Co Ltd v East Indian Produce Co Ltd* [1973] 2 Lloyd's Rep 515.

[91] *Dunlop Pneumatic Tyre Co Ltd v Selfridge & Co Ltd* [1915] AC 847. Indeed a sub-buyer, as 'a third party' under the Contracts (Rights of Third Parties) Act 1999, may enforce particular terms in the main contract between the seller and the buyer, provided that the contract should state that the sub-buyer could, or that the contract confers a benefit on the party that is clearly identified. See Bridge, *Benjamin's Sale of Goods*, n 3 above, paras 17-080, 17-085; Beale, *Chitty on Contracts*, n 1 above, para 44-437.

[92] MG Bridge, 'Markets and damages in sale of goods cases' (2016) 132 *LQR* 405, 420.

[93] *H Parsons (Livestock) Ltd v Uttley Ingham & Co Ltd* [1978] QB 791; *Henry Kendall & Sons v William Lillico & Sons Ltd* [1969] 2 AC 31; *Ashington Piggeries Ltd v Christopher Hill Ltd* [1972] AC 441. See also *Kasler and Cohen v Slavouski* [1928] 1 KB 78; *Biggin & Co Ltd v Permanite Ltd* [1951] 1 KB 422.

[94] *Arnhold Karberg & Co v Blythe, Green Jourdain & Co* [1916] 1 KB 495, 510, 514.

[95] *Hindley & Co Ltd v East Indian Produce Ltd* [1973] 2 Lloyd's Rep 515.

[96] The seller's duty is often defined as making or procuring a reasonable carriage contract: *Houlder Bros & Co Ltd Commissioner of Public* [1908] AC 276, 290; *Tsakiroglou & Co Ltd v Noblee Thorl GmbH* [1961] 2 All ER 179. See also, Bridge, *Benjamin's Sale of Goods*, n 3 above, para 19-041; Bridge, *The International Sale of Goods*, 4th edn (Oxford, OUP, 2017) para 4.108.

string, due to breach of section 32(2) or breach of other contractual undertakings concerning the description or condition of the goods, the seller in the last contract, being the buyer in the penultimate contract, will seek to indemnify himself from his own seller up the string for the loss imposed under the last contract, and this will continue until the liability in question reaches the first buyer, regardless of the length of the string.[97,98] Therefore, the first buyer will seek to put this liability back on the shoulders of the initial seller/shipper, who is in fact the source of the defect both under the carriage and the sale contract.

Where this is the case, in order for the first buyer to recover from the seller for the liability rolled back up the string,[99] the first condition is that the probability of resale should have been within the contemplation of the parties at the time of the contract.[100] It is trite law that under c.i.f. sales, it is not uncommon practice to resell the goods before or while afloat.[101] It is especially true that the probability of resale increases when the seller is under a duty to tender a bill of lading, which may hint at the possibility of resale, owing to its transferable feature. For instance, where the first contract of sale is on FOB terms, the seller is normally under a duty to tender a transferable document, namely a bill of lading. When this is the case, there is also no difficulty in assuming that the buyer may resell the goods. The second condition is that it should also be within the contemplation of the initial seller and his buyer that each contract in the string will include the same or similar undertakings in respect of the description or condition of the goods, rendering the initial buyer (as a seller), and each sub-buyer (as seller) liable to their own buyers for breach of their corresponding contracts.[102] It has already been stated above that c.i.f. sales are contracts for sale of goods through performance of the documents. Before the goods reach their destination, they might be sold multiple times through documents and will often be sold on identical or similar undertakings as to the description or condition of the goods, without any variation. It is trite law that not being the initial seller would not exempt an intermediate seller from being in breach of his undertakings to his own buyer.[103] Indeed, it might

[97] *Biggin v Permanite* [1951] 1 KB 422, 432; *Kasler v Slavouski* [1928] 1 KB 78.

[98] Instead of multiple actions, each party in the string may also seek to join their contractual parties to the existing action. See *Henry Kendall & Sons v William Lillico & Sons Ltd* [1969] 2 AC 31; *Ashington Piggeries Ltd v Christopher Hill Ltd* [1972] AC 441.

[99] The first buyer may recover from the seller not only the loss arising from dangerous goods, but also the costs of defending the sub-buyer's claim against him in court. *Kasler v Slavouski* [1928] 1 KB 78, 89; *Godley v Perry* [1960] 1 WLR 9, 16–17. Additionally, the buyer may be entitled to recover the loss, even if he reasonably settled with his buyer out of court, provided that it was reasonable to settle and that the amount was reasonable. See *Biggin v Permanite Ltd* [1951] 2 KB 314, 320 (CA); *Comyn Ching & Co Ltd v Oriental Tube Co Ltd* [1979] 17 BLR 56; *Siemens v Supershield Ltd* [2009] EWHC 927, [64].

[100] *R & H Hall Ltd v WH Pim Junior & Co Ltd* (1928) 33 Com Cas 324; (1928) 30 Ll L Rep 159 (The sale contract was on c.i.f. terms). See also *Hammond Co v Bussey* (1887) 20 QBD 79; *Patrick v Russo-British Grain Export Co* [1927] 2 KB 535; *GC Dobell Co v Barber and Garratt* [1931] 1 KB 219; *Biggin v Permanite* [1951] 1 KB 422 (High Ct) (reversed on other grounds [1951] 2 KB 314 (CA)).

[101] *Hall v Pim* (1928) 30 Ll L Rep 159, 161.

[102] *Kasler v Slavouski* [1928] 1 KB 78, 85; *Biggin v Permanite* [1951] 1 KB 422, 433–34.

[103] *Hindley & Co Ltd v East Indian Produce Ltd* [1973] 2 Lloyd's Rep 515.

be argued that variations or exemption clauses in one of the contracts in a string may break the link between the contracts and prevent the loss from rolling back further up the chain. However, unlike for market loss,[104] for other consequential losses such as physical damage, the courts can be said to have rarely allowed such variations to break the link in the chain of sales.[105] Even if a variation is allowed in one of the contracts in the string in relation to description or any other undertaking as to the condition of the goods, the courts sometimes have not considered it material, but rather have allowed the claim, provided that the loss resulted from a defect in the goods which was covered by the description or undertakings in the initial seller's contract as well as in the other contracts in the string.[106] Thus, even if there exists a variation in one of the contracts in the string, so long as it is proved that the loss resulted from the initial seller's breach under the contract, the first buyer would probably be entitled to recovery from the seller for the cumulative loss that he inherited from the successive sub-buyers in the string. This might be the case even if one of the sub-contracts in the string included an exemption clause with regard to the condition of the goods or latent defects in them; such clauses in sub-contracts may not enable the initial sellers to exempt themselves from liability.[107]

III. Conclusion

This chapter, by following the causal link established between the seller's breach and the loss imposed on the buyer under the 1992 Act consequent upon the damage caused by the goods, has sought to examine whether his loss is considered too remote under the rule of remoteness and whether it can be recovered as a consequential loss in the light of the law of damages applicable to sale of goods cases. It is suggested that it can be recovered and is more likely to fall within the first limb of the rule of remoteness than the second one. When applying the rule of remoteness, the courts approach the link between the breach and the loss with common sense. Particularly under sale contracts on shipment terms, the courts, without conducting in-depth analysis, take into consideration only simple factual

[104] *Dexters Ltd v Hill Crest Oil Co (Bradford) Ltd* [1926] 1 KB 348, 359.

[105] *Biggin v Permanite* [1951] 1 KB 422, 433. For a similar view, see *British Oil and Cake Co Ltd v Burstall & Co* (1923) 39 TLR 406, 407.

[106] Bridge, *Benjamin's Sale of Goods*, n 3 above, para 17-083; Beale, *Chitty on Contracts*, n 1 above, para 44-436.

[107] The courts strictly interpret such exemption clauses, particularly in chain sales. In *Henry Kendall v William* [1969] 2 AC 31, where two contracts in a chain sale included exemption clauses in relation to latent defects, such clauses were held not to exempt the initial c.i.f. sellers from liability. See also *Ashington Piggeries* [1972] AC 441 and *Pinnock Bros v Lewis and Peat Ltd* [1923] 1 KB 690, 696–99, where the sellers argued that, given the exemption clause regarding latent defects in the sub-contract, they were not liable to their buyers for the loss that the buyers inherited from their sub-buyers. However, the sellers were eventually found liable.

causation between the loss and the breach in allowing claims for consequential losses under the rule of remoteness. The case law appears to show that the courts often allow claims for such losses under CIF and FOB sales where relevant. In that regard, particularly considering the buyer's innocence in the present context, perhaps the courts may adopt a more relaxed approach to allowing recovery than they would normally do under CIF and FOB sales. Especially considering that section 32(2) includes an autonomous reference to damages, it might come in handy for the courts to interpret this section extensively so as to allow recovery of the buyer's loss as a direct loss rather than a consequential one. As an effective alternate route to claim, the analogy established with the principle accepted in *Lambert v Lewis* could be put to use in favour of the buyer against the seller.

9

Non-contractual Remedies

I. General

The propositions made in Chapters seven and eight may create a remedy for the buyer/transferee under the sale contract against his immediate seller for liability for dangerous goods inherited under the carriage contract. Having said that, these propositions have yet to be tested before the courts, and they might fall short in providing an adequate remedy for the buyer against his immediate seller. Even if complete solutions are ensured under the sale contract, this does not necessarily eliminate the need for an examination of an alternative remedy on an alternative legal basis. For instance, the buyer might be in a less favourable position in a contractual action against his seller owing to practical difficulties such as an intervening insolvency or a lack of available assets. Thus, the buyer might be forced to have to look for redress elsewhere for his loss. Where this is the case, he may seek his right to remedy on an alternative legal basis against potential alternative parties. Therefore, to provide an alternative remedy to his potential contractual action, non-contractual actions which might be executable in favour of the buyer, will be discussed in this chapter. We shall begin (in section II) with the Civil Liability (Contribution) Act 1978 (the 1978 Act) – where the right to contribution between wrongdoers is available by way of statute – to see whether the buyer/transferee could be entitled to claim from the shipper/initial seller for contribution in respect of his loss. In the section III, we shall look into tort actions, which may be put to use for the benefit of the buyer against the initial seller/shipper.

II. Propositions for Recovery under the Civil Liability (Contribution) Act 1978

A. Basic Scheme of the Act

Where A1 and A2 are jointly or severally, or both jointly and severally liable to B for the same damage, A1 may find himself liable to B for the entire damage incurred by B on the basis that B may seek to recover damages from A1 only. Having taken into account his own interest, B wishes to proceed his claim against a party that has the biggest pockets and the most readily realisable assets. This might appear to be fair to B but not to A1. Where this is the case, A1 would seek to claim contribution from A2. Common law was not sympathetic to contribution between several wrongdoers who were liable for the same damage, unless there was an express or implied contribution agreement.[1] Such a right to contribution arises only by way of statute under English law.[2] Section 1(1) of the 1978 Act[3] states: 'any person liable in respect of any damage suffered by another person may recover contribution from any other person liable in respect of the same damage (whether jointly with him or otherwise)'.[4] Section 6(1), on the other hand prescribes that

> a person is liable in respect of the damage for the purposes of this Act if the person who suffered it … is entitled to recover compensation from him in respect of that damage (whatever the legal basis of his liability, whether tort, breach of contract, breach of trust or otherwise).[5]

Therefore, the Act provides a right to contribution among wrongdoers, even if liability arises from a different cause of action,[6] such as where one is liable in tort and another for breach of contract[7] or for breach of trust.[8] The rationale behind the Act is to ensure that a wrongdoer would not be unjustly enriched, when his liability to a third party has been discharged by a claimant who is also liable to the same third party.[9] Liability, in respect of the 1978 Act, means a liability that has been or could be established in an action filed in England and Wales, even if the rules of private international law indicate that foreign law is to be applied to

[1] *Merryweather v Nixon* (1799) 8 TR 186; 101 ER 1337; *Farebrother v Ansley* (1808) 1 Camp 343; 170 ER 979; *Wilson v Milner* (1810) 2 Camp 452; 170 ER 1215; *Weld-Blundell v Stephens* [1920] AC 956; *Hardy v Motor Insurers' Bureau* [1964] 2 QB 745, 768.

[2] The Civil Liability (Contribution) Act 1978. The Commonwealth countries like Australia, Singapore and Hong Kong adopted the provisions of the 1978 Act in their corresponding statutes: the Wrongs Act 1958 (Victoria, Australia); the Civil Law Act (ch 43) (Singapore); Civil Liability (Contribution) Ordinance (Cap 377) (Hong Kong). Thus, the relevant provisions in these statutes are substantially the same as the 1978 Act. On the other hand, the Law Reform Act 1936 (NZ), based on the UK's Law Reform (Married Women and Tortfeasors) Act 1935, is still in force in New Zealand, and thus only applicable to tortfeasors.

[3] The 1978 Act repealed and replaced the Law Reform (Married Women and Tortfeasors) Act 1935. See Law Commission, *Law of Contract: Report on Contribution* (Law Com No 79, 1977). On the Act see generally, HG Beale, *Chitty on Contracts*, 33rd edn (London, Sweet & Maxwell 2021) para 17-029 ff; M Jones, *Clerk & Lindsell on Torts*, 23rd edn (London, Sweet & Maxwell, 2020) para 4-13 ff.

[4] For materially same sections in other Commonwealth jurisdictions, see s 23B of the Wrongs Act 1958 (part IV) (Vic); s 15 of the Civil Law Act (ch 43) (Singapore); s 3 of the Civil Liability (Contribution) Ordinance (Hong Kong).

[5] For substantially identical sections in other Commonwealth jurisdictions, see 23A of the Wrongs Act 1958 (part IV) (Vic); s 19(1) of the Civil Law Act (ch 43) (Singapore); s 2(3) of the Civil Liability (Contribution) Ordinance (Hong Kong).

[6] *Royal Brompton NHS Trust v Hammond* [2002] UKHL 14; [2002] 1 WLR 1397, [41].

[7] *Thomas Saunders Partnership v Harvey* (1989) 30 Con LR 103, 121; *Prekookeanska Plovidba v Felstar Shipping Corporation and Others (The Carnival)* [1994] 2 Lloyd's Rep 14; *Eastgate Group Ltd v Lindsey Morden Group Inc* [2002] 1 WLR 643, 646; *Heaton v AXA Equity and Law Life Assurance Soc plc* [2002] 2 AC 329, 335. Where two parties are liable for breach of contract, see *Co-operative Retail Services Ltd v Taylor Young Partnership* [2002] UKHL 17.

[8] *Friends' Provident Life Office v Hillier Parker May & Rowden* [1997] QB 85, 99–104.

[9] *Dubai Aluminum Co Ltd v Salaam* [2002] UKHL 48; [2003] 2 AC 366, [76], per Lord Hobhouse.

solve any issue in dispute.[10] A claim for contribution under the 1978 Act is hence considered *sui generis*, since '[it] creates a cause of action in its own right, the ambit of which is to be discerned from the terms of the Act itself.'[11]

So far as liability for dangerous goods imposed on the CIF or FOB buyer[12] under the Carriage of Goods by Sea Act 1992 (the 1992 Act) is concerned, the shipper/seller's liability would not be extinguished and both the shipper/seller and the buyer/transferee would become jointly liable to the carrier.[13] The carrier would then have an option to pursue his claim against either or both, depending on who he considers to have the deepest pockets or the most easily realisable assets within the reach of the carrier. However, once the buyer comes under liability for this, he would justly seek to redeem his loss and to recover this from the party from whom he inherited it, namely the shipper/seller.[14] This has yet to be tested before the courts and therefore it is as yet unknown whether the buyer would be entitled to claim contribution under the 1978 Act for his liability inherited from the shipper/seller[15] who is the source of the liability. In the following sections, we shall look into the questions of whether the buyer is entitled to claim contribution in respect of his loss under the 1978 Act from the shipper/seller, and if so, what proportions would be just and equitable between them.

B. Notion of Same Damage and Same Victim

In order for a claim for contribution to succeed under the 1978 Act, there are some conditions to be satisfied. The first condition is that the potential contributor and the claimant should be liable to the same party.[16] Put differently, the damage caused by the potential contributor and by the party seeking contribution must have been suffered by the same victim.[17] It is immaterial whether their liability

[10] Section 1(6) of the 1978 Act. See also *RA Lister Co Ltd v EG Thomson (Shipping) Ltd* [1987] 1 WLR 1614; *Virgo Steam Ship Co SA v Skarrup Shipping Corp (The Kapetan Georgis)* [1988] 1 Lloyd's Rep 352. But for a different view on the choice of law issue in Australia, see *Fluor Australia Pty Ltd v ASC Engineering Pty Ltd* [2007] VSC 262 (Australia).

[11] *The Kapetan Georgis* [1988] 1 Lloyd's Rep 352, 357. See also *CF Harvey v RG O'Dell Ltd* [1958] 2 QB 78, 107 noted with approval in *Ronex Properties Ltd v John Laing Construction Ltd* [1983] QB 398, 407.

[12] Indeed the buyer could be liable for dangerous goods as an original party as well, where he is the shipper under bare FOB and sometimes under classic FOB types.

[13] By s 3(3) of the 1992 Act. For the potential non-contractual liability of the buyer to the carrier, see generally Chapter 6.

[14] This was exactly what the buyer sought to do against the shipper/seller in *Borealis AB v Stargas Ltd and Others (The Berge Sisar)*. The liability ultimately was not transferred to the buyer though, *The Berge Sisar* [2001] UKHL 17, [15].

[15] Apart from the shipper, sometimes the charterer can also be liable: *Chandris v Isbrandtsen-Moller* [1951] 1 KB 240. Therefore, it will be discussed below whether the buyer can claim contribution from the charterer under the 1978 Act, where the charterer is liable for dangerous goods against the shipowner.

[16] By s 1(1) of the 1978 Act.

[17] *Birge Construction Ltd v Haiste Ltd* [1996] 1 WLR 675, 680, 682.

to the same victim arises at the same or different times.[18] Thus, in the present context there is no apparent issue with fulfilling the first condition in respect of the buyer's claim for contribution, since he as the claimant, and the shipper/seller as the potential contributor would become liable to the same party, namely the carrier, under the 1992 Act for liability arising from dangerous goods,[19] despite the fact that the buyer's liability may arise at some time after the seller's.

The second condition is that the party seeking contribution and the potential contributor should be liable for 'the same damage'.[20] 'Damage' is considered synonymous with 'harm' or 'loss' and 'the same damage' does not therefore have a broad interpretation.[21] In *Royal Brompton Hospital NHS Trust v Hammond (No 3)*,[22] the House of Lords held that the words 'liability in respect of the same damage' should be given only their natural and ordinary meaning 'without any glosses, extensive or restrictive'.[23] The ordinary meaning of 'the same damage' was formulated by Lord Bingham in that case. According to his formulation, A1's claim for contribution by A2 depends upon the damage, loss or harm for which A1 would be liable to B corresponding (even if some of it) with the damage, loss or harm for which A2 would be liable to B. This appears to accord with the equity of the situation, in which it seems only fair that A2 makes a contribution to A1 of a fair portion of what both A1 and A2 owe in law to B.[24] Put simply, the formulation requires overlapping; that A1 should be liable to B in respect of the damage which corresponds with the damage for which A2 is liable to B. Also the fact that the measure of damages can be different in contract from tort does not alter the fact that the damage is the same for the purpose of the 1978 Act.[25]

Assume that A1 and A2 are supposedly liable to B in respect of some damage, harm or loss. When either A1 or A2 pays a sum to B on account of their respective liability, unless that payment operates to reduce the liability of the other to B, the damage caused by them cannot be regarded as 'same' so as to fall within the scope of the 1978 Act. Returning to the buyer's claim for contribution from the shipper/seller for liability for dangerous goods, it is submitted that his case is one to which the 1978 can be applied. First, section 3(1) of the 1992 Act clearly indicates that the buyer can only become subject to 'the same liabilities' of the shipper under that contract, as if he had been a party to that contract. As stated above, contribution can be claimed under the 1978 Act whatever the legal basis of liability, whether tort or breach of contract. In the present context, when the buyer as transferee is

[18] *Re Securitibank Ltd* [1986] 2 NZLR 280, 287–88.
[19] By s 3(1) and (3) of the 1992 Act.
[20] By s 1(1) of the 1978 Act.
[21] *Royal Brompton v Hammond* [2002] UKHL 14; [2002] 1 WLR 1397, [6].
[22] [2002] UKHL 14; [2002] 1 WLR 1397.
[23] ibid, [27].
[24] ibid, [6].
[25] *Eastgate Group Ltd v Lindsey Morden Group Inc* [2001] EWCA Civ 1446; [2001] 2 All ER 1050; [2002] 1 WLR 643.

considered liable to the carrier for dangerous goods under the 1992 Act, he statutorily becomes party to the same contract that the shipper already is party to, and subsequently inherits the identical liability of the shipper, in respect of the same damage caused by dangerous goods. Whatever damage is caused by dangerous goods, they would become jointly liable for the same damage to the carrier under the same contract via section 3(1) of the 1992 Act. According to the formulation of Lord Bingham, there is therefore no reason why their liability should not be considered the 'same damage'; once the buyer makes payment to the carrier on account of his liability arising from dangerous goods as provided by section 3(1) of the 1992 Act, such a payment will operate to reduce or extinguish the liability of the shipper/seller to the carrier. To support this argument, an analogy can be made with *The Kapetan Georgis*,[26] where an explosion occurred on board the vessel from a cargo of coal during its carriage. The shipowners pursued their claim against the time charterers for the loss caused by the shipment of dangerous goods. Following the shipowners' claim, the charterers joined the shippers in the proceedings and made a claim based on tort as well as under the 1978 Act against the shippers, alleging that the shippers were also liable to the shipowners for the same damage arising from their shipment of dangerous goods. Hirst J held that the time charterers were entitled to contribution from the shippers under the 1978 Act.[27] The learned judge, without delving into whether it was 'the same damage' or not, held that both the charterers' and the shippers' liability was considered to be in respect of 'the same damage'. The case shows that when the charterer and the shipper become liable to the carrier for a shipment of dangerous goods, albeit under different contracts, the damage caused by those goods is regarded as 'the same damage' under the 1978 Act. When the buyer is regarded as a transferee who inherits the same liability for the same damage from the shipper under the same contract, it is arguable that their liability could be considered to be in respect of the same damage for the purpose of the 1978 Act.

The Kapetan Georgis may also provide some assistance for the buyer's claim for contribution from alternative parties by way of analogy. In the case, the charterers' claim against the shipper under the 1978 Act was held to be sound by the court. Where a similar case arises, the shipper could be entitled to contribution from the charterer, where the latter is also held responsible for the same damage incurred by the shipowner. It would follow that if the buyer inherits the shipper's liability under the 1992 Act, – provided that the charterer is also in breach of a contractual/non-contractual duty to the carrier regarding the shipment of dangerous goods, as was the case in *The Kapetan Georgis* – their liability can be considered to be in respect of the same damage for the purpose of the 1978 Act, on the basis that the charterer's and the shipper's liability for dangerous goods would already be

[26] [1988] 1 Lloyd's Rep 352.

[27] ibid, 359. As Hirst J reached a decision in tort, his decision on the 1978 Act is considered only obiter.

regarded as arising from 'the same damage'. Where this is the case, the buyer may be entitled to an alternative contribution claim under the 1978 Act against the charterer as well as the shipper/seller, to the extent of the charterer's responsibility for the damage in question. Apart from this, during shipment of dangerous goods, alongside the shipper, other parties (like the bare FOB seller or the supplier who has no contractual relation with the carrier) can be found liable to the carrier in tort for dangerous goods, as they may have caused or contributed negligently to the damage or loss arising from the shipment of dangerous goods.[28] Providing they are responsible for the damage in question, the buyer/transferee may have also an alternative claim for contribution from those parties alongside the shipper/seller under the 1978 Act, where those parties are considered liable to the carrier.

C. Apportionment of Liability

When A1 and A2 are subject to liability for the same damage to the same party as discussed above, the subsequent question becomes one of the relative proportions of that liability as between A1 and A2 under the 1978 Act. The apportionment of liability is of considerable significance, as a good deal of money may ride on this issue. Where A1 seeks to recover contribution from A2, section 2(1) of the 1978 Act prescribes that the amount of contribution recoverable from any person 'shall be such as may be found by the court to be just and equitable having regard to the extent of that person's responsibility for the damage in question'.[29] In order for apportionment to be 'just and equitable', the court assesses the relative responsibility of the parties, which involves consideration of the causative relevance of their respective acts and omissions and their relative blameworthiness.[30] Thus, section 2(2) of the 1978 Act gives great flexibility to the courts in deciding whether to exempt any person from liability to make contribution or to order a party to contribute what amounts to a complete indemnity.[31]

[28] See *Losinjska Plovidba v Transco Overseas Ltd (The Orjula)* [1995] 2 Lloyd's Rep 395. This analogy may also be of some assistance to the bare FOB buyer or classic FOB buyer who is named as the shipper in the bill of lading. If the non-contractual seller causes or contributes to the damage arising from dangerous goods during or prior to shipment, when the buyer as the shipper becomes subject to liability to the carrier from the shipment of those goods, as was the case in *The Orjula*, if the buyer/shipper can prove that his seller's negligent act or fault contributed to the damage in tort, the buyer may have a contribution claim against his seller under the 1978 Act.

[29] For identical provisions in other Commonwealth jurisdictions, see also s 24(2) of the Wrongs Act 1958 (part IV) (Vic); s 16(1) of the Civil Law Act (ch 43) (Singapore); s 4(1) of the Civil Liability (Contribution) Ordinance (Hong Kong).

[30] *Madden v Quirk* [1989] 1 WLR 702, 707; *Downs v Chappell* [1996] 3 All ER 344, 363; *Davies v Swan Motor Co (Swansea) Ltd* [1949] 2 KB 291, 326; *Randolph v Tuck* [1962] 1 QB 175, 185; *The Miraflores and The Abadesa* [1967] 1 AC 826, 845; *Brown v Thompson* [1968] 1 WLR 1003, 1008; *Baker v Willoughby* [1970] AC 467, 490.

[31] *Saipem SpA and Conoco (UK) Ltd v Dredging VO2 BV and Geosite Surveys Ltd* [1993] 2 Lloyd's Rep 315; *Resource America International Ltd v Platt Site Services Ltd* [2004] EWCA Civ 665. For complete indemnity awards, see *Nelhams v Sandells Maintenance Ltd* [1996] PIQR 52; *The Sincerity S* [1996] 2 Lloyd's Rep 503; *Ryan v Fildes* [1938] 3 All ER 517; *Semtex Ltd v Gladstone* [1954] 1 WLR 945.

So far as the shipper/seller and the buyer/transferee's liabilities are concerned, there is the question of how the court will apportion liability between them so that it is considered just and equitable. Although apportionment under the 1978 Act is on a case-by-case basis, in the present context, the case between those parties can be more straightforward than it might be thought it would be. The assessment of relative responsibility requires consideration of both blameworthiness and the causative relevance of the respective acts and omissions of the parties. Returning to the core of liability arising from dangerous goods, in most cases it arises from the acts or omissions of the shipper before or during shipment. No exhaustive list of examples is given but the most common ones are that the shipper may not have enabled the carrier to take the necessary precautions to carry the goods safely[32] or that the goods may have been insufficiently packed.[33] On the other hand, unlike the shipper, in overseas sales, the buyer/transferee would be unlikely to have any physical nexus with the goods or instigate the shipment. He in most cases takes no part in shipment as transferee and it is likely that he would not even become party to the carriage contract under the bills of lading until sometime after shipment. While liability for dangerous goods often arises from the acts or omissions of the shipper/seller, it would be implausible to argue that any of the buyer/transferee's actions or omissions would have any causative relevance to the damage to the carrier.[34] If any, the only act done by the buyer would be to exercise his contractual rights against the carrier, which would make him liable to the carrier by way of transfer under section 3(1) of the 1992 Act. This, however, can hardly be said to have any causative relevance to the damage caused by dangerous goods. It is therefore submitted that since the shipper/seller is solely responsible for shipment of such goods, his acts and omissions could be said to be the sole source of the damage incurred by the carrier.[35] The buyer would not have become liable by way of transfer if it had not been for the shipper's acts or omissions in the first place. The buyer's liability is subordinate to the shipper/seller's, as he would only inherit it under the 1992 Act as a result of exercising his contractual rights. Had the shipper/seller not been liable to the carrier initially, the buyer would not have had liability transferred to him subsequently, despite triggering section 3(1) of the 1992 Act.[36] It would follow that the existence of such liability did not depend upon

[32] *Compania Sud Americana de Vapores SA v Sinochem Tianjin Import and Export Corporation (The Aconcagua)* [2011] 1 Lloyd's Rep 683. See also *Mediterranean Freight Services Ltd v BP Oil International Ltd (The Fiona)* [1994] 2 Lloyd's Rep 506. See also *Northern Shipping Co v Deutsche Seereederei GmbH and Others (The Kapitan Sakharov)* [2000] 2 Lloyd's Rep 255.

[33] *Brass v Maitland* (1856) 6 E & B 470; 119 ER 940; *Bamfield v Goole & Sheffield Transport* [1910] 2 KB 94; *Great Northern Railway v LEP Transport* [1922] 2 KB 742.

[34] Unless he has instigated the shipment or participated during it, but this would make him liable directly to the carrier without triggering the 1992 Act.

[35] Indeed the shipper often instructs independent contractors to fulfil the duty of shipment on his behalf. However, this would not relieve the shipper of liability caused by his contractors' acts or omissions.

[36] For an analogy, see *Shah v Gale* [2005] EWHC 1087.

the buyer's subsequent inheritance of it under the 1992 Act. Put simply, without the buyer being subject to this liability by way of transfer, the shipper/seller alone would still become liable as a result of his own acts or omissions during or prior to shipment. Therefore, in assessing the causative relevance of their respective acts and omissions, the shipper's breach of contract is said to be the sole blameworthy conduct, compared to the buyer's which would occur only subsequently and in no way can be said to have contributed to the damage. However, a question arises at this point: What if the shipper/seller has no apparent fault in the damage caused to the carrier? Where neither the shipper nor the carrier knows or ought reasonably to be aware of the dangerous nature of the goods, and accordingly the shipper has no apparent fault during shipment, this would not relieve the shipper of liability, since his liability is strict in nature.[37] His liability does not depend upon his acts or omissions or the knowledge available to him.[38] Where this is the case, liability would fall on the shipper rather than the carrier, purely as a result of the legal allocation of blameworthiness between the carrier and himself, on the ground that the shipper would have better means of knowledge of the goods.[39]

Where the causative potency is not apparent, in order to apportion liability sometimes the courts take account of the moral blameworthiness of the parties and may find that one is greater than the other.[40] When there is no apparent act or omission of the shipper causing the damage, as is the case between the shipper and the carrier, the shipper/seller should be treated as the sole morally blameworthy party vis à vis the buyer. In so finding, the same rationale as lies behind the strict liability of the shipper against the carrier can be applied between the buyer/transferee and the shipper/seller when allocating blameworthiness under the 1978 Act. Between the carrier and the shipper, the carrier is accepted as the more innocent party than the shipper, given that the latter has better means of knowledge of the goods. There is no reason why this should be different between the shipper/seller and the buyer/transferee, who is no doubt at least as innocent as the carrier is, and has played no part during or prior to shipment. This inference can also be supported analogously with vicarious liability cases where the employer, albeit innocent, becomes liable for the wrongful act of his employee.[41] For instance, in *Dubai Aluminum v Salaam*,[42] it was held by the House of Lords that the innocence of the vicariously liable employer was not a defence against the apportionment to him of liability under the 1978 Act. As with the shipper's strict liability for dangerous goods, vicarious liability does not depend on the fault of the employer and his innocence is considered immaterial. It was considered by the House of Lords that

[37] *Brass v Maitland* (1856) 6 E & B 470; 119 ER 940; *Effort Shipping Co Ltd v Linden Management SA (The Giannis NK)* [1998] AC 605; [1998] 1 Lloyd's Rep 337.

[38] ibid.

[39] ibid.

[40] *Furmedge v Chester-le-Street District Council* [2011] EWHC 1226.

[41] *Briess v Woolley* [1954] AC 333; *Ryan v Fildes* [1938] 3 All ER 517; *Semtex Ltd v Gladstone* [1954] 1 WLR 945; *KD v Chief Constable of Hampshire* [2005] EWHC 2550.

[42] *Dubai Aluminum v Salaam* [2002] UKHL 48; [2003] 2 AC 366.

the feature of vicarious liability is not whether the party concerned is at fault but whether he is answerable for the damage caused.[43] By analogy, whether at fault or not, the shipper can be said to be answerable to the carrier – even where he is also not aware of the nature of the goods – for damage and loss arising from dangerous goods. Therefore, as with the vicarious liability cases, having no fault or omission should not be a defence for the shipper/seller and he should be the one who is considered blameworthy against the buyer.

The contribution regime under the 1978 Act exists to correct as far as possible unjust enrichment at the expense of another.[44] Under the Act a person should only be liable to the extent that his wrongdoing is causative and has contributed to the damage in question. In seeking 'just and equitable' apportionment having regard to the buyer's responsibility for the damage, where there is no wrongdoing or blameworthy conduct on his part and where he could in no way be said to have contributed to the carrier's loss, the buyer should be entitled to a complete indemnity from the shipper/seller. There are the questions of whether there are alternative defendants from whom the buyer might claim contribution, such as a charterer, an initial seller or a supplier who has no contractual relation with the carrier, and if so, whether this would affect the the buyer's entitlement to obtain a complete remedy from the shipper/seller. Given that the buyer would still be considered as having perpetrated no wrongdoing which could in any way be considered the cause of the loss to the carrier, it is probable that having alternative defendants would not affect his complete recovery. However, this may change the apportionment among the defendants themselves, since the court should assess their relative responsibility for the loss caused to the carrier.

There is another question of what would happen if one of the defendants – for instance, the shipper/seller – were insolvent or likely to become insolvent or beyond the practical reach of the law. Where this is the case, the defendants who are actually available before the court would bear the burden of the entire liability.[45] This follows from the fact that the trial judge can only apportion the damages between those defendants available before the court and cannot consider the causal contribution of a party who is not before the court.[46] However, in a case like this, although the buyer's full recovery would technically appear to be secure, this may not always be the case in practice. Under section 2(3) a defendant's contribution is limited to what he would have been liable to pay to the claimant. Thus, for instance, where the shipper/seller is not before the court but the

[43] ibid, [154].

[44] ibid, [76].

[45] ibid, [71], [167]; *Mayfield v Llewelleyn* [1961] 1 WLR 119. However, as to s 7(3), nothing in the 1978 Act can alter the effect of an express contractual provision or an indemnity. For instance, where one party's liability is limited to a certain amount by the contract agreed with the victim, that party will not be required to make contribution more than this agreed amount.

[46] *Dubai Aluminum v Salaam* [2002] UKHL 48. Unless there is a clear mistake in principle or fact, the trial judge's decision on apportionment will unlikely be altered by an appellate court. See *Fitzgerald v Lane* [1989] AC 328; *Worlock v SAWS (A Firm)* (1983) 22 BLR 66.

initial seller or the supplier who is liable in tort is, the measure of damages might differ between the contract and tort. If the buyer/transferee became liabile for pure economic loss, he would not be able to recover it from those who are liable in tort, given that they would not become liable for pure economic loss in tort but only for loss consequent upon physical damage.[47] Accordingly, the buyer could only seek contribution from them in respect of those heads of loss for which they were already liable in tort.[48] Put differently, he would not be able to recover from them beyond what they would themselves have been liable to pay to the carrier in tort, regardless of how much his total liability is to the carrier under the contract.

D. Joinder of the Shipper/Seller or Other Potential Parties

In the present context, the buyer/transferee may invoke the 1978 Act for contribution, in practice, in four different situations. First, where the carrier has sued both the shipper/seller and the buyer/transferee as co-defendants, the buyer may request the court to apportion liability for the damage caused by reference to the 1978 Act.[49] Second, where the carrier has sued the buyer as the sole defendant, the buyer may be entitled to issue third-party proceedings[50] against the shipper/seller or other alternative defendants if any, in order to join them to the action.[51] Third, where the carrier has sued and won a judgment against the buyer as sole defendant, the buyer is still allowed to bring a separate action for contribution against the shipper/seller later.[52] Fourth, where the buyer has made a bona fide out-of-court settlement with the carrier for the loss, he is still entitled to bring a separate action for contribution against the shipper/seller.[53] However, he will need to prove that he would have been liable to the carrier, assuming that 'the factual basis of the claim against him could be established'.[54]

There is, however, a defence available to the shipper/seller in section 1(5) of the 1978 Act against joining third-party proceedings. If he can prove that there is

[47] *The Orjula* [1995] 2 Lloyd's Rep 395. For liability of the initial seller who has no contractual relation with the carrier, see Chapter 4. For example, where liability arises from *legally* dangerous goods causing detention of the vessel, such loss would not be recoverable under the 1978 Act from those that are liable in tort, since such a loss is considered pure economic loss.

[48] For the difference between contract and tort in dangerous goods cases in terms of heads of loss, see *The Orjula* [1995] 2 Lloyd's Rep 395.

[49] *Payne v British Time Recorder Co Ltd* [1921] 2 KB 1; *Pride of Derby and Derbyshire Angling Association Ltd v British Celanese Ltd* [1952] 1 All ER 1326; *Diboll v City of Newcastle upon Tyne* [1993] PIQR 16.

[50] By virtue of rule 20 (mostly called Part 20 proceedings) of the Civil Procedure Rules 1998 (CPR).

[51] *McCheane v Gyles (No 2)* [1902] 1 Ch 911; *British Racing Drivers' Club Ltd v Hextall Erskine & Co* [1996] 3 All ER 667.

[52] *West v Buckinghamshire County Council* [1985] RTR 306. Foreign courts' judgments do not give any right to claim contribution under the 1978 Act: *Société Nationale Industrielle Aérospatiale v Lee Kui Jak* [1987] AC 871, followed in *Bouygues v Caspian (No 5)* [1997] 2 Lloyd's Rep 533, 540. See also *Airbus Industrie GIE v Patel* [1997] 2 Lloyd's Rep 8.

[53] Section 1(4) and (5) of the 1978 Act.

[54] Section 1(4).

a pre-existing judgment given in England & Wales between him and the carrier in his favour for the liability in question, such a decision would be considered conclusive evidence against the potential claims for contribution.[55] Nevertheless, albeit technically possible, such a defence appears to fall short for the shipper/seller in practice, because the buyer would in any event only claim for contribution for a pre-existing liability of the shipper/seller that the buyer would inherit from him by way of transfer under the 1992 Act.

When there is a claim for contribution with no international element, contribution claims under the 1978 Act can readily be brought before the English courts. However, when there is an international element, the courts may need to serve out of jurisdiction for third-party proceedings where the proposed defendant is a necessary or proper party to that claim.[56] Sale contracts on FOB and CIF terms contain strong overseas elements, as parties can often be of different nationalities. Particularly in the case of chain sales, the shipper/initial seller and the end buyer are unlikely to have any contractual proximity with each other. The carriage contract is often concluded with a carrier who is also of a different nationality. The contract between the shipper/seller and the carrier may not always include an exclusive English law and jurisdiction clause. It may sometimes contain an exclusive arbitration clause or a clause that gives force to a foreign law to govern the carriage contract between them. It may therefore have limited or no connection at all with England and the court may not be able to exercise forum conveniens discretion over disputes between the carrier and the shipper/seller, as there might be a more appropriate forum available to the parties under that contract. Where this is the case, the question of whether the buyer would be able to join the shipper/seller before the English courts for a contribution claim arises, where he as transferee becomes liable to the carrier via the 1992 Act for dangerous goods transported under that carriage contract. To put it simply, the presence of a more appropriate forum or arbitration clause between the carrier and the shipper raises the issue of whether such clauses could be set aside by the courts, and accordingly the 1978 Act could have an overriding effect so as to allow the buyer's claim for contribution against the shipper.

The case law overwhelmingly suggests that the 1978 Act can be applied directly without assessing how closely the contribution claim is connected with English law.[57] In *The Benarty*,[58] the cargo owners claimed before the English courts against

[55] By virtue of s 1(5), foreign court judgments do not establish such conclusive estoppel. See A Briggs, 'The International Dimension to Claims for Contribution: Arab Monetary Fund v Hashim' (1995) *LMCLQ* 437, 440.

[56] CPR Rule 6.20(3A).

[57] *The Kapetan Georgis* [1988] 1 Lloyd's Rep 352; *The Golden Mariner* [1989] 2 Lloyd's Rep 390; *The Berge Sisar* [1997] 1 Lloyd's Rep 635; *Bouygues Offshore SA v Caspian Shipping Co (No 3)* [1997] 2 Lloyd's Rep 493; *RA Lister Co Ltd and Others v EG Thomson (Shipping) Ltd and Another (No 2) (The Benatry)* [1987] 1 WLR 1614; *Arab Monetary Fund v Hashim (No 3)* [1991] 2 AC 114; *Petroleo Brasiliero SA v Mellitus Shipping Inc (The Baltic Flame)* [2001] EWCA Civ 418; [2001] 1 All ER 933. For a different approach adopted in Australia, see *Fluor Australia Pty Ltd v ASC Engineering Pty Ltd* [2007] VSC 262.

[58] *The Benatry* [1987] 1 WLR 1614.

the shipowner and the charterer for the damage negligently caused to the cargo. Subsequently, the shipowner claimed for contribution under the 1978 Act from the charterer. Although the bill of lading included an exclusive Indonesian law and jurisdiction clause, the court allowed the claim under the 1978 Act without assessing how closely the case was connected to English law.[59] In *Arab Monetary Fund v Hashim*,[60] where the case had almost no connection with English law, Chadwick J held that although in principle a claim for contribution is governed by the law that has closest connection with the claim, the 1978 Act displaced that rule and has an overriding effect. In *The Kapetan Georgis*[61] the shipowner claimed against the charterers, who were a US company, for the damage caused to the vessel by the shipment of dangerous goods. In turn, the charterers made a claim for contribution under the 1978 Act against the shippers who were a Canadian company. Although the carriage contract evidenced in the bill of lading between the shipowner and the shipper contained a Hamburg arbitration clause, this was not considered an obstacle to the charterer's contribution claim against the shipper under the 1978 Act. More significantly, Hirst J held that the 1978 Act establishes a statutory cause of action in its own right; 'the ambit of which is to be discerned from the terms of the Act itself'.[62] He went on to add that there was nothing in the Act to restrict its scope to liabilities only incurred in England and Wales. He further opined: 'on the contrary it seems to me that s 1(6) with its references to private international law, is a small pointer in favour of an international dimension'.[63] This was later supported by the Court of Appeal in *The Baltic Flame*.[64] In that case, the cargo owners brought an action against the shipowner alleging that the goods were damaged after shipment. Subsequently, the shipowner joined the charterer for contribution for the damage caused to the goods and, in turn, the charterer brought a contribution claim against the shipper under the 1978 Act in respect of his potential liability to the shipowner. However, the bill of lading between the shipowner and the shipper contained a London arbitration clause, and subsequently the latter sought to reject the court's exercise of the forum conveniens discretion over his case. Potter J, who delivered the judgment extensively held:

> … the 1978 Act is strictly territorial in scope. However, it is unequivocal in its application to all proceedings brought in England, and there is nothing in the Act, or in

[59] For a similar case, see also *Bouygues Offshore SA v Caspian Shipping Co (No 3)* [1997] 2 Lloyd's Rep 493; where the owner of a barge which was lost in South African waters while under tow sued the charterer of the tug in England. Subsequently the charterer sought to join a South African port authority as a third party to claim contribution for its potential liability under the 1978 Act. Colman J, without assessing how closely the case was connected to English law, held that amalgamation of all the litigants in one forum should override other countervailing considerations.

[60] [1991] 2 AC 114.

[61] [1988] 1 Lloyd's Rep 352.

[62] ibid, 357.

[63] ibid.

[64] [2001] EWCA Civ 418; [2001] 1 All ER 933.

particular in s 1(6) to limit the right of contribution to liabilities incurred in England and Wales.[65]

The judgment, outlining that the 1978 Act has an overriding effect and should apply regardless of application of foreign law, is indeed supported by the words of section 1(6): 'it is immaterial whether any issue arising in any such action was or would be determined (in accordance with the rules of private international law) by reference to the law of a country outside England and Wales.' The sub-section does not require English courts to have jurisdiction over the claim between the shipper and the shipowner, and there is nothing in the Act to make its applicability dependent upon the governing law of the contract between the victim (the shipowner) and the potential contributor (the shipper/seller). In support of this, Potter J opined that the Act applies, even if the potential liability for contribution has yet to be established in an action in England or Wales. What matters is that liability could have been established for the same damage, had the contributor been sued in England or Wales. That is also true when considering the facts of the case, since the charterer of the *Baltic Flame* was not bound – in seeking contribution from the shipper – by the arbitration clause in the bill of lading concluded with the shipowner. In fact, the charterer's position was vulnerable in the case. Otherwise, the 1978 Act would be unlikely to render the shipper responsible for a potential contribution to the charterer, since the shipper was not party to arbitration proceedings. Similarly to *The Baltic Flame* case, in *The Berge Sisar*, where the carrier sued the buyer/transferee for liability for dangerous goods under the 1992 Act, subsequently the buyer sought to join the shipper/seller (who would have been originally responsible for this liability) to claim for contribution under the 1978 Act. Although the bill of lading between the carrier and the shipper contained an arbitration clause, as with the other authorities outlined above, Waller J on similar grounds held that the right to claim for contribution under the 1978 Act superseded the right conferred by the arbitration clause, and accordingly the shipper/seller should be joined.[66]

When considering a claim for contribution under the 1978 Act, the courts are said to have exercised forum conveniens discretion without assessing how closely the case is connected with English law. In so doing any countervailing facts against the convenience of the English forum, which would otherwise come into play, are outweighed. Therefore, it seems probable that the buyer's right to recover under the 1978 Act supersedes any right conferred by the contractual choice of a foreign law or arbitration clause between the shipper and the carrier, and the courts can be said to readily allow the buyer/transferee's proceedings against the shipper/seller.

[65] [2001] EWCA Civ 418, [36].
[66] *The Berge Sisar* [1997] 1 Lloyd's Rep 635.

III. Suggestions on Tort Actions

Propositions for action against the buyer's immediate seller under the sale contract were made in Chapter seven, in order to provide a solution for the buyer facing dangerous goods liability inherited from the shipper/seller. There might be a need for different legal bases for the buyer's claim, since these suggestions have yet to be tested before the courts, and ultimately they might be incapable of providing a wholly adequate remedy against his seller. Also, the fact that the buyer has a contractual proximity with the shipper/seller and an effective remedy against him under the contract will not be a bar to an alternative action in tort.[67] In any case, the end buyer/transferee may or may not have any contractual relationship with the original seller/shipper, since chain sales are not uncommon in international trade. Given that the shipper is the source of liability arising from dangerous goods, the buyer may wish to sue him directly. However, he will not be entitled to bring a contractual action against the shipper/seller,[68] given the doctrine of privity of contract.[69] Thus, this section will seek a potential effective remedy in tort for the buyer/transferee's inherited liability for dangerous goods which might be put to use against the shipper/seller.

It is a general principle that an action for negligence can only succeed where the claimant has a proprietary interest in the goods at the time the damage occurred.[70] Accordingly, as a matter of law, this principle bars recovery of pure economic loss in negligence, unless the claimant was the owner or the person entitled to their possession.[71] Where the buyer/transferee incurs contractual liability arising from dangerous goods for physical damage to the carrier's vessel, his loss can only be categorised as economic, as he has no proprietary interest in the vessel. Thus, the buyer could be said to have no hope of redress in tort at first sight. Nevertheless, without disputing the validity of this long-established principle, where the claim is part of a chain originating in a claim for physical damage, the application of this principle may be set aside, having regard to the decision of the House of Lords in *Lexmead v Lewis*[72] in which the relevant dicta of Lord Diplock on this are as follows:

> I should not wish the dismissal of the dealers' appeal to be regarded as an approval by this House of the proposition that where the economic loss suffered by a distributor in the chain between the manufacturer and the ultimate consumer consists of a liability to pay damages to the ultimate consumer for physical injuries sustained by him, or

[67] *Clarke v Army and Navy Co-operative Society Ltd* [1903] 1 KB 155.

[68] Indeed the bare or classic FOB buyer who is also the shipper does not fall within this group unless he re-sells the goods further in the chain.

[69] *Dunlop Pneumatic Tyre Co Ltd v Selfridge & Co Ltd* [1915] AC 847.

[70] *Candlewood Navigation Corporation Ltd v Mitsui OSK Lines Ltd* [1986] AC 1; *Leigh & Sillivan Ltd v Aliakmon Shipping Co Ltd (The Aliakmon)* [1986] AC 785; [1986] 2 Lloyd's Rep 1.

[71] ibid.

[72] *Lexmead (Basingstoke) Ltd v Lewis and Others* [1982] AC 225; [1985] 2 Lloyd's Rep 17.

> consists of a liability to indemnify a distributor lower in the chain of distribution for his liability to the ultimate consumer for damages for physical injuries, such economic loss is not recoverable under the Donoghue v. Stevenson principle from the manufacturer.[73]

The dicta of Lord Diplock were later applied in *The Kapetan Georgis*[74] by Hirst J, which can assist in the buyer's hope of redress against the shipper/seller by way of analogy. The facts of the case are not conceptually different from the buyer/transferee's position. The claimants were the owners of *The Kapetan Georgis*, which was time-chartered to the defendants. The cargo of coal which was allegedly dangerous due to being excessively gaseous was loaded by the shippers. Several days later, an explosion on board the vessel occurred resulting in damage and loss of life. The shipowners brought a claim against the charterers for damages for breach of contract arising from the shipment of dangerous goods. In turn, in case they would be held liable to the shipowners, the charterers claimed against the shippers in tort that the shippers owed a duty to take reasonable care that the loaded coal was not dangerous and they were thus negligent in shipping excessively gaseous coal.[75] In following the dicta of Lord Diplock, Hirst J held that when the case features a physical damage claim somewhere up the chain and a claimant who became liable for that physical damage caused by a third party's tortious act, the long-established principle may not apply, and therefore the loss of the claimant may not be considered a purely economic loss.[76] As a result, he held that the charterers were entitled to claim in tort against the shippers for their liability to the shipowners, which resulted from the negligent act of the shippers.[77]

Following these judgments, without abolishing the long-established principle, an exceptional rule appears to have emerged: when the claimant incurs a legal liability for physical damage to someone else's property and if the proximate cause of the damage to that property is a third party's negligence, the general rule can be set aside and the claimant may have an effective claim against that third party in tort. In *The Kapetan Georgis*, the charterer became liable to the shipowners for the physical loss of the vessel, and the proximate cause of that loss was the shipper's negligent shipment. Accordingly, the exception came into play and did not require the charterer to have a proprietary interest in the vessel whatsoever to claim in tort, and his loss was not categorised as pure economic loss but a loss consequent upon that physical loss. If liability for dangerous goods could be advanced successfully in tort against the charterer as it was in the case, there is no reason why the same should not apply in favour of the buyer/transferee whose position is conceptually similar as against the shipper/seller. As with the charterer in *The Kapetan*

[73] *Lexmead v Lewis* [1982] AC 225, 278. Jones, *Clerk & Lindsell on Torts*, n 3 above, para 4-32.
[74] [1988] 1 Lloyd's Rep 352.
[75] The charterers also made a claim for contribution under the 1978 Act, which has already been discussed above.
[76] [1988] 1 Lloyd's Rep 352, 356.
[77] ibid.

Georgis, when the buyer becomes liable as transferee under the 1992 Act for physical damage to the carrier's vessel caused by the shipment of dangerous goods, the proximate cause of that damage would be the negligence of the shipper, not the buyer/transferee's.[78] In both scenarios, the shipper is in breach of the bill of lading contract with the carrier due to the dangerous nature of the goods and neither the buyer nor the charterer has contractual proximity with the shipper/seller but both come under legal liability to compensate for the physical damage caused to the carrier as a result of the shipper's tortious acts or omissions. Also, neither the buyer nor the charterer plays a part during or prior to shipment. Like the charterer, the buyer as transferee would have no proprietary interest in the vessel but pursues his loss consequent upon the physical damage to the vessel.[79]

In order for the buyer/transferee to be entitled to claim in tort against the shipper/seller under this exception, the buyer must be subject to liability for physical damage to the carrier's vessel, where the proximate cause of that damage is the shipper/seller's negligence. When he becomes subject to liability under the 1992 Act for the shipment of dangerous goods, he does so not as a result of his actions but because of the shipper's breach in shipping dangerous goods. There is no reason why his claim should not be considered as part of a chain which originates in a claim for physical damage. The exceptional rule created by the House of Lords in *Lexmead v Lewis* is that when the claimant comes under legal liability for physical damage to someone else's property, and if the proximate cause of the damage to that property is the third party's negligence, the general rule can be set aside and the claimant may have an effective claim against that third party in tort. On this ground, as with the charterers in *The Kapetan Georgis*, once the buyer/transferee comes under liability to compensate the carrier via the 1992 Act for physical damage caused by dangerous goods and the proximate cause of this damage is the shipper/seller's (third party's) negligence or omissions in shipment of dangerous goods, the general rule should be set aside and the buyer should be allowed redress in tort against the shipper/seller for such liability.

Indeed, one may argue against the rule created in *Lexmead v Lewis* and *The Kapetan Georgis* on the basis of abolishing the general rule. However, neither Lord Diplock in *Lexmead v Lewis* nor Hirst J in *The Kapetan Georgis* disputed the validity of the general rule. Instead, they created an exception, which can be distinguished, and its application can be restricted to such peculiar cases.[80] As Lord Macmillan opined in *Donoghue v Stevenson*, which is one of the landmark cases on tort: 'The criterion of judgment must adjust and adapt itself to the changing circumstances of life. The categories of negligence are never closed'.[81] In support

[78] It is immaterial whether it resulted from the negligence of an independent contractor acting as an agent of the shipper, since the duty to the carrier falls on the shipper.

[79] See *Muirhead v Industrial Tank Specialties Ltd* [1986] QB 507; [1986] AC 177.

[80] Neither the Privy Council nor the House of Lords mentioned the exception established in *Lexmead v Lewis* in the two subsequent cases as to the general rule. See, respectively, *Candlewood Navigation Corporation Ltd v Mitsui OSK Lines Ltd* [1986] AC 1; and *Leigh & Sillivan Ltd v Aliakmon Shipping Co Ltd (The Aliakmon)* [1986] AC 785; [1986] 2 Lloyd's Rep 1.

[81] [1932] AC 562, 619.

of this, Lord Pearce said in *Hedley Byrne & Co Ltd v Heller & Partners Ltd*: 'How wide the sphere of the duty of care in negligence is to be laid depends ultimately upon the courts' assessment of the demands of society for protection from the carelessness of others'.[82] Thus, the categories of negligence are regarded as dynamic and there is always room to create new duty of care situations.[83] Perhaps on these grounds, both *Lexmead v Lewis* and *The Kapetan Georgis* can be said to have stretched the existing principles in tort to adjust the law to the circumstances of international trade.

There might be also some criticism of this exception on the basis of the 'floodgates' argument,[84] namely that the courts might show some reluctance to allow recovery of economic loss in tort claims, as this would open the floodgates to claims. The underlying reason is that there might be indeterminate liability to a large number of plaintiffs.[85] Nevertheless, the floodgates argument was disapproved by the House of Lords in *Junior Books v Veitchi*[86] on the basis that wrongdoers should not be allowed to avoid liability caused by their wrongdoings. In any case, as was the case in *The Kapetan Georgis*, once the number of plaintiffs is limited to those who are liable to the owner of the property, the floodgates argument could no longer be viable. In the present context, the floodgates argument would have no room for application, as liability is not irreversible under the 1992 Act, and therefore the number of plaintiffs is only limited to the end buyer/transferee that irrevocably inherits liability.

IV. Conclusion

Suggestions have been made in this chapter under the 1978 Act and in tort to provide non-contractual solutions for the buyer/transferee pursuing a remedy for his inherited liability for dangerous goods. The rationale behind the Act is to ensure that the wrongdoer is not unjustly enriched, where his liability to a third party has been discharged by a claimant that is also liable to the same third party.

[82] [1964] AC 465, 536.

[83] On the similar view, see Jones, *Clerk & Lindsell on Torts*, n 3 above, para 8-05.

[84] See the US case of *Ultramares Corporation v Touche, Niven & Co* 255 NY 170; 174 NE 441 (1931) and *Spartan Steel & Alloys Ltd v Martin & Co (Contractors) Ltd* [1973] QB 27. See also *Muirhead v Industrial Tank Specialties Ltd* [1986] QB 507; [1986] AC 177. Another criticism can be made on the basis that the shipper/seller may not know who the ultimate buyer will be in chain sales, thus he may not also know to whom his duty is owed. However, tort law on this point is clear: it is not required that there must be a specific person to whom the duty is owed when the negligence occurs, the duty can be potential or contingent or owed to a general class: *Grant v Australian Knitting Mills Ltd* [1936] AC 85, 104; *Farrugia v Great Western Ry Co* [1947] 2 All ER 565, 567. In *The Kapetan Georgis*, there was not even a dispute on this point as to whether the shipper should have known the charterer as an identified person. Therefore the shipper is not required to know the end buyer as an identified person. By reason of the transferability of bills of lading, he can be said to owe that duty to a general class of holders of the bill who have an interest in the goods.

[85] *Ultimares Corporation v Touche, Niven & Co* 174 NE 441, 444 (1931).

[86] *Junior Books Ltd v Veitchi Co Ltd* [1982] 3 All ER 201; [1983] 1 AC 520, 532, 545.

On the grounds discussed above, it is arguable that the buyer/transferee may have an arguable claim under the 1978 Act against the shipper/seller or other alternative parties. Although it might appear to be difficult at first sight to bring an overseas shipper/seller before the English courts where there is a more appropriate forum, the case law predominantly proves otherwise. The courts may show readiness to apply the 1978 Act, even if there are other countervailing factors weighing against the convenience of the English forum, like the choice of foreign law or arbitration clause. Although there appears to be no technical problem with the claim of the buyer under the 1978 Act, it is not without some practical difficulties. For instance, the shipper/seller may not have any asset within the reach of the court or he might be insolvent or untraceable. An overseas shipper/seller may refuse to join the proceedings in England, even when a court orders him to do so. Another possibility might be that the buyer may not be able to seek declaratory recognition of the judgment in his favour given in England, in the country in which the shipper/seller has assets, and accordingly the buyer may not be able to effectively recover in practice.

So far as the buyer's claim in tort is concerned, he may have a hope of redress under the exception created by *Lexmead v Lewis* and *The Kapetan Georgis* against the shipper/seller for his liability for physical damage to the carrier's vessel or other cargoes on board where the proximate cause of the damage is the shipper's negligence. Although it is an exception to the general rule, the courts may be reluctant to set aside the general rule and refuse to apply the exception. However, considering the position of the buyer/transferee, particularly if he has no practical remedy in a contractual action, it is submitted that the courts should show readiness to apply this exception against the shipper/seller in order that he is not unjustly enriched where he is actually the source of liability. However, the fact that there is an action available in tort does not necessarily follow that it is without difficulties. First, an overseas third-party shipper/seller may not readily accept joining a tort action in England or he might be untraceable. Even if he joins, the buyer must himself prove that the proximate cause of the damage to the carrier is the negligence of the shipper/seller. However, it is trite law that the shipper becomes strictly liable to the carrier for the shipment of dangerous goods regardless of his omissions or actions. Where this is the case, the buyer may have difficulty in proving that the shipper's negligence caused the damage to the carrier if he is not negligent. Accordingly, he may not be entitled to claim in tort against the shipper. Even if the buyer proves the shipper's negligence, he may not be able to obtain full recovery against him, given that heads of loss might differ under the contract and in tort. Regardless of heads of loss against the carrier under the contract, the buyer can only recover economic losses consequent upon physical damage and he is not entitled to recover pure economic loss in tort actions. Similar practical problems mentioned in respect of the 1978 Act may arise in tort actions as well. The seller/shipper may not have any realisable assets within reach or the buyer may encounter difficulties in the country in which the seller/shipper has realisable assets in seeking declaratory recognition and enforcement of the judgment given in England in favour of him.

10

Conclusion

I. Outcomes and Proposed Solutions

The task of this work has been to explore the allocation of liability for dangerous goods between the seller and the buyer under CIF and FOB contracts, providing an in-depth study of the issue of carriage of dangerous goods in the context of international trade law. In doing so, it has discussed whether and to what extent the law of international sale of goods can provide any assistance in the re-allocation of liability between the buyer and the seller. In addition to its contractual analysis, it has sought to offer suggestions for non-contractual mechanisms to the same end.

Chapter one highlighted the modern landscape of many different dangerous goods. It is almost impossible to transport them today with the outdated principles of the nineteenth and the early twentieth centuries without any incidents. As a result of this, as shown in Chapter two, the existing international efforts regulating the maritime transport of dangerous goods are far from simple, being composed of multiple layers of rules buried in detail. Chapter two also discussed the effectiveness and implementation of these regulations, which will be referred to once again at the end of this chapter when evaluating the efforts of the industry, including all the stakeholders engaged in the transport of dangerous goods. However, prior to doing so, it is worth elaborating once again on the conclusions and the recommendations in the main chapters (Chapters three to nine) to see whether the status quo of the law is up to the task without being subject to any radical changes.

A. Dangerous Goods not Confined to 'Dangerous Goods'

We saw in Chapter two that dangerous goods are classified in certain categories in the international dangerous goods regulations. However, Chapter three proves that under English law, be it common law or the Hague/Hague-Visby Rules, dangerous goods are not confined to these categories, but go beyond the lists provided in these regulations. The word 'dangerous' is not restricted to inherently dangerous goods, and dangerousness is conceptually taken into account as a combination of surrounding circumstances together with the nature of the cargo. Thus, even the shipper of the most innocuous goods could be subject to liability for dangerous goods, unless necessary measures are taken for their carriage. In that respect, we have also seen that the approach adopted by the English courts has been profoundly influential within the major shipping Commonwealth countries. So far as the liability regime is concerned under English law, regardless of whether it arises under the Rules or common law, the shipper comes under strict liability to the carrier, even if he bears no fault at all concerning the shipment. In this regard, in the shipping countries making use of the Hague/Hague-Visby Rules, like the US and the Nordic countries, their interpretation of article IV rule 6 is similar to the English approach, although there are some differences in other aspects. As for the Commonwealth countries, the English case law can be said to have been vastly influential. As a result, the implementation of the rule 6 provision is substantially the same as the English interpretation. Chapter three also showed that a unanimous approach is adopted by the major shipping countries to the strictness of liability for dangerous goods, which will be commented on once again in the end of this chapter.

B. Seller Justifiably Attracts Liability at the Shipment Stage

Chapter four, in discussing the question of whether it is the seller or the buyer as the shipper that attracts liability arising from dangerous goods under FOB and CIF sales, concluded that it is not entirely possible to find a single rule under CIF and FOB contracts to identify who the shipper is. Having said that, under CIF and many FOB sales, at the shipment stage, the case law shows that liability often justifiably falls on the seller/shipper as the source of the defect rather than the buyer, regardless of the former being designated in the bill of lading as agent of the buyer. So far as CIF sales are concerned, there is no difficulty in generalising that it is almost invariably the seller, as both wet and dry shipper, who is subject to liability vis-à-vis the carrier. Even if he is regarded as agent of the buyer in making the carriage contract (which would be a very exceptional case under CIF sales) this will not relieve him of liability against the carrier. Unlike in CIF sales, offering a single inflexible rule under FOB contracts is not without difficulties. Under bare and classic FOB sales, where the buyer concludes the contract and is named as the shipper in the bill, it is the buyer that becomes subject to liability under the contract. However, it has also been advocated in Chapter four that the non-contracting seller may not be immune from liability, as, under FOB sales he can be party to a separate implied contract with the carrier in which he could be subject to liability. Indeed, some reservations have been put forward regarding the proposition, as it might prove difficult to put into practical effect by the courts, which may arguably feel reluctant to impose dangerous goods liability on the seller under the implied contract where there is an original party subject to liability under the bill of lading. However, it has been suggested that the non-contracting seller should not be allowed to avoid liability, particularly where his actions are the source of damage and loss and the buyer is not worth suing. The chapter also championed the idea of imposing liability in tort on the non-contracting seller, where he is the source of the fault or negligence, despite the fact that there are only a limited number of cases reported showing that the non-contracting seller can have this liability imposed on him.

So far as classic FOB and FOB 'with additional duties' contracts are concerned, the discussion in Chapter four proved that a case-specific analysis is necessary to ascertain the identity of the shipper under these contracts. Where the seller negotiates the carriage contract and is named as the shipper in the bill, and he has no interest in being party to the carriage contract on shipment, the courts appear to have adopted an approach that the seller may have been named as shipper in the contract as an agent of the buyer. Accordingly, the bill of lading can be said to have evidenced a contract only between the buyer and the carrier. However, when dealing with liability arising from dangerous goods, this approach may have been justifiably set aside and the courts are apparently inclined to hold the seller/named shipper liable as principal rather than the buyer, even if the facts of the case indicate otherwise. The author is of the opinion that the approach taken by the courts in the present context is correct, on the basis that the seller is said to be better placed to know the goods that he sells and have the closest nexus with them both physically and contractually – albeit being named as agent – prior to shipment, compared to the buyer who has no proximity with the goods and takes no part in the shipment stage of the process.

C. Liability is Transmissible to the Buyer at the Delivery Stage Probably Only under the Contract

As discussed in Chapter four, under CIF and many FOB sales,[1] it is often the seller who is subject to liability to the carrier for dangerous goods under the carriage contract at the shipment stage. However, through the anti-privity devices introduced in English law (previously the 1855 Bills of Lading Act, and now the 1992 Carriage of Goods by Sea Act), the buyer is allowed to become party to the carriage contract concluded by the seller so as to enjoy rights therein against the carrier. This, however, comes along with a burden in the form of the principle of mutuality, which is not only concerned with the transfer of rights, but also with the imposition of contractual liabilities. Therefore, the buyer is not offered immunity from liabilities under the carriage contract, if he wishes to exercise his rights therein. Having said that, liability for dangerous goods was never transferred to the buyer/consignee under the 1855 Act, despite the fact that it was also based on the principle of mutuality, like its successor. Thus, the practical question forming the main substance of Chapter five was whether liability arising from dangerous goods would be transmissible from the seller/shipper to the buyer/transferee under the carriage contract by means of the 1992 Act. The chapter, in addressing this

[1] Save for the bare and the classic FOB where the buyer is the shipper named in the bill of lading.

question, concluded that liability for dangerous goods is transmissible from the seller/shipper to the transferee/buyer under the 1992 Act. The chapter contended that there appears to be no injustice done in transferring this liability to the buyer via the mechanism of the 1992 Act. First, under the Act, he will not be subject to liability unless he wishes to exercise his contractual rights. It follows that there is no automatic imposition of liability at the time contractual rights are transferred. Second, we have seen that the courts have so far sought to ensure the balance by restrictively interpreting the imposition mechanism of the 1992 Act in favour of the buyer/transferee, who will often be entitled to avoid liability[2] by trading transferable bills of lading, even if liability is incurred preliminarily. So far as dangerous goods liabilities are concerned, they can be disproportionate when damage to or total loss of a vessel, other cargoes and even loss of life may result, and the shipper may not have any or sufficient assets within reach. The rights of third parties are a matter of commercial necessity. On the other hand, liabilities of third parties are a matter of policy. English law, in terms of carriage contracts, is based on the principle of mutuality, and justifiably favours the protection of the carrier in order to reduce the risk of insolvency under the tri-partite relationship by giving the carrier a right to redress against the transferee/buyer – who is the prime reason behind the shipment, as those goods are ultimately carried for his benefit. For these reasons, Chapter five concludes that liability for dangerous goods is transmissible.

Since the 1992 Act came into force, the Act can be said to have ironed out the deficiencies of its predecessor and there has been almost no need to rely on other common law actions outside the contract, given that it has created a comprehensive contractual regime between the carrier and the transferee/buyer who is not the shipper. The Act, however, has not abolished the common law actions and does not govern the law outside the contract. We saw in Chapter four that at the shipment stage the non-contracting seller may be subject to liability to the carrier in tort and under an implied contract. Chapter six sought to address a very similar question arising at the final stage of the voyage: whether the buyer could be subject to liability for damage or losses arising from dangerous goods under the common law actions, where there is no contractual nexus between the carrier and the buyer at the delivery stage. In addressing this question, Chapter six concluded that unlike his counterpart, the buyer appears to enjoy immunity from liability for dangerous goods at the delivery stage where there is no contract governing his relationship with the carrier. This is arguably the correct outcome, as he is neither at fault nor in a position at the delivery stage to contribute to causes leading to dangerous goods incidents. Under the *Brandt v Liverpool*-type implied contract, the buyer is probably not at risk of attracting liability for dangerous goods. Nor will he be in danger of being sued for liability just because he holds a document of title that gives constructive possession of the goods. So far as the rules of tort are concerned, the buyer/consignee, unlike the seller/wet shipper, is said to enjoy protection against carriers, unless he took part prior to or during shipment in a manner to

[2] Unless an irreversible step is taken by the buyer; for instance taking delivery of the goods.

cause damage or loss. On the other hand, to a degree, the buyer at the delivery stage might be at risk of being subject to liability under a bailment action. Albeit unlikely, as discussed in Chapter six, under some exceptional circumstances, the buyer/consignee can sometimes be considered the bailor. However, the courts may justifiably be reluctant to impose such liability on the buyer/consignee under bailment if there is a contract governing his relationship with the carrier. In such a case, it would be unlikely that shipowners would be allowed to circumvent the mechanism of section 3(1) in the presence of a contractual regime. Having said that, the chapter recommended – not without some hesitation – a proposition that where the buyer becomes the bailor as a result of actual attornment established upon his demanding or taking delivery of the goods, the courts should show more readiness to render the buyer/attornee liable, particularly where the carrier has only a minimal chance of gaining redress from the shipper due to practical difficulties, such as the latter having no assets within reach. Given that buyers would normally have been subject to liability under section 3(1) on demanding and taking delivery of the goods under the contract, the courts should not allow buyers to take advantage of the absence of a contract, when they wish to exercise their rights by demanding or taking delivery of the goods under the bailment.

D. Contractual Recovery by the Buyer

In Chapters five and six, we saw that liability for dangerous goods is more likely to be transferred under the contract than via the non-contractual mechanisms. The transfer of liability, however, begs a further question, which has yet to be addressed under English law: whether the buyer would have an effective remedy to recover his loss from the seller. In addressing this question, the book has offered both contractual and non-contractual propositions in Chapters seven, eight and nine. So far as the contractual solutions are concerned, the buyer should first prove a causal link between his loss and breach of the seller under the sale contract, if he is to be entitled to a remedy. In doing so, some propositions advanced in Chapter seven may be of use. These are based on the implied conditions of the 1979 Sale of Goods Act, such as description or satisfactory quality of the goods, which are not without difficulties, as they might depend on the facts of individual cases. It was discussed that the buyer may not always be able to invoke one of the implied conditions, if the facts do not prove the link between the buyer's loss and the seller's breach. Therefore, the propositions put forward on the implied conditions of the 1979 Act may not fit every case, and accordingly they are unlikely to offer a holistic solution. The chapter, however, championed as the main proposition that section 32(2) can be put to use to tackle this issue completely under the terms of the sale contract. Under CIF and many FOB sales,[3] by virtue of section 32(2),

[3] This is not the case where the buyer himself concludes the carriage contract under the bare FOB and sometimes under classic FOB sales.

the seller is under a duty to conclude the carriage contract evidenced in the bill of lading on behalf of the buyer on usual terms[4] in the specific trade concerned by providing all necessary precautions for safe carriage of the goods[5] and conferring substantial continuous protective rights throughout the voyage.[6,7] His duty to conclude a reasonable carriage contract has three separate limbs and once he fails any of these limbs, he will be considered in breach of section 32(2). Under the first limb 'contract on usual terms', in the absence of an express term in the sale contract concerning 'the usual thing' in a certain line of business, the courts may imply a term into the sale contract, if the contract is to be deprived of its business efficacy which requires that a party should not be deprived of substantially the benefit that he is supposed to receive under the contract according to the intent of the parties.[8] The 'usual thing' in the carriage of dangerous goods is that the goods ought to be afforded the necessary precautions their nature requires for their safe transport. If the goods are not duly treated with all the required measures and the buyer accepts the goods at the port of discharge, he would not have any right of recovery against the carrier, but in fact would be subject to liability arising from them when exercising his contractual rights under the carriage contract.[9] If no term is implied into the sale contract indicating that the goods should be provided with all necessary precautions for their safe carriage, the buyers would be deprived of any substantial remedy under the sale contract. Indeed, the courts will often be reluctant to imply a term into the contract except for rare situations where the business efficacy of the contract so requires. However, it is unjustifiable to argue the contract would have any sort of business efficacy in the present context, where the buyer had no remedy either against the seller under the sale contract, or against the carrier in the carriage contract, but rather a liability imposed on him. The proposition made under the first limb is not without difficulties. However, under the second and the third limbs, it was submitted in Chapter seven that the buyer may have a better claim. When discussing the second limb 'the contract must be appropriate to grant sufficient protection to the goods', it was shown that there is a strong correlation between loss of or damage to the goods and the lack of necessary precautions for the safe carriage of the goods. The examples of dangerous goods cases given in the chapter proved that when the carriage contract

[4] *Ceval Alimentos SA v Agrimpex Trading Co Ltd (The Northern Progress)* [1996] 2 Lloyd's Rep 319; *Tsakiroglou & Co Ltd v Noblee Thorl GmbH* [1961] 2 All ER 179; [1962] AC 93; *Finska Cellulosaforeningen (Finnish Cellulose Union) v Westfield Paper Co Ltd* (1940) 68 Ll L Rep 75; *TW Ranson Ltd v Manufacture d'Engrais et de Produits Industriels Antwerp* (1922) 13 Ll L Rep 205; *Burstall & Co v Grimsdale and Sons* (1906) 11 Com Cas 280.

[5] *Texas Instruments Ltd v Nason (Europe) Ltd* [1991] 1 Lloyd's Rep 146; *Gatoil International Inc v Tradax Petroleum Ltd (The Rio Sun)* [1985] 1 Lloyd's Rep 350; *Thomas Young and Sons Ltd v Hobson and Partners* (1949) 65 TLR 365; *BC Fruit Market Ltd v The National Fruit Co* (1921) 59 DLR 87.

[6] *Hansson v Hamel & Horley Ltd* [1922] 2 AC 36.

[7] By virtue of s 32(2) of the 1979 Act.

[8] *Hongkong Fir Shipping Co Ltd v Kawasaki Kisen Kaisha* [1962] 2 QB 26, 70.

[9] By virtue of s 3(1) of the 1992 Act.

fails to provide for any necessary measure that the nature or characteristics of the goods require, not only does this result in damage to the carrier, but also loss of or damage to the goods is a very likely outcome. Since the lack of a particular measure that the goods require may give rise to damage to the goods, it would follow that the contract has failed to afford the protection the goods require for their preservation during the sea voyage. Put simply, had the goods been provided with the necessary precautions, loss or damage would not have occurred. This also proves that those measures concerning the safe carriage of dangerous goods are not only vital for preventing damage to the vessel, the environment and loss of lives, but also necessary for the preservation of the goods themselves during transit. Therefore, the author is strongly of the opinion that a contract that fails to afford necessary measures that the goods require for their survival, would fail to grant sufficient protection to the goods, and accordingly such a contract would probably be considered as failing to satisfy the second limb of section 32(2). For this reason, it is also submitted that such a bill of lading tendered will also fail to satisfy the third limb 'the contract must confer substantial protective rights', since the buyer would be unlikely to have any substantial rights against the carrier in the carriage contract. The buyer would not be entitled to sue the carrier for damage to the goods, because the seller has failed to inform the carrier of the required precautions for the goods and the carrier cannot be considered in breach of an obligation that is not found in the contract. In fact, instead of substantial rights, the buyer would inherit liability for dangerous goods by means of the 1992 Act, if he took delivery of the goods or made a claim against the carrier.

Section 32(2) has been judicially considered very little before the courts and the position of the buyer, which this book is concerned with, appears to have never been pursued in litigation in this regard. The position of the sub-section, however, has been preserved under English law as well as in major shipping Commonwealth countries like Australia, New Zealand, Canada, Hong Kong and Singapore for well over a century, though it has never really been given much attention. Nevertheless, it still stands and is the law, albeit dormant in nature. It might be perhaps put to use as advocated in this work for the benefit of the buyer. Considering the fact that the courts often maintain a restrictive approach in transferring liability for dangerous goods to the buyer, the propositions on section 32(2) made throughout Chapter seven may become more viable devices for the courts to interpret it in a wider sense, once the buyer has liability actually and irreversibly imposed on him.

If these propositions happen to fall short in providing a desired effect, it is submitted – not without some hesitation – that section 32(2) perhaps could be amended so as to cover such a loss of the buyer, particularly considering the fact that this is not something unexecuted before under English law. Under the 1855 Act regime, the buyers of undivided bulk cargoes could not sue their carriers, if the goods were lost or damaged during transit, as the buyer would not obtain any legal title to sue. Although, this problem originated under the 1855 Act, it has been extensively overcome by the amendments made in the Sale of Goods

Act (Amendment) 1995.[10] Similarly to this, if the desired consequences are not obtained with the current wording of section 32(2), the sub-section might be amended so as to cover such a loss of the buyer.

Perhaps, as an alternative to all these recommendations, a short-cut but an effective solution can be produced by the parties to the sale contract themselves. In overseas sales, although traders frequently use standard forms or descriptions, owing to freedom of contract they are granted almost absolute flexibility to incorporate terms into their contracts for allocating their risks and responsibilities. Thus, there seems to be nothing to prevent the contracting parties from including a clause in which the seller would indemnify the buyer against any claim concerning any damages and expenses incurred by the carrier as a result of the shipment of dangerous goods and the seller would thus reimburse the buyer for his loss against the carrier consequent upon the transfer of liabilities arising from the shipment of dangerous goods via the 1992 Act. It would follow that such an indemnity provided in the sale contract would likely be employed to shift the buyer's loss back onto the seller in the present context, as effect would be given by the courts to this tailor-made term as a result of freedom of contract. In practice, though, such a solution for buyers may fail to materialise, as sellers, depending on their bargaining power, would probably be eager to negotiate against including such a term in their contract to keep their risks as limited as possible.

Chapter seven discussed that there might be a causal link between the loss inherited by the buyer consequent upon the damage caused by dangerous goods and the seller's breach under the sale contract. However, this does not necessarily mean that all damages are recoverable, despite them flowing from that breach, as it is trite law that the loss must not be considered too remote to recover. Therefore, in the light of the law of damages applicable to sale of goods cases, Chapter eight sought to address the question of whether the buyer's loss is too remote to be recovered under the rule of remoteness. The discussion in the chapter suggested that the buyer's loss in the present context would likely be recoverable under the rule of remoteness. The courts approach the link between the breach and the loss with common sense, when applying the rule of remoteness. Especially so far as sale contracts on shipment terms are concerned, they appear to take into consideration only simple factual causation between the loss and the breach, in allowing claims for consequential losses under the rule of remoteness. The case law shows that the courts seem to have a relaxed approach and often allow such consequential losses under CIF and FOB sales where available. In that regard, concerning the position of the end buyer, who is not at fault whatsoever in the present context, perhaps the courts may even adopt a more relaxed approach than they would normally do under CIF and FOB sales. Particularly considering the wording of section 32(2) and its autonomous reference to damages, it might come in handy for the courts

[10] See ss 16 and 18 rule 5 of the 1979 Act.

to interpret this sub-section extensively to allow recovery of the buyer's loss as a direct loss rather than a consequential one in relation to the breach. As an effective alternate route to a claim, the analogy set out in Chapter eight with the principle established in *Lambert v Lewis*[11] could be readily utilised in favour of the buyer against the seller.

E. Recovery under Non-contractual Mechanisms

Chapters seven and eight recommended propositions for a remedy for the buyer/transferee under the contractual mechanism against his immediate seller for liability for dangerous goods inherited under the carriage contract. As these propositions have yet to be tested before the courts, it is unknown whether they would provide an adequate solution for the buyer against his immediate seller. Therefore, the buyer would be better placed if he had a further option for redress based on an alternative legal basis against potential alternative parties. Thus, Chapter nine came up with alternative solutions for recovery, under non-contractual actions, such as via the Civil Liability (Contribution) Act 1978, and in tort. As far as the 1978 Act concerned, it was submitted that the buyer may have an arguable claim under the 1978 Act against the shipper/seller or other alternative parties, like charterers. The rationale behind the Act is to ensure that the wrongdoer will not be unjustly enriched, where his liability to a third party has been discharged by a claimant that is also liable to the same third party. It would not be wrong to say that there is probably no party better suited to the rationale of the Act than the buyer in the present context, and it may seem more practical to sue the seller/shipper directly as the source of liability than his immediate seller as well. Having said that, a successful claim for the buyer under the 1978 Act is not without some practical difficulties. The seller/shipper may not have any or sufficient realisable assets within the reach of the court or he might be insolvent or untraceable. Alternatively, given the absence of a contract between them, an overseas seller may refuse to join the proceedings in England. A further problem could be that there might be a failure to obtain declaratory recognition, in the country in which the seller/shipper has assets, of the judgment given in England in favour of the buyer.

As for the buyer's claim in tort, under the exception introduced in *Lambert v Lewis* – which requires that in order to have an arguable claim, the claimant must be subject to liability for physical damage caused to a third party's property, where the proximate cause of the damage is the negligent act or fault of the defendant – it is arguable that the buyer's claim fitting the formulation of this exception might be successfully pursued against the seller/shipper. Particularly if the buyer has no

[11] *Lexmead (Basingstoke) Ltd v Lewis and Others (Lambert v Lewis)* [1982] AC 225; [1985] 2 Lloyd's Rep 17.

practical remedy in contractual actions, perhaps the courts may show some readiness to apply this exception in a more relaxed regime against the shipper/seller in order for him not to be unjustly enriched when he is actually the source of liability. However, as with the 1978 Act, an action in tort is not without difficulties for the buyer. First, an overseas third-party shipper/seller may not readily accept being joined in a tort action in England. Even if he joins, the buyer must prove that the proximate cause of the damage to the carrier is the negligence of the shipper/seller. However, it is trite law that the shipper becomes strictly liable to the carrier for the shipment of dangerous goods regardless of his negligence or actions. Where this is the case, the buyer may have difficulty in proving the shipper's negligence giving rise to the damage to the carrier, if the shipper is in fact not negligent or at fault. Even if the buyer proves the shipper's negligence, the difficulty is that the seller/shipper may not have any realisable assets within reach or the buyer may encounter difficulties in the country in which the seller/shipper does have realisable assets in seeking declaratory recognition of the judgment given in England in favour of him. It is also worth adding that the buyer may not be entitled to full recovery in a tort action, given that heads of loss available in a claim in tort might differ from the ones under the contract, and accordingly he may not be able to recover pure economic losses that he might have incurred under the contract.

The book offers non-contractual solutions only in the alternative to the contractual ones. Perhaps it might seem more practical for buyers to bring a claim against the direct source of liability under a non-contractual action. However, the author is of the opinion that the contractual actions should be favoured over the non-contractual ones in the present context by reason of the potential practical difficulties summarised above. Buyers might be discouraged by the fact that pursuing such a claim in the context of string sales could prove difficult, and at first sight it might seem unjust under string sales. However, there is no injustice done, for two particular reasons. First, the Sale of Goods Act 1979 provides a system of strict liability for defective goods meaning that although a seller in a chain of sales may not be personally at fault, he may still be liable towards his buyer, given the fault of the initial seller. Sales on shipment terms are generally considered as sale of goods through performance of the documents, and often in string sales, commodities are sold multiple times on identical or similar terms before arrival at their destination. Accordingly, not being the initial seller would not prevent an intermediate seller from being in breach of his contractual duties towards his buyer. That situation is peculiar to these contracts. Second, when the ultimate buyer recovers his loss from his immediate seller under the last contract, the loss will not irreversibly attach to his seller. This is probably the case even if there is a variation in one of the contracts in the string, as the courts appear to have maintained a restrictive approach against allowing a variation. The intermediate sellers in string sales will join or pursue their claims against their immediate sellers, which will eventually and justifiably reach back to the initial seller/shipper who is the source of this liability.

II. A Holistic Approach

Nevertheless, against all these conclusions given above, it might still be argued that English law is not up to the task in terms of liability for dangerous goods, as the strict liability regime is based on a case from the nineteenth century, the Hague Rules were originally enacted in the early twentieth century, and the Hague-Visby Rules were only amended roughly 50 years ago. As advocated throughout this work, the status quo of English law in the present context *could be* regarded as up to the task, if it is to put into effect as recommended in this work. As far as the strict liability regime is concerned, it might seem somewhat outdated, as it originated in the case of *Brass v Maitland* that was decided in 1856. However, the policy behind the decision – that the shipper has the better means of knowledge in relation to the nature and character of the goods that he sells (including its properties and the specific dangers associated with it) than the carrier to whom the goods are presented[12] – still holds great importance and is arguably the correct policy for a number of reasons. First of all, although the strict liability regime was first established in 1856 in *Brass v Maitland*, it was approved only roughly 24 years ago by the House of Lords in *The Giannis NK*.[13] Second, the shipper often is the seller of the goods[14] and as the party who sells the goods, he can be arguably said to have the closest nexus with the goods both physically and contractually prior to carriage. In respect of physical proximity, loading responsibilities are mostly allocated to the shipper. For instance, when a substance classified as dangerous in the IMDG Code is shipped, his duty does not end as soon as he puts the goods over the ship's rail. The seller as shipper, is not only bound to provide a dangerous goods transport document containing all the necessary safety information required by the Code, but also undertakes to see that the goods are properly packed, marked and labelled. So far as his contractual nexus with the goods is concerned, as was discussed in Chapter seven, under CIF and many FOB sales,[15] the seller as shipper, is under a duty to conclude the carriage contract evidenced in the bill of lading on behalf of the buyer on the usual terms applicable[16] in the specific trade concerned by providing all necessary precautions for safe carriage of the goods[17] and conferring

[12] *Brass v Maitland* (1856) 6 E & B 470; 119 ER 940.

[13] *Effort Shipping Co Ltd v Linden Management SA (The Giannis NK)* [1998] AC 605; [1998] 1 Lloyd's Rep 337.

[14] On this see generally, Chapter 4.

[15] This is not the case where the buyer concludes the carriage contract under a bare FOB contract and sometimes under classic FOB sales. On this see generally, Chapter 4 above.

[16] *Ceval Alimentos SA v Agrimpex Trading Co Ltd (The Northern Progress)* [1996] 2 Lloyd's Rep 319; *Tsakiroglou & Co Ltd v Noblee Thorl GmbH* [1961] 2 All ER 179; [1962] AC 93; *Finska Cellulosaforeningen (Finnish Cellulose Union) v Westfield Paper Co Ltd* (1940) 68 Ll L Rep 75; *TW Ranson Ltd v Manufacture d'Engrais et de Produits Industriels Antwerp* (1922) 13 Ll L Rep 205; *Burstall & Co v Grimsdale and Sons* (1906) 11 Com Cas 280.

[17] *Texas Instruments Ltd v Nason (Europe) Ltd* [1991] 1 Lloyd's Rep 146; *Gatoil International Inc v Tradax Petroleum Ltd (The Rio Sun)* [1985] 1 Lloyd's Rep 350; *Thomas Young and Sons Ltd v Hobson and Partners* (1949) 65 TLR 365; *BC Fruit Market Ltd v The National Fruit Co* (1921) 59 DLR 87.

substantial continuous protective rights throughout the voyage.[18,19] It should not be forgotten that the shipper presents his goods, often sold by him, to a party who has no nexus with them whatsoever prior to shipment, and that party agrees to carry these goods with the risks associated with them based on only the information provided by the shipper. It is not uncommon that dangerous goods may cause catastrophic incidents resulting in loss of lives, total loss of the vessel and damage to the environment. And if it were not for strict liability, shippers would have been able to avoid liability caused by dangerous goods presented by them and the carrier would have been left without any sort of remedy, once the shippers proved that they did not know the nature and character of their own goods. In this regard, the law appears to be based on the correct policy. This could also be supported by the fact that as shown in Chapter three, the major shipping nations have substantially the same or similar strict liability regimes for shipment of dangerous goods today, proving that a uniform approach has been adopted on the matter. So far as the Hague/Hague-Visby Rules are concerned, no doubt they have their own longstanding issues, and questions over their flawed applicability to modern problems of the global shipping industry are unavoidable. However, in terms of liability for dangerous goods, the Rules are not as problematic as the other issues, since the relevant provision is consistent with the strict liability regime. In support of this, the corresponding provision on liability for dangerous goods of the Rotterdam Rules, which used to be considered the heir apparent to the Hague/Hague-Visby Rules until recently, is also based on the strict liability policy.[20] Considering the fact that the Rotterdam Rules were only drafted in 2008, this proves that there was no intention to alter the strict liability regime.

Indeed a policy based on a nineteenth-century case might seem questionable or out-dated concerning its application to the contemporary relationship between the shipping parties, as *Brass v Maitland* dealt with apportionment of liability for dangerous goods only between the shipper and the carrier. And this argument is not completely unfounded. Liability for dangerous goods originates under the carriage contract, arising from the cargo destined for a third party, who is often the buyer/consignee, and carriage contracts are concluded for the benefit of that third party, creating a tri-partite relationship between the shipper/seller, the carrier and the consignee/buyer. Thus, there is no doubt that the law established in *Brass v Maitland* is one-angled, as it does not deal with the buyer/consignee's position against the carrier. The buyer, as consignee, would have avoided liability in *Brass v Maitland*, as he was not privy to the carriage contract with the carrier. Rights and liabilities of the buyer/consignee against the carrier under the carriage contract had first been dealt within the 1855 Bills of Lading Act, which had its own issues around failure to fill the contractual gap between the consignee and the carrier.

[18] *Hansson v Hamel & Horley Ltd* [1922] 2 AC 36.
[19] By virtue of s 32(2) of the 1979 Act. On this see generally, Chapter 7.
[20] Art 32 of the Rotterdam Rules.

This issue was only ironed out by the enactment of the 1992 Act.[21] The buyer under the 1992 Act could only be subject to liability for dangerous goods alongside the shipper, based on the principle of mutuality that if a third party wishes to take the benefit of the carriage contract, he should also bear the corresponding burdens therein. Under the Act therefore, he is not automatically subject to liability unless he seeks to exercise his contractual rights. By making the carrier entitled to sue both the shipper/seller and the consignee/buyer for the same liabilities, the policy of the 1992 Act connotes the rationale behind the principle: the carrier should be protected at all times under the tri-partite relationship, on the basis that he is the most innocent and remote party regarding the goods that are the source of damage or losses incurred by him. This is also arguably true in the context of sale of goods law; the buyer as transferee may have a closer link with and an interest in the goods, which may justify his potential liability under the tri-partite relationship. As was discussed in Chapter seven, by virtue of section 32(2) of the 1979 Act, under CIF and many FOB contracts,[22] the seller is under a duty to make or procure a contract of carriage on behalf of the buyer. Section 32(2) expressly indicates that the seller concludes this contract 'on behalf of the buyer',[23] whether he concludes it as principal or as agent of the buyer. Where the seller/shipper – even as original party – drafts all the details in the contract and makes all arrangements to enable the carrier to take necessary precautions to carry the goods safely, he does all this for the benefit of the buyer/transferee on behalf of him under section 32(2). This once again proves that the contract of carriage is a contract for the benefit of a third party, namely the buyer.[24] In support of this, by virtue of section 45(1) of the 1979 Act, when delivered to the carrier, goods are deemed to be in the course of transit for the purpose of transmission to the buyer. This is to say, the carrier obtains and carries the goods not only on behalf of the buyer but also for the benefit of the buyer. All these factors appear to prove that the buyer can be regarded as the prime reason behind the shipment. Therefore, enabling the carrier to sue both parties to the carriage contract for damage incurred by reason of dangerous goods via the 1992 Act appears to have improved the one-angled strict liability regime of *Brass v Maitland* by including the buyer/consignee, who is the prime beneficiary behind the carriage of these goods.

However the law detailed above is only responsive after a dangerous goods incident occurs and it may only be put to use afterwards to compensate for the injured parties' losses as justly as possible. However, focus should be on preventing or at least reducing the number of dangerous goods incidents from happening on the high seas. To do so, some preventive measures need to be taken. As shown

[21] The 1855 Act was repealed by the 1992 Act.

[22] The exception is bare FOB and some classic FOB contracts. See *Pyrene v Scindia* [1954] 2 QB 402; *Scottish & Newcastle Int'l Ltd v Othon Ghalanos Ltd* [2008] UKHL 11.

[23] Section 32(2) of the 1979 Act.

[24] See also s 32(1) of the 1979 Act which prescribes that delivery of the goods to the carrier is prima facie deemed to be delivery to the buyer.

in Chapter two, dangerous goods regulations are not without issues, as sometimes they may be ineffective to a degree. The inherent ineffectiveness of the Codes is regularly sought to be corrected by the International Maritime Organization with the assistance of the stakeholders involved in the transport of dangerous goods. This, however, does not entirely address the issue. The CTU Code is a non-mandatory instrument setting out guidance on best practice for the handling and packing of cargo transport units for carriage by road and sea. It is applicable to the entire carriage operations and includes guidance for packing and handling cargo as well as discharging and unpacking cargo transport units. It was introduced as a non-mandatory instrument in 2014 to tackle the lack of guidance in the industry. However, given that it is non-mandatory, the Code has yet to be incorporated or acknowledged widely around the world. Thus, perhaps one way of reducing non-compliance and increasing enforcement would be making the CTU Code a mandatory international instrument so that Member States would be forced to incorporate it into their national laws. As much as this will add another layer to the compendium of dangerous goods regulations, as shown in Chapter one, with the infinite variety of dangerous goods carried by sea, these goods cannot be handled and carried today employing the out-dated principles of the twentieth century. Nevertheless, this alone would not be sufficient to tackle the issue at its core, as the concern is that making an instrument mandatory does not automatically have it followed thoroughly in practice. The vast majority of incidents involving dangerous goods show that non-compliance is the underlying reason, which results from lack of awareness and knowledge of dangerous goods regulations, poor packing or handling practices, and fraudulent misdeclarations/ non-declarations. Therefore, the elephant in the room is the lack of adequate enforcement and implementation undermining effectiveness of the international dangerous goods regulations.

The diagnosis for solution is that focus should be on training and educating all the parties involved in the transport of dangerous goods, in order to increase their competence. However, this requires greater engagement by some stakeholders including national governments, if the industry is willing to reduce the number of incidents substantially. To start with shippers of dangerous goods, as liability rests with them, they should establish a safety culture at corporate level to ensure that the cargo presented to the vessel by them will be in compliance with dangerous goods regulations. This can only be achieved if their employees are trained to a certain level of competence corresponding to their job description. A similar responsibility lies with carriers. They should also provide their employees, including their shore-based personnel engaged in the transport of dangerous goods, with regular training for effective and functional implementation of dangerous goods regulations in order to keep pace with changes and updates in regulations and practice. This would enable them to more effectively identify misdeclarations/ non-declarations, poor packing and handling practices of shippers prior to shipment. However, the author is strongly of the opinion that the greatest responsibility lies on the shoulders of national governments. It is a must-do for port authorities and enforcement agencies that they should increase paperwork checks, inspections and controls via a sufficient number of competent personnel who have training specific to their particular job description so as to be able to implement national and international regulations rigorously. A rigid control and monitoring system at ports would likely ensure effective implementation and enforcement of these regulations, which would have a domino effect in changing the safety culture of stakeholders engaged in the transport of dangerous goods. A cargo of dangerous goods failing inspection at the port of shipment due to non-compliance with the relevant regulations would no doubt put pressure on the stakeholders in the supply chain, starting from shippers, all the way down to their contractors and suppliers. This would, in the long run, encourage or to put it more bluntly, force these actors to have training to a certain level of competence so as to comply with these rules effectively. This might arguably hold the key to enhancing safety and reducing the number of dangerous goods incidents by indirectly forcing each stakeholder to improve their enforcement standards. Perhaps another suggestion to improve effective implementation would be for competent bodies, approved by national governments, to deliver a mandatory training programme to all the stakeholders involved in the transport of dangerous goods. However, in that respect success might be limited to national level, as this would entirely depend on governments' own policies to tackle the issue, since not every government across the world has the resources to fund such a policy, or they may choose to leave the issue to the industry to address.

An additional measure would be that governments might introduce substantial fines for non-compliance with dangerous goods regulations, which could perhaps have a deterrent impact on each stakeholder. Indeed, shippers are subject to liability for dangerous goods, if they fail to warn carriers of the nature and characteristics of their goods. However, the shipper or his assets could be out of reach of the governing jurisdiction. Therefore, he might avoid liability. Nevertheless, incorporation of deterrent fines by national governments at national levels for non-compliance by a stakeholder who operates in that country could put pressure on that stakeholder to implement dangerous goods regulations effectively, as they would be readily reachable by individual governments. This book ultimately champions the idea that incidents involving dangerous goods can only be successfully prevented from happening with effective enforcement and implementation of the relevant regulations, which can only be achieved by the adoption of a comprehensive as well as a pragmatic approach by all the stakeholders engaged in the carriage of dangerous goods, including national governments as advocated above. The Audit Scheme of the IMO (IMSAS) perhaps can be effectively put to use, if it is really to be used as a tool to ensure implementation of compulsory instruments of the IMO with high standards. As shown in Chapter two, according to the Fifth Consolidated Audit Summary Report 2021 (CASR) of the IMSAS, some Member State authorities were found to have failed to adequately regulate, control and supervise practices related to handling of dangerous goods. By the Paris Memorandum of Understanding on Port State Control (Paris MoU), so as to reduce the operation of vessels with a poor performance, each year a 'White, Grey and Black' (WGB) list is published in the

Annual Report, ranking flag states from best to worst, based on the total number of inspections and detentions over a three-year period for flags with at least 30 inspections during that period.[25] Perhaps, a similar list could be published under the Audit Scheme, ranking Member States based on the total number of checks, inspections and their overall performances in terms of compliance with the IMO's dangerous goods regulations. This would surely put some pressure on Member States to do better altogether and ensure that the relevant regulations are applied rigorously.

Perhaps one solution would be adopting a similar approach to that taken to the carriage of nuclear materials and radioactive wastes, so that the transport of dangerous goods would have an autonomous regime segregating them from other goods. However, it is submitted that this does not appear to be feasible for a number of reasons. First, nuclear materials and radioactive wastes are much easier to identify and there are only certain types suitable for sea carriage. Unlike nuclear materials, dangerous goods are not limited to those listed in the relevant regulations. As was discussed in Chapters one, two and three, these regulations are not conclusive about what is considered dangerous; neither will they be decisive on the subject, as even the most innocuous-looking cargo could create danger to the vessel. Also, compared to dangerous goods, nuclear materials only account for a very low volume of transported goods and there are not many carriers available in the global shipping industry to transport nuclear materials and radioactive wastes by sea. For these reasons, having a separate regime might *seem* to be working for carriage of nuclear materials by sea. However, considering the ever-increasing proportion of dangerous goods carried by sea each year and the fact that they are unsuitable to be squeezed into stringently defined limits as shown in Chapters one, two and three, governing dangerous goods with an isolated regime would be unlikely to address the present issues in the transport of dangerous goods by sea.

[25] www.parismou.org/detentions-banning/white-grey-and-black-list.

BIBLIOGRAPHY

Books

Aikens, R, Lord R, Bools, MD, *Bills of Lading*, 3rd edn (London, Informa, 2020).
Beale, HG, *Chitty on Contracts*, 33rd edn (London, Sweet & Maxwell, 2021).
Bell, AP, *Modern Law of Personal Property in England and Ireland* (London, Butterworths, 1989).
Bools, MD, *The Bill of Lading: a Document of Title to the Goods: an Anglo-American Comparison* (London, LLP, 1997).
Bridge, MG, *Benjamin's Sale of Goods*, 11th edn (London, Sweet & Maxwell, 2020).
—— *The International Sale of Goods*, 4th edn (Oxford, OUP, 2017).
Cooke, J, Young, T, Ashcroft, M, Taylor, A, Kimball, J, Martowski, D, Lambert, L, Sturley, M, *Voyage Charters*, 4th edn (London, Informa, 2014).
Debattista, C, *Sale of Goods Carried by Sea* (London, Butterworths, 1990).
Debattista C and Hornyold-Strickland F, *Debattista on Bills of Lading in Commodities Trade*, 4th edn, (London, Bloomsbury Publishing, 2021).
Edelman, J, Colton, S, Varuhas, J, *McGregor on Damages*, 21st edn (London, Sweet & Maxwell, 2020).
Eder, B, Foxton, D, Berry, S, Smith, C, Bennett, H, *Scrutton on Charterparties and Bills of Lading*, 24th edn (London, Sweet & Maxwell, 2019).
Gaskell, N, Asariotis R, Baatz, Y, *Bills of Lading: Law and Contracts* (London, LLP, 2000).
Jones, M, *Clerk & Lindsell on Torts*, 23rd edn (London, Sweet & Maxwell, 2020).
Lorenzon, F (ed), *Sassoon: C.I.F. and F.O.B. Contracts*, 6th edn (London, Sweet & Maxwell, 2017).
Mark, M, *Chalmers' Sale of Goods Act 1979*, 18th edn (London, Butterworths, 1981).
Palmer, NE, McKendrick, E, *Interests in Goods*, 2nd edn (London, LLP, 1998).
—— *Palmer on Bailment*, 3rd edn (London, Sweet & Maxwell, 2009)
Peel, E, *Treitel on the Law of Contract*, 15th edn (London, Sweet & Maxwell, 2020).
Sassoon, DM, *Sassoon: C.I.F. and F.O.B. Contracts*, 4th edn (London, Sweet & Maxwell, 1995).
Schmitthoff, CM, *The Law and Practice of International Trade*, 12th edn (London, Sweet & Maxwell, 2012).
Tetley, W, *Marine Cargo Claims*, 4th edn (Toronto, Cowansville, 2007).
Todd, P, *Bills of Lading and Bankers Documentary Credits*, 4th edn (London, Informa 2007).
—— *Cases and Materials on International Trade Law* (London, Sweet & Maxwell, 2003).
Treitel, GH, Reynolds, FMB, *Carver on Bills of Lading*, 4th edn (London, Sweet & Maxwell, 2017).
Watts, P, *Bowstead and Reynolds on Agency*, 21st edn (London, Sweet & Maxwell, 2017).

Journal Articles

Aikens, R, 'Which Way to Rome for Cargo Claims in Bailment When Goods Are Carried by Sea?' (2011) *LMCLQ* 482.
Bassindale, J, 'Title to Sue under Bills of Lading: the Carriage of Goods by Sea Act 1992' (1992) *JIBL* 414.
Baughen, S, Campbell, N, 'Apportionment of Risk and the Carriage of Dangerous Cargo' (2001) 1 *Int'l ML* 3.
—— 'Bailment's Continuing Role in Cargo Claims' (1999) *LMCLQ* 393.

—— 'Bailment or Conversion? Misdelivery Claims against Non-contractual Carriers' (2010) *LMCLQ* 411.
—— 'Obligations of the Shipper to the Carrier' (2008) 14 *JIML* 555.
—— 'Sue and be Sued? Dangerous Cargo and the Claimant's Dilemma' (2006) 5(4) *S&TLI* 14.
—— 'The Legal Status of the Non-contracting Shipper' (2000) 1 *IJOSL* 21.
Beatson, J, Cooper, JJ, 'Rights of Suit in Respect of Carriage of Goods by Sea' (1991) *LMCLQ* 196.
Bradgate, R, White F, 'The Carriage of Goods by Sea Act 1992' (1993) 56 *MLR* 188.
Bridge, MG, 'Markets and damages in Sale of Goods Cases' (2016) 132 *LQR* 405.
Briggs, A, 'The International Dimension to Claims for Contribution: Arab Monetary Fund v Hashim' (1995) *LMCLQ* 437.
Campbell, N, 'Defining the Frontiers of the Bill of Lading Holder's Liability – the Berge Sisar and the Aegean Sea' [2000] *JBL* 196.
Curwen, N, 'The Problems of Transferring Carriage Rights: an equitable solution' [1992] *JBL* 245.
Davenport, B, 'Reform to Bill of Lading Law – Some Implications for Banks' (1992) *JIBFL* 305.
Davies, JM, 'What is reasonable contract' (2003) 3(4) *Lloyd's Shipping & Trade Law* 1.
Devlin, P, 'The Relation between commercial law and commercial practice' (1951) 14 *MLR* 249.
Dowrick, FE, 'A Jus Quaestium Tertio by Way of Contract in English Law' (1956) 19 *MLR* 374.
Faber, D, 'The Problems Arising from Multimodal Transport' (1996) *LMCLQ* 503.
Ferris, C, 'The Carriage of Goods by Sea Act 1992' (1992) 3 *ICCLR* 432.
Gelgec, A, 'Banks' Liability for Demurrage' (2018) 18 *Lloyd's Shipping & Trade Law* 5.
—— 'Identifying the Shipper under Bills of Lading' Case analysis *MVV Environment Devonport Ltd v NTO Shipping GmbH & Co KG (The MV Nortrader)* [2020] EWHC 1371 (Comm) (2020) 26 *JIML* 229.
—— 'Challenging the Impact of FIOST Clauses on Cargo Interests' (2021) 6(1) *University of Bologna Law Review* 29.
Girvin, S, 'Bills of Lading and Straight Bills of Lading: Principles and Practice' [2006] *JBL* 86.
—— 'Carriage by Sea: the Sea Transport Documents Act 2000 in Historical and Comparative Perspective' (2002) 119 *South African Law Journal* 317.
—— 'Shipper's Liability for the Carriage of Dangerous Cargoes by Sea' (1996) *LMCLQ* 487.
Gower, LCB, 'F.O.B. Contracts' (1956) 19 *MLR* 417.
Howard, T, 'The Carriage of Goods by Sea Act 1992' (1993) 24 *JMLC* 181.
Humphreys, G, Higgs, A, 'An Overview of the Implications of the Carriage of Goods by Sea Act 1992' [1993] *JBL* 61.
Lebhun, J, 'Practising CIF and FOB today' (1981) 1 *ETL* 24.
Lee, DYH, Sooksripaisarnkit, P, 'The Straight Bill of Lading: Past, Present, and Future' (2012) 18 *JIML* 39.
Lorenzon, F, 'When is a CIF Seller's Carriage Contract Unreasonable?' (2007) 13 *JIML* 241.
McMeel, G, 'Straight Bills of Lading in the House of Lords – the Rafaela S' (2005) *LMCLQ* 273.
Mildon, D, Scorey, D, 'Liabilities of Transferees of Bills of Lading' (1999) *IJOSL* 94.
Murphy, J, 'The Merits of Rylands v Fletcher' (2004) 24 *OJLS* 643.
Negus, R, 'The Negotiability of bills of lading' (1921) 37 *LQR* 442.
Newark, FH, 'Non-Natural User and *Rylands v Fletcher*' (1961) 24 *MLR* 557.
Nolan, DP, 'The Distinctiveness of *Rylands v Fletcher*' (2005) 121 *LQR* 421.
Reynolds, B, 'Further Thoughts on the Carriage of Goods by Sea Act 1992 (UK)' (1994) 25 *JMLC* 143.
Reynolds, FMB, 'The Carriage of Goods by Sea Act 1992 Put to the Test – the Berge Sisar' (1999) *LMCLQ* 161.
—— 'The Carriage of Goods by Sea Act 1992' (1993) *LMCLQ* 436.
Rose, FD, 'Liability for Dangerous Goods *(The Giannis NK)*' (1998) *LMCLQ* 480.
Sabapathy, S, 'Falling Market and Remoteness' (2013) *LMCLQ* 284.
Sassoon, DM, 'Application of FOB and CIF Sales in Common Law Countries' (1981) 16 *ETL* 50.
—— 'The Origin of F.O.B. and C.I.F. Terms and the Factors Influencing their Choice' [1967] *JBL* 32.
Stallybrass, W, 'Dangerous Things and the Non-Natural User of Land' (1929) 3 *CLJ* 376.
Stiggelbout, M, 'Contractual Remoteness, 'scope of duty' and Intention' (2012) *LMCLQ* 97.

Tettenborn, A, 'Tort Liability and environmental responsibility' (1996) *LMCLQ* 8.
—— 'Transferable and Negotiable documents of title – a Redefinition?' (1991) *LMCLQ* 538.
Thomas, R, 'Bills of Lading – The Position of Holders and Intermediate Holders Under the English Carriage of Goods by Sea Act 1992' (2001) 5 *Int'l ML* 165.
Todd, P, 'Bank As Holder Under Carriage of Goods by Sea Act 1992' (2013) *LMCLQ* 275.
—— 'Bank As Holder Under Carriage of Goods by Sea Act 1992' (2015) *LMCLQ* 155.
—— 'Bill of Lading as Document of Title' [2005] *JBL* 762.
—— 'The Bill of Lading and Delivery: the Common Law Actions' (2006) *LMCLQ* 539.
Treitel, GH, 'Bills of lading and Implied Contracts' (1989) *LMCLQ* 162.
—— 'Bills of Lading: Liabilities of Transferee' (2001) *LMCLQ* 344.
—— 'Exemption Clauses and Third Parties' (1955) 18 *MLR* 172.
—— 'The Legal Status of Straight Bills of Lading' (2003) 119 *LQR* 608.
Wee, P, 'Contractual Interpretation and Remoteness' (2010) *LMCLQ* 150.
Weir, T, '*Rylands v Fletcher* Reconsidered' (1994) *CLJ* 216.

Chapters in Edited Books

Baughen, S, 'Charterparty Bills of Lading Cargo Interests Liabilities to the Shipowner' in R Thomas (ed), *The Evolving Law and Pratice of Voyage Charterparties* (London, Informa, 2009).
Gelgec, A, 'Clause Paramount and Its Impact on Package Limitation Figures' in M Musi (ed), *New Challenges in Maritime Law* (Bologna, Bonomo, 2015), 147.
—— 'Separation of Actual and Physical Possession of Bills of Lading under English Law' in F Berlingieri and M Musi (eds), *Maritime, Port and Transport Law: Current Scenarios and Emerging Issues* (Bologna, Bonomo, 2017), 1.
—— 'Who Attracts the Dangerous Goods Liability under CIF and FOB Contracts?' in S Zunarelli and M Musi (eds), *Current Issues in Maritime and Transport Law* (Bologna, Bonomo, 2016), 29.
Mustill, M, 'Carriers' Liabilities and Insrance' in K Gronfors (ed), *Damage from Goods* (Gothenburg, Tullbergs Klippan, 1978), 69.
Reynolds, FMB, 'Bills of Lading and Voyage Charters' in R Thomas (ed), *The Evolving Law and Practice of Voyage Charterparties* (London, Informa, 2009), 210.
Wooldridge, F, 'The Kinds of F.O.B. Contracts' in F Fabricius (ed), *Law and International Trade Recht und Internationaler Handel* (Frankfurt, Athenaum Verlag, 1973), 388.

Miscellaneous

'A white paper by National Cargo Bureau', US National Cargo Bureau (2020). www.natcargo.org/Holistic-Approach-For-Undeclared-Misdeclared-And-Other-Non-compliant-Dangerous-Goods_White-Paper-by-NCB.pdf.
'An insight into the causes and prevention of cargo fires', *Maritime Risk International* (December 2017).
'Cargo liquefaction – still a problem; still taking lives', *Maritime Risk International* (May 2012).
'Dangerous solid cargoes in bulk; DRI, nickel and iron ores', *A selection of articles previously published by Gard AS* (January 2014) www.gard.no/Content/6227919/Dangerous%20solid%20cargoes%20in%20bulk%20June%202011.pdf.
'IUMI Position Paper – Firefighting systems on board container vessels', *The International Union of Maritime Insurance* (2017).
'Making bunkering safe', *Maritime Risk International* (December 2019).
'Mis-Declaration in 27 percent of the incidents', *Maritime Risk International* (October 2016).
'Putting out the fires', *Maritime Risk International* (December 2019).

Hansard

Carriage of Goods by Sea Bill Deb 4 February 1992, col 234.

Encyclopedias

Halsbury's Laws of England (2019) vol 91Sale of Goods and Supply of Services, para 191.

Theses

Josephine Thörnroos, 'The Contracting Shipper's Strict Liability in the Carriage of Dangerous Goods by Sea' (Master thesis, University of Helsinki 2019).

Law Commission Reports

Law Commission, *Rights of Suit in Respect of Carriage of Goods by Sea* (Law Com No 196, Scot Law Com No 130, 1991).

Law Commission, *Law of Contract: Report on Contribution* (Law Com No 79, 1977).

Other Reports

The Bahamas Maritime Authority, *MV Bulk Jupiter Report*, (Official No 8001956, 2015).

Websites

www.cinsnet.com/about-cinsnet.

www.cinsnet.com/wp-content/uploads/2017/11/CINS-Cocoa-Butter-Guidelines-January-2018-Final.pdf.

www.cinsnet.com/wp-content/uploads/2018/01/Calcium-Hypochlorite-Guidelines-CINS-IGPI-Version-3-January-2018.pdf.

www.cinsnet.com/wp-content/uploads/2019/11/CINS-DG-Stowage-Considerations-Final.pdf.

www.cinsnet.com/wp-content/uploads/2021/04/CINS-IG-Seed-Cake-Guidelines-Version-3-April-2021.pdf.

www.gard.no/Content/24227347/CINS_IGPI_GuidelinesCarriageCharcoalCarbon.pdf.

www.gov.uk/government/publications/carriage-of-dangerous-goods-guidance-note-16/thameslink-southern-and-great-northern-tsgn-2014-franchise-agreement.

www.ichca.com/cargo-integrity-group.

www.imo.org/en/MediaCentre/MeetingSummaries/Pages/CCC-7th-session.aspx.

www.imo.org/en/MediaCentre/MeetingSummaries/Pages/MSC-103rd-session.aspx.

www.imo.org/en/MediaCentre/PressBriefings/Pages/38-bauxite-CCC.aspx.

www.imo.org/en/OurWork/Safety/Pages/CTU-Code.aspx.

www.irclass.org/technical-circulars/fire-safety-hazards-associated-with-wood-pellets.
www.bulkcarrierguide.com/cement-handling.html.
www.bulkcarrierguide.com/coal-hazards.html.
www.bulkcarrierguide.com/coal-hazards-&-safety-considerations.html.
www.bulkcarrierguide.com/iron-ore.html.
www.gard.no/web/news/article?p_document_id=28440601.
www.nautinst.org/uploads/assets/uploaded/d865b674-d59d-4255-8d7b462811d48043.pdf.
www.parismou.org/detentions-banning/white-grey-and-black-list.
www.skuld.com/topics/cargo/solid-bulk/agricultural-cargoes/transportation-of-wheat.
www.skuld.com/topics/cargo/solid-bulk/general-advice/wood-pellets-and-risk-of-fire.
www.tis-gdv.de/tis_e/ware/getreide/weizen/weizen-htm/#schaedlingsbefall.
www.ttclub.com/-/media/files/tt-club/birpit/book-it-right-and-pack-it-tight---amendment-39-18.pdf.

Working Papers

'Radioactive Materials Transport the International Safety Regime – An Overview of Safety Regulations and the Organisations Responsible for their Development', *World Nuclear Transport Institute* (July 2006).

INDEX

www.ingramcontent.com/pod-product-compliance
Lightning Source LLC
Chambersburg PA
CBHW071301180926
51613CB00001B/102